Cinéma-monde

Cinéma-monde
Decentred Perspectives on Global Filmmaking in French

Edited by
Michael Gott and Thibaut Schilt

EDINBURGH
University Press

Edinburgh University Press is one of the leading university presses in the UK. We publish academic books and journals in our selected subject areas across the humanities and social sciences, combining cutting-edge scholarship with high editorial and production values to produce academic works of lasting importance. For more information visit our website: edinburghuniversitypress.com

© editorial matter and organisation Michael Gott and Thibaut Schilt, 2018
© the chapters their several authors, 2018

Edinburgh University Press Ltd
The Tun – Holyrood Road
12 (2f) Jackson's Entry
Edinburgh EH8 8PJ

Typeset in Monotype Ehrhardt

A CIP record for this book is available from the British Library

ISBN 978 1 4744 1498 2 (hardback)
ISBN 978 1 4744 1499 9 (webready PDF)
ISBN 978 1 4744 1500 2 (epub)

The right of the contributors to be identified as authors of this work has been asserted in accordance with the Copyright, Designs and Patents Act 1988 and the Copyright and Related Rights Regulations 2003 (SI No. 2498).

Contents

List of Figures	vii
Notes on Contributors	ix
Acknowledgements	xiv

Introduction: The Kaleidoscope of Cinéma-monde   1
Michael Gott and Thibaut Schilt

Part I From Local to Global: The Cinéma(s)-monde(s) of Auteurs and Actors

1. *Site 2:* Style and Encounter in Rithy Panh's Cinéma-monde   25
   Joseph Mai
2. Globalisation, Cinema and Terrorism in Rachid Bouchareb's Films: *London River, Baton Rouge* and *Little Senegal*   45
   Mireille Rosello
3. Guerrilla Filmmaking with Rachid Djaïdani   65
   Laura Reeck
4. Globalisation, Cinéma-monde and the Work of Abderrahmane Sissako   85
   Dayna Oscherwitz
5. The Career of Actress Hafsia Herzi: Crossing Borders, Challenging Barriers   110
   Leslie Kealhofer-Kemp

Part II Voyages, Limits and Borders

6. Lost at Sea or Charting a New Course? Mapping the Murky Contours of Cinéma-monde in Floating Francophone Films   131
   Michael Gott
7. The Beautiful Fantasy: Imaginary Representations of Football in West African Cinema   155
   Vlad Dima

8   Merry Christmas in No Man's Land: European Borders,
    Language Barriers and Front Lines in Christian
    Carion's *Joyeux Noël*   175
    Gemma King
9   An Ostrich, a Backhoe and a few Ski-Doos: Tracking the Road
    Movie in Quebec and Beyond   192
    Thibaut Schilt
10 Accented Mappings of France in a Globalised World: *Le
    Havre* (2011) and *Samba* (2014) through the Lens of Cinéma-
    monde   216
    Leïla Ennaïli

Part III Hubs and Spheres of Production

11 Activist Cinéma-monde in Paris: Filming Foreigners in the
    French Capital   239
    Alison Rice
12 Cinema Made in Liège: A 'Hub' of Francophone Belgian
    Filmmaking   257
    Jamie Steele
13 'Images of Diversity': Film Policy and the State Struggle for
    the Representation of Difference in French Cinema   282
    Michelle Stewart
14 Youth and *Média-engagé:* Is This West Africa's
    Heterolinguistic Cinéma-monde?   304
    Carina Yervasi

Epilogues
Worlds Within; In the World   323
Bill Marshall
Cinéma-monde as a Call to Arms   336
Lucy Mazdon
Cinéma-monde and the Transnational   341
Will Higbee

Index   357

Figures

1.1	Yim Om and her son	37
1.2	Boy flying a kite in *Site 2*	40
2.1	Ousmane and Elizabeth on a public bench in a park in London	53
2.2	Ousmane praying under olive trees in the south of France	56
3.1	The beginnings of the canvases for the 'Wandering' exhibit in *Encré*	74
3.2	Activating spectatorship through a *jeu de regards* in *Rengaine*	77
4.1	Dramane leaves behind the narrative of global prosperity	92
4.2	Jihadists make movies: the film within a film in *Timbuktu*	103
5.1	Rym and her stepfather Slimane in *La Graine et le mulet*	111
5.2	Hafsia Herzi as Loubna/Esméralda in *La Source des femmes*	120
6.1	Alice and shipmates gaze over the Mediterranean	141
9.1	Benoît and Maryse sit in front of their mother's light machine in *En terrains connus*	202
9.2	Ahmed prepares to ride a Ski-Doo for the first time in *L'ange de goudron*	206
10.1	Wilson playfully acts out a TV advertisement on a suspended platform as Samba looks on	226
10.2	A close-up of a sensationalist headline in *Le Havre*	230
11.1	Anne looks on as a fellow passenger stands up to her aggressor on the metro	244
11.2	Bahia exudes compassion as she helps an elderly couple into a metro car	251
12.1	The PIL facility in Liège, with slag heaps in the background, highlighting the city's coal-mining heritage	270
13.1	Still from the climax of *Beur sur la ville*	282
13.2	Diversity in the Republican classroom; still from *Fracture*	292
13.3	Still from *Aïcha*, featuring sympathetic and strong female and Muslim characters	293

13.4 Still from *Qu'Allah bénisse la France* echoing the multi-racial composition of Mathieu Kassovitz's *La Haine* 296
14.1 Young activists with homemade signs attend a rally in early 2011, *Y en a marre/Fed-Up* (Adams Sie, 2013, Senegal) 306
14.2 Young participants cheer and hold up their brooms at the end of a rally in Ouagadougou in *'Le Balai Citoyen': Smockey et Sams'K le Jah veulent assainir le Burkina!* (Droit Libre TV, 2013, Burkina Faso) 316

Notes on Contributors

The Editors

Michael Gott Phd is Associate Professor of French and Film and Media Studies at the University of Cincinnati, where he teaches courses in European Studies, Film and Media Studies, and French-language culture and cinema. He is the author of *French-language Road Cinema: Borders, Diasporas and 'New Europe'* (Edinburgh University Press, 2016) and co-edited *Open Roads, Closed Borders: The Contemporary French-Language Road Movie* (2013) and *East, West and Centre: Reframing European Cinema Since 1989* (Edinburgh University Press, 2014). Michael has published articles and book chapters on French, Czech, Belgian, African and European cinemas.

Thibaut Schilt Phd is Associate Professor of French at the College of the Holy Cross in Massachusetts, where he teaches courses in francophone and European cinema, gender studies, and French language and culture. He is the author of the monograph *François Ozon* (2011). In 2013, he co-edited with Michael Gott the volume *Open Roads, Closed Borders: The Contemporary French-Language Road Movie*, published with Intellect Press. He has published several articles on French-language road movies and queer cinema.

Contributors

Vlad Dima PhD is an Assistant Professor at the University of Wisconsin, Madison. He has published over thirty articles, mainly on French and francophone cinemas, but also on francophone literature, American cinema and television. His first book, *Sonic Space in Djibril-Diop Mambety's Films* (2017), is forthcoming with the Indiana University Press. He is currently working on a second project titled, *The Beautiful Skin: Clothing, Football and Fantasy in West African cinema, 1964–2014*.

Leïla Ennaïli PhD is an Assistant Professor of French at Central Michigan University where she teaches French language courses as well as courses on migration and francophone studies. She obtained a PhD in 2011 from the University of Illinois. Her dissertation examines the intersection between representations of foreigners in France and the development of France's national borders from 1870 to today. She has recently worked on films depicting migrants in Calais, France and in Paris. She has published articles on Didier Daeninckx's novel *Galadio* and Ali Magoudi's novel *Un Sujet français*. Dr Ennaïli's research interests include migration studies, French and francophone literature and cinema, and identity discourses.

Will Higbee PhD is Professor of Film Studies at the University of Exeter (United Kingdom). He is the author of *Mathieu Kassovitz* and *Post-Beur Cinema* and co-editor of *De-Westernizing Film Studies* and *Studies in French Cinema: UK Perspectives 1985–2010*. He has published numerous articles on contemporary French and Maghrebi cinema, as well as on issues of national, transnational and diasporic cinemas. He is the Principal Investigator on the Arts and Humanities Research Council-funded Transnational Moroccan Cinema research project.

Leslie Kealhofer-Kemp PhD is Assistant Professor of French and Film at the University of Rhode Island. Her current research focuses on representations of minorities, and particularly minority-ethnic women, in France in cinema and on television, as well as on the films and careers of actors and actresses of North African and West African origin in France. She is the author of *Muslim Women in French Cinema: Voices of Maghrebi Migrants in France* (2015). Her work has also appeared in journals such as *The French Review*, *Modern and Contemporary France*, *Studies in French Cinema*, and *Contemporary French Civilization*.

Gemma King PhD is Lecturer in French Studies at the Australian National University. She received her PhD as a *cotutelle* from the University of Melbourne and the Université Sorbonne Nouvelle-Paris 3 in 2015. Her research focuses on contemporary French cinema, investigating the rise of multilingual film in France and the relationship between language use and social power. Her work has been published in *Contemporary French Civilization*, *The Australian Journal of French Studies* and numerous edited volumes, and her book *Decentring France: Multilingualism and Power in Contemporary French Cinema* is forthcoming.

Joseph Mai PhD is Associate Professor of French at Clemson University, where he also teaches in the World Cinemas programme. He is the author of *Jean-Pierre and Luc Dardenne* (2010), the recently completed *Robert Guédiguian* (2017) and articles exploring ethics and aesthetics in (primarily French) literature and film studies.

Bill Marshall PhD is Professor of Comparative Literary and Cultural Studies at the University of Stirling, Scotland, having previously held posts at the Universities of Southampton and Glasgow, and served as the Director of the Institute of Modern Languages Research in the School of Advanced Study, University of London. He is the author of: *Victor Serge: The Uses of Dissent* (1992), *Guy Hocquenghem: Beyond Gay Identity* (1997), *Quebec National Cinema* (2001), *André Téchiné* (2007), and *The French Atlantic: Travels in Culture and History* (2009). He has also edited books on *Musicals – Hollywood and Beyond* (2000), *Montreal-Glasgow* (2005), and a three-volume Encyclopedia on *France and the Americas* (2005). His current project is on the 'Uses of Prehistory' in modern and contemporary French culture.

Lucy Mazdon PhD is Chair in Film Studies at the University of Southampton. She has published widely in the fields of French and transnational film and television. Her publications include *Encore Hollywood: Remaking French Cinema* (2000), *France on Film: Reflections on Popular French Cinema* (2001), *Je t'aime, moi non plus: Franco-British Cinematic Relations* (2010) and *Sex, Art and Cinephilia: French Cinema in Britain* (2012, both with Catherine Wheatley).

Dayna Oscherwitz PhD is Associate Professor of French and Francophone Studies and Chair of World Languages and Literatures at Southern Methodist University in Dallas, Texas. She is author of *Past Forward: French Cinema and the Post-Colonial Heritage* (2010), co-author of *The Historical Dictionary of French Cinema* (2006), and co-editor of *The Western in the Global South* (2015). She has also published numerous articles and book chapters on French and African cinema.

Laura Reeck PhD is Professor of French at Allegheny College in Meadville, Pennsylvania. Her research interests include postcolonial literary categories; the Beur/*banlieue* literary and cultural field; the harkis in literature; ethnic minorities and film/filmmaking in France. She is the author of *Writerly Identities in Beur Fiction and Beyond* (2011). Recent articles have appeared in *Contemporary French and Francophone Studies*, *Francophone Postcolonial Studies*, *Hommes et Migrations*, *Sefar*, and in the edited volume *A Practical Guide to French Harki Literature* (ed. Moser, 2014). She is co-editor with Kathryn Kleppinger of *Post-Migratory Cultures in Postcolonial France* (forthcoming in 2018).

Alison Rice PhD is Associate Professor of French and Francophone literature and film at the University of Notre Dame. She has published a number of articles, interviews and translations, as well as two books. *Time Signatures: Contextualizing Contemporary Francophone Autobiographical Writing from the Maghreb* (2006), closely examines the writing of Hélène Cixous, Assia Djebar, and Abdelkébir Khatibi. *Polygraphies: Francophone Women Writing Algeria* (2012), focuses on Maïssa Bey, Marie Cardinal, Hélène Cixous, Assia Djebar, Malika Mokeddem, Zahia Rahmani and Leïla Sebbar. Her current project, 'Francophone Metronomes: Worldwide Women Writers in Paris,' is an in-depth study of women writers of French from around the world, complemented by filmed interviews.

Mireille Rosello PhD teaches at the University of Amsterdam in the department of Literary and Cultural Analysis and the Amsterdam School for Cultural Analysis. She focuses on globalised mobility and queer thinking. Her latest works are a special issue of the journal *Culture, Theory and Critique* (on 'disorientation', coedited with Niall Martin, 2016); an anthology on queer Europe, *What's Queer about Europe? Productive Encounters and Re-Enchanting Paradigms* (coedited with Sudeep Dasgupta, 2014) and a collection of articles on multilingualism in Europe (*Multilingual Europe, Multilingual Europeans*, coedited with László Marácz, 2012). She is currently working on rudimentariness.

Jamie Steele PhD has held the posts of Associate Lecturer and Lecturer (E&S) at the University of Exeter (United Kingdom). Dr Steele completed his PhD in Film in early 2014. His PhD thesis – entitled 'The Transnational Regional in Francophone Belgian Cinema' – focuses on film policy as well as a macro- and micro-economic analysis of the industry to consider the perceived imbalance between Belgian and French cinema. He currently has a publication contract with Edinburgh University Press for his first monograph on contemporary francophone Belgian cinema with a particular focus on the Dardenne brothers, Bouli Lanners, Olivier Masset-Depasse, Joachim Lafosse, and Lucas Belvaux.

Michelle Stewart PhD is Associate Professor of Cinema Studies and founding Chair of the School of Film and Media Studies at Purchase College-SUNY. She received her PhD from the University of Minnesota in Cultural Studies & Comparative Literature. Her dissertation, 'Sovereign Visions: Native North American Documentary', investigates the development of Native North American filmmaking as a creative form of cultural activism that is tied to a political programme of cultural revival, self-determination, and national sovereignty. With Pam Wilson (Reinhardt College), she co-edited *Global Indigenous Media: Cultures, Practices, and Politics* (2007). Her most recent research concerns film policy and minority cinema in Europe, with an emphasis on the filmmaking of North African and West African immigrants in France. She has been a Fulbright Scholar, Kempner Distinguished Professor at Purchase, and a fellow at the Institute for Advanced Studies in Marseille.

Carina Yervasi PhD is Associate Professor of French and Francophone Studies and associate faculty in Black Studies and Film and Media Studies at Swarthmore College. She teaches and researches francophone media representations of youth and resistance, feminisms, and diasporas. She has published on Belgian cinema and feminism in *SITES*, on the films of Burkinabé Dani Kouyaté and urban youth culture in *Research in African Literature*, and on French cinema in *Film and History*. At present, she is working on a manuscript about narratives of displacement in contemporary francophone West African media.

Acknowledgements

Michael Gott and Thibaut Schilt thank all the authors who contributed to this volume, as well as the staff at the University of Edinburgh Press, especially Eddie Clark, Gillian Leslie, Rebecca MacKenzie and Richard Strachan. Special thanks are due to each of our three epilogue writers for agreeing to contribute a response to our volume under tight time constraints. We are also grateful to Frédérick Pelletier for giving us permission to use a still from his film *Diego Star* for the book cover.

Michael Gott would like to thank the Taft Research Center and the Center for Film and Media Studies at the University of Cincinnati, Leslie Kealhofer-Kemp, Joe Mai and the students in his Spring 2016 seminar on the topic of 'Cinéma-monde' for their insightful weekly discussions of many of the films covered in the volume.

Thibaut Schilt thanks the Department of Modern Languages and Literatures at the College of the Holy Cross, as well as Elena Past, Marie McDonough and Vinay Swamy.

INTRODUCTION

The Kaleidoscope of Cinéma-monde

Michael Gott and Thibaut Schilt

The first cinema awards specifically dedicated to internationally produced francophone films were created in 2013, under the supervision of the then Canadian-based Association Trophées Francophones du Cinéma (or ATFciné), with the assistance of filmmakers and organisers of film festivals and national film awards working in Belgium, Senegal, Quebec and France. The initiative behind these film awards is unique in that it brings together a variety of film industries and national cinemas, and is inclusive in its definition of 'francophone',[1] expanding the geographical limits of what is customarily considered the francophone world and formally recognising an increasing number of films that combine French with many other languages or do not contain any French at all. Such inclusivity has not yet been fully extended to the academic realm, where divisions between French and francophone categories linger. An article entitled 'Cinéma-monde? Towards a Concept of Francophone Cinema' by Bill Marshall (2012) represents the most significant and promising step in that direction. In it Marshall calls for increased critical attention to develop the concept of 'francophone film' in both French and Film Studies, 'given the remappings necessary both in relation to the global and transnational turn in analysing film and in rear guard attempts to assert French and other cultural nationalisms that also take place' (2012: 51). For Marshall, francophone cinema, by decentring French-language cinema studies, 'dramatically focuses attention on four elements: borders, movement, language, and lateral connections' (2012: 42).

This collection seeks to build upon Marshall's intervention and those of other scholars who have theorised transnational and world cinemas and to extend and adapt the debate that erupted after the publication of the 2007 manifesto 'For a *littérature-monde* in French' (Barbery et al.) from literature to cinema. Whereas Marshall employs 'cinéma-monde' in his title, he adorns it with a question mark and only refers back to the term again once in the text. In its place he opts for the concept of 'francophone' cinema derived from the Deleuzian concept of 'francophonising', an active verb that outlines a minorising of a heretofore centred notion of 'French' cinema (2012: 44). Despite what Dominique Wolton describes as *la Francophonie*'s capacity to 'valorize cultural diversity as a central phenomenon of globalization' (2006: 20), we have chosen to use 'cinéma-monde' to describe our approach to cinema, primarily as a means to transcend a 'francophone' label that is problematic in a variety of ways. The *littérature-monde* manifesto prompted scholars and authors alike to examine the continued validity of the francophone discursive category. Though 'francophone' was initially an optic through which to 'de-centre a model of French studies that was focused exclusively on the Hexagon' (Hargreaves, et al. 2010: 2), it also enabled a two-tiered dichotomy that often relegated literature and films made in France and those made in its former colonies to discrete categories. Moreover, to say simply 'francophone' runs the risk of eliding both European French-language productions – most notably but not exclusively from Belgium and Switzerland – and diversity within the Hexagon that is not derived from the colonial or, as the manifesto signers argued, neo-colonial (Hargreave, et al. 2010: 2). Florence Martin, in the latest scholarly intervention to engage with the term 'cinéma-monde' – in this instance through a case study of Maghrebi film – suggests that it may offer a way to 'help scholars steer away from *francophonie* altogether' (2016: 474).[2]

This collection is the first to examine contemporary cinema within a wilfully broad 'French-language' category and aims to explore the opportunities and limitations of adopting the label of 'cinéma-monde' (as opposed to francophone, transnational, or world cinema) as a critical framework or optic through which to approach a flexible corpus of films that are linked to the francophone world by some combination of linguistic or cultural affinities, geographic contacts, production connections, or reception networks. Cinéma-monde, as considered in the fourteen chapters and three epilogues in this collection, is not mapped exclusively along the boundaries of French-speaking countries, regions, or zones. It may be multilingual, or in some cases contains very little French but holds some other connection to the world of French-language cinema. The links generated by and generating cinéma-monde might be narrative, cultural, symbolic, practical, or financial. Concepts such as Randall Halle's 'interzones' (2014; see Chapter 6 in this volume) or Mary Louise Pratt's 'contact zones' (2010) offer particularly useful ways to think about the connections engendered in cinéma-monde. Crucially, those authors do not neglect the economic component that often frames various forms of contact. Halle insists that films be approached as products as well as art and offers an analysis of how transnational cinematic apparatuses function. Pratt suggests that 'trading posts' are a key site of exchange (along with border cities) and emphasises the often asymmetrical quality of these exchanges. If cinéma-monde seeks to level the analytical playing field by decentring 'French' film studies, we acknowledge that economic conditions that affect funding and distribution of film projects are far from level. Indeed, as Kathleen Newman argues in the context of transnational cinema, 'all relations between center and periphery are uneven' (2010: 10). What Halle terms the 'neo-orientalism' of European film funding (2010) refers to economic relations that affect cinematic storytelling. As Martin points out, the plural appellation *cinémas du monde* that is represented annually at the Cannes film festival and disseminated by French networks with global reaches, is also a political instrument:

> Hence the *cinémas du monde* are but an extension of the French state, a political instrument officially designed 1) to strategically maintain the use of the French language and culture throughout the former colonies and beyond; and 2) spread messages and sponsor films that, although not always in French, promote the ideals of the French Republic. (2016: 463)

We intend to expand the discussion of these concepts by analysing production networks and films in which filmmakers, production teams, actors, and narratives are situated within and/or move to, from, through and beyond diverse regions of the French-speaking world. This includes Quebec, Belgium, the Caribbean, North Africa, sub-Saharan Africa, the Middle East, Southeast Asia, and transnational regional spaces within France that defy strictly national and linguistic categories. We will focus in particular on exploring the porosity of various kinds of borders in and around francophone spaces and the ways in which languages and identities 'travel' in contemporary cinema. Cinéma-monde, as we understand it, does not simply designate cinema in French from outside of France. Nor does it exclude France. While the French market looms large in the production equation and Paris continues to exert a magnetic pull on filmmakers, France and its capital by no means represent the centre of cinéma-monde. Thus we will consider how global production and reception of cinema allows us to 'look sideways to lateral networks that are not always readily apparent', a gesture that opens the door to an exploration of the 'relationships among different margins' (Lionnet and Shih 2005: 1–2). The city of Montreal, for example, where the National Film Board of Canada has its headquarters and where the aforementioned ATFciné was originally based, thrives as an ever more robust cinema hub, producing francophone films that are gaining significant attention outside the borders of Quebec and are often co-produced with other francophone partner countries.

The ATFciné awards are an intriguing if perhaps ultimately unsatisfying starting point for discussions of what types of parameters might be applied to a more flexible, inclusive and diverse approach to French-language cinematic production. The association was founded in Montreal in 2012 by Henry Welsh, a former producer of the Québécois *Prix Jutra* award ceremony (renamed in 2016 Gala Québec Cinema/*Prix Iris*). Its offices are now based in Paris and Abderrahmane Sissako, whose film *Timbuktu* (see Chapter 4) won the 2015 *Trophée*, is currently president. The stated objective of the ATFciné is to present an annual 'panorama of the diversity of cinematic production from nations in *la Francophonie*' (ATFciné). To this end the association holds an annual awards ceremony televised on TV5 monde in rotating cities of the francophone world – the first three ceremonies were held in Dakar, Paris and Abidjan – accompanied by screenings of the films nominated for awards. Another aim is to provide funding on a competitive basis to support local film projects in the nation hosting the award. The criteria determining eligibility of individual films is worthy of attention for the flexible definition it sketches of what makes a film 'francophone'. To qualify for an ATFciné award a film must contain dialogue that is at least 50% in French or another language spoken in the country of production, which must be one of the 54 full members of *l'Organisation internationale de la francophonie*. Membership, then, comprises both 'francophone' or partly French-speaking nations (Canada, the Ivory Coast, Belgium, Switzerland, Tunisia), countries that retain a small postcolonial francophone presence (Cambodia, Lebanon, Vietnam) and yet others with primarily symbolic cultural connections to the French language or France (Armenia, Egypt, Greece, Romania). Added to this is the potentially vague proviso that the director must attest that he or she speaks French '*correctement*'. If these guidelines do go some way in widening our mental space of what francophone cinema is and might be, they nonetheless exclude some films that undoubtedly should be part of a conversation about cinéma-monde. For example, *Transylvania* (2006, France) by Tony Gatlif, a major transnational French director, might not be included because while made and set in Romania, the international troupe of actors primarily converse in English. Likewise a film such as *Le voyage du ballon rouge/Flight of the Red Balloon* (2007, France/Taiwan), by Hou Hsiao-Hsien, would be disqualified despite being set in Paris and featuring a major French actress (Juliette Binoche) because Hou does not speak French.

If a classification system based on *les Trophées francophones* is not entirely satisfactory, the films figuring amongst the nominees represents a diverse line-up that seems destined to provoke the kind of categorical 'slippages' that Marshall (2012: 39) suggests are positive. The *Trophées* list includes films in Amazigh; Arabic; Armenian; Dioula; English; English, Greek, and Serbian; French and Arabic; Khmer; Haoussa; Lingala; Luxembourgish and English; Mauritian Creole; Malgache; Malinké; Mooré; Vietnamese; Wolof; sign language; and Romanian. Even in cases when French mingles with other languages within the dialogue, it is immediately clear that the label 'francophone' does not adequately contain these films.

Lateral connections like those evoked by Marshall in his article that launched the cinéma-monde discussion and by Lionnet and Shih in their conception of 'minor transnationalism' are evident in many of the films shortlisted for the *Trophées*. A film such as *Spartiates* (2015) by Swiss director Nicolas Wadimoff, nominated for best documentary, about a martial arts club in the *banlieue* of Marseille, demonstrates the behind the scenes links that contribute to the creative inspiration and production contexts of cinéma-monde. The trajectory of the Geneva-born Wadimoff is particularly illustrative of decentred, lateral francophone connections because he studied film in Montreal and made his first feature film, *Clandestins* (1997, Switzerland/Canada/France/Belgium) with Québécois director Denis Chouinard (see Chapters 6 and 9 for more on Chouinard). If *Spartiates* is an example of a film project with transnational roots and a decidedly local focus, Franco-Senegalese director Dyana Gaye's *Des étoiles/Under the Starry Sky* (2013, France/Belgium/Senegal), a 2014 nominee, is an example of how cinema reflects increasingly varied trajectories within and beyond the francophone world. The narrative of this multilocal film with dialogue in English, French, Italian and Wolof criss-crosses between Dakar, New York, and Turin, in the process demonstrating that the postcolonial axis (France–Senegal in this case) is no longer the sole or even the primary trajectory for French speakers.

Accented Cinemas: from Elvis Gratton to Hamid Naficy

In Quebec directors Pierre Falardeau and Julien Poulin's 1985 cult classic *Elvis Gratton: le King des Kings*, the titular character is questioned by a French man sitting near him on a plane: 'Vous êtes canadien? Vous avez l'accent . . .' [Are you Canadian? You have the accent . . .]. The response from Elvis and his wife is both humorous and telling on a number of levels:

> 'Elvis' Gratton: Moé, je suis un Canadien québécois, un Français canadien-français . . . Un Américain du Nord français, un francophone Québécois canadien . . . Un Québécois d'expression canadienne-française française . . .

Linda Gratton: On est des Canadiens américains francophones d'Amérique du Nord
... Des Franco-Québécois ...

Their French interlocutor is justifiably perplexed by the complexity of this response to his query about identity, which is both patronising and simplistic (many Québécois would not identify themselves primarily as Canadian). The verbal gymnastics that Elvis and his wife engage in as a means of explaining their identities as francophone Quebecers become the object of ridicule for Falardeau and Poulain, who created the buffoonish Elvis as a caricature of anti-independence voters after the failed 1980 Quebec independence referendum. This contorted construction of self – premised on the desire to avoid a simpler identity as 'Québécois' – is qualified and hyphenated to the point of incomprehensibility and absurdity. Beyond the particular political context that grounds this scene, the exchange is germane to our discussion of cinéma-monde in two ways. First, it puts on display the difficulty of naming complex identities that cannot be summed up by a national label and the incessant need of individuals and communities to label themselves. This is something that most of the characters, actors, and directors under consideration in this volume are likely to grapple with. Secondly, it reveals a tendency that we aim to counter with our cinéma-monde approach: the relegation of so-called 'accented' French to the margins of the French-speaking world (or indeed of France). Case studies in the following chapters involve speakers of French from around the world, including Quebec, Africa and Europe, who communicate with other francophones but also sometimes fail to make themselves understood due to differences within the French language. A number of the films covered involve lateral connections between different places and different accents from the French-speaking world. With his film *Congorama* (2006, Canada/Belgium/France; discussed in Chapter 9), Québécois director Philippe Falardeau tells a story that links Canada and Belgium (and the Congo), bypassing France as political cinematic statement that is in part a reaction to what he perceives as the linguistic intolerance of the French film industry. Falardeau denounces the expectation that Belgian and Québécois actors and actresses working in Metropolitan France must hide their accents (Castiel 2006).

Our conception of cinéma-monde is not limited to spaces outside the Hexagon. Regional accents have largely been an unacceptable mark of distinction from a 'standard' French that is synonymous with Paris and the French film industry. In an interview in support of his 2016 film *Chouf*, Marseille-based director Karim Dridi made a point similar to Falardeau's when he protested that French cinema has a 'Parisian accent' and suggested that an actor from the nation's second city is expected to lose his or her accent in order to get work.³ Dridi contends that this attitude overlooks an 'enormous' amount of linguistic inventiveness in Marseille, where the regional French is inflected with words drawn from languages including Arabic, Comorian and Romany (RFI 2016). *Chouf*, funded by the CNC, expresses this diversity with its Arabic title transcribed into Latin characters and is a still too rare example of diversity in French cinema.

Several of our contributors turn to Hamid Naficy's incisive work on 'accented cinema' in order to frame their analysis of decentred cinema. This volume, both directly and filtered through Marshall's call to 'put the accent back' in French-language cinema (2012: 45), takes some important cues from Naficy's formulation. We propose that cinéma-monde should be delineated in a fashion similar to 'accented cinema', which does not refer to a cohesive category but to a 'cinematic formation' that Naficy identifies in 'disparate and dispersed pockets around the globe' (2001: 4). Like 'accented cinema', cinéma-monde is also elaborated in relationship to a centre: 'If the dominant cinema is considered universal and without accent, the films that diasporic and exilic subjects make are accented' (2001: 4). One could make the case that every film considered in this volume is to some extent 'accented' in relation to French cinema. Marshall argues for an expansion of Naficy's premise to a wider context of francophone film, including a diversity of voices from within French cinema that are, for a variety of reasons, peripheral (2012: 44). Marshall's conception of 'accent' in cinema does not necessarily hinge on outsider status vis-à-vis the industry, or even on an interstitial relationship – 'astride and in the interstices', as Naficy puts it (2001: 40) – and includes space for films made and distributed within normal industry channels such as *Bienvenue chez les Ch'tis / Welcome to the Sticks* (Dany Boon, 2008, France). Although a French-only production, Boon's box office sensation generates several levels of 'lateral' connections. Marshall cites the use of the Picard dialect, whose terrain extends beyond the border with Belgium, and brings up a comparison with a film from Quebec with a similar premise, Jean-François Pouliot's 2003 *La Grande Séduction / Seducing Doctor Lewis* (2012: 45). Such juxtapositions of francophone films, Marshall contends, opens the door to 'fruitful comparisons' and 'through their multiplication of perspectives pluralise the whole debate' (2012: 46).

To put the accent back, then, is 'to say that the Francophone cultural and linguistic world is interesting only when all its accents, contexts, and mixings are *made audible*' (Marshall 2012: 45; original emphasis). To make diversity audible through accents widely conceived is a foundational premise of our cinéma-monde project. Yet if we believe that this is a good starting point, it is not enough. Returning to Elvis Gratton, the example of a connection made because of shared language helps to illustrate the basic contours of what cinéma-monde might look like. In a practical sense, for research, teaching or viewing, cinéma-monde is a label under which to combine and compare films (and other media) from diverse geographic sources that are linked to a francophone linguistic, and also cultural, world or worlds. However, if a cinéma-monde approach might resonate, it is not simply because we identify encounters such as that between a Frenchman and a Quebecer on screen or behind the scenes in the production of a film, even if one enquires about the other's accent. This exchange on a plane leaves the Frenchman with no particular new insight; the accent, life and identity of his Québécois fellow passenger is just as opaque and odd to him as it was before their exchange. Cinéma-monde becomes more than a potentially useful classification when the encounter, in this case the explanation of Québécois identity, sparks solidarity, or at least recognition of a shared experience. The two (or more) interlocutors must forge some sort of connection via a common marginal or alternative position or a shared ethic. We will return to this idea in the following section.

Delineating Cinéma-monde

So far, using the example of the ATFciné, we have sketched out a conception of cinéma-monde as a category that is broader and more flexible than 'francophone'. Adding the question of accents to the conversation highlights our desire to also focus on diversity within the spaces of francophone cinema. A cinéma-monde approach, then, would simultaneously be concerned with expanding a francophone discursive category and emphasising the linguistic and cultural diversity that might be hidden behind that term if it is understood in binary terms or as derivative from French colonialism. Before outlining a few more parameters that have informed this collection, it is important to emphasise that we are not forwarding cinéma-monde as a static category or classification. Instead, we prefer to view it as an optic or framework through which to approach a flexible corpus. Each of the films, filmmakers, actors and locations in this book could be approached in a number of ways. Cinéma-monde is just one optic through which we can examine their relationships to other parts of the world or their internal diversity. In Chapter 8, Gemma King draws on Mireille Rosello's conceptualisation of 'mosaic Europe' (2012: 215) as a space where language difference is overcome but not eliminated in encounters between individuals. While the concept is apt to King's examination of *Joyeux Noël* (Christian Carion, 2005, France/Germany/UK/Belgium/Romania/Norway/Japan/USA), and certainly many other films that fall under our purview, in a wider cinéma-monde context we would prefer a kaleidoscope over a mosaic as a metaphor. The layers of a kaleidoscope are not fixed but shift, and various images become clear or are seen under different light as the instrument is turned and light refracted. Cinéma-monde is also kaleidoscopic because it involves looking at the world through a particular yet variable and adjustable optic. As stated already, in our understanding, cinéma-monde is not a concept coterminous with the boundaries of French-speaking nations or zones, nor is it exclusively extra-hexagonal. It may be multilingual, or in some cases contains very little French but holds a link to the production apparatus of French-language cinema or nurtures a cultural connection with the francophone world. It might float within and across fluid margins. It might also be confronted and divided – indeed increasingly so – by less permeable boundaries, such as the official borders of the European Union. The concept should allow us to bring together a variety of film industries and national cinemas, and be inclusive in its definition of 'francophone', expanding the geographical limits of what is customarily considered *la Francophonie*, which is depicted as a 'heterolingual' space (Sanaker 2010), and formally recognising an increasing number of films that combine French with many other languages. Multiple nodes must be considered in any construction of a meaningful theory of cinéma-monde; these include production, narrative, the economic context, and the migration of films, filmmakers, and protagonists. Lastly, but crucially, if these films are well-suited to examine the 'fuzzy and flexible border crossings' (Iordanova 2010: 68–69) that have unmoored French cinema from its national context and what Shohat and Stam (2003: 1) call a 'web of connectedness' that links places, they also account for the unequal relations of power involved in such networks and in global mobilities in general (Tarr 2007: 3). As Nataša Ďurovičová observes In *World Cinemas, Transnational Perspectives*, the 'trans-' prefix 'implies relations of unevenness and mobility' (2010: x)

In comparison to the 'world cinema' and 'transnational cinema' categories, cinéma-monde is slightly less broad in its purview. Cinéma-monde is transnational, and it is of the world or greatly concerned with the world and with others. However, our conception of *monde*, as the French term suggests, is more limited by design to include linguistic and cultural connections that belong to what we would like to call 'franco-zones'. Similar to 'contact zones' (Pratt 2010), franco-zones are physical spaces within or across francophone or non-francophone countries or even virtual, ideational spaces where these cultural and linguistic connections might occur.

In their introduction to the collection *Theorizing World Cinema*, Lucia Nagib, Chris Perriam and Rajinder Dudrah note the major downside of the 'world cinema' label: 'the "problems" with world cinema start with the name itself . . . [which] has given origin to a highly questionable, though enduringly popular, opposition between the American mainstream and the rest of the world' (2012: xix). In order to avoid the trap of this duality, they engage with a 'polycentric' approach to cinema (2012: xxii). As we have already stated, one of the primary aims of taking a cinéma-monde approach is the desire to avoid similar dichotomies, in this case between the French industry and films made at least partly outside of that production and funding apparatus. As the following chapters make clear, from the Paris-set 'activist' films concerned with interactions between denizens of the capital and outsiders (Chapter 11) to the culturally and cine-industrially marginal 'guerrilla filmmaking' of Rachid Djaïdani (Chapter 3), a decentred perspective and approach to cinema need not be entirely situated in a peripheral space. Other contributors engage with resolutely peripheral spaces, such as Dakar and Ouagadougou (Chapter 14). What links the above chapters and many of the films explored in the volume's corpus are the gestures of solidarity, ethics or interest in others that they contain. Much like David Damrosch's (2003) definition of 'World Literature' (see Chapter 1), cinéma-monde is fundamentally about 'encounters' between different cultures and perspectives (2003: 5). This type of encounter would be the counterexample to Elvis Gratton's humorous but unproductive exchange described in the previous section: to be meaningful, encounters must involve what Galt and Schoonover in their collection *Global Art Cinema* label (cinematic) 'openness', a stance that as Laura Rascaroli notes is related to a good deal of anxiety in a post-crisis Europe and a post-9/11 world (2013).

To different degrees – or different 'scales', to use Hjort's term (2010: 13) – these encounters and connections are all transnational. Moreover, cinéma-monde, much like 'littérature-monde', as Thérèse Migraine-George puts it in her book on the latter topic, can be a site of 'renewed transnational debates' on identity and ethics (2013: ix). In a similar vein, Hjort argues that the value of cinematic transnationalism is derived from its 'resistance to globalization as cultural homogenization' (2010: 15). Likewise, cinéma-monde is resistant to homogenising forces and attuned to accommodation or at least acknowledgement of differences. It must also be stated that even when potentially meaningful encounters result, the transnational is not *a priori* positive, liberating, celebratory, or virtuous (Ezra and Rowden 2006: 9; Hjort 2010). There are a number of reasons that people and languages come into contact. Causes for connections and situations that necessitate a lingua franca include travel and migration, but also war, terrorism, commerce, illicit trade, trafficking and espionage. Espionage is behind the French dialogue – alongside Russian and English – in Christian Carion's Moscow-set spy film *L'affaire Farewell/Farewell* (2009, France). Global trafficking brings the francophone Lithuanian protagonist in Sarunas Bartas's *Indigène d'Eurasie/Eastern Drift* (2010, France/Lithuania/Russia), a film that includes dialogue in French, Lithuanian, Polish and Russian, to Paris and a small port town in France as well as to Moscow and Vilnius. In Carion's *Joyeux Noël* war is the pretext for dialogue across national boundaries.

Franco-zones and Hubs: Production and Diffusion

The decentring process at play in cinéma-monde recognises, as we have already mentioned, the presence of 'franco-zones' within which exist a series of 'hubs' that are laterally connected to one another with no singular centre. These hubs, which collectively comprise and delineate cinéma-monde, are free to associate with multiple 'partners' at once in an organic fashion. Put another way, the identity of cinéma-monde, even though itself a compound term, should be understood as an alternative to strictly bilateral, hyphenated connections (Franco-Senegalese, Belgo-Québécois etc.). Instead, its components are protean and interchangeable. This decentring occurs at the level of production, funding and promotion (and indeed, prizes, as the ATFciné awards attest), but also within the films themselves. Alongside her discussion of Ismaël Ferroukhi's transnational, multilingual, internationally-produced road movie *Le Grand Voyage/ The Great Journey* (2004, France/Morocco/Bulgaria/Turkey), Mireille Rosello suggests that 'just as a new "*littérature-monde*" [. . .] seems to be displacing the old "Francophone" category, new films treat France or Frenchness as one of the multiple nodes in an individually reinvented global network' (2011: 260). The same remark can be made of the aforementioned *Des étoiles*, produced by France, Belgium and Senegal and set in New York, Dakar and Turin, as well as many other contemporary road movies (and 'floating films'; see Chapter 6), which are inherently multilocal and thus, in narrative terms, the ultimate decentred films.

When it comes to production and financing, cinéma-monde is composed of numerous hubs of various sizes, an assemblage of usually, but not always, francophone cities or regions that are crucial to its existence and sustenance. Belgium's thriving, bilingual film industry comprises, on the francophone side, the Brussels region and, as Chapter 12 attests, an increasingly important cinema made and produced in Liège and whose films are set in the city itself, its suburbs, and the wider Walloon region. Similar, if more modest, systems of support exist in Switzerland and Luxembourg. Within metropolitan France, a number of strong production and funding hubs outside the Paris/Île-de-France region have developed around Lyon/Rhône-Alpes, in Nord-Pas-de-Calais, and in Provence, among others, and 'regional directors' (such as Bruno Dumont and Dany Boon in the north, Diane Kurys and Gaël Morel in Lyon, Karim Dridi and Robert Guédiguian in Marseille/L'Estaque, for example) have emerged. The Quebec film industry, based in Montreal, is strong and self-sufficient, despite its difficulties (with some exceptions) penetrating the francophone film market outside of its borders (see Chapter 9 for further details). Though some decline in production and (notoriously) in the number of operating movie theatres can be recognised in both North and sub-Saharan Africa (Marshall 2012: 40–41), Senegal, Morocco, Burkina Faso and Chad are important filmmaking hubs for cinéma-monde and, as Chapter 14 argues in the case of West Africa, for the activist video-making of *média-engagé*. With regard to francophone sub-Saharan African cinema specifically, Dominic Thomas asserts that its films are connected to a social, economic and political structure of interaction with France and other francophone European nations that effectively blurs the lines of demarcation between the films made on the two continents and results in 'a complex network of transversal influences' (2009: 142). This fluid, dialogic relationship between multiple actors within the film industry encapsulates the spirit of cinéma-monde. Not all of the production that makes up cinéma-monde emanates from what we have described as a hub. Indeed, 'franco-zones' encompassed in the following chapters include places such as Cambodia, London and New York, which are not significant sites of cinéma-monde production.

The promotion and diffusion of the francophone world's cinematic output is ensured by film festivals worldwide, many of which are exhibiting signs of an increasingly transnational tendency. Among them are the Festival panafricain du cinéma et de la télévision de Ouagadougou (FESPACO), the Festival international du film francophone de Namur, the Festival du cinéma méditerranéen de Bruxelles (CINEMAMED), the Festival international de cinéma méditerranéen de Montpellier (Cinémed), the COLCOA French Film Festival (based in Hollywood, California), the Marrakech International Film Festival, the Festival international du cinéma francophone en Acadie (FICFA; held in Moncton, New Brunswick), the Festival du film francophone de Vienne (sponsored by UniFrance), the Rencontres internationales des cinémas arabes (Marseille), the Journées Cinématographiques de

Carthage, the Festival du film francophone d'Angoulême, and the Bucharest International Film Festival (BIFF, which has a special 'film francophone' award). Evidently, these festivals vary greatly in both importance and influence; and some of them (like that of Austria) do not give out prizes and only screen films. Nonetheless, they create 'contact points' both within and outside the franco-zone and collectively reshape the map of cinéma-monde.

In the next and final section of this introduction, we provide a brief summary of each of the fourteen chapters present in this collection. While we made every possible effort to render visible as many layers as possible of the kaleidoscope that is cinéma-monde in the space we were allotted, we had to leave out, however reticently, many crucial representatives. We mention some of them in passing in this introduction, and others are named, also briefly, in the ensuing chapters. Let us refer to more of them here. While Hafsia Herzi is the only actor whose border-crossing, polyglot attributes are examined in detail in this volume (see Chapter 5), similar claims could be made about Lubna Azabal, Hiam Abbass, Sabrina Ouazani, Saïd Taghmaoui, Ronit Elkabetz, Zinedine Soualem, Isaka Sawadogo, Mehdi Nebbou, Linh Dan Pham, and Nadia Kaci, among others. In addition to the individual directors whose cinema is analysed in some detail in the ensuing chapters, we would like to recognise others who shape the contours of cinéma-monde in important ways: Karim Dridi, Ilmaar Raag, Amos Gitai, Otar Iosseliani, Alain Gomis, Raoul Peck, Nabil Ayouch, Lionel Baier, Ursula Meier, Greg Zglinski, Fernand Melgar, Chantal Akerman, Trần Anh Hùng, Nicolas Wadimoff, Onur Karaman, Oliver Laxe, Leyla Bouzid, Nadir Moknèche, Nadia El Fani, Merzak Allouache, Rafi Pitts, Christophe Karabache, Kalthoum Bornaz, Emir Kusturica (also as an actor), Narjiss Nejjar, Radu Mihaileanu, Tony Gatlif, Danis Tanovic, Ismaël Ferroukhi, and Abdellatif Kechiche. Collectively, these actors and directors come from, work in, or culturally associate with nations that include Lithuania, Georgia, Mexico, Belgium, Tunisia, Romania, Israel, Bosnia and Herzegovina, Haiti, Vietnam, Iran, Spain, Serbia, Turkey, Quebec, Switzerland, Lebanon, Morocco, France and Algeria.

In addition to this list of directors with at least a small corpus of work, we may reference individual films that delineate cinéma-monde in compelling ways, either because they contain some French dialogues but are not immediately recognisable as 'francophone', or because they contain no French at all, but are considered 'French' because of how they were produced, or who directed them. In the former category, let us mention Philippe Aractingi's *Sous les bombes/Under the Bombs* (2007,

France/Lebanon/UK) and *Mirath/Heritages* (2013, Lebanon/United Arab Emirates/France/Switzerland/Germany); Fanny Ardant's *Cendres et sang/Ashes and Blood* (2009, France/Romania/Portugal) and *Cadences obstinées/Obsessive Rhythms* (2013, France/Portugal); *Rabat* (Victor Ponten and Jim Taihuttu, 2011, Netherlands); *Le Voyage en occident/Journey to the West* (Ming-liang Tsai, 2014, France/Taiwan); and *Smrt u Sarajevu/Death in Sarajevo* (Danis Tanovic, 2016, France/Bosnia and Herzegovina). In the latter category, films worth noting are *Xenia* (Panos Koutras, 2014, Greece/France/Belgium) and especially *Mustang* (Deniz Gamze Ergüven, 2015, France/Germany/Turkey/Qatar), a film with dialogue entirely in Turkish that represented France in the Best Foreign-Language Film category at the 2016 Academy Awards. Another category that bears mentioning is that of films produced in Quebec that primarily feature dialogue in indigenous languages. The dialogue in *Avant les rues/Before the Streets* (Chloé Leriche, 2016, Canada) is primarily in Atikamekw, interspersed with bits of French. Leriche's film might circulate as 'Canadian' (as when it screened at the Berlin Film Festival in 2016), within francophone contexts as Québécois production, and across North American and global indigenous communities as a film that addresses some of the shared concerns of those communities. The above is clearly not an exhaustive list. Yet another type of film that might fit in the cinéma-monde conversation is Jacques Audiard's *Dheepan* (2015), a French production with a transnational narrative trajectory and far more dialogue in Tamil than in French.

From Cambodia to Timbuktu: Decentred Perspectives on Global French-language Cinema

The topics, themes and individual films covered in the fourteen chapters of this collection constitute an extensive, but in no way exhaustive, representation of the 'decentred perspectives' on world cinema in French (among a multitude of other languages) that we intended to highlight in this project. The enclosed essays contribute to an initial definition and demarcation of the parameters of cinéma-monde via an exploration of a diverse range of cinematic productions that include feature films, short films, documentaries as well as *reportages* produced on mobile phones. Together, our contributors travel around a vast and varied cinéma-monde, whether on land or on water, making pit stops in Thailand, London, Morocco, Louisiana, Quebec, New York City, Mali, Liège, Normandy, Senegal, Palestine, Poland, Algeria, Provence, Paris, Tunisia, Iraq, Sète, Brussels and Burkina Faso, among other locales. Some of the films analysed here – whether fiction films or documentaries produced for television, the cinema, or online distribution – were directed by veteran, critically-acclaimed auteurs, by experimental filmmakers, or by relative newcomers, and cover all of the primary regions where francophone cinema is made today.

The volume is divided into three sections organised thematically and each containing four or five essays. Part I, entitled 'From Local to Global: The *Cinéma(s)-monde(s)* of Auteurs and Actors', focuses on four individual international directors and one particularly versatile actress, all of whom contribute in crucial ways to a reshaping, as well as a remapping (both literal and figurative), of a French-produced cinema that is both local and global. In Chapter 1 Joseph Mai examines the 'rigorously local' filmmaking of Franco-Cambodian director Rithy Panh. The author remarks that Panh's committed cinema insists on recording the everyday yet far from ordinary lives of the victims of the Khmer Rouge regime in the director's native country as well as in refugee camps in neighbouring Thailand. Mai focuses his attention on *Site 2* and argues that this documentary is a particularly noteworthy representative of cinéma-monde in its ability to create an 'encounter' that renders the site of the film tactile to the viewers while simultaneously challenging their geopolitical understanding of the world. Rachid Bouchareb's multilocal, multilingual filmmaking is the focal point of Chapter 2, in which Mireille Rosello examines the 'global vision' of this French director of Algerian descent, whose oeuvre critiques, among other things, the traditional Western view on terrorism. In her analysis of three particular films, Rosello contends that cinema, globalisation and terrorism are inextricably linked in Bouchareb's cinematic interpretation of the world. Chapter 3 is dedicated to what Laura Reeck terms the 'guerrilla filmmaking' of Rachid Djaïdani. She discusses the 'minorised' and 'minority' hexagonal cinema of the Franco-Algero-Sudanese activist writer turned filmmaker, whose experimental documentary and fiction films challenge French cinema to reinvent itself in a way that would enable outsiders to be welcomed into its inner circle. In Chapter 4 Dayna Oscherwitz compares and contrasts Abderrahmane Sissako's better-known films with the English-language novels of the Afropolitanism movement, whose African-born characters all share a familiarity with the realities of the Global North. Oscherwitz surveys the most celebrated films of the Mauritanian-born, Malian-raised, Russian-trained, French-based director, demonstrating how they dispute the universal narrative on globalisation and concomitantly root themselves in the specific context of francophone Africa. Leslie Kealhofer-Kemp concludes Part I with a close look at the impressive global career of the young French actress Hafsia Herzi, whose unique cinematic ability to cross national borders and challenge barriers, whether linguistic, cultural, or otherwise, is the focus of Chapter 5. The author considers the filmography of the actress, who is of Maghrebi origin and grew up speaking both French and Algerian Arabic, and discusses Herzi's career choices as well as the press's reception of her films, ultimately contending that her body of work cannot be divorced from either Metropolitan France or so-called francophone cinema.

Part II, 'Voyages, Limits and Borders', comprises discussions of individual films that collectively delineate and define cinéma-monde, whether in the themes they tackle, the journeys upon which they embark, or the cross-national realities of their production. Each chapter analyses narrative voyages by land and sea through, from, to, or across francophone linguistic zones; or assesses post-border crossing representations of migrants and refugees in France. In Chapter 6, Michael Gott centres his attention on the aquatic attributes and political implications of 'floating francophone films', which all take place on a variety of vessels, whether docked or at sea. The author argues that water in these films constitutes both 'hard' and 'soft' borders (Eder 2006), creating multiple productive 'points of contact' between disparate regions of the world while also segregating European and North American francophone zones from non-European spaces. In Chapter 7 Vlad Dima investigates the representation of football in the films of three contemporary West African directors, Moussa Touré (Senegal), Abderrahmane Sissako (Mali), and Mahamat Saleh Haroun (Chad). Dima draws connection between the ubiquity of the sport in many parts of the world (a veritable 'football-monde') with cinema's own universal potential, and constructs a psychoanalytical model for neocolonial subjectivity as it emerges from what the author calls 'the clutches of fantasy'. In Chapter 8 Gemma King provides a close reading of a film that assembles a multinational cast of characters in one place, Christian Carion's international co-production *Joyeux Noël* (2005). Based on the true story of the 1914 Christmas truce, the film engages in an optimistic interpretation of the *non-lieu* (a concept King borrows from Marc Augé) as a productive space for transnational interaction and multilingual communication. This depiction of the European space, the author opines, provides a meaningful way of conceptualising cinéma-monde. Chapter 9 focuses on the cinema of Quebec and its relatively young but incredibly rich industry. Using three twenty-first-century road movies produced and directed in Quebec as case studies for assessing the position of the francophone province within cinéma-monde, Thibaut Schilt contends that contemporary Quebec cinema looks simultaneously inward toward its own history and current reality, and outward, as global factors inexorably shape its relationship to others, and significantly impact its future. In Chapter 10 Leïla Ennaïli examines two recent films about illegal immigration to or through France, Aki Kaurismäki's *Le Havre* and Eric Toledano and Olivier Nakache's *Samba*, in an attempt to engender new ways of envisioning French space and French identity. Expanding Hamid Naficy's concept of 'accented cinema', the author considers the two films as exemplars of cinéma-monde (and the hyphen at the centre of this compound word) in how they remap the position of France within a globalised world.

Part III, 'Hubs and Spheres of Production', examines specific cinematic zones and assesses the cultural and fiscal policies and political engagement that often combine to provide the impetus for the creation of films. These productions often exemplify the ethical imperative in cinéma-monde, and refugees, exiles and activists are front and centre in most of the following chapters. Contributors analyse the networks and nodes within which a wide array of films are inspired, funded, produced and disseminated. Chapter 11 turns to the French capital as the location for the activist filmmaking of Michael Haneke, Coline Serreau, Michel Leclerc and Catherine Corsini. Alison Rice asserts that by portraying individuals whose otherness is the main cause of their suffering in the not always bright City of Lights, the four films under discussion denounce the shortcomings of a society that often fails to celebrate the crucial contributions of foreign-born individuals. In Chapter 12 Jamie Steele zeroes in on Liège as a pivotal hub of francophone Belgian filmmaking. The author traces the history of the Walloon city and highlights its increasing importance within the Belgian film industry, as it houses film production companies, film institutions, funding agencies, distributors and film festivals, and since the 2000s has witnessed, on the heels of the Dardenne brothers' politically engaged cinema, the emergence of a new group of young filmmakers. Michelle Stewart explores in Chapter 13 the state-sponsored *Images de la diversité* fund, which aims to represent cultural diversity and promote equal opportunity in French filmmaking. The author takes stock of the films produced since the creation of the fund, ultimately recognising its success in facilitating the creation of often multilingual films by women and underrepresented minorities with hyphenated identities. Part III ends with Chapter 14, in which Carina Yervasi takes us to West Africa in order to investigate the heterolinguistic cinema of the region. Focusing on what she designates as *média-engagé*, a collection of politically-engaged documentaries, videos and *reportages* produced by young activist citizens in Burkina Faso and Senegal, the author analyses four documentaries and concludes that their very presence ought to expand our understanding of cinéma-monde so that it embraces what it might otherwise disregard as marginal forms of filmmaking.

And finally, the volume concludes with three separate epilogues by film scholars Bill Marshall, Lucy Mazdon and Will Higbee, who respond to the issues and ideas raised in the introduction and various chapters and provide their own reactions to the concept of cinéma-monde. The goal of this section is to build on and respond to the chapters in this volume and in some cases fill in areas not explored in depth in the introduction and fourteen chapters.

In the first epilogue, Marshall suggests that 'cinéma-monde always came with a question mark: it was a hypothesis, a heuristic device, conjuring up a "what would happen if" we looked at francophone film production through a slightly different lens' (page 323). Testing this optic on a varied corpus of films produced or co-produced in Quebec and following lines that can be drawn from these examples towards other places and contexts, Marshall charts out a map of the possibilities of cinéma-monde. In his analysis of the circulation of middlebrow films such as Jean-Jacques Annaud's *La Guerre du feu/Quest for Fire* (1981, Canada/France) and *La Grande Séduction* (Jean-François Pouliot, 2003, Canada), Marshall highlights the persistence of the national within a cinéma-monde framework. Remakes of *La Grande Séduction,* for example, highlight Marshall's broader point that 'connections can be formed in terms of parts of wholes, in other words of the *worlds within* Quebec or French national cinema' (page 328).

In the second epilogue, Mazdon considers cinéma-monde as an urgent 'call to arms' at a time when western nations tend to choose populism over openness to others. After arguing that the Oscar win of Asghar Farhadi's *Forushande/The Salesman* (2016, Iran/France) and its director's powerful speech *in absentia* assert the vital role of film 'in the deconstruction of nationalism and other forms of oppression and exclusion' (page 337), the author contends that cinéma-monde crucially contributes to this deconstruction in its rejection of a homogeneous 'French' national cinema. She concludes by proposing a fourth area of inquiry not present as a distinct category here but which could be the focus of a future volume, that of reception.

In the third and final epilogue, Higbee contends that cinéma-monde is best approached as a subset of transnational cinema. He develops this argument using the example of contemporary Moroccan cinema, 'arguably the Maghreb's most important national cinema' (page 347). 'Thinking-through the "transnationality" of cinéma-monde', Higbee suggests, offers a way to bring crucial cultural, linguistic, political and economic relationships into critical focus. Taking a slightly different approach from that espoused by Marshall, Higbee argues that cinema has been transnational from its very inception and recent trends in production and circulation of film have made it 'virtually impossible to think or theorise cinema solely within the framework of the nation-state' (page 344).

Notes

1. With the exception of direct quotes, we have opted to spell 'francophone' with a lower case throughout this volume. While we recognise that the word tends to be capitalised in English, especially when referring to the academic field of 'Francophone Studies' (a loaded and potentially problematic term) and the nonacademic (and political) concept of 'Francophonie', we opted not to make an orthographic distinction between the varying uses of the word. We thus use 'francophone' indiscriminately, including as a mere synonym to 'French-speaking'.
2. Florence Martin's article 'Cinéma-monde: de-orbiting Maghrebi cinema', published in *Contemporary French Civilization*, was the first comprehensive examination of the topic since Marshall's essay. In the piece Martin considers how the latter delineates cinéma-monde but also investigates the first use of the term by French political scientists, Josepha Laroche and Alexandre Bohas. As Martin points out, they employ cinéma-monde in a very different fashion, using it to describe the globalised Hollywood-based media environment against which the French television channel *Canal +* developed.
3. There are examples of French films that feature characters with pronounced Provençal accents, such as Marcel Pagnol's classic 1930s 'Marseille Trilogy', and more recent examples such as Claude Berri's diptych *Jean de Florette* and *Manon des sources/Manon of the Spring* (1986, Switzerland/France/Italy) and Yves Robert's diptych *La gloire de mon père/My Father's Glory* and *Le château de ma mère/My Mother's Castle* (1990, France). However, these are exceptions in the French cinematic landscape, and the main actors in these films often force or fake their southern accent to play the part. For more on actors who are compelled to erase their regional accent to reach success, see Hafsia Herzi's case in Chapter 5.

Works Cited

ATFciné (no date), 'Objectifs', <http://www.trophees-francophones.org/objectifs> (last accessed 10 January 2017).

Augé, Marc (1992), *Non-lieux: Introduction à une anthropologie de la surmodernité*, Paris: Seuil.

Barbery, Muriel et al. (2007), 'Pour une "*littérature-monde*" en français', *Le Monde des Livres*, 16 March, p. 2.

Castiel, E. (2006), '*Congorama*: Dualité génétique', *Séquences*, 245, pp. 30–1.
Damrosch, David (2003), *What is World Literature?*, Princeton: Princeton University Press.
Ďurovičová, Nataša, and Kathleen E. Newman (2010), *World Cinemas, Transnational Perspectives*, New York: Routledge.
Eder, K. (2006), 'Europe's Borders: The Narrative Construction of the Boundaries of Europe', *European Journal of Social Theory*, 9:2, pp. 255–71.
Ezra, E. and T. Rowden (2006), 'General introduction: What is transnational cinema?', in E. Ezra and T. Rowden (eds) (2006), *Transnational Cinema: The Film Reader*, London and New York: Routledge, pp. 1–12.
Galt, Rosalind and Karl Schoonover (eds) (2010), *Global Art Cinema: New Theories and Histories*, Oxford: Oxford University Press.
Gott, Michael and Thibaut Schilt (eds) (2013), *Open Roads, Closed Borders: The Contemporary French-Language Road Movie*, Bristol: Intellect Press.
Halle, R. (2010), 'Offering Tales They Want to Hear: Transnational European Film Funding as Neo-Orientalismin', in Rosalind Galt and Karl Schoonover (eds), *Global Art Cinema: New Theories and Histories*, pp. 303–19.
Halle, Randall (2014), *The Europeanization of Cinema: Interzones and Imaginative Communities*, Champaign: University of Illinois Press.
Hargreaves, Alec G., Charles Forsdick and David Murphy (eds) (2010), *Transnational French Studies: Postcolonialism and Littérature-monde*, Liverpool: Liverpool University Press.
Hjort, M. (2010), 'On the Plurality of Cinematic Transnationalism', in Nataša Ďurovičová and Kathleen E. Newman (eds), *World Cinemas, Transnational Perspectives*, New York: Routledge, pp. 12–33.
Iordanova, D. (2010), 'Migration and cinematic process in post-cold war Europe', in D. Berghahn and C. Sternberg (eds), *European Cinema in Motion*, Basingstoke: Palgrave Macmillan, pp. 50–75.
Laroche, Josépha, and Alexandre Bohas (2005), *Canal + et les majors américaines: une vision désenchantée du cinéma-monde*, Paris: Éditions Pepper/L'Harmattan.
Lionnet, Françoise and Shu-mei Shih (2005), *Minor Transnationalism*, Durham, NC: Duke University Press.
Martin, F. (2016), 'Cinéma-monde: de-orbiting Maghrebi cinema', *Contemporary French Civilisation*, 41:3–4, pp. 461–75.
Marshall, B. (2012), 'Cinéma-monde? Towards a Concept of Francophone Cinema', *Francosphères*, 1:1, pp. 35–51.
Migraine-George, Thérèse (2013), *From Francophonie to World Literature in French: Ethics, Poetics, and Politics*, Lincoln: University of Nebraska Press.
Nagib, Lucia, Chris Perriam and Rajinder Dudrah (eds) (2012), *Theorizing World Cinema*, London: I. B. Tauris.
Naficy, Hamid (2001), *An Accented Cinema: Exilic and Diasporic Filmmaking*, Princeton: Princeton University Press.
Newman, K. (2010), 'Notes on Transnational Film Theory', in Nataša Ďurovičová

and Kathleen Newman (eds), *World Cinemas, Transnational Perspectives*, New York: Routledge, pp. 3–11.

Pratt, Mary Louise (2010), *Imperial Eyes: Travel Writing and Transculturation*, London: Routledge.

Radio France International (2016), <http://www.rfi.fr/emission/20160528-cinema-cannes-festival-farhadi-client-dridi-chouf-babinet-swagger> (last accessed 10 January 2017).

Rascaroli, L. (2013), 'Becoming-minor in a sustainable Europe: the contemporary European art film and Aki Kaurismäki's *Le Havre*', *Screen*, 54:3, Autumn 2013.

Rosello, Mireille (2009), 'We, the Virtual Francophone Multitudes? Neo-Barbarisms and Micro-Encounters', in Elizabeth Mudimbe (ed.), *Empire Lost: France & its Other Worlds*, Lanham: Lexington Books, pp. 47–67.

Rosello, M. (2011), 'Ismaël Ferroukhi's Babelized Road Movie', *Thamyris/Intersecting*, 23, pp. 257–76.

Sanaker, John K. (2010), *La rencontre des languages dans le cinéma francophone: Québec, Afrique subsaharienne, France-Maghreb*, Quebec City: Presses de l'Université Laval.

Shohat, E. and R. Stam (2003), 'Introduction', in Ella Shohat and Robert Stam (eds), *Multiculturalism, postcoloniality, and transnational media*, New Brunswick: Rutgers University Press, pp. 1–18.

Tarr, C. (2007), 'The Porosity of the Hexagon: Border Crossings in Contemporary French Cinema', *Studies in European Cinema*, 4:1, pp. 7–20.

Thomas, D. (2009), 'Africa/France: Contesting Space', *Yale French Studies*, 115, pp. 141–53.

Wolton, Dominique (2006), *Demain la francophonie*, Paris: Flammarion.

Part I
From Local to Global: The Cinéma(s)-monde(s) of Auteurs and Actors

CHAPTER 1

Site 2: Style and Encounter in Rithy Panh's Cinéma-monde

Joseph Mai

It is tempting to dismiss the *littérature-monde* manifesto as a last gasp of *la Francophonie*, a French refusal to accept cultural and colonial decline, or the dying embers of a lost rivalry with the Anglo-Saxon world. But *littérature-monde*, especially when we stand in a globalised culture, can also remind us of our lack of universality: our most capacious words – words like 'world' – are in fact of limited and relative scope. In the Anglo-American world, employing the term *littérature-monde*, a phrase synonymous with but qualitatively different from its English equivalent, supports David Damrosch's assertion that 'World Literature' cannot be the 'plenum of all literature' (Damrosch 2003: 4). Instead, thinking through the concept of *littérature-monde* sends us in the direction of Damrosch's own definition of World Literature, in which totality is replaced by encounter and circulation: World Literature would consist of 'all literary works that circulate beyond their culture of origin, either in translation or in their original language (Virgil was long read in Latin in Europe)' (5). World Literature would be an encounter between one culture and another, between a reader and a book from elsewhere, frequently requiring the mediation of translation and the invention of new forms, without exhaustion of possibilities. *Littérature-monde* would remind us that there are many paths toward other worlds.

To consider cinéma-monde as another form of circulation, happening in a space between cultures, challenges us to rethink the relation between dominant and emerging cinemas. With good reason, theorists of world cinema have often been concerned with the cultural and economic dominance of Western cinema: cinéma-monde should lead us inevitably to discussions of French colonisation and its afterlives. But to look at cinéma-monde as an encounter also allows us to appreciate, as Dudley Andrew (2004) argues, how the stylistics of Western cinemas have been adapted and repurposed around the world, similar to how techniques of the novel have travelled around the earth. The cinemas of former colonies should not be thought of as simple derivations or as extensions of French cinema's reach into the world, in a way that evokes a narrow definition of *la Francophonie*. If the origin of cinéma-monde is in the encounter, and distinct from technology and artistic technique, then cinéma-monde will give rise to new forms more oriented to how we intersect with the film as viewers.

Of the many tools we have for understanding the encounter with filmmakers from faraway places with complex histories and geographies, maps can be among the most helpful. Dudley Andrew has argued for the use of what he calls an 'Atlas of World Cinema', and gives examples of several types of maps that we can use to decipher the geopolitical, economic, cultural, and linguistic issues that can inform our encounter with films from elsewhere.[1] But Andrew and others also recognise some pitfalls of relying on maps. First, each map has its own ideological 'slant' or 'bias': it parses the world in just one manner, according to this economic or demographic factor or that political border, and so it requires counterbalance and flexibility. Andrew proposes 'multiple yet differentiated maps' in order to overcome this inflexibility (political maps, economic maps, topographical maps, etc.). Similarly, wanting to move beyond the familiar frameworks of colonisation and the 'Francophone' film, Bill Marshall prefers a less rooted and systematic thinking, along the lines of Édouard Glissant's metaphor of the 'archipelago'. This perspective also demands different types of maps: 'it is evident that the term [cinéma-monde] dramatically focuses attention on four elements: borders, movement, language, and lateral connections' (Marshall 2012: 42). The atlas, in its multiplicity, is never 'totalising' or rigid for it is focused on encounter.

There is a second related weakness, for a reliance on maps may put the viewer at an undue distance from individual works of cinema. David Damrosch criticises Franco Moretti's recommendation that much of the work of literary history become 'second hand': 'are students of world literature really going to have to leave the analysis of actual works to specialists in national literatures, as Moretti proposes?' (Damrosch 2003: 25–26). Andrew also warns of the risk of 'retreating to the distance demanded by the protocols of social science' (Andrew 2004: 15). Maps trade in statistics, lines and interpretations; but they miss the qualitative difference that is afforded by the close attention to texts, written or filmed, in the encounter. Andrew expresses this attention as a different type of map: the 'orientation map'. He also calls it an 'interior map' and associates it with 'cognitive maps' (2004: 15). Perhaps it is no map at all, but a way of seeing otherwise.

The benefit of this latter type of map is that it 'encourages a dialectical understanding of culture and of one's place in it' (Andrew 2004: 15).

It draws critically on analysing how a film creates point of view for the viewer (Andrew finds that point of view is inexplicably neglected by Moretti). Point of view implicates the viewer in the film, creates a relation between the viewer and another world. One can and should describe point of view: it can be close or distant, fragmented or encompassing, direct or oblique, cold or warm, or characterised by a host of relational adjectives. It is perhaps because, with cinéma-monde, we are dealing with works made in places that previously may have had little to do with 'our' world that Andrew favours the term 'tactile' to describe this relation. Cinéma-monde gets us to understand other territories in ways that bring out their multiplicity: it 'brings us precisely to the earth, this earth on which many worlds are lived and perceived concurrently' (Andrew 2004: 21). Cinéma-monde takes us out of our 'world' – our particular way of inhabiting our temporal and spatial existence, our habit of seeing everything as a universal monolith (i.e. as World Cinema) – and makes us conscious of our own 'global situation' and our own 'geopolitical orientation' (2004: 15–16). We perceive things newly and are aware of our own place: one of the strengths of the cinema is this ability to show 'the intricate rapport, both tactile and relational, that makes up "Life on Earth"' (2004: 22). The relationality of this encounter would perhaps best be described as ethical, but would not be disconnected from other intellectual and political implications.

Keeping in mind Marshall's less rooted notion of identity, the definition of cinéma-monde as an encounter, and Andrew's 'tactile' point of view and self-awareness, we can forward some observations about viewership in the film that I propose to analyse here, Rithy Panh's *Site 2* (1989, France/Germany). Rithy Panh was born in Cambodia, in 1962, eight years after Cambodian independence from France. Panh did not speak French as a child and learned it later, in France, after arriving there in 1979. He was thus raised in a post-colonial Cambodia, during a period where France had lost almost all of its cultural influence: today 96% of Cambodians speak Khmer, whereas only 2% speak French as a foreign language and merely some 800 speak it as their first language. *Site 2* is set in a UN refugee camp between Cambodia and Thailand, and is filmed almost entirely in the Khmer language. At the same time, Panh has lived in France and Cambodia, is a dual citizen, was trained in France as a filmmaker, and *Site 2* was funded by French and German production companies. The film was immediately subtitled in French, and its primary production company now offers an English version as well. Surely Panh intended for Khmer-speaking audiences in Cambodia and in the diaspora to view the film; but given the production history and the difficulties of film exhibition in Cambodia we can also assume that Panh counted on a large percentage of non-Cambodians and 'Westerners' among his viewers. Of course the director's intentions and production history cannot account for viewership, which in this case appears quite diverse and is open to many different global and linguistic worlds. Inspired by the concept of cinéma-monde, my analysis here is informed by but not limited to a particular idealised viewer crossing borders into another culture whose history and geography is largely unfamiliar.

I will argue that *Site 2* taps deeply into the conception of cinéma-monde as an encounter for three main reasons. First, maps are a great aid to understanding the stakes involved in Panh's work, in part because of the Khmer Rouge's own perverse conception of mapping and geography and in part because of Rithy Panh's own displacement through history under the form of war, genocide, and finally migration. Second, the style of *Site 2* emphasises a sensuous experience of the refugee camp in which it is set, providing the viewer from elsewhere with an awareness of place that more abstract maps cannot provide. Third, this experience has a profound effect on viewers whose attitude toward refugee camps such as Site 2 conforms to an understandable if superficial 'sympathy' or an unexamined ideology of Human Rights. The film challenges the viewer to a deeper encounter that shakes his or her confidence in *idées reçues* while inspiring new emotions and ethical thinking.

Revolutionary Words and Non-places

Rithy Panh's itinerary has in large part resulted from shifting geopolitical maps and Cambodia's unfortunate place on them. As Ben Kiernan describes it, mid-twentieth-century Cambodia was a fairly insulated country, culturally and ethnically homogenous, mainly Theravada Buddhist, somewhat 'mummified' by French colonial rule, and divided into a rural world of subsistence rice farming and an urban world producing 'a few goods for the world market' (Kiernan 1996: 5). After independence in 1954 and during the rule of Norodom Sihanouk until 1970, Phnom Penh quickly modernised, through the expansion of education, long neglected under the French. Rithy Panh's father, a former senator and a Chief of Staff for several Ministers of Education, participated in this effort. As Gleeson points out, Sihanouk was also a film director himself, having made a number of popular genre films that borrow Western techniques to give a positive national representation to both contemporary Cambodia (at a time it was referred to as the 'Pearl of Asia') and the 'traditional Indo-Khmer mythologies from the former golden age of Angkor' (Gleeson 2009: 271). Throughout Sihanouk's rule, traditional Communist groups challenged power, but were usually divided among themselves and dealt with effectively by Sihanouk, and by the late 1960s these groups were almost non-existent. Panh was born into this world.

Sihanouk's rule ended with a coup from the authoritarian Right, led by the American-supported Lon Nol in 1970. This repressive situation, along with the destabilisation caused by massive American B-52 carpet-bombing campaigns in Eastern Cambodia, swelled the ranks of a new radical Communist group, the Khmer Rouge, led by a French-educated vanguard including Ieng Sary and Pol Pot (born Saloth Sary). Lon Nol proved incapable of stopping the Khmer Rouge: after a bloody campaign, the Khmer Rouge (KR) entered Phnom Penh in 1975 and founded Democratic Kampuchea. Driven by a drastic ideological purity, they immediately imposed a wartime economy, mass population displacements, summary executions, etc.

I would like to emphasise two important themes in the Khmer Rouge's campaign to radically transform Cambodian society, both of which have a profound effect on Rithy Panh's experience, as he recounts in his memoir, *L'élimination/The Elimination* (2012). The first step of the Angkar (Pol Pot's party organisation) was a radical ideological re-education of the population. Intellectuals (and simply wearing glasses could qualify one as an intellectual) and property owners, like Panh's father, were immediately redefined as 'New People', in opposition to the 'Base People' of the countryside, and were forced to undergo severe re-education. Central to the shift of worldview for the Khmer Rouge was a new use of language. Indoctrination required a strange newspeak that combined ideological slogans, songs, neologisms and redefined archaic terms. Locard (2004) gives a full account of the language of a great leap forward, by which the Angkar attempted to clean the cultural slate. The title of Panh's memoir evokes this language disconnected from people's daily lives. Perhaps the most emblematic term of his memoir is 'kamtèch': an unfamiliar word that meant 'to kill', but really denotes 'to reduce to dust', or to eliminate every trace.

The second, though related, theme in this social transformation is a radical re-organisation of space, beginning with mapmaking. The geographer James A. Tyner has called this the 'unmaking of space' and the creation of 'placelessness.'[2] Tyner describes how the central planners of the Khmer Rouge created new maps drawn according to their radical project, including a frequently reproduced national map that replaced traditional topographically or socially defined spaces with seven geographical zones divided into numbered administrative sectors (Tyner 2008: 124). For Tyner this cartography was an attempt to eliminate 'identifying features' that contribute to a sense of place and reduce all areas of Kampuchea to sameness. The Pol Pot regime was entirely committed to imposing revolutionary cartography on millions of people. They began by evicting city dwellers from their homes. Panh's family was turned out of its home, often separated, forced to abandon personal possessions and to wander the countryside and participate in collective farming; one by one they died of starvation, disease, or despair. Ironically, given the Angkar's obsession with central planning, the map of Panh's movements through Cambodia is completely erratic and illogical. He eventually was forced to work in a Khmer Rouge 'hospital' where his main occupation was burying victims who died from the improper care and unsanitary conditions of 'revolutionary medicine'.

The arrival of Vietnamese troops in late 1978 and the fall of Phnom Penh in January 1979 did not bring order to Democratic Kampuchea. Panh, again in a way that was exemplary of many other Cambodians, made his way toward Thailand, where he spent months in a United Nations Border Relief Operation (UNBRO) refugee camp just across the border. From there, in 1979, at age 16, he joined some family in France and became a part of the Cambodian diaspora. Not without difficult adjustments, he completed secondary school and continued on to the national film school, the Institut des hautes études cinématographiques (IDHEC, now La Fémis), where he seems to have been influenced by direct cinema and the auteurs associated with modernism.

The Geographies of Site 2

When Panh returned to Cambodia a decade later to make his first film, *Site 2*, geography on the Thai border was still a mess. In 1979, Pol Pot and other KR leaders (the party was not banned and was still considered a legitimate party by the UN) had fled to the jungles near the border, the Vietnamese in pursuit. Fighting continued officially until 1989 (including a major offensive in 1984), but skirmishes continued up until and beyond the Paris Peace Agreement of 1991. The UN recognised, in the great numbers of Cambodians fleeing starvation and the advancing Vietnamese army, an immense humanitarian crisis. UNBRO was founded to set up and administer camps to shelter people from imminent harm.

Given their origins in the Khmer Rouge aftermath, it is tempting to view the refugee camps as neutral, temporary, or liminal entities, even as non-spaces. But they were not empty of socio-political forces. The anthropologist Lindsay French has shown, in a doctoral dissertation essential for anyone interested in this film or the UNBRO camps, that a number of counterbalanced political forces determined both the layout and location of Site 2, the largest of the camps. These interests made a complex mixture of 'interactions and structures' that French describes as 'several geographies' (French 1994: 66). First there was the UNBRO ideology, often formulated by the 'barang' or Westerners (including many French nationals – the term 'barang' coming from the Khmer pronunciation of 'français') – concerned with the situation. The UNBRO was guided by a commitment to humanitarianism and the principles of the Universal Declaration of Human Rights, adopted by the UN in 1948. Its main goals in the numerous border camps, were to administer the basic life needs of food, water, shelter and protection, and to provide primary education and information concerning human rights and the UNBRO mission.

There were other interests as well. As French explains, the UNBRO did not operate freely, and had to work with the Thai government to locate the camp. The Thais did not want the camp too far inland, and insisted that it be nestled in a space close to a mountain range and near the border. There were also bandits and smugglers that inhabited the mountains. On the other side of the border were more danger and more interests: the Khmer Rouge, pursued by Vietnamese troops, and fields of landmines. The Thai government also did not want to encourage long-term stays in the camp and so provided bare-bone amenities and minimal protection. Created in 1978 and taken down in 1993, Site 2 was a cramped space: 7.8 acres with a population that fluctuated between 140,000 and as many as 190,000. Some inhabitants, like Panh, were able to escape the situation for another country; but many others remained despite the threats of violence, uneven supplies, and restricted space, for up to a decade. Eventually two markets, a primary school, and the UNBRO organised entertainment and leisure activities served the camp. Among the barang, the Thai, the Khmer Rouge and the Vietnamese, the inhabitants of the camp sought to eke out a semblance of normality.

Filming Words, Rebuilding Space: Yim Om's Point of View

At first Rithy Panh had three days of access to the Site 2 camp, but successfully obtained two additional weeks. In the film, Panh spends almost no time directly on the structure of the camps: beyond a quick reference to its size and population, and despite the rather neutral title of the film, there is no voice-over or subtitles providing factual information about its history or layout. Instead he spent much of his time narrowing the camp down to a single perspective, that of Yim Om, her family (mainly her children), her memories, and her daily experiences. And yet the story of the Khmer Rouge years comes through her story.

Just after the film's titles we see a fixed shot of a ripening rice field as Yim Om tells of her childhood: born in the village of Prey Mlou, in the Hok Andoet district of Takeo province, south of Phnom Penh, Yim grew up in a large house with a tile roof and a happy family. She worked in the nearby rice fields and can describe in detail the number of paddies she worked and the number of bags she could gather per harvest. If Panh's early childhood took place in the modernising world of Phnom Penh, Yim Om belongs to the long, unchanging, traditional world of the Cambodian countryside. But ensuing history tears Yim Om from this national idyll and sets her on the road to a more disputed and inhospitable space. First the Lon Nol's 1970 coup against Sihanouk forced her to leave her province and take to the road. Her monologue gives dramatic details that bring the flight to life. She and her husband left in the middle of the night with their children and a few beef cattle, sleeping in forests and fearing the American carpet bombers (Yim's sector was one of the most brutally bombed by the Americans before the Khmer Communists took it over). Later the Khmer Rouge liberated her village, but the family was forced to return and farm it collectively. In 1974, Pol Pot executed her father and then her brother. In 1979 they again took flight: she lists the unfamiliar names of villages and districts, a disordered movement from southern Cambodia to the Thai border in the northeast. Then camp names appear in her description: Svay and Thamr Pouk, where she has a child; more camps; a son killed by a water truck; attacks on the most recent camp while her husband was studying at the city of Ampil; more flight, more bombs, then Prey Chan and Site 8, which, following more bombs, was folded into Site 2, where they finally arrive with nearly nothing. Moretti's mapping of the European novel shows that novels taking place near national borders seek to recuperate margins into national identity (Moretti 1998: 35–38). Here at the margins of Cambodia, even slightly outside Cambodia but not in any official national territory, the refugee camp is the narrative space of a failed nation.

The film thus focuses on the lived experience of a single person. It does so, however, in a particular way, emphasising what Panh has called '*la parole filmée*' (Panh 2011). The type of language [*parole*] implied here is diametrically opposed to that used by the Khmer Rouge: it is a plain, vernacular or 'popular' language in which individuals – both victims and perpetrators in Panh's other work – recount their stories (see Torchin 2014: 36). But it is also a language *filmed*; *mise en scène* is wholly dedicated to conveying this particular individual's manner of existing in language. Light, framing, and sound make the film a portrait of Yim Om. The film begins with a medium close-up portrait of her face; she is in her thirties or forties, and looks tired. She stands in front of a bamboo wall and the right side of her face is cast somewhat in shadow, but the left side has bright, soft light falling on it from a natural light source. The camera is at her level. She has not yet spoken, but when she does a bit later we will see her from a three-quarter angle, again at her level, this time the light softly brightening her entire face. The light and framing, typical of Panh's filming of people, casts Yim in a sympathetic way, underscoring her individuality and her humanity. Several commentators have observed the importance of the 'humanising' effect of Panh's work in the post-Khmer Rouge period (Gleeson 2009: 172; Hamilton 2013: 175).

Panh also uses sound to emphasise Yim's particular way of speaking. In a style directly opposed to most documentary, he uses long sequence shots without cuts or shot-countershot arrangements to film Yim speaking. Because of this a number of pauses, hesitations, repetitions and changes of mind punctuate her discourse: a viewer must listen with patience. The effect lifts language out of the logical or 'explanatory' mode of most documentary; it reseats language in the body, the lived experience, a language situated in *parole* as opposed to a simple communicative strategy: 'I wanted the viewers to hear a rhythm that envelops everything that goes into poetry, both the word and its meaning' (Panh 2008: 24). Style becomes ethics, as if Panh were attempting to create a form open to receiving Yim Om's own breath, since it has been taken away by years of the Khmer Rouge, war, and displacement: 'I feel like I am killing someone if I take away her breath ... If you do not respect breath, you respect nothing' (26).[3]

There is also an intimate connection between the voice track and the non-diegetic musical tracks written by Panh's long-time collaborator, Marc Marder. Panh brought Marder, a New Yorker living in Paris, to Cambodia so that he might hear a number of sounds: the Khmer language, Cambodian musical instruments, ambient noises, and the varied sounds of rice fields. Marder composed with a Western string bass, but was equally inspired by these local sounds and instruments. His music combines a slightly hoarse undertow, a minimal and low wind instrument (possibly a harmonica or a Cambodian instrument), and a deep but soft drum. It has slow rhythm and a squeaky, simple, repeated melody, like a hesitant voice. It tells no story at all, bears no linguistic signification, but echoes Yim's words and refracts them toward emotion: sadness, hope, resignation, and often fear. With these techniques Panh singles Yim out as a complete speaking body.

As we have seen, the Khmer Rouge's revolutionary strategy included a recasting of language, but also an effacement of previous space and its reorganisation into the spaces they considered necessary for war Communism. For Tyner, this leads to a 'weakening of the identity of places' that had previously been defined through traditions, social practices, and other types of representations (Tyner 2008: 139). Along with Yim Om's story and voice, Panh also conveys her efforts to re-establish a personal space, even in Site 2. Lighting and framing again play a role in conditioning the viewer's experience of Yim's space at the beginning of the film. We soon realise that this shot is actually staged in Yim's house, which is lit up by natural light coming through windows and through gaps in the walls. Sound adds to this effect. As Panivong Norindr has pointed out, a rich soundtrack of everyday sounds plays an important role in this film and its follow up, *La terre des âmes errantes/ The Land of Wandering Souls* (2000, France [Norindr 2010]). We hear, off-screen, the low hum of voices, mainly playing children, as well as the sounds of bicycles, stamping feet, music, and other ambient noises that make up a constant counterpoint to the image throughout the film. Like the lighting, this soundtrack makes the representation of private space fragile and constricted: the exterior and the public constantly impinges even inside the home.[4] Through sound, Panh brings us a tactile sense of what it is like to be ourselves in a space that is private but impinged upon from the outside: as much as images, sound defines a territory, brings it to life for the viewer' (Panh 2008: 27). Remarkably, at least in terms of the use of light and sound, it is by creatively integrating her paltry material conditions – the flimsiness of the houses and the lack of solitude – that Panh emphasises Yim's individual humanity.

Panh's camera gives the viewer a glimpse at how Yim Om and others attempt to reconstruct a sense of place in the camp by performing daily acts of life and social practice. This 'orientation map' (the map that makes her world *tactile*) begins with a tour through her home, in direct counterpoint to the story she told of her capacious childhood house. She describes each room, points out the nylon bag where she and her husband keep their clothes, where she keeps the rice and water, the kitchen and the latrines: no space is wasted. She also shows the UNBRO booklet in which records are kept of her food and water rations. The film concentrates on domestic activities – cooking, eating, bathing and praying – as Yim and her family go through daily life. Panh and his camera operator follow her with a handheld camera, moving deftly and zooming in attentively on objects and spaces as she discusses them. The camera only cuts when we move to a new space and not according to a division of spaces by an external logic. Fragments of movement and sound are perceived rapidly and in the margins, but we are locked in on Yim.

This concentration continues even as Panh ventures into broader, more collective or abstract spaces. The film explores, for instance, the makeshift economy of Site 2, which Lindsay French describes in depth. The inhabitants make trips to the two markets, the Thai market and the poorer camp market. Yim describes changes in the UNBRO's allotment system; seemingly minor bureaucratic modifications requiring major readjustments to ensure the survival of the family. Their economy has different classes: those who receive money from outside, especially from relatives in the US or elsewhere have a better existence than those who cannot supplement what the camp can offer. There are also the extremely deprived and precarious who risk life by leaving the camp to find work or gather firewood. The economy even provides space for some leisure activities: a concert organised by the UN or Sunday strolls on the dyke for those who have time. Hanging over this economy is the sharp contrast with memories of Yim Om's rural past and the collective farming of Democratic Kampuchea. Again these scenes are shot in ways that do not allow for an outside, encompassing view. The water delivery is filmed, for example, through fragments and sequence shots: we glimpse the water truck arriving, watch buckets being filled, a man climbing onto the truck, children playing, and we watch two girls fill their buckets and walk them all the way back to their home. The close-up panning shots of the hoses typify the style: these hoses come from somewhere and lead to somewhere but we are locked in on the hoses themselves.

Panh is particularly concerned to represent issues related to children in the camp. Unsurprisingly we see them through Yim's point of view, at home helping her cook for instance, but we also see them at school, in the streets, and at work. Their problems are typical of the camp: illness (Yim's own child is sick with a fever and earache) with inadequate medical supplies; dangerous living conditions; looming malnourishment; but also boredom. They are also affected by class inequities: some, in abject poverty, collect plastic bags (identical to those found in any cheap grocery store) for the merchants, washing those that are broken in a dirty stream so that they can melt them down to petrol, which they sell door-to-door for paltry sums. The tenacity of the children and their precarious lives figures in several scenes. For example, it is palpable in the children's inventiveness, even the melting of the bags or the *bricolage* of a kite out of throwaway materials. It is also in the way the young kids help their parents, cooking the salted fish or fetching water during the daily delivery. Once again image and sound filters this experience through Yim (who explains what they are doing, sometimes in voice-over) and by following the children around in sequence shot.

Uncertainties

In my introduction, following Dudley Andrew's lead, I suggested that cinéma-monde, when understood as an encounter, in addition to making some part of the world of the film tactile to the viewer, could make us conscious of our own 'geopolitical orientation'. Panh fosters this sense of self-awareness from the beginning of the film, in a manner that evokes the modernist techniques of someone like Alain Resnais, one of the few filmmakers he has mentioned as an influence. As Yim tells her story, Panh periodically interrupts with a series of ten inserts, sometimes extremely brief, most lasting no more than a second: a house out of focus and obscured by bamboo; a curtain pulled back to show a child indoors; a kite made of plastic; a boy curled up on an outdoor floor; a man at the extreme right of the frame under a grey sky; a shot from a similar angle on the sky with a bicycle going by; a water pipe; a hand swinging a rope hanging from a beam; a winding mountain road. These shots destabilise the viewer and point to irremediable gaps between what Yim recounts of her past and images from the camp that we will subsequently recognise. Then, as Yim tells us about the bombing of Site 8 and the family's final move to Site 2, a long-duration left-to-right pan over the surrounding landscape establishes the camp for the first time: as it moves it reveals triangular roofs emerging from the ground, then rows of houses, roads, larger buildings, covers the entirety of the camp until eventually arriving at the reservoir. We have come into the camp, but the view is fragmented and elliptical: we do not come with a sense of mastery.

This uncertainty of the viewer's position reflects the fragility of Yim Om's efforts to recreate a sense of place and time in the camp. This is illustrated, for instance, in the strange temporal fold that Yim Om seems to occupy in the important scene in which she discusses transmission and her children. Throughout, she speaks nostalgically of a childhood that haunts her thoughts and dreams, but a childhood that is, in her view, irrevocably lost. On several occasions she states bluntly that she has no hope for her own future. However, her remaining children still have some kind of life in front of them and her judgment of their time is more ambiguous. In one scene her daughter tells of how she has grown up in the camps for the past ten years. She describes rice cultivation in remarkable detail, but only because she has heard her mother telling stories about planting, spacing, and harvesting. She has no memories of Cambodia, and recounts horrifying dreams of the Vietnamese forces bombing the camp and her being separating her from her parents.[5] Yim can only transmit a knowledge that has no practical content for her children in the hope that

Figure 1.1 Yim Om and her son.

they may someday come out of the camp. There is a continual action 'as if' regular life may return. On the other hand, she cannot remember how many camps she has brought them to, and that hope remains dim. Panh's simple *mise en scène* allows for these complicated subjective temporal modes to inhabit the screen even as Yim Om attempts to create a normalised transmission of values and lifestyle.

The film makes the viewer confront Yim's perplexity through the use of the camera. As she speaks, Yim's young son stands by her side listening, in an image of transmission. The hand-held camera moves gently, reminding us that we have an embodied, human perspective on the scene, that we seek a visual connection to her words, a place from which to understand her. As she explains her hopelessness, the boy wanders off, and the camera moves in on her face alone (see Figure 1.1). The boy, however, is just in the back room, barely separated, and so the camera pulls back out to show both again, him in the background, somewhat out of focus, close and yet separated from her. Then the camera moves in again on her. This extremely attentive point of view seeks out the relation between the two, but it hesitates undecidedly, at a loss, just as Yim contradicts herself as she speaks about the future. A coherent relation between the two seems impossible within the spatial and temporal suspension of the camp.

The same type of ambiguity colours scenes in which camp inhabitants seek to construct more collective social practices and institutions. Yim wants to give her children an education so that they have some way of integrating a post-camp world. In this she reflects the efforts of the UNBRO to supply a primary education, considered by the UN (and the vast majority of people, though not everyone in the camp) to be a basic human right. An early, extended scene shows the children arriving in straight lines at school. The children's disciplined formation, combed hair, and bright, clean clothes contrast wildly with their habitual experience in the camp, and with the fact that we often see them working. The camera pans across the school windows as they sing indoors: *frère Jacques* in Khmer.

Suggestively, given this chapter's (and this volume's) interest in mapping, the scene concentrates on a geography lesson: a little girl in a prim dress stands before a map with a stick, pointing out the directions on a map while the other kids, dressed in clean clothes as opposed to the frequently shirtless kids around the camp, repeat obediently and loudly after her. A boy answers the teacher that there are many rice paddies in Battambang, and then points out the town on a map. The teacher reminds them that they now know 'our country' very well, and invites them to find it on a map of the hemisphere: an older girl points it out on the map, and when the teacher asks the name of the country she is pointing at she replies 'Cambodia'. Education is not rejected in this scene; and yet how absurdly out of touch French songs and national political maps can be within what Yim Om calls at least three times 'the land of others' and once 'the land of refugees.' There is here a caution against the 'distant' use of mapping versus the proximity of encounter that works like *Site 2* can provide. This proximity gives the viewer a sense of Yim Om's attempt to rebuild place, but it also acknowledges that her attempts are incomplete, that space remains abnormal. When the neatly appointed children arrive at the school in straight lines, the camera focuses strangely on their shadows in the dirt road, suggesting, in a manner similar to Yim Om's multiple relations to transmission, that the exercise is somewhat unreal, fragile, a serious attempt at constructing a spatial practice that could easily be read as a mere simulacrum, a mere shadow.

This ambiguity should prove troubling to the viewer, especially (though not only) the 'Western' viewer, for it extends to the entire ideology of human rights as it is presented in the film, as we can see if we pay close attention to another complex scene toward the end of the film. Panh was present in the camp on December 10th, 1988, during an UNBRO-organised celebration of Human Rights Day, commemorating the adoption of the Declaration of Human Rights forty years earlier by the UN. The scene begins as another normalised moment in the family's life: dressed in their nicest clothes they go out into the public space, filled with people and amplified music. A group of balloons flies overhead, and people joke about the Rights of Man being carried away. We hear an English voice over a loudspeaker, eventually translated into Khmer: 'many children have never seen an elephant. This gentle giant is the mascot of . . .' There enters an elephant draped in a blue banner proclaiming the commemoration of the Rights of Humankind and carrying a man on its back. Just as the animal passes in front of the camera, Yim's voice-over begins. She was filled with hope on this day. The camera tracks across a number of hung drawings showing memories of camp inhabitants in naïve and direct style, scenes of arrest, torture, and shooting, as people point out details and explain, an allegory in miniature of many of Panh's films. Yim hopes, in contradiction with her earlier pessimism, that people will respect each other, respect the elderly and the children, honour Buddhism, give forgiveness and liberate these camps.

But for the first time in the film Yim's voice cracks from emotion: that very evening, she explains, two grenades fell in the camp, injuring some women just next to her own house, and she is afraid that next time it could be her. Her voice-over combined with the kitschy images of the celebration come into tension; the UN celebration oscillates between a genuine celebration of and yearning for Human Rights and superficial window dressing.[6] We should be clear, however, about this effect. Just as one does not come away from the film thinking that education is futile, one does not come away from these scenes thinking that human rights and the hopeful future they represent are worthless. The UN is not summarily dismissed as some empty barang *mission civilisatrice*. The next day children are seen dressing each other in a blue tarpaulin and pretending to be an elephant with other kids riding on their back. Their play is ambiguous but not cynical; there is great resilience in these children, who continue to read at night and joyfully fly their homemade kite against a blue sky, in the face of a fragile existence (see Figure 1.2).

In fact there are experiences, such as Yim's constant fear, that only the inhabitants of the camp can fully apprehend. Violence was a daily experience. Yim describes acts of violence that result from people having nothing to do and living in cramped quarters. Threats also came from outside, the bandits in the mountains and the Vietnamese army and Khmer Rouge fighters across the nearby border, especially at night. This was a part of camp life that the UN and NGO workers knew about, but did not experience. Yim points out that the international workers must leave the camp at the first sign of trouble, the first sound of an explosion, and at night, a fact

Figure 1.2 Boy flying a kite in *Site 2*.

confirmed independently by Lindsay French who, though working eleven months in the camp, was permitted to spend only one night inside. Panh filmed at least one night in the camp as well, and explores this fear from a point of view that importantly suggests the viewers' limited knowledge of fear. We see dark shots lit up only by candles – people washing, a child reading (in continuity with the effort to educate), praying, finally the baby. Then the camera moves out of the fragile home into the night. Marder's music is ominous and disquieting, without being macabre. It is extremely dark on the road that goes by Yim's house, which is lit up only by a handheld lamp carried alongside the tracking camera. As spectators we have in fact walked this route before, earlier in the film, during the daytime. The camera moves ahead slowly, panning from side to side, and we feel a jolt of fear when the light suddenly reveals a human figure. There happens to be no danger tonight: the light picks out a smiling woman and even children. But the camera does not continue as far down the road as it had earlier in the film; rather it cuts to a black screen to end the film. This premature cut reflects our difference as viewers from the inhabitants of the camp: one night is not every night, and we return to the safety of our screening room. Panh's cinéma-monde makes us aware of our separateness from their experience, of the limits of our empathy, of the shortcomings of our (supposed) ideology of human rights, of our own 'world' on a much more diverse earth.

Shamelessly Tactile

Tracking shots, sequence shots, details and fragments, shadows and light: these stylistic techniques seem to dialogue with French modernist filmmaking, an influence that has been the target of some mild criticism. Carrie Tarr, working in a strictly anti-colonial perspective, groups Panh in a category of filmmakers whose dependence on French funding may require self-censorship, or as she puts it: 'the reliance on French funding and French audiences means that films made by overseas or metropolitan minority filmmakers may be unable to make significant challenges to dominant French discourses' (Tarr 1997: 61). Tarr singles out films that appeal to art-cinema audiences and that display an *auteurist* or experimental style, which Tarr considers 'escapist' or self-exoticising. She cites *Gens de la rizière/Rice People* (1993, Cambodia/France/ Switzerland/ Germany) as a work in which Panh 'sidesteps a critique of the effects of empire in his films, concentrating instead on the lived experience of his indigenous subjects' (1997: 64).

This critique (and it should be noted that it is made in passing and not based on Panh's work as a whole) seems to miss the mark in two important ways. First, Panh's films do criticise empire quite directly, though perhaps nowhere so explicitly as in his more recent made-for-television film *La France est notre patrie/ France is Our Homeland* (2015, France), in which he critically deconstructs archival images of the French colonial presence in South-East Asia. At the same time, Panh finds direct condemnation too facile, and too superficial. As he has explained in relation to a follow-up film to *Site 2, La terre des âmes errantes*, a position of 'denunciation' might offer 'temporary relief to Western spectators but would change nothing in the underlying problem' (Panh 2008: 10–11).

Secondly, local experiences are extremely valuable to those who approach cinéma-monde as an encounter. Such encounters can throw into question the point of view that underlines both empire and its denunciation: the very idea that we come to a film with the proper answer. One way of formulating this is as a destabilisation of 'Western' subject positions vis-à-vis 'Eastern' experiences. Barbé-Petit detects, for instance, in Panh's adaptation of Marguerite Duras's *Un barrage contre le pacifique/ The Sea Wall* (2008, France), a similar opposition, according to which the Western Cartesian tradition attempts (and fails) to impose a technical and humanistic mastery over the untameable rice paddies of the Cambodian landscape (Barbé-Petit 2014: 258). Similarly, in a recent article on *Le papier ne peut pas envelopper la braise/Paper Cannot Wrap Ember* (2007, France), Leslie Barnes also refers to Panh's style as a pre-emptive measure against a false sense of 'epistephilia'. For Barnes a position of empathetic superiority or political righteousness toward the prostitutes filmed by Panh would feed a fantasy of knowledge. The film, according to Barnes, resists dogmatic positions concerning the agency and exploitation of these sex workers. Barnes concludes:

> Rather than posit an understanding of prostitution as victimisation or self-determination, Panh's film focuses on the intimate corporeal and emotional experiences of the prostitute – her pastimes, family pressures, worries and betrayals – and asks his viewer not only to accept, but to identify with the contradictory nature of her existence. Panh does not seek to educate his viewer . . . (Barnes 2015: 63)

For a viewer this means being emotionally engaged 'without any sense that by watching the film we are participating in a solution to the problem' (2015: 63).

Site 2 produces a similar effect. The film does not offer an answer to the question of Site 2 or suggest what we should do about refugee camps at all. It tells us neither to reject nor to embrace our beliefs. It is much more concerned that we encounter, with whatever beliefs we hold, the inhabitants of the camp in their world and with their point of view. Though abstract maps help us understand the history and geography of Cambodia and places like Site 2, Panh is much more concerned with the interior map of the encounter. His stylistics remind one of a passage from the journal of the Belgian filmmaker Luc Dardenne: 'When the intellectual with a wide perspective reproaches the filmmaker for looking at things through the wrong end of the lorgnette, we should feel no shame' (Dardenne 2015: 42). This image of the lorgnette reseats the cinema in the 'narrow gaze' of a person, 'of flesh and blood limited by birth and death' on other 'individuals limited by their birth and their death' (2015: 42). Likewise, Rithy Panh's film brings the viewer into proximity, transforms maps into sensuous images, removes viewers from abstract trains of thought, and sends them toward poetic, affective, and ethical concerns.

Notes

1. Franco Moretti's work (1998) on mapping World Literature is a compelling model, and one that greatly informs Andrew's work.
2. See Tyner (2008), chapters 4 and 5.
3. 'J'ai l'impression de tuer quelqu'un si je lui enlève sa respiration . . . Si on ne respecte pas la respiration, on ne respecte rien . . .' It is not by coincidence that film ends on a short poem by René Char that serves as a brief, nervous portrait of Yim: Falling asleep in life, / Awakening by life, / Knowing death / Leaves us destitute, / Our mind plagued, / Our sides wounded ['s'endormir dans la

vie, / s'éveiller par la vie, / savoir la mort, / nous laisse indigent, / l'esprit rongé, / les flancs meurtris.'] Yim is at times in a lull, wounded, lacking and worn in spirit, but she also grasps restlessly onto life.
4. Domestic space is of course flimsy and constricted: the house lets light through the thatch roofs; the bamboo walls are thin; the interior walls are made of recycled cardboard; space is precious.
5. Lindsay French confirms that the loss of transmission was an important worry to people across the camp.
6. An effect amplified by the globish English of the speaker and the show of the elephant. It is worth noting that the speaker is right concerning the elephants: though they historically roamed through Cambodia, there are now very few left, especially in the wild (this one obviously is captive), and those that are exhibited are frequently abused. It is another sign of a lost tradition.

Works Cited

Andrew, Dudley (2004), 'An Atlas of World Cinema', *Framework: The Journal of Cinema and Media*, 45:2, pp. 9–23.

Barnes, Leslie (2015), 'Objects of pleasure: Epistephilia and the sex worker in Rithy Panh's *Le Papier ne peut pas envelopper la braise*', *French Cultural Studies*, 26:1, pp. 56–65.

Barbé-Petit, Françoise (2014), 'Rithy Panh chez Margeurite Duras: Un barrage contre l'oubli, au cœur de l'orient', in F. de Chalonge, Y. Mével and A. Ueda (eds), *Orient(s) de Marguerite Duras*, Amsterdam: Rodopi, pp. 251–64.

Damsrosch, David (2003), *What is World Literature?*, Princeton: Princeton University Press.

Dardenne, Luc (2015), *Au dos de nos images II*, Paris: Seuil.

French, Lindsay (1994), *Enduring Holocaust, Surviving History: Displaced Cambodians on the Thai-Cambodian Border, 1989–1991*, PhD Dissertation, Harvard University.

Gleeson, Erin (2009), 'The Presence of the Past', *Contemporary Visual Art + Culture Broadsheet*, 38:4, pp. 271–3.

Hamilton, Annette (2013), 'Cambodian Genocide: Ethics and Aesthetics in the cinema of Rithy Panh', in Axel Bangert, Robert S. C. Gordon and Libby Saxton (eds), *Holocaust Intersections: Genocide and Visual Culture at the New Millenium*, Leeds and Philadelphia: Maney, pp. 170–90.

Kiernan, Ben (1996), *The Pol Pot Regime*, New Haven: Yale University Press.

Marshall, Bill (2012), 'Cinéma-monde? Towards a concept of Francophone cinema', *Francosphères*, 1:1, pp. 35–51.

Locard, Henri (2004), *Pol Pot's Little Red Book: The Sayings of Angkar*, Chiang Mai: Silkworm Books.

Moretti, Franco (1998), *Atlas of the European Novel 1800–1900*, London: Verso.

Norindr, Panivong (2010), 'The Sounds of Everyday Life in Rithy Panh's Documentaries', *French Forum*, 35:2–3, pp. 181–90.

Panh, Rithy (2011), *L'élimination*, Paris: Grasset.
Panh, Rithy (2008), *La parole filmée. Pour vaincre la terreur*, in *Le cinéma de Rithy Panh*, Éditions Montparnasse.
Tarr, Carrie (1997), 'French cinema and post-colonial minorities', Alec Hargreaves and Mark MicKinney (eds), *Postcolonial Cultures in France*, London and New York: Routledge, pp. 59–63
Torchin, Leshu (2014), 'Mediation and Remediation: *La parole filmée* in Rithy Panh's *The Missing Picture (L'image manquante)*', *Film Quarterly*, 68:1, pp. 32–41.
Tyner, James A. (2008), *The Killing of Cambodia: Geography, Genocide and the Unmaking of Space*, Aldershot: Ashgate.

CHAPTER 2

Globalisation, Cinema and Terrorism in Rachid Bouchareb's Films: *London River*, *Baton Rouge* and *Little Senegal*

Mireille Rosello

What does Rachid Bouchareb's *London River* (2009, UK/France/Algeria) – but also the director's earlier films – tell us about the intersection of globalisation, terrorism and cinema? Given the intimate relationship between recent forms of terrorism and the media, cinema, one of the most powerful distributors of popular stories, does not have a choice but to participate in a cultural struggle about how to understand and represent terrorism (Kellner 2003 and 2005; Pludowski 2007; Finnegan 2007). Many voices have suggested that the terrorist attacks against the twin towers in New York were instantly legible as a typical Hollywood movie (King 2005: 47–59). Wheeler Winston Dixon, author of a collection of essays on *Film and Television after 9/11* cites film critic David Thompson and Lawrence Wright, author of the script of the 1998 film *The Siege*. The former is reported to have said 'There was a horrible way in which the ghastly imagery of September 11 was stuff we had already made for ourselves as entertainment first' (qtd in Dixon 2004: 10), while the latter stated that the events were 'cinematic in a kind of super-real way. It was too Hollywood' (qtd in Dixon 2004: 9).

Thus 9/11 is constructed as a turning point in the history of cinema and of the world. All future terrorist attacks are now supposed to have their original cinematographic script: some kind of generic Ground Zero is the standard for future stories. Conversely, all future media performances including movies now have to reckon with an implicit benchmark. The cinematographic spectacularisation of the attacks on US soil has had irreversible consequences for global cinema. First of all, two powerful myths about the globalisation of cinema and terrorism have backed each other up: 'Hollywood' aka CNN was the reference for international news coverage sending images of terrorism around the world. As a result, even more than before, Hollywood imagined itself as the mandatory global norm. All films about terrorism would now by default be compared to such performances. Secondly, terrorism as an object of representation became both taboo and inescapable: its absence in contemporary films is structuring and remarkable – they fall into the categories of about or not about terrorism.[1]

Thirdly, and perhaps even more distressingly for filmmakers or creators in general, the idea that the terrorist attack 'was' cinematic erased the distinction between what happened and all the obviously but invisibly politicised representations. The simultaneous occurrence of the event and of the distribution of images erased the process of narrativisation that goes into the creation of any story, fiction or non-fiction film. In terms of representational politics, 'mass mediated' terrorism and 'terrorist spectaculars' (Nacos 2003: 23; Nacos 2007) hijack the distinction between the story and storytelling techniques and challenge movies to achieve the same illusion of effective pseudo-self-evidence.

To exaggerate, I could say that all films are now global because terrorism imposes an artificially global (US driven) grammar over cinema. And it is not very reassuring to refine the formulation by saying, perhaps more accurately, that films are now potentially all global in the face of terrorism because they are made for audiences who will be expected to be familiar with an event that many describe as cinematic: 9/11. Cinema, the global and terror are now inextricably entangled.

London River, Bouchareb's 2009 film, seems to be the perfect example of this phenomenon. Terrorism could have been both the theme and the narrative grammar capable of explaining the global character of that work of art. Bouchareb's choice to set the story in London right after the July 2005 attacks makes the timeliness and topicality of his film both unremarkable and potentially controversial. It would seem counterintuitive to claim that *London River* is not a film about terrorism. After all, the title of the interview that the director granted to Stuart Jeffries for *The Guardian* is 'Rachid Bouchareb: My Film about the 7/7 London Bombings' (Jeffries 2010). The film follows two characters who desperately look for their missing children after the bombings. When Brenda Blethyn (whom Bouchareb had already noticed in Ken Loach's *Secret and Lies*) was asked to play the role of one of the main protagonists, she hesitated to participate in the mediation of the tragedy. Alerted by her agent that Bouchareb was making a film 'about 7/7', she remembers thinking: 'oh no, I don't want to do that. It's too recent history, and it seemed like sacrilege' (Film4.com). She implies that the film was breaking a taboo: her formulation suggests that fiction has a sacred duty to not intervene too early. On the other hand, many reviewers criticised the film for its sentimental plot and absence of solid political analysis (French 2010; Thomas 2010). Stephen Holden, writing for the *New York Times* goes as far as saying that 'This movie is not concerned with history or politics' (Holden 2011). As for Kaleem

Aftab, he accuses the film of pandering to an international audience and of being suitable for six-years olds (Aftab 2009). In other words, there was no 'sacrilege' but rather a selling out to a form of globalisation that individualises and depoliticises.

Most of the negative comments are, however, paradoxical: critics are favourably impressed that Bouchareb replaced sensationalism with an intimate and personal story, but then, they criticise that individual story for being apolitical. And this apparent contradiction has to do with the fact that their readings focus exclusively on the plot and then find the film predictable, didactic or too politically correct (Douin 2009). To be fair, if the plot is the only object of scrutiny, it is difficult to disagree: if we summarise *London River* as the story of a Christian European and a Muslim African who get to know each other, overcome their differences and become friends, it is hard to be excited about the allegorical structure of the binary opposition between two stock characters of contemporary history. The mother is prejudiced and Islamophobic, assuming that her daughter was manipulated by her Muslim lover. And only slowly will she accept that the man whom she encounters is, like her, looking for a missing child, a victim of the terrorist attack.

My point is that this film is political in a way that is not acknowledged by such criticism. *London River* approaches the fraught terrain of terrorism/global/cinema from an angle that is precisely 'political' if we adopt Jacques Rancière's definition of 'le politique' and understand it as the moment where the stakes of the debate and the distribution of the sensible are being negotiated (Rancière 2004). If we do not read or watch for the plot but become aware of the protocol that governs the perspective and enables a certain story to unfold, then it is possible to examine the ways in which the film refuses to let global terror function as a generic constraint or at least resists the pressure to adopt such grammar. What I call here grammar, protocol or generic constraint add up to the overall frame that will instruct the spectator either to ignore those who are not deemed worthy of our attention or to focus on individuals that we will construct as victims or perpetrators. The frame is what, generally, makes concepts and object appear or disappear. More generally and perhaps more crucially, the frame accounts for who counts as what Judith Butler calls 'grievable lives' in her 2009 *Frames of War*. At the beginning of the introduction ('Precarious Life, Grievable Life') she explains that she is

> seeking to draw attention to the epistemological problem raised by this issue of framing: the frames through which we apprehend or, indeed, fail to apprehend the lives of others as lost or injured (losable or injurable) are politically saturated. They

are themselves operations of power. They do not unilaterally decide the conditions of appearance but their aim is nevertheless to delimit the sphere of appearance itself. (Butler 2009: 1)

In the case of cinema, the camera constitutes one of what Butler calls 'operations of power' to the extent that it implicitly asks the spectator to agree with what is treated as relevant, important, worth seeing, or relegated to invisibility.

The film offers us the possibility to define terrorism as a discourse that insists on becoming the primary logic of any narrative. In order to take advantage of that possibility, however, it is necessary to watch the film politically, by which I mean obliquely: focus on the framing device rather than the plot, and on details rather than the global picture. If we do so, *London River* becomes a film that chooses to make sense of the world from a vantage point that refuses to be compromised by the myth of global terrorism, and that shares that vantage point as a gift to the audience. *London River* is therefore less 'about' terrorism than about the possibility to resist the cinematographic storytelling conventions that over-determine the terror/global/cinema nexus.

The Function of Terrorism and the National in Bouchareb's Films

The over-determination in question functions as the equivalent of perspective in a Renaissance painting. We do not even have to agree on how to define terrorism for it to occupy the function of a vanishing point on the canvas that films will only then have to fill. Like an Oulipian constraint, a perspective line does not predict what the theme of the painting or the poem will be. It is, however, a structure that both limits and enables the deployment of certain narrative elements.

Therefore, I propose to focus more specifically on those elements of *London River* that are more vulnerable to the presence of a pre-imposed cinematographic frame: the representation of space and of the characters' religious practices. Space, or rather the spatial rootedness of the protagonists is crucial because, as in a painting, some places in the film will seem closer to or further from an imagined centre, smaller or more relevant, or relegated to the status of unimportant detail. As for the filmic construction of religious practices in a transnational setting, it intervenes in a situation where Islam, as the chaotic point where culture meets religion and race, has become one of the mandatory building blocks of any narrative influenced by global terrorism discourses. Yet, before focusing on the spatial framing and the representation of religion in *London River*, I propose to look back at Bouchareb's earlier films because they provide clues as to how the director can successfully occupy a different place in this fraught landscape.

Terrorism, when used as the name of a paradigmatic global frame, occupies a function analogous to that of the concept of the nation(al). National cinema supposes a naturalisation of the bond between a national culture (presumed relatively homogeneous in terms of historical legacy, geographical contours and linguistic abilities) and a corresponding public. A national audience is imagined as implicitly sharing such references. Terrorism is one of the concepts that functions both as a representational matrix and a theme. And for Bouchareb, the necessity to work against a constraining hegemonic frame is not new: he belongs to a community of filmmakers who already had reasons to question their relationship to the idea of the national. His relationship to the idea of the national – and specifically to France and Frenchness, has never been straightforward. For a director of Algerian origin born in France during the Algerian War, France was never the implicit and naturalised home whose hegemonic culture and values are expected to be shared, even if only as references. Bouchareb's French films all have an 'accent' (Naficy 2001). He was never national.[2]

And even more interestingly, his 'accent' is not immediately recognisable. On the one hand, Bouchareb belongs to a generation of directors whose works have questioned the hegemonic French perspective line and who have (sometimes) been provisionally reincorporated into the system of representation. It was the case in France in the 1980s and 1990s when a cluster of directors troubled the idea of Frenchness by focusing on disenfranchised *banlieues* and on the figures of (at first male) children of African immigrants.[3] The dissident national French hero was a young male disenfranchised by his ethnicity and/or class and the spatial signature of that type of figure was the depressing high-rise neighbourhoods where spectacular or endemic violence is expected.

Bouchareb could have been a part of that movement. Instead, his way of filming his relationship to Frenchness was never quite in sync with that of his contemporaries. His first feature, *Baton Rouge* (1985, France), so often cited as one of the first *beur* films, is in fact slightly idiosyncratic: the director's focus is on *banlieue* youths but he precisely takes them out of the ghetto. The geography of this rearranged national space is transnational: Bouchareb films three Parisian *banlieue* friends in the United States, far from the archetypal French peri-urban zones. Baton Rouge, instead, is the backdrop of their adventure. It is also the city of blues rather than of urban rap (the audioscape that accompanies so many *banlieue* films). Here Baton Rouge is not constructed as an alternative francophone space where the protagonists would be more French because perceived as more authentic by a historically displaced French minority. Instead it is an elsewhere where the relationship to the national may be reinvented, a space, as Bouchareb puts it in an interview, where the 'characters would not be seen as *beurs* but as individuals with all their hopes and dreams' (Bouchareb qtd in Derderian 2003: 115). Bouchareb's early films (and plots) are already examples of transnational rather than minority French cinema, which sets him apart from the movement of *beur* directors who, as Lanzoni suggests, have achieved national and therefore indirectly international recognition by now, but as French directors (Lanzoni 2015).

When he filmed *Baton Rouge*, Bouchareb was not, however, turning his back on the preoccupations of his contemporaries and looking for a (probably illusory) escapist cinematographic or supra-national space. He explored the same cultural, political and ethnic issues as *beur* directors (Hargreaves 2011; Higbee 2007b: 39). His rethinking of the national was already global in a very idiosyncratic way since rather than reinterpreting Frenchness through the more and more recognisable postcolonial prism, he carefully avoided the potentially binary Maghreb-France axis. He never proposed some cosmopolitan version of the global as a solution to his questions about the national: in *Baton Rouge*, the characters are quickly confronted with the limits of the American dream: when money runs out, they have to bum train rides or steal and they end up being deported by the immigration police. In *Poussières de vie* (a 1994 film produced in France and set in Vietnam), Bouchareb also highlights local difficulties rather than exploring an exotic destination, focusing on the children born to Vietnamese women and American soldiers who returned to the United States. Global mobility is not presented as a form of liberation and is not the alternative to the issues that *banlieue* youths confront in France. Yet, the narratological building blocks and especially the filming of space and the focalisation are different are different from what is typically found in *beur* or *banlieue* films of the period.

Little Senegal (2001, Algeria/France/Germany) is an interesting model of what will later happen in *London River*. Here America is both the destination and the origin since the film is about the main protagonist's quest to find his ancestors, taken from Senegal to the new world more than two hundred years before the story starts. Alioune, who has long worked as a tour guide in a slavery museum, will now embody the history that he has been explaining to tourists. *Little Senegal* thus begins in Gorée, currently one of the districts of Dakar, Senegal, but also an island from which slaves were shipped to the new world. For Bouchareb, that liminal space is the organisational principle of a struggle over what constitutes a nation (historically and geographically). The film starts in Africa and continues in the US yet the 2001 film was subtly but firmly participating in the French debate about the function and place of the colonial past, and especially the legacy of slavery.[4] But there again, Bouchareb complicates a Franco-French or francophone debate. The main protagonist, whose job is to guide American tourists around the museum of slavery, ends up rewriting the Middle Passage, retracing the steps of one branch of his enslaved family. The character's trajectory combines and therefore defamiliarises two grand narratives picked up in books written more than ten years apart: Paul Gilroy's *The Black Atlantic* (1993) and Christopher Miller's *The French Atlantic Triangle* (2008). *Little Senegal* refuses, however, to imagine transnational racialised lines of alliance. Delphine Letort notes that the character of African origin is shown to be alienated from the African-American community and that the film is sceptical about the ability of a globalised diaspora to come to terms with the legacy of French colonialism, the history of slavery and the postcolonial condition (Letort 2014).

One element of *Little Senegal* is worth mentioning here as a transition to *London River* because the two films share the same lead actor: just as Bouchareb both deals with the issues that *banlieue* youths confront but also refuses to systematically assign them to what could be misconstrued as their 'natural' environment, he chooses, as the main protagonists of his films, actors who sabotage any attempt to map identity politics over the characters' trajectory. Both in *Little Senegal* and *London River*, the screen is powerfully occupied and defined by Sotigui Kouyaté, who does not fit the profile of the typically young and sometimes amateur actors found in films portraying ethnic minorities. Born in Mali to a long and illustrious family of griots, he is famous for his work with Peter Brook (especially *The Mahabharata*). A tall and thin black body whose posture is always erect, Kouyaté's presence exudes dignity and a remarkable sense of entitlement. Contrary to the figure of the spontaneous male (and now female) *banlieue* youths, whose explosiveness is sometimes blamed, sometimes feared, and sometimes explained, translated or justified,[5] Kouyaté appears as a timeless, almost mythical old wise man.

When one of the building blocks of the global discourse on terrorism is the profiling of ethnicised subjects or the racialisation of cultural and religious factors, the choice of an actor by the film director testifies to the difficulty of navigating the troubled waters that separate the materiality of the body and representational politics. By stating that he wrote his scenario for his actors (Jeffries 2010), Bouchareb reminds us that there is no pre-existing empty frame that would have to be filled by people who correspond to our mental stereotypes of who, for example, is a potential victim and who is a potential perpetrator of terrorism.

The Remapping of Global and Local

London River is a global story that locally rearranges – rather than erases or reinforces – the traditional global opposition between the South and the North. The main protagonists of the films are the parents of two young people whom they have not been able to reach after hearing the news that a terrorist attack had been perpetrated in London. The film follows them on their quest for their missing children but also for a way to make sense of a world that has become incomprehensible to them. From one point of view, the two heroes may look like archetypes: black and white, the African man and the European woman, the Muslim and the Christian. But the male protagonist, who is originally from Mali, has lived in France for so long that he is completely estranged from his son, who was raised in Africa and is now studying in London. As for the representative of the Global North, she lives in Guernsey, a tiny island situated in the English Channel off the coast of Normandy, whose position allegorizes the geographical and political ambiguities of the borders of Europe. London is thus identified as eccentric to these two regional points of reference: Guernsey and the South of France.

The film opens on the deserted green cliffs of Guernsey, accompanied by the sound of waves and of Elisabeth Sommers humming to herself as she walks alone on a small path overlooking the sea. That image is then matched by a bird's eye view of another rural landscape, and this time the soundtrack emphasises cicadas. A black man is seen alone in the middle of an olive grove. In a series of tightly arranged crosscutting shots, the characters are then embedded in their symmetrical natural environments, the horizontality of the sea beyond Elizabeth responding to the verticality of the tall elms that surround Ousmane. The establishing shots that introduce the two protagonists are thus almost didactic in their insistence on constructing them as symmetrical: in these first scenes, both are presented as rural characters from the North. Both are presented as connected to the land: she takes care of a small farm; he is a forester in the South of France. They are alone in a landscape that constitutes a meaningful spatial identification marker. The traditional opposition between the rural poor from the Global South and the Western(ised) inhabitants of the global cities of the North is replaced by a shared rootedness in the materiality of the soil.

Figure 2.1 Ousmane and Elizabeth on a public bench in a park in London.

Elizabeth is shown to be feeding animals, picking salads. Later in the film, when the two characters have warmed to each other, this connection is officially recognised as what makes sense of their world: as tragic as they are, the events in London and terrorism in particular are not the paradigm of meaningfulness.

Whereas at the beginning of the film Elizabeth clearly mistrusts Ousmane and treats him as a potential terrorist, she eventually apologises to him. This is one of the most interesting and perhaps optimistic scenes of *London River*. Both characters are seated on a public bench in a park (see Figure 2.1). Quietly, Elizabeth admits that she suspected Ousmane's son of having manipulated her daughter. To which he answers, with disarmingly honesty and a lack of defensiveness that confers dignity to this powerful character, that he had also feared the worst and did not rule out that his child was responsible for the attacks. Both characters are in fact acknowledging that they are estranged from their children. Jane never told her mother about her relationship and Ousmane did not raise his son and does not know him. Terrorism is what has brought them to a specific neighbourhood in London, away from their rural homes. But in that particular moment, it is their relationship to the land that connects them in a differently global way.

In this scene filmed in a park, the two characters have managed to momentarily ruralise London by moving away from the bustling neighbourhood where their children shared a flat. In this quiet area, the protagonists talk about their jobs as respectively farmer and forester.[6] Elizabeth comments on the fact that Ousmane's hands, like hers, are scarred by his work. Both parents know that their children would not have made the same choice. Elizabeth says that her daughter is ashamed of her mother's hands, the hands of an old farmer. And when Ousmane explains that his job consists of keeping elms alive, a battle he is losing, Elizabeth is capable of not only following the conversation but also adding a meaningful detail to that ecology of thinking: the last elms, she says, still grow in Guernsey. The allusion to 'griffures' (scratches), 'blessures' (wounds), the 'fight against the death of trees' are a moment of diversion, a pause during which a new type of unspectacular war becomes important. Ousmane is confronted by and talking about the 'slow violence' whose link with globalisation is subtly and powerfully suggested in this scene (Nixon 2011).

That conversation is also crucial for the globalised audience to understand the meaningfulness of the last two scenes of the film. Ousmane, asked by one of his colleagues what they must do about the elm, reluctantly gives him the order to fell it and refuses to watch. We now know what that episode means to him. The last shot shows Elizabeth hoeing her field with a strength that comes from anger and grief after a few seconds of contemplating the sea as the temptation of an ultimate refuge against her pain. The fight against the disappearance of the elms, the physically demanding preparation of a vegetable patch acquire a new dimension. The dynamic of terrorism, with its own logic of violent, spatial and temporal reconfiguration is pushed to the background, and the film invites us to reassess the importance of issues that were, until now, relegated to the status of meaningless details.

Global Signs of the Religious

Just as places are filmed in a way that refuses to adopt contemporary frames of reference, Islam, and religion in general, are presented from the very first scenes from a very specific point of view. The place that religion occupies in the story is the object of a double re- and de-emphasis, a gesture that, far from being a movement away from political issues, constitutes *London River*'s political stance. A film about terrorism that does not talk at all about Islam or rather presents Islam as a difference that does not make a difference is itself remarkable because it refuses to fall into the trap of having to choose between accusation and justification.

The logic of the film insists that Islam only matters in the context of the terrorist/global/cinema nexus if one is already constrained by Islamophobic scripts that have, paradoxically, nothing to do with Islam. When the terrified mother discovers that her daughter's flat is in a neighbourhood where the Arabic language is omnipresent and where bodies are darker than her own, she calls her brother and complains that the place is 'crawling with Muslims'. It is almost too painfully obvious to make the point that she does not know whether she has met a Muslim yet and is only paraphrasing the dominant discourse that conflates Arabic, Arabs, religion, culture and race. It does not exonerate the character from the accusation of crass prejudice but her reaction is contradicted by all the other visual elements that have introduced religion until then.

Long before Elizabeth meets Ousmane, the spectator has been told that he is a Muslim but has also been presented with his religion in a way that makes it strictly equivalent to Elizabeth's Christian background. Instead of treating Christianity as the obvious European religion and therefore the unmarked background on which Islam stands out as the foreign cultural element, *London River* uses the establishing shots to treat the characters' religions as differences that should not make more difference than the geographical settings in which they are contingently presented. The first scenes of the film, which have organised the protagonists' spaces, have already added the religious to the frame. Islam and Christianity were thus forcefully paired as symmetrical.

Contrary to a myth that treats Europe as secular and its immigrants as deeply and archaically religious, the film present its characters as deeply engaged in their own religious rituals. The first time we see Elizabeth, she is walking towards a small church and we hear, in quick succession, a very short quotation from the minister's sermon and the voices of the small community singing in unison (although her voice is emphasised in the soundtrack). As for Ousmane, the first shot shows him praying among olive trees (see Figure 2.2) and two close-ups on his hands show his rosary and then ritual ablutions. He is physically alone and she is also symbolically isolated – no visual allusion is made to any interaction between Elizabeth and the other churchgoers. Both are religious but in a way that does not focus on communities and belonging. Bouchareb does not represent the dominant ethnic European as secular, a choice that is perhaps even more significant for a French audience than on the international scene.

Once again, Bouchareb departs from films whose representation of Islam is linked to a national discourse. As Michel Cadé recently showed in his study of the role of religion in *beur* and *banlieue* cinema, Islam, until the beginning of the century, is practically absent from representations of culturally Muslim communities (Cadé 2011). Only gradually do allusions to religious practices appear in films, suggesting the possibility to accreditate the existence of a non-controversial 'Islam de France'.[7]

In *London River*, the treatment of religion is hardly realistic: the symmetry between Elizabeth and Ousmane's rituals is highlighted, stylised.

Figure 2.2 Ousmane praying under olive trees in the south of France.

Islam and Christianity are intertwined by a visual transition that no element of the plot justifies. Both in Guernsey and in the South of France, Christianity is the pretext to mention both love and persecution. In Guernsey, the minister is heard reading a text from Matthew (5:43) about loving those who persecute us. In a crosscutting shot, we see Ousmane, who has just been introduced as a Muslim, sitting alone, peacefully, in the shade of an old chapel. Islam and Christianity are seen as inseparable to the extent that both religions are also cultural references in the same region. The voice of History, a disembodied didactic narrative, intervenes from the outside: we hear the voice of a tour guide commenting on the fact that in the twelfth century, whole communities were eliminated in Flanders, Rhenania and Champagne. The historical reference to the Cathars (whose sites have now become tourist destinations) may well be unrecognisable to an international or even national audience but visual clues still suggest violence in that peaceful chapel: Ousmane is sitting in front of a medieval painting representing the persecution of people thought to be heretic. And due to the tight editing, the image is still very close to the allusion to the 'love your enemies' sermon but also to the vision of a beautiful black body praying alone in an idyllic landscape. A further connection between Christianity and Islam as well as between the characters who have not yet met each other is deliberately established by a confusing and rather unrealistic visual transition: as the guide announces that they are going to visit the 'garden', a close-up on stone crucifixes removes the spectator from the geographical space that Ousmane occupies and takes us to the island. When the shot becomes larger, we realise that we are in the little cemetery where Elizabeth came to talk to her dead husband. The symbol of Christianity has been used as a mode of transportation between the two spaces, the two protagonists, and the two religions.

Later in the film, the allusions to Islam and Christianity practically disappear altogether. Ousmane is seen praying once more in his hotel room for a few seconds but any other reference is indirect and linked to the search for the two children. The visits to the mosque are part of the quest: the imam distributes flyers with the addresses and telephone numbers of hospitals. His main dramatic function is that he can speak French and that can therefore work as a hyphen between Ousmane (who speaks no English) and the men and women who might have known his son. Just as the crucifix created a relatively artificial and therefore all the more remarkable visual bridge between the South of France and the island and between the two faiths, the imam's unexplained native fluency connects that which other traditional scenarios would present as a priori separate and self-contained.[8]

The camera is not visually interested in the mosque as a place of worship. At no point does Bouchareb present us with the stereotypical image of a community of Muslim men praying together. Religion is clearly articulated as one of the possible identification markers of a multicultural and internally diverse Europe.[9] But the film proposes one of the most idealised definitions of secularism: a system that allows religions to coexist and cohabit. The earlier allusions to love and hate nuance this apparently optimistic picture but the representation is also an implicit response to or a comment about militant forms of French 'laïcité' that tend to focus on and object to the most public manifestations of Islam. *London River* neither ignores its characters' faiths nor turns their religion into a cultural identity.

Conclusion

What are the consequences of altering the frame of global terrorism? Bouchareb's intervention into what remains a conceptual minefield suggests that if cinema alters the parameters used to represent the actors, it participates in a reorganisation of the world defined as a concept that competes with the state, the nation, the local, the global or '*le monde*' in French.

The ways in which *London River* frames terrorism posits the existence of an implied audience that is neither French nor francophone but global in very specific ways. The presence of two parents whose children will never be seen because they have already disappeared before the beginning of the story interpellates us spectators as either dead (like the young victims) or in mourning (like the parents).[10] Such modes of identification are more relevant than categories such as Africa and Europe, the Global South and the Global North, minority or dominant ethnic, Islam and Christianity or even male and female. This is not to say that religion, nationality, gender or class are treated as irrelevant, on the contrary, we are asked to become more aware of how such constructions constitute framing devices and to connect with them in more nuanced and self-conscious ways. To that extent, Bouchareb's films contribute to the emergence of a kind of transnational cinema that privileges what Higbee calls movements of 'transvergence' (Higbee 2007a). If we are capable of empathy with the main protagonists, it has to happen on the basis of alliances that are not national, nor even post-colonial. If this film is 'francophone,' it is not in the sense that has been used to describe films made by or about minority speakers of French who need to question the supremacy of the Hexagon, the former *métropole*, in a word, Paris, as having appropriated the place of the centre.

Bouchareb manages to make us understand what francophone means when it is distinct from Anglophone rather than as opposed to (hexagonal) French. In *London River*, when the characters express themselves in French, they speak neither as the representatives of the old imperial centre (France) nor as the former colonised francophone periphery. French is a sort of imperfect lingua franca between the two characters only because one of them (Ousmane) does not understand English, the national language of the country where the story takes place. Paradoxically, Elizabeth's rudimentary French is presented as the bridge that connects her to Ousmane, whose French connects him as much to Africa as it does to France.

But Ousmane and Elizabeth are also global in specifically local ways. No one in the film is entitled to speak for the universal; both protagonists are simultaneously extremely local and globalised by forms of grief that are compounded by the difficulty of making sense of their spatial, conceptual disorientation.

The categories that generate stereotypes (religion, place of origin, ethnicity) are never ignored and the film is not an attempt to universalise the representation of mourning. Instead, it globalises mourning in a way that precisely takes into account the historical and political situation of the main characters.[11] If *London River* succeeds in troubling the cinema/global/terrorism nexus, it is not so much because of what the film shows as what it chooses not to show, and also because it makes the spectator aware of the structuring absences – a possibility itself opened up by the change of perspective inaugurated by the very first scenes. By inviting the viewer to become aware of what is or could be a centre, a periphery, an identity or a coincidence, a detail or the main point of a story, *London River* avoids a number of archetypal narratives.

Bouchareb's focus on two grieving parents who did not know each other before the beginning of the story enables him to relegate the figure of the terrorist to a visual and political elsewhere. The perpetrators never become characters. Narratologically speaking, after an attack covered by global media and works of fiction, a number of generic conventions are attractive because they allow the storytellers to talk about the terrorists who must be found, named and accounted for. They become the main protagonists of the tale that subsequently needs the conventions of detective fiction. Bouchareb articulates a critique of the dominant Western gaze on terrorism by representing the terrorists in a certain way.[12] The issue of thematisation is yet another narratological level.

By refusing to even mention the terrorists, Bouchareb frees the spectators from a recognisable set of options: we do not have to choose between, or combine a number of, plausible scripts: neither the film nor the audience must demonise or 'humanise' the suicide bombers (Martin 2007), nor does *London River* provide a narrative of causality that would make their actions historically or politically understandable. I argue that this impossibility is precisely what creates a politicised global audience: the film avoids to work from within narrative logics that are, regardless of their attempt to condemn or understand the terrorists, both authorised and limited by a perspective of surveillance.[13] As spectators freed from that particular set of options, we are left with the task of reinventing what it means to grieve politically from a different perspective.

Notes

1. The force of the taboo is clear when the blurring between fiction and the reality of politics is judged unbearable: after the attacks in Paris in November 2015 the theatrical release of Nicolas Boukhrief's *Made in France* (2015, France) was cancelled.
2. And I am here deliberately creating an echo to the title of Latour's 1991 book, *We Have Never been Modern*.
3. Examples of this trend include *Prends 10 000 balles et casse-toi/ Take Your Ten Thousand Francs and Get Out* (Mahmoud Zemmouri, 1981, France/Algeria), *Le thé au harem d'Archimède/Tea in the Harem* (Mehdi Charef, 1984, France), *La Haine* (Mathieu Kassovitz, 1995, France), *Hexagone* (Malik Chibane, 1994, France), *Douce France* (Malik Chibane, 1995, France), *Raï* (Thomas Gilou, 1995, France), *Bye-Bye* (Karim Dridi, 1995, France/Belgium/Switzerland), *Salut cousin!/Hi Cousin!*, Merzak Allouache, 1996,

France/Algeria/Belgium/Luxembourg), *Le gone du Chaâba/The Kid from Chaaba* (Christophe Ruggia, 1997, France). For films that focus on female protagonists, one has to wait until the turn of the century: *Inch'Allah dimanche* (Yamina Benguigui, 2001, France/Algeria), *Dans la vie* (Philippe Faucon, 2007, France), *Tout ce qui brille/All That Glitters* (Géraldine Nakache and Hervé Mimran, 2010, France); see also Tarr 2009 and 2013.
4. 2001 is also the year of the so-called Taubira law that recognises the slave trade and slavery as a crime against humanity. See also Blanchard et al. 2005; Hourcade 2013.
5. See Abdellatif Kechiche's *L'Esquive* (2004, France): the focus of the films is on adolescents who must memorise Marivaux's *Le Jeu de l'amour et du hasard* to perform the play at school. Oscillating between Marivaux's eighteenth-century French and contemporary French, the film debunks the stereotype of the illiterate and uncouth youth whose language is rudimentary at best and often aggressive. The film presents the exchanges between the characters as highly ritualised language games (See Blatt 2008, Bastide 2004, Nettelbeck 2007).
6. For a compelling and precise analysis of how London itself is filmed (and how the symbol of the bridge is emphasised in a decidedly unspectacular way), see Tarr 2016.
7. Cadé mentions films such as Philippe Faucon's *Dans la vie* (2007, France) and Rabah Ameur-Zaïmech's most recent work: whereas Islam is simply absent from the director's first film *Wesh Wesh, qu'est-ce qui se passe?* (2001, France), the connection between religion and work place is integral to *Dernier maquis* (2008, France/Algeria).
8. Critics have of course noticed that the Londoners' ability to speak French in this film is slightly implausible or 'contrived' as Collinson puts it (Collinson 2010). Having cast some of the actors who already worked with him on *Indigènes/Days of Glory* (2006, Algeria/France/Morocco/Belgium), Bouchareb could take advantage of a francophone Muslim police officer (Mathieu Schiffman) and of a francophone imam (Sami Bouajila). For a remarkably rich and precise analysis of how French, English, Arabic and Mandinka function in the film, see Smith 2013.
9. Africa is never filmed, never shown not even as the subject of dreams or flashback sequences.
10. In Bouchareb's *La route d'Istanbul/The Road to Istanbul* (2016, Algeria/France/Belgium), the main role is again occupied by the figure of a parent but this time the film focuses on another aspect of the terrorism/global cinema – radicalisation. Here, 'Elizabeth' is a Belgian mother whose teenage daughter has vanished. When the police discover that she has crossed the border and is headed for Turkey, the mother decides to follow her to what seems to be the most plausible destination: Syria and ISIS territory.
11. 'Many people think that grief is privatising, that it returns us to a solitary situation and is, in that sense, depoliticising. But I think it furnishes a sense of political community of a complex order, and it does this first of all by

bringing to the fore the relational ties that have implications for theorising fundamental dependency and ethical responsibility' (Butler 2004: 22).
12. Elaine Martin argues that by 'subtly shifting concepts of "we" and "they" while stressing causality, history and temporality', Third Cinema films implicitly respond to the critique made by Edward Said in his 1988 *The Essential Terrorist* – a text in which he points out that the terrorist is always the other and the concept is based on an erasure of history and causality (Martin 2012; Said 1988).
13. Compare with the well-known scene in Gillo Pontecorvo's *La bataille d'Alger/The Battle of Algiers* (1966, Italy/Algeria) in which recruits are taught how to deal with terrorism and are made to watch the film of a checkpoint: at the very moment when soldiers are bullying an old man because they suspect that his suitcase contains explosives they allow the woman who carries the bomb to walk right past them. The spectator has, by then, become an insider and recognises that unless one knows who the terrorists are, it is impossible to identify them. Similarly, Philippe Faucon's *La désintégration/ The Disintegration* (2011, France/Belgium) narrativises the gradual evolution of an ordinary citizen who slowly becomes a jihadist. In both cases, the purpose of the camera is to make the spectators understand how 'they' function, regardless of what this knowledge would imply.

Works Cited

Aftab, K. (2009), 'London River: The Film of the 7/7 Bombing,' *The Independent* (17 February) <http://www.independent.co.uk/arts-entertainment/films/features/london-river-the-film-of-the-77-bombing-1623696.html> (last accessed 7 July 2017).

Bastide, B. (2004), 'Review of Abdellatif Kechiche's *L'Esquive*', *Artelio* (January).

Blanchard, Pascal, Nicolas Bancel, and Sandrine Lemaire (2005), *La Fracture coloniale*, Paris: La Découverte.

Blatt, A. (2008), 'The Play's the Thing: Marivaux and the 'Banlieue' in Abdellatif Kechiche's *L'Esquive*,' *The French Review*, 81:3, pp. 516–27.

Butler, Judith (2009), *Frames of War: When is Life Grievable*, London: Verso.

Butler, Judith (2004), *Precarious Life: The Powers of Mourning and Violence*, London: Verso.

Cadé, M. (2011), 'Hidden Islam: The Role of the Religious in Beur and Banlieue Cinema in France', in Sylvie Durmelat and Vinay Swamy (eds), *Screening Integration: Recasting Maghrebi Immigration in Contemporary France*, Lincoln and London: University of Nebraska Press, pp. 41–57.

Collinson, G. (2010), 'Review of *London River*' (9 October), <http://www.flickeringmyth.com/2010/10/british-cinema-london-river-2009.html> (last accessed 7 July 2017).

Derderian, R. (2003), 'The Banlieues as Lieux de Mémoire: Urban Space Memory, and Identity in France', in Pierre Lagayette, *Géopolitique et mondialisation: La relation Asie du Sud-Est/Europe*, Paris: Presses Universitaires de la Sorbonne, pp. 107–20.

Dixon, Wheeler Winston (2004), *Film and Television after 9/11*, Carbondale: Southern Illinois University Press.

Douin, J.-L. (2009), '"London River": une rencontre sous le signe du deuil,' *Le Monde* (22 September) <http://www.lemonde.fr/cinema/article/2009/09/22/london-river-une-rencontre-sous-le-signe-du-deuil_1243397_3476.html#0eypI3zgJZbR7xMS.99> (last accessed 7 July 2017).

Film4.com (ND) Interview with Rachid Bouchareb and Actress Brenda Blethyn, [No Author] <http://www.film4.com/special-features/interviews/blethyn-bouchareb-on-london-river> (last accessed 7 July 2017).

Finnegan, Lisa (2007), *No Questions Asked. News Coverage Since 9/11*, London: Praeger.

French, P. (2010), 'Review of *London River*', *The Guardian* (11 July) <http://www.theguardian.com/film/2010/jul/11/london-river-film-review> (last accessed 7 July 2017).

Gilroy, Paul (1993), *The Black Atlantic: Modernity and Double Consciousness*, Cambridge, MA: Harvard University Press.

Hargreaves, A. (2011), 'From Ghettoes to Globalization: Situating Maghrebi-French Filmmakers', In Durmelat, Sylvie and Vinay Swamy (eds), *Screening Integration: Recasting Maghrebi Immigration in Contemporary France*, Lincoln: University of Nebraska, pp. 25–40.

Higbee, W. (2007a), 'Beyond the (Trans)national: Towards a Cinema of Transvergence in Postcolonial and Diasporic Francophone Cinema(s)', *Studies in French Cinema*, 7:2, pp. 79–91.

Higbee, W. (2007b), 'Re-presenting the Urban Periphery: Maghrebi-French Filmmaking and the "banlieue" Film', *Cinéaste*, 33:1, pp. 38–43.

Holden S. (2011), 'In Wake of Terror Attacks, Unlikely Bonds,' *The New York Times* (6 December) <http://www.nytimes.com/2011/12/07/movies/london-river-stars-brenda-blethyn-review.html?_r=0> (last accessed 7 July 2017).

Hourcade, R. (2013), 'L'esclavage dans la mémoire nationale française: cadres et enjeux d'une politique mémorielle en mutation', *Droit et cultures*, 66:2.

Jeffries, S. (2010), 'Rachid Bouchareb: My Film about the 7/7 London Bombings.' *The Guardian* (6 July) <http://www.theguardian.com/film/2010/jul/06/rachid-bouchareb-london-river-interview> (last accessed 7 July 2017).

Kellner, Douglas (2003), *From 9/11 to Terror War: Dangers of the Bush Legacy*, Lanham: Rowman and Littlefield.

Kellner, Douglas (2005), *Media Spectacle and the Crisis of Democracy*, Boulder, CO: Paradigm Press.

King, G. (2005), '"Just Like a Movie?" 9/11 and Hollywood Spectacle', *The Spectacle of the Real: From Hollywood to 'reality' TV and beyond*, Bristol: Intellect Press, pp. 47–59.

Lanzoni, R. F. (2015), 'A National Recognition for Beur Cinema: Rachid Bouchareb and Abdellatif Kediche', in *French Cinema: From Its Beginnings to the Present*. New York: Bloomsbury, pp. 465–79.

Latour, Bruno (1993), *We have never been modern* [1991], translated by Catherine Porter, Cambridge, MA: Harvard University Press.

Letort, D. (2014), 'Rethinking the Diaspora through the Legacy of Slavery in Rachid Bouchareb's *Little Senegal*,' *Black Camera*, 6:1, pp. 139–53.

Martin, E. (2012), 'Films about Terrorism, Cinema Studies and the Academy', in Di Leo Jeffrey, and Mehan Uppinder, *Terror, Theory and the Humanities*, Ann Arbor: Open Humanities.

Martin, E. (2007), 'The Global Phenomenon of "Humanizing" Terrorism in Literature and Cinema', *CLCWeb: Comparative Literature and Culture*, 9.1.

Miller, Christopher (2008), *The French Atlantic Triangle*, Durham, NC: Duke University Press.

Nacos, B. (2003), 'Terrorism as Breaking News: Attack on America', *Political Science Quarterly*, 118:1, pp. 23–52, <http://www.jstor.org/stable/30035821> (last accessed 7 July 2017).

Nacos, Brigitte (2007), *Mass-Mediated Terrorism: The Central Role of the Media in Terrorism and Counterterrorism*, Lanham: Rowman and Littlefield.

Naficy, Hamid (2001), *An Accented Cinema: Exilic and Diasporic Filmmaking*, Princeton: Princeton University Press.

Nettelbeck, C. (2007), 'Kechiche and the French Classics: Cinema as Subversion and Renewal of Tradition', *French Cultural Studies*, 18:3 (October), pp. 307–19.

Nixon, Rob (2011), *Slow Violence and the Environmentalism of the Poor*, Cambridge, MA: Harvard University Press.

Pludowski, Tomasz (ed.) (2007), *How the World's News Media Reacted to 9/11: Essays from around the Globe*, Spokane, WA: Marquette Books.

Rancière, J. (2004), *The Politics of Aesthetics: The Distribution of the Sensible*, translated by Gabriel Rockhill, London and New York: Continuum.

Said, E. (1988), 'The Essential Terrorist', in Said, Edward and Christopher Hitchens (eds), *Blaming the Victims: Spurious Scholarship and the Palestinian Question*, London: Verso, pp. 149–58.

Smith, A. (2013), 'Crossing the Linguistic Threshold: Language, Hospitality and Linguistic Exchange in Philippe Lioret's *Welcome* and Rachid Bouchareb's *London River*', *Studies in French Cinema*, 13:1, pp. 75–90.

Tarr, C. (2013), 'From Riots to Designer Shoes: *Tout ce qui brille/All that Glitters* (2010) and Changing the Representations of the Banlieue in French Cinema', in *New Suburban Stories*, Dines, Martin, and Timotheus Vermeulen (eds), London: Bloomsbury, pp. 31–40.

Tarr, C. (2009), 'Community, Identity and the Dynamics of Borders in Yasmina Yahiaoui's *Rue des Figuiers* (2005) and Karin Albou's *La Petite Jérusalem* (2006)', in Nadia Kiwan and Helen Vassallo (eds), *International Journal of Francophone Studies*, 12:1, pp. 77–90.

Tarr, C. (2016), 'The Mediation of Difference in *London River* (Rachid Bouchareb

2009)', in Barta, Peter and Phil Powrie (eds), *Bicultural Literature and Film in French and English*, London: Routledge, pp. 60–74.

Thomas, S. (2010), 'Review of Rachid Bouchareb (Dir.), *London River*', *Literary London: Interdisciplinary Studies in the Representation of London*, 8:2 (September), <http://www.literarylondon.org/london-journal/september2010/thomas2.html> (last accessed 7 July 2017).

CHAPTER 3

Guerrilla Filmmaking with Rachid Djaïdani

Laura Reeck

In the first issue of the literary and culture journal *Francosphères*, Bill Marshall (2012) contributed a call to reshape the field of French Film Studies in 'Cinéma-monde? Towards a Concept of Francophone Cinema'. When compared with the 2007 'Pour une "littérature-monde" en français' manifesto from which it derives, cinéma-monde becomes at once an extension and an inversion of what the signatories of the manifesto proposed. While the signatories suggested that it was time to sign the 'death certificate' of francophone literature in a view to making all French-language literature belong to the same category of 'littérature-monde en français', Marshall cites the shortcomings in the manifesto's line of argument: its Parisian-centredness, the tenuous relationship between the signatories, and its failure to address the many variants of the French language (2012: 35). In a reversal, Marshall offers that 'Francophone cinema' could account for all French-language films, and in his essay the concept of cinéma-monde becomes synonymous with 'Francophone cinema' – the category of 'francophone' being the very one the signatories of the manifesto sought to dismantle.

Marshall does not stop with a static category, but rather conceptualises it by transforming it into a verb, 'francophonising,' which leads to the 'minorising' of French national cinema through emphasis on four key elements, 'borders, movement, language, and lateral connections' (2012: 42). Through their lens, maintains Marshall, 'Francophone cinema' has the ability to inflect the dominant and pervasive view and reception of French national cinema, and along with it the field of French Film Studies. At the same time, by virtue of the fact that 'Francophone cinema' covers the topography of the world, the conceptual category is meant to call attention to the global-ness of cinema as an industry and product. This conceptualisation of 'Francophone cinema' with minorising as its primary operation can be seen as synonymous with cinéma-monde until the end of the article when Marshall suggests that perhaps the moment should be seen as 'post-Francophone' (51), therein turning the synonym on its head and leaving the definition of cinéma-monde open.[1]

While Marshall gives some attention to hexagonal filmmaking in his discussion by suggesting that *The Artist* (Michel Hazanavicius, 2011, France/USA/Belgium) and *Bienvenue chez les ch'tis/Welcome to the Sticks* (Dany Boon, 2008, France) belong to cinéma-monde because of their 'accents', and gives a nod in passing to *beur* cinema, a filmic category that dates back to the 1980s, no sustained attention is given to the wealth of minority filmmakers in France today, many of whom are bringing a different aesthetic and vision to French cinema. By referencing 'accent', Marshall connects to Hamid Naficy's *An Accented Cinema* (2001), though he turns a broad conceptualisation of a cinematic voice and style very quickly and literally into a question of linguistic accent and dialect. Here a critical elision is that Naficy uses 'accented cinema' in the specific case of filmmakers who have been displaced, who live in diaspora, or who live as postcolonial ethnic minorities within a majority population. This last positionality should not be abstracted and gives accented cinema its specificity. Though Marshall pays it no real attention, he does reference a gap important to it, seen here to be productive and creative, 'where Frenchness can be questioned, interrogated, even reinvented, from the so-called margins and peripheries' (47). This liminal space can be seen as the outside of the inside.

What a case study of Rachid Djaïdani's guerrilla filmmaking brings to a discussion of cinéma-monde – still in need of dimensions – is an instance of minorised (and minority) hexagonal filmmaking. In the rush to globalness, Djaïdani recalls how hexagonal France is as multilayered, complex, and vital as anywhere else. His guerrilla filmmaking depends upon the most local and intimate means of production and falls outside national production networks and circles, all the while making claims to French national cinema and, somewhat paradoxically, being seen as such in its international reception while not being supported by French film institutions. In what follows, I explore the way in which Djaïdani engages in a self-reflexivity in his filmmaking that queries the boundaries of French national cinema from the outside of the inside. In the first section, I highlight the main features of Djaïdani's filmmaking. Then, I examine his two documentaries, both of which focus on artist-outsiders – in one case Djaïdani himself – as they confront institutional discrediting and aim to re-establish themselves. Finally, I use his fiction feature *Rengaine/Hold Back* (2012, France) as an example of a film that excavates the dangers of clan-like mentality between ethnic and religious groups in France as it decentres tropes of filmic Paris. As a whole, Djaïdani's guerrilla filmmaking offers a challenge to French cinema to reinvent itself, which involves letting outsiders in.

Situating Rachid Djaïdani, Situating Guerrilla Filmmaking

Born to an Algerian father and an Algero-Sudanese mother in a Parisian *banlieue*, mason then boxer Rachid Djaïdani published three novels before turning to filmmaking.[2] Not long after the publication of his first novel, *Boumkoeur* (1999), Bernard Pivot invited him to appear on the literary talk show *Bouillon de culture*. His 'I write to exist' in response to Pivot's 'How did you get the idea of writing a book?' has become oft-referenced in discussions on the development of the field of *banlieue* writing. Djaïdani begins his first cinematic undertaking, a self-filmed documentary entitled *Sur ma ligne* (2006, France), with his introduction to the literary world on Pivot's programme and concludes with the dramatic and interruptive call to action that he offered at the end of the same show, 'Go ahead. Do it, guys. I did it. Make your mark'. In this way, Djaïdani chose to frame his film with the start and finish of the show that first presented him publicly as an author. With *Sur ma ligne*, screened at the 8th Biennale des cinémas arabes at Paris's Institut du Monde Arabe in 2006, and then chosen for screening by the Association du cinéma indépendant de sa diffusion (ACID) at Cannes in 2007, in addition to affirming his literary authorship, Djaïdani emerged as a film auteur.

In documentarist Ali Akika's estimation, '*Sur ma ligne* is a breath of fresh air for anyone who's suffocating under the constant stream of clichés used by people desperately trying to sell us a stale world'. From the outset, Djaïdani's filmmaking has been unusual, fresh, and iconoclastic.[3] In 2010, Djaïdani was invited to participate in Festival Pocket Films held at the Forum des Images in the French capital, then in its fifth year, as a guest filmmaker. He filmed the nine months of his wife's pregnancy and the birth of their daughter on his mobile phone camera, reducing them to a 26-minute film, *La Ligne brune* (2010, France), selected for the 2012 edition of the Dubai film festival. Importantly, while shooting it, Djaïdani filmed against the backdrop of the 2009 debate on French nationality initiated by then Minister of Immigration, Integration, National Identity and Mutually-Supportive Development Eric Besson, in this way merging the personal and the political, something Djaïdani has repeated across his filmic production. Another film challenge and instance in which Djaïdani brought together the personal and the political was his made-for-TV documentary film, *Quinquennats* (2013, France), one of three 90-minute documentary films commissioned by Canal+ along with Agnès Jaoui and

Denis Podalydès for a series called 'Faites tourner!'.[4] Djaïdani chose to feature his parents in their daily lives against the backdrop of both the 2002 and 2012 presidential campaigns: on the Front National and its presence in the second round of the presidential election in 2002, Djaïdani's father responds 'It doesn't concern me' to his mother's 'The FN wants to put us in huts!'. Though a high level of disaffection for politics prevails in *La Ligne brune* and *Quinquennats*, this does not mean that Djaïdani is indifferent; rather, he rejects political life and influence as they exist today in France, and more broadly the status quo.

Perhaps the clearest expression of Djaïdani's guerrilla filmmaking is found in his first fiction feature, *Rengaine*, which was shot predominantly with family members and friends, no budget, without a licence to film, and on the streets with no lighting. With no script, and thus no demonstrable project, Djaïdani could not get the necessary licence to be recognised by the Centre national du cinéma et de l'image animée (CNC), and thus could not request any funds or sponsorship. Filmed over nine years and generating over 400 filmed hours that Djaïdani edited down, *Rengaine* follows a contested love story between Dorcy, a Black Christian French man, and Sabrina, an Arab French women of Muslim heritage. It has been billed a modern-day *Romeo and Juliet*. When *Rengaine* was chosen for the 2012 Directors' Fortnight at Cannes, Djaïdani had another project in the works: filming his artist friend, Yassine Mekhnache (one of the brothers in *Rengaine*, notably seen 'tagging' an aluminium panel) on a quest to find new gallery representation. With *Encré* (2015, France), Djaïdani shot over 100 hours of film, which he edited down to 73 minutes, once again with no licence to film and no financial support. It was first screened at the Cinéma du Réel film festival in Paris in March 2015, and then shown at the 2016 Journées internationales du film sur l'art at the Louvre.

At Cannes, *Rengaine*, a film made on the most local of levels, garnered international acclaim and recognition when it won the International Critics Prize (FIPRESCI). Several months later, it was awarded the d'Orano prize for a first film at Deauville. And before *Rengaine* was nominated for Best First Film in 2013 at the Césars, it had been announced as part of New York's MoMA New Directors/New Films 2013 line-up. Though Djaïdani could be seen as an outsider to the film establishment in France and a relative unknown entity in film scholarship, in which he is understudied, his films have benefited considerably from the global circulation of film, namely through film festivals.[5] His case exemplifies some of the tensions alive between mainstream, experimental, national, and transnational cinema, so that while experimental cinema like Djaïdani's does not fit neatly with French national and mainstream cinema, it does appeal on the global film circuit (i.e. in film festivals and international film events). Its primary contradiction to national cinema is that it does not operate within institutional parameters, and its primary contradiction to mainstream cinema is that its aesthetic and production modes differ markedly.

In this way, Djaïdani's filmmaking complicates Will Higbee's (2013) argument in *Post-Beur Cinema* that North African immigrant and Maghrebi-French filmmaking turned to national and mainstream cinema over the early part of the twenty-first century.[6] For Higbee, 'mainstream' means using standard and conventional norms for filming – 'editing, lighting, narrative conventions, sound design, genre' (2013: 28) as well as institutional practices for production and distribution. To arrive at his conclusion, Higbee considers film budgets, the number of entrants and critical reception, including film awards. Djaïdani provides a point of contrast for Higbee's argument: with no budget, unpaid and largely non-professional actors, and not respecting any of Higbee's norms for filming, he has managed to attract critical acclaim, most especially at international film festivals, while largely being skipped over (at least in the institutional sense) and drawing small niche audiences in the national context. In reference to *Rengaine*, Djaïdani has said of his tenuous position: 'So from the very beginning I wasn't part of the system [. . .] but I want in [. . .] I want to tell them, "Let us in". But if from the outset they close the doors, and they say, "what he does is illegal". . .' (Djaïdani 2012). Djaïdani includes himself in a class of guerrilla filmmakers in France who continue to face institutional obstacles to production and distribution and who are shaping a new type of French cinema. In reference to similar films produced in a similar timeframe, *Donoma* (Djinn Carrenard, 2010, France) and *Rue des cités* (Carine May and Hakim Zouhani, 2011, France), Djaïdani has said: 'There's a new cinema that's emerging with new faces and, at the same time, today, it just so happens that the three films that have gotten attention are by two Arabs, a French woman, and a Black man, who are still outside the schools, who are outside the system' (Reeck 2013). Put succinctly, he wants inclusion in French national cinema while retaining his unique filmic signature that puts pressure on its bounds and dimensions.[7]

An investigation of the overlay of the local and global, the national and transnational, the vertical and the horizontal undergirds Françoise Lionnet and Shu-mei Shih's 'minor transnationalism', in which the national, local, and global cohabitate and produce different configurations and expressions across space and time (2005: 6). Minor transnationalism offers an alternative to 'major' transnationalism by drawing particular attention to practices that 'occur in the nonspaces of boundaries and borders, spaces which are nonetheless infinitely expansive and full of possibilities' (19). Minor transnational subjects do not necessarily benefit from unfettered and unlimited global movement and access; in contrast to the global nomadic subject, 'minor transnational subjects are inevitably interested in their respective geopolitical spaces, often waiting to be recognised as "citizens" to receive the attendant privileges of citizenship' (8). Further, Lionnet and Shih contradict the way in which 'major' transnationalism assumes that 'ethnic particularity and minorised perspectives are contained within and easily assimilated into the dominant forms of transnationalism' (7). So while minority cultures within a given space should be seen as an integral part of it, they fall betwixt and between when major transnationalism opposes dominant and resistant modes and keeps binary oppositions such as North/South, from above/from below, from inside/from outside intact. For them, minor transnationalism includes a crosscutting transversalism in evidence through 'micropractices' (8) and 'lateral network structures' (7). Minor transnationalism valorises what grows up from below, the 'gap' as imagined by Marshall. If minor transnationalism provides the general conceptual terrain on where to locate Rachid Djaïdani's guerrilla filmmaking, Hafid Naficy's 'accented cinema' (2001) provides particular conceptual terrain. Across three subcategories – exilic, diasporic, and postcolonial ethnic and identity filmmaking – Naficy signals how the positionality of these three groups of filmmakers creates an accent – or unique cinematic voice, style, and themes, in sum a unique cinematic language. And so, a backhistory of migration as well as the diversity and difference of the filmmakers vis-à-vis the dominant society and culture in which they live are conditions for accented cinema. While he affirms there is no perfect similarity between the experiences of someone living in exile and someone living in diaspora, Naficy emphasises that both people are similarly deterritorialised. As for postcolonial ethnic filmmaking, it retains a different relationship to place, one more anchored in the 'here and now' (15), though deterritorialised in its own right.

In a Deleuzian vein, Naficy characterises accented cinema not just as a minority cinema, but also as a minor cinema, which is to say a political or claims-staking cinema within a majority cinema. Because of its position vis-à-vis majority cinema, accented cinema offers a critique of the dominant cinema: 'By its artisanal and collective mode of production, its subversion of the conventions of storytelling and spectator positioning, its critical juxtaposition of different worlds, languages, and cultures, and its aesthetics of imperfection and smallness, it critiques the dominant cinema' (2001: 26). In lieu of industrial means for producing a film, accented filmmaking often depends on the return of the author, who is frequently required to contribute to the production of his or her film.[8] As a result, the filmmaker has a direct and visible impact on the film, in some cases going so far as to act in it. Finally, Naficy references a doubleness among accented filmmakers that should not go unnoticed: 'From the cinematic traditions, they acquire one set of voices, and from the exilic and diasporic they acquire another' (22). This results in a double consciousness that translates to the accent of their films, whether in double-structured narratives or the treatment of 'time, space, and causality' (22). It also means that accented filmmakers often work on two levels, within and around their films – a doubling that introduces self-reflexivity to the films.

Close-ups on Artist-Outsiders in *Sur ma ligne* and *Encré*

Through their dual interests in artists and artistic outsidedness, *Sur ma ligne* and *Encré* work around artistic invention and reception, while applying pressure to traditional documentary form and expression. Both films are experimental in nature, in part because of Djaïdani's vision and in part as a result of the way they were produced. Though Naficy prefers to focus on fiction features in his ranging study, his attention to the documentary form arises in his discussion of 'experimental accented films', which he qualifies through an artisanal, 'home-made' quality that they have due to lower grade film and material. Such films tend to be made by a young generation of filmmakers who have been 'born or bred in diaspora' (2001: 22). Naficy's assessment of how they compare to accented feature films fits very closely to the present examination: 'experimental accented films are more hybridised than the feature films in their intentional crossing and problematisation of various borders, such as those between video and film, fiction and nonfiction, narrative and non-narrative, social and psychic, autobiographical and national' (22). With his documentaries, Djaïdani seems particularly attuned to the porous lines between fiction and nonfiction, and also between identity and performance.

In *Sur ma ligne*, Djaïdani films himself from winter 2001 to spring of 2003 as he writes his second novel, *Mon nerf* (2004). In his bedroom in Carrières-sous-Poissy, Djaïdani most often appears alone in the camera's frame, tortured by the act of writing as he alternates between restlessness and sleeplessness, once appearing like a Buddhist monk who has renounced the outside world. Throughout he embellishes his own performance and captures the few allowed into his space of writing as they perform for the camera: his mother dances and sings when she visits him; he sets up a faux interview with a friend who has been asked to diagnose his computer's failings. Dressed in a bathrobe as he exits the shower, he offers the lone moment of truth-seeking to the film in the comic mode: 'And it's the truth we're after', Djaïdani claims holding his index finger to the air in a seemingly authoritative gesture, but then he quickly qualifies, 'Well, anyhow, if I'm having fun, everyone should be having fun'. It connects with Naficy's assertion that, in accented cinema, identity occupies the fore, but as a process of becoming or a 'performance of identity' (6).[9]

As mentioned earlier, *Sur ma ligne* begins and also concludes with clips from Djaïdani's appearance on Bernard Pivot's *Bouillon de culture*. In other words, he frames the documentary with these already filmed black-and-white sequences, showing one representation of his authorship. The rest of the film, in colour and in real time, is a second representation of his authorship. What we see in the colour portion is the portrait of an artist; one struggling with the human emotions of self-doubt, elation, humility, ambivalence, one unsure of how to proceed in the world of publishing and unanchored when he hands his manuscript over to publishers. While Djaïdani learns about and films the bounds of his authorship, he also experiments with filmmaking. However, this experimentation does not empty the film of meaning or message: we must watch to the end when Djaïdani has seen his novel through the production process and finds himself signing a stack of books for the French publishing house Seuil. He engages his counterpart, François de Closets, in a conversation and explains that while he was in the process of securing a contract with Seuil for *Boumkoeur*, he was accused of not having written the novel and was asked to tell the truth about its authorship, with the suggestion that he had hired a ghostwriter a defining instance of what Djaïdani (2007) calls 'discrimination intellectuelle'.[10] With this backstory in mind, *Sur ma ligne* becomes the proof of his authorship.

The anecdote about Djaïdani's disavowal at Seuil, which could have been the beginning of *Sur ma ligne*, mirrors the notional beginning of *Encré*. Once again, the film follows an artist-outsider whose world we enter in medias res. Director of the Cinéma du Réel film festival, Maria Bonsanti (2015) commented on *Encré*'s resonance with fictional film: 'The film is engaging and displays a quasi-fictional quality in the way in which it travels with the spectator until the moment when the artist filmed by Djaïdani manages to get exhibited in New York'. At the outset of *Encré*, in a voice-over to a night scene in which Yassine (who goes by the nickname Yaze) Mekhnache's paintings are being unloaded into a new studio space, Yaze is told by his gallerists, 'I think we have to stop working together [. . .] We like you just fine, Yaze, but it's your lifestyle [. . .] I'm sorry to say it, but among all the artists we work with, we've only got a problem with you'. In this rendering of him as the lone problem among the artists they represent, Yaze wonders what they have done for him, given that they did not sell any of his work. Then, with a shot in broad daylight and in direct address to the camera, Yaze announces a new departure – an artistic and cultural road trip that takes artist and filmmaker to New York via Morocco.

Obstacles are nothing new to Yaze, who began his artistic career as a graffiti artist in Lyons, France. No longer in school at the age of fourteen, Yaze applied to enter Lyons's Beaux Arts but was not admitted based on the fact that he had no high school diploma and graffiti art was not seen as an art form. Somewhat audaciously, he decided to set up a studio across the street and began focusing on abstract human portraits. When he could, he informally interviewed instructors entering the Beaux Arts building on technique and form. In the context of *Encré*, re-establishing himself means that Yaze has to find a new gallerist. When he and two younger friends, both minorities at a largely white event, visit the Foire Internationale d'Art Contemporain (FIAC) together, Yaze expresses a particular interest in meeting Kamel Mennour, an 'ethical' gallerist with 'integrity'. One of his friends tells Mennour's story from his first sales job in the Darty electronics and home-furnishings store, where he sold framed poster art. Their conversation then turns to the artists on display, 'The artists are always the same ones. There's no interest in finding new talents, you know, new faces'. This is why Mennour stands out in representing less-established artists such as Kader Attia and Mohamed Bourouissa alongside some of the world's most internationally well-known artists, such as Daniel Buren and Anish Kapoor; he breaks the chain of social reproduction. Yaze's friend continues: 'He takes a risk and show things that are really worth it [. . .] Not just those artists who already made a name for themselves, but also those who are doing something new and have not yet been discovered'. In the same sequence, we see Yaze as he turns to look up at a neon light instalment that reads 'Etrangers partout' ('Foreigners/Outsiders everywhere'). It is this outsidedness to the system that Yaze knows he is up against and must conquer.

What follows in the next section of the film are two remarkable painting sequences. The first begins with extra-diegetic cello and piano music that accompanies the first artistic gestures in the film as Yaze begins applying paint to large canvases on a wall. The camera goes in and out of focus before the scene changes, and the music becomes part of the diegesis. Yaze is now listening to François and Sylvain Rabbath as they continue their piano and cello duet in an apartment living room. The second painting

Figure 3.1 The beginnings of the canvases for the 'Wandering' exhibit in *Encré*.

sequence follows Yaze's visit with his father, himself an artist, but one who is content with reproducing Venetian water scenes and postcard-like casbahs. For Yaze, painting is altogether different – it was his first and remains his preferred language. In the second painting sequence, Yaze stands above his canvas with Djaïdani shooting from a God's-eye perspective: Yaze looks like Jackson Pollock, and perhaps more fittingly still Jean-Michel Basquiat, at work in transforming a blank canvas into a wash of vibrant and communicating colours and strokes.[11]

In preparation for his New York show at the Catherine Ahnell gallery, Yaze first travels to Marrakech, a section that offers stunning visuals and unfiltered sound. It begins with an extreme close-up side view of Yaze's face as he drives several Moroccan women to a rural cultural centre. To begin their work together, Yaze traces lines and areas on a canvas that the women embroider with gold and silver thread in a stitch commonly seen on traditional Moroccan women's dresses. Large-scale canvases emerge, with non-geometric shapes that together seem to be a new ordering of the continents.

We will not see these to their completion in step-by-step fashion: we see them hanging on a clothesline in Morocco, and the next time we see them, they are finished products being carried into the gallery (see Figure 3.1). What seems to interest Djaïdani more in this instance is the response they elicit on the streets of New York as passers-by inquire and comment on their origins in Morocco; he never lets art lie far from personal interactions and response.

A linear narrative with clear progression and spatial-temporal markers does not figure in Djaïdani's documentary filmmaking. His films never progress through the unfolding or reconstituting of an historical narrative. Further, computer screens or superimposed shots with time-lapse photography interrupt real time and image; voice-overs narrate scenes to which they do not correspond fully. This mediation sends us back to the documentary-fiction scale that Djaïdani navigates and upon which he improvises. In lieu of an historical narrative, Djaïdani's documentary films advance through recurring themes and motifs, image-sets, and sequences. What is more, whether a close-up on his wife's pregnancy, the writing of his second novel, or Yaze's painting toward an art show, Djadaïni's filmic content depends upon portraiture, giving his films an intimate and personal resonance. And yet, though painting these portraits happens in slow-time over an extended process or unfolding, the narrative progression and camerawork is jumpy and restless, and the editing produces lacunas that require patience and watching until the end – much like with the dénouement of a fiction feature. When Yaze travels to Morocco, the film abruptly cuts from the streets of Paris to a ruralscape in Morocco; and similarly, when Yaze travels to New York City, nothing within the film's diegesis marks the physical journey or the time it takes; there is merely a cut to the new setting.

Such lacunas stem in part from the fact that Djaïdani shoots a disproportionate number of hours of film, which he then edits down to unusually short films. Interestingly, this creative process reflects Yaze's remarks as his gallery show is about to open in New York at the end of *Encré*: 'What hangs on the walls goes beyond what I could have imagined [. . .] I create a work of art and then ask myself questions afterwards [. . .] On opening night, I'm a spectator as well'. Djaïdani's methods reveal the same about his filmmaking. In reference to *Rengaine*, Djaïdani has compared himself to a self-made painter who resembles Yaze: 'I'm a painter (if I may say so) who had to prepare his canvas by himself, find his artistic references, and find a way – both financially and in terms of a process – to create a portrait, which is what this film is' (Reeck 2013). And so, *Sur ma ligne* and *Encré* are the filmic inscriptions of artist-outsiders working to safeguard their signatures while also striving for recognition. In these documentaries, both Djaïdani and Mekhnache appear as autodidacts, and by the end both sit at a critical juncture, a breakthrough moment – Djaïdani as a writer, Mekhnache as a painter.

Seeing Paris's Many Faces and Facets in *Rengaine*

While the return of the author to filmmaking is literal with *Sur ma ligne*, it continues to be important in the case of *Rengaine*. The location of the accented filmmaker vis-à-vis the accented film can be a physical location in the film, a figurative presence, or a personal investment, whether financial or as an actor. Given the nature of the guerrilla project in *Rengaine*, filming with no budget and over nine years, Djaïdani had to be invested both financially and physically in his film: 'I shot it by myself. It was me, my camera, the actress was my wife, some guys I know, my friends. The kids are my nephews and the mother is my friend's mother' (Reeck 2013). But in all cases, Naficy characterises accented filmmakers in terms of the impact of their personal histories on their films: 'Accented filmmakers are not just textual structures or fictions within their films; they also are empirical subjects, situated in the interstices of cultures and film practices, who exist outside and prior to their films' (2001: 4). With *Rengaine*, Djaïdani explores a theme not often seen in French cinema – interethnic and interreligious taboo and prejudice, through which we see the importance of Djaïdani's personal history in the fact that his parents form an interethnic couple.

Rengaine is a family drama that takes a bold look at the divisions and dynamics that lead to clan-like mentality operating in and as a pack, and what happens when a character, in this case an Arab French woman, decides to assert her individuality.[12] Originally called '40 frères', the film features Sabrina, played by Djaïdani's wife Sabrina Hamida, who has fallen in love with a Black Christian man, Dorcy, played by Stéphane Soo Mongo. They decide to get married, but when news of this circulates among Sabrina's 40 brothers (a nod to the 40 thieves in *Ali Baba*), and especially when her older brother Slimane, played by Slimane Dazi, learns of the impending marriage and seeks to thwart it, Sabrina confronts the suspicion and prejudice of her entourage. This basic plot line fits with what Naficy says about accented films made by postcolonial ethnic filmmakers: he claims that because of their unique positionality, their films tend to feature 'conflict between descent relations, emphasising bloodline and ethnicity, and consent relations, stressing self-made, contractual affiliations' (2001: 15). Broadly, *Rengaine* deconstructs hard-edged stereotypes held by one racial or ethnic group about another. At the same time, the film decentres tropes of filmic Paris, the consequence of which is the minorising of the proverbial City of Light, here filmed largely in the dark.

With accented cinema, Naficy highlights the importance of spectatorship, suggesting that spectators of accented films must have recourse to

Figure 3.2 Activating spectatorship through a *jeu de regards* in *Rengaine*.

'watching, listening ... reading, translating, and writing' (2001: 4) to meet the films on their own terms: the active spectator goes hand in hand with the return of the author and authorship to filmmaking. In *Rengaine*, the importance of spectatorship is highlighted through the eyes and *le regard*, but the perspective we are given is often partial or mitigated, as in numerous instances scenes are shot through rear-view mirrors or through a window and, apart from Sabrina and Dorcy, very rarely do characters in the film look into each other's eyes. Even *tête-à-têtes* are filmed through alternating one-shots of the characters. Our spectatorship gets activated and challenged as we look for and work to understand what Djaïdani wanted to show: 'I wanted to show the faces of Paris – people's mugs. For me, from the very moment that I pick up a pen or camera, it's already a political act. It gives me the power to show all the people I know, their daily lives, those who never appear in films that are exported' (Reeck 2013). As Djaïdani hones in on the many faces of Paris, and particularly those lesser-seen in film, one definitional feature of the camera work is the extreme close-up.[13]

In this regard, an important sequence within a quick juxtaposition of shots at the beginning of the film features Slimane. Reciting the names of each brother, Slimane arrives at the 40 brothers in his family only by counting himself twice, and thus by eliding one of the brothers. This missing brother proves critical and the omission only becomes clarified at the end of the film.

In this sequence, eyes, and gazes, dominate in extreme close-up: Slimane and a not yet identified woman stand in front of a mirror (see Figure 3.2). In a dark room filled with shadows, we see Slimane, who is looking towards the unidentified woman, through a mirror image. The *jeu de regards* that Djaïdani creates disorients the spectator: this is a technique that Djaïdani employs throughout – destabilising the spectators so that they to work to find their bearings, ultimately re-locating themselves.

Accented cinema often contains a degree of self-reflexivity as film commenting on filmic attributes or filmmaking, one that is pronounced and meaningful in *Rengaine*. On the one hand, such themes as seeing and watching, as well as the theme of performance (e.g. Dorcy is an aspiring actor, and all forms of performance find expression in the film – miming, dancing, acting) point to embedded filmic properties. On the other, throughout *Renagine*, there is an obvious appraisal of French cinema, and a concomitant adjusting of it.[14] At one point, one of Dorcy's friends declares: 'in France right now, we're not innovators [. . .] we're followers.' This is precisely where Djaïdani intervenes with his filmmaking: the need for invention and creation serves as a refrain across his oeuvre broadly and as he works around tropes of filmic Paris, which he mines on his own terms, in *Rengaine* specifically.

For his part, Naficy underscores the deterritorialisation at work in accented cinema and how it recaptures and transforms space and place. Somewhat paradoxically, as Naficy clearly states, 'Because they are deterritorialized, [accented] films are deeply concerned with territory and territoriality' (2001: 5). In *Rengaine*, which explores the exacerbated territoriality of communities, ethnicities, and religions, one of the most noteworthy presences in the film is the city of Paris itself, which Djaïdani manages to deterritorialise. We are brought into the city through the limits imposed by guerrilla filmmaking: with unfiltered sound and background noise, we hear it, which gives the film an intimacy, immediacy, and even urgency at times. Through the constant movement of his camera, Djaïdani evinces a mobility that is tantamount to a right to the city as he maps a particular decentred geography. Though *Rengaine* does go to the centre of Paris, with shots of Slimane on the Pont des Arts looking toward Notre-Dame and location shooting at Les Halles, most of the film is shot in northern Paris (e.g. Gare du Nord, Pigalle, Les Buttes Chaumont, Montmartre). This is a slight decentring coupled with still more decentred choices that Djaïdani made about filmic Paris, perhaps first and foremost the fact that the film is largely shot outside at night. This was not purely by choice because he lacked a licence to film, but nonetheless this gives an unusual look and feel to the film.

Of particular note in this last respect is a night scene filmed under the Bir Hakeim bridge that features a love relationship about which the other characters know nothing: Slimane has been involved with a Jewish woman by the name of Nina, the same woman who appears in *Rengaine*'s first sequence.[15] Here Nina and Slimane confront the difficulties in their relationship: Nina wants their 'secret' to end; Slimane admits he is inhibited by Nina being Jewish. This could be seen as the key love story in *Rengaine*; it significantly deepens Slimane's character; it creates two parallel narratives, a double-structure that captures Naficy's assertion that stylistically accented cinema turns on fragmentation and a critically juxtaposed narrative structure (2001: 4). Djaïdani has agreed to the importance of the clandestine love story between Slimane and Nina: 'Now, that's where I wanted to take it one step further to something even more transgressive and violent [. . .] So Slimane's transgression goes further because he is in a relationship with a Jew. And, suddenly, in the theatre, everyone goes quiet' (Reeck 2013). In addition to the powerful interreligious dynamic that this scene raises in the revelation of the relationship between Slimane and Nina, the way that Djaïdani films and understands this scene is worth noting: 'when they're there, we could have slowed down, and done a "Oh, look, they're next to the Eiffel Tower." But, we didn't, because we don't give a damn about the Eiffel Tower' (Reeck 2013). Instead of a wide shot panning over to the Eiffel Tower that would lend itself to 'postcard Paris', Djaïdani prefers to focus on the intensity of the troubled relationship between Slimane and Nina, virtually effacing the outline of the bridge. Instead of focusing on lit monuments by night, he focuses on faces in the dark.

In another bridge scene at night, Djaïdani appropriates the history of French cinema, returning to the same bridge under which Arletty stands with Louis Jouvet in *Hôtel du Nord* (Marcel Carné, 1938, France).

> And, at the same time, for us French, we're not far from the bridge of Arletty, 'Atmosphère? . . . Qu'est-ce qu'elle a ma gueule?' [*Hotel du Nord* (1938)]. It's a mythic bridge for French cinema. [. . .] And so, these are the symbols that we integrated into the film. We appropriated the history of French cinema, 'Atmosphère, atmosphère . . . Qu'est-ce qu'elle a ma gueule? Est-ce que j'ai une gueule d'atmosphère?' We take it up from there. I appropriate classical cinema through several references to say, 'Atmosphère? That's us'. To say that we are taking over the references. We are the new France. (Reeck 2013)

In an enigmatic sequence with piano music on the soundtrack, the camera pans along the lights bordering the Canal Saint-Martin as Dorcy and Sabrina walk hand in hand. In showing his attention to all the faces and facets of Paris, and especially those lesser seen, Djaïdani locates a new France. Here, as with Naficy, deterritorialisation is not an evacuation or emptying out, but rather a reorganisation and reconceptualisation. Djaïdani accomplishes this reterritorialisation by presenting a crosscutting view of Paris that stands to strike the spectator as known and unknown, acknowledged and unacknowledged, above ground and underground.

Towards the end of the film, Slimane has affirmed his intention to marry Nina and to father her children. Throughout the film, the only person to know about the love relationship between Slimane and Nina is the fortieth brother, Nacer, the missing name at the beginning of the film, who appears at its end. He is gay and has been banished from the family by Slimane, who has taken on the role of 'le grand frère', because of the taboo that homosexuality represents. In one of the final sequences, Nacer appeals to Slimane to let Sabrina pursue her relationship with Dorcy, pointing to Slimane's own hypocrisy. This confrontation, in which the film's tension reaches an apex, unlocks something in Slimane, who will ask for Dorcy's forgiveness in the final scene of the film. In this way, the end of *Rengaine* resonates with redemption, and two interethnic, interreligious relationships will endure, providing a new twist on *Romeo and Juliet*, and perhaps more fittingly still *West Side Story* (Jerome Robbins and Robert Wise, 1961, USA). With a topic that has more often than not been reduced to pat stereotypes in romantic comedies, Djaïdani unearths and denounces the interethnic prejudice that keeps or forces people and communities apart; he deconstructs the pride and honour of clan in favour of characters who have been made to feel as outsiders but who dare, nonetheless, to cross boundaries.

Conclusion

At present, like Djaïdani the writer at the end of *Sur ma ligne* and Yaze at the end of *Encré*, Djaïdani the filmmaker sits at a threshold. In the summer of 2015, he completed shooting *Tour de France* (2016, France), a road movie starring Gérard Depardieu and the Maghrebi-French rapper Sadek as they travel through the perimeter of France visiting its port cities, an important geographical periphery. For the first time, he filmed with the approbation of the Centre and had a budget to pay the actors, but his mode of filmmaking outside on location with very little apparatus, his interest in art – in this case the painter Joseph Vernet – and music, as well as a sense of continuous movement endures. The film premiered at the 2016 Directors' Fortnight at Cannes to mixed reviews. There is some sense that *Tour de France* lost the freshness that Djaïdani's guerrilla films have (e.g. Ehrlich 2016, Sotinel 2016). Time will tell if he will be able to retain his unique signature while working within French film institutions.

As for Djaïdani's guerrilla filmmaking, it provides a particularly interesting case in the hypothesis of a cinéma-monde because of its localness, here and now-ness (Naficy 2001: 15), and use of 'micropractices' (Lionnet and Shih 2005: 8) – ranging from self-filming to using family and friends as actors to self-financing, spontaneous on location shooting, and Facebook-page publicity – on the one hand, and its global-ness in terms of its circulation and acclaim on the other. It makes claims to French national cinema; at the same time as it reroutes mainstream aesthetic modes and production practices; at the same time as it has reached international audiences in Dubai, Italy, Morocco, and New York and has been prized by international film critics. As such, Djaïdani's is a minor cinema in communication with a major cinema as it points the way toward a version of French cinema that is interested in the personal and the political, being at home and in the world, and new ways of seeing and receiving the creative process, especially when it is experimental or fringe. Its place within the geography of cinéma-monde is that of minorised (and minority) hexagonal film with a true and compelling accent originating in Djaïdani's positionality as a postcolonial ethnic filmmaker.

Notes

1. My concern with now making 'Francophone cinema' inclusive of all French-language cinema is that it is counter-intuitive. 'Francophone cinema' has been used for more than twenty years to reference an external periphery to hexagonal French-language cinema and contains an unevenness in its points of reference (i.e. European French-speaking countries vs post-colonial French-speaking countries). Adjusting its notional dimensions to be inclusive (a centre) after having been exclusive (a periphery) for so long seems insufficient.
2. Djaïdani's first exposure to filmmaking occurred on the set of Mathieu Kassovitz's *La Haine* (1995, France). When asked to reflect back on that experience in 'Vingt ans après *La Haine*, les cités, toujours grandes absentes des écrans' (Ferenczi 2015), Djaïdani said about the opportunity, which presented itself just as he had been suspended from his vocational-technical high school: 'The film shoot saved my life. It was the first time we saw people who didn't look like us; it was poetry descending upon our housing project'.
3. In our 2012 interview, Djaïdani explained that he uses the same Panasonic dvx100be as Lars von Trier. Interestingly, Djaïdani could be seen to adhere to all but one of the tenets laid out in the Dogme95 manifesto (i.e. he names himself in the credits as the filmmaker, breaking tenet 10 of the manifesto), the key elements of which are: no artifice or props in location shootings; no sound filter and only music that corresponds to the scenes shot in the film; a hand held camera that films in colour; and no unnecessary action, especially

no violent action. We could use this observation to situate him within avant-garde filmmaking.
4. On its website, Faites tournez! describes its enterprise as follows: 'Faites tourner was born of a desire to invest a new creative field – short films – in order to experiment with new narratives, to let a diverse range of sensibilities express themselves, to experience reality differently'.
5. Elizabeth Ezra and Terry Rowden (2006) have explored this phenomenon: 'Central to the creation of this [global] cine-literacy has been the proliferation of film festivals as an alternative means of film distribution and presentation' (3). They then offer: 'Transnational distribution in its many forms unmoors films from their immediate contexts, thereby allowing them to circulate much more freely than ever before, i.e. to "migrate"' (7). In this way, films obey a unique logic as they can be distributed internationally in simultaneity with or even before national distribution (or sometimes in the absence of national distribution).
6. While Higbee points to an important trend, very few women filmmakers are mentioned in the study, which leads one to wonder if they are not making films or if they continue to face barriers. Also, in recent history, Mehdi Charef struggled to get his *Graziella* (2015, France) into theatres. It was only through the substantial financing of the Gavras's – the producers of the film – that it was distributed. Also of note is Rabah Ameur-Zaïmeche's *Histoire de Judas/Story of Judas* (2015, France), which, while it received critical attention, got a very small audience. An important point of note and distinction that needs further examination is the mainstreaming of comedies versus the mainstreaming of dramas.
7. Higbee importantly references such a complex position in his study: 'filmmakers of Maghrebi origin working in France in the 2000s have increasingly questioned the boundaries between national, transnational and diasporic cinema at the same time as their films demand, either implicitly or explicitly, a reconsideration of the very difference (religious, ethnic, and cultural) that has traditionally been seen as a barrier to their successful integration into French society' (2013: 3).
8. One of the ironies here is that by their very nature and difference to mainstream practices, such filmmakers resist collectivisation and categorisation: 'By and large, they operate independently, outside the studio system of the mainstream film industries, using interstitial and collective modes of production that critique those entities. As a result, they are presumed to be more prone to the tensions of marginality and difference. While they share these characteristics, the very existence of the tensions and differences helps prevent accented filmmakers from becoming a homogeneous group or a film movement' (Naficy 2001: 10).
9. Elsewhere, I have studied *Sur ma ligne* in detail (see *Writerly Identities in Beur Fiction and Beyond*, 2011, pp. 138–44), analysing it in terms of Bill Nichols's 'performative documentary', which has obvious points of connection to

Naficy's 'accented cinema', and could be considered one variant of experimental accented film.
10. In an article in *Libération*, Djaïdani is quoted using this terminology to refer to his treatment by Seuil editors: 'When I brought in the manuscript of my first book (the best-seller *Boumkoeur*), the lady at the publishing house asked me suspiciously if I had really written it, says Djaïdani. This intellectual discrimination angered me, so for my second novel, I got a basic camera to film myself' (Daum 2006).
11. These two artist biopics have definite resonance with *Encré*, largely because of the methods of their artists. Numerous scenes from each communicate squarely with *Encré* as Yaze, standing over his canvas, shows the physicality of painting.
12. Often when inter-ethnic and inter-racial relationships get explored on the big screen, it is in a romantic comedy, in which stereotypes abound and direct the plot (e.g. *Le Ciel, les oiseaux, ta mère; Qu'est-ce qu'on a fait au Bon Dieu?*). *Rengaine* contradicts this as a suspenseful dramatic film.
13. Here it is important to know that while making *Rengaine*, the director consulted Hervé Sneid, the film editor of *Delicatessen* and more recently *Mesrine*. When Sneid watched *Rengaine* in an early iteration, he noted that the filmmaking was not yet cinematic, which led Djaïdani to stop filming and ask himself what makes cinema cinematic: 'And at one point, I understood what cinema is – *le regard*, the eyes. And that's when I returned to shooting the film, and ended up reshooting some scenes' (Djaïdani 2012).
14. In order to support inventiveness and newness, Djaïdani has imagined different ways of working, corresponding in part to new technologies; he asks for more spontaneity in filmmaking and that those making decisions trust in a process and a vision, and not in a script alone. He envisions a commission within the CNC that would evaluate films 'on the basis of a pitch, a few words and a basic framing, who can help a new generation of filmmakers to emerge. Filmmakers who come from the countryside, and those who come from the *banlieue*, and those from Paris who didn't necessarily have the chance to be born with a silver spoon, with all the advantages' (Reeck 2013).
15. The Bir Hakeim bridge has been featured in a range of films and has become a trope of filmic Paris, often with métro trains running over it (e.g. *Zazie dans le métro*, *Last Tango in Paris*, *Un Indien dans la ville*, *Munich*, and *Inception*).

Works Cited

Akika, A., Review of *Sur ma ligne*, <http://www.lacid.org/sur-ma-ligne> (last accessed 21 November 2015).

Bonsanti, M., 'Le film documentaire: antidote au fanatisme', interview with Maria Bonsanti, 13 March 2015, <http://www.culturecommunication.gouv.fr/Actualites/En-continu/Le-film-documentaire-antidote-au-fanatisme> (last accessed 15 November 2015).

Bouillon de culture, presented by Bernard Pivot, 26 February 1999. France 2.
Daum, P. (2006), 'La Mise au poing de Rachid Djaïdani,' *Libération.fr*, 20 July, <http://next.liberation.fr/culture/2006/07/20/la-mise-au-poing-de-rachid-djaidani_46502> (last accessed 13 November 2015).
Ehrlich, D. (2016), '"Tour de France" Is A Half-Hearted "Gran Torino" Remake Starring Gérard Depardieu As Clint Eastwood.' *IndieWire*, 15 May, <http://www.indiewire.com/2016/05/cannes-review-tour-de-france-is-a-half-hearted-gran-torino-remake-starring-gerard-depardieu-as-clint-eastwood-290570> (last accessed 17 July 2016).
Ezra, Elizabeth and Terry Rowden (2006), *Transnational Cinema: The Film Reader*, London: Routledge.
Faites tourner!, <http://television.telerama.fr/tele/documentaire/faites-tourner,12996571,emission49568370.php> (last accessed 13 November 2015).
Ferenczi, A. (2015), 'Vingt ans après *La Haine*, les cités, toujours grandes absentes des écrans', *Télérama*, 1 June, <http://www.telerama.fr/cinema/vingt-ans-apres-la-haine-les-cites-toujours-grandes-absentes-des-ecrans,112366.php> (last accessed 1 November 2015).
Higbee, William (2013), *Post-Beur Cinema: North African Émigré and Maghrebi-French Filmmaking in France since 2000*, Edinburgh: Edinburgh University Press.
Lionnet, Françoise and Shu-mei Shih (eds) (2005), *Minor Transnationalism*, Durham, NC: Duke University Press.
Marshall, B. (2012), 'Cinéma-monde? Towards a Concept of Francophone Cinema', in *Francosphères*, 1:1, pp. 35–51.
Naficy, Hamid (2001), *An Accented Cinema: Exilic and Diasporic Filmmaking*, Princeton: Princeton University Press.
Nichols, Bill (2001), *Introduction to Documentary*, Bloomington: University of Indiana Press.
Reeck, Laura (2011), *Writerly Identities in Beur Fiction and Beyond*, Lanham: Lexington Books.
Reeck, Laura (2013), Interview with Rachid Djaïdani, Paris, *Bomblog*, 11 April 2013, <http://bombmagazine.org/article/7160> (last accessed 13 July 2016).
Sotinel, T. (2016), '"Tour de France": Gérard Depardieu se met au hip-hop', *LeMonde.fr*, 15 May, <http://www.lemonde.fr/festival-de-cannes/article/2016/05/15/tour-de-france-gerard-depardieu-se-met-au-hip-hop_4920050_766360.html> (last accessed 18 July 2016).

CHAPTER 4

Globalisation, Cinéma-monde and the Work of Abderrahmane Sissako

Dayna Oscherwitz

Malian/Mauritanian director Abderrahmane Sissako is one of the most acclaimed and well-known film directors in Africa, particularly francophone Africa. His films, including *La Vie sur terre/Life on Earth* (1998, Mali/France/Mauritania), *Heremakono/Waiting for Happiness* (2002, France/Mauritania), and *Bamako* (2006, Mali/France/USA) are among the most widely distributed African films in Europe, the UK, and North America, and *Timbuktu* (2014, Mauritania/France), his most recent film, is one of the most fêted and one of the highest grossing African films of all time. Despite Sissako's relative success in both award and box office terms, the overall reception of his films has been mixed; for example, his films have been accused of depicting Africa in a way that reinforces stereotypes of the continent prevalent in the Global North (Adesokan 2010; Beau 2015; Cessou 2014). The divergent responses to Sissako's work derive from a type of clash between the transnational orientation of his films, and an idea of African cinema as a 'revolt against colonialism, and then against neo-colonialism, dependency, and euro-centrism' (Harrow 2007: 1). This critical paradigm, which David Murphy has described as cinematic regionalism, rooted in 'a reductive opposition between Western and African culture' (2006: 28), derives from francophone African post-independence politics and an accompanying aesthetics of liberation. This regionalism evolved as an attempt to correct the role the cinematic image had played in supporting and sustaining French colonial-era policies and hierarchies (Tcheuyap 2006: 9–11), and it was seen as a method of creating plurality and equality in filmic production and in global relations.

Sissako's films, with their global reach, their relative commercial and critical success, and their divergence with respect to received, established notions of African film production both resemble and anticipate the collection of English-language novels that Taiye Selasi in 2005 termed 'Afropolitan', as well as the francophone concepts of *littérature-monde* and cinéma-monde that Afropolitanism inspired. In that respect, it is useful to consider Sissako's work in terms of its relationship to these other transnational, cosmopolitan models of cultural production, and to examine the modes through which all of these interrogate global power dynamics in the face of globalisation.

Afropolitanism is a transnational literary and artistic concept used to designate people of African parentage with deep, experiential ties to Africa, Europe, and North America; it was applied to Selasi's writing, as well as to other novels written by Anglophone writers of African heritage whose works centre on characters with intimate knowledge of the urban centres of the Global North.[1] Like these novels, Sissako's work articulates what Achille Mbembe terms 'the presence of the elsewhere in the here and vice versa' (2007: 28), the entrance of Africa into the age of globalised dispersion and circulation. In many ways, however, Sissako's films constitute a 'francophone' alternative to the predominantly Anglophone Afropolitanism, and as precursor to the francophone concept of cinéma-monde.

One central divergence among Afropolitan novels, Sissako's films, and the films of cinéma-monde is the trajectory and orientation of the central characters in the works. Afropolitan novels typically record migration through individual stories that move 'out of Africa' and they often convey this through the unified, if multifaceted, consciousness of a single protagonist. Hence in Afropolitan novels, Africa is typically a point of origin, and the endpoint or destination is a capital city or major metropolis in the Global North. Moreover, Afropolitan novels often function as a type of African, cosmopolitan bildungsroman that represents and celebrates transnational movement and individual class mobility, and they may therefore indirectly validate dominant discourses of development, which see African nations and other areas of the Global South as primitive versions of Western nations. This apparently uncritical representation of the unequal relationship between Africa and the Global North sometimes found in these novels has, for that reason, led various critics of the novels to accuse them of standing for 'empty style and cultural commodification' (Santana 2013).

Sissako's films, on the other hand, tend to reject linear, unified narrative and the representational model of classical film aesthetics. They have no clear protagonist, and the characters in them have incomplete trajectories. The intended direction of the characters in the films is just as often somewhere in Africa as somewhere beyond. African towns and cities and the cities of the Global North are, in these films, points of origin, points of destination, or midway points on a journey somewhere else. Cinéma-monde is a label applied to transnational filmmakers who work in a francophone, transnational context and whose work actively contemplates the porous borders and migratory circulations of the contemporary, globalised era (Marshall 2012). The concept builds upon previous models of transnationalism in cinema, including Hamid Naficy's concept of 'accented' or exilic/diasporic filmmaking that retains the 'accent' of the country of origin. Sissako's films and other global, transnational films express the relationship between Africa and the Global North as polycentric, emphasising journeys more than destinations. They, therefore, 'highlight crossings and itineraries, and challenge claims of plenitude made by languages and cultures' (Marshall 2012: 35). Sissako's films are also deeply visual, using a montage of divergent images and contexts to reflect upon the processes of globalisation. They reject, however, the rising plot structure and developmental narrative paradigms of Afropolitan novels in favour of a migratory and circulatory structure more in keeping with the narratives of cinéma-monde.

Uneven Prosperity, Linear Trajectories and Cinematic Circulation

Cinéma-monde, transnational cinema, and Sissako's films are byproducts of globalisation, understood as 'the integration through international trade of markets in goods and services [. . .] financial integration through international trade in assets [. . .] international outsourcing of services and international movement of persons' (Frankel 2006: 1), the consequence of which was the promise of increased economic interdependence that would ostensibly be distributed relatively equally among participating nations (Marquardt 2005). All of these films and novels are cultural products that circulate in the transnational economy, functioning as symbols of national cultural capital, and as discursive spaces in which socio-political realities are reflected and dissected. As such, these novels and films occupy a unique position in the global capitalist system, having the capacity to observe, record and critique the very workings of the system in which they circulate (Oscherwitz 2015).

Cinema, specifically, was used as a tool of domestication by European colonisers during the colonial era (Barry 2004; Genova 2013); it has been a key force in the creation of American cultural dominance, through Hollywood's expansive distribution networks – created and sustained by aggressive trade negotiations – and it has shaped the perceptions and images of Africa that circulate throughout the world (Higgins 2012). Film has also been a central front in the articulation of African political and cultural identities and a site of economic contestation and control. The French, for example through the Consortium audiovisuel international, Fonds sud, and other funding mechanisms, have remained actively engaged in film production in West and North Africa, and this has raised questions, from the early days of African filmmaking, about the consequences of such economic participation or control over the process of creation and representation and about whether such funding mechanisms ultimately locate creative control over much of African film production in France.[2]

Film, therefore, and its circulations through the transnational marketplace, raises important questions about freedom and balance in the globalised world. Films from francophone Africa circulate more freely in France than they do in many African countries, and films from France or Hollywood circulate more freely in Africa than francophone African films, even if, in the post-Nollywood era, other African media forms are distributed widely on the continent. These issues of funding, circulation, and distribution are central to critical readings of African films and function as the central markers of a film's identity, both in terms of production and categorisation.

Funding, production, and distribution in cinema are complex and negotiable processes, and they interact with the dynamic personal trajectories and fluid creative practices of certain filmmakers to produce a body of work that is not easily localisable, either in terms of production and distribution or in terms of aesthetic or thematic rootedness. In certain respects, as Susan Hayward has suggested, cinema has always been transnational (1993: 20). From the silent era, for example, studies were targeting an international marketplace that was easily accessible before the coming of sound, as there was no language barrier to overcome. Co-productions in the early decades of commercial film production were also commonplace, and countries with major film infrastructure, such as France and the United States, have consistently been aggressive in marketing and distributing their films internationally.

In the 1990s and 2000s, however, critical attention turned to filmmakers whose personal and artistic trajectories were transnational and whose impetus for cross-border filmmaking was something other than a desire to carve out as large a commercial market as possible. 'Independent' filmmakers, who were often expatriates or immigrants, began, in relatively large numbers, making films that reflected the crossings and displacements of their own personal trajectories. The work of such filmmakers, as Will Higbee has noted, has often been seen as transnational, because it involves and depicts cross-border migration (2007: 80), but many critical paradigms for interpreting transnational production fail to take into account film's engagement with the global politics governing relationships between Global North and Global South and/or the intimate relationship between what is now termed globalisation and the processes of colonisation and decolonisation of which it is an extension (Higbee 2007: 80; Hall 1991: 19–21). Thus, classifying Sissako and filmmakers like him as 'transnational' because their works cross borders fails to sufficiently emphasise the ways in which their filmmaking deliberately positions itself outside of any specific national culture. It also does not do full justice to the complexities or intricacies of deliberately migratory filmmaking practices or the implicit critiques of the networks of power and resources of global film production and distribution that underpin such practices.

Transnational Aesthetics and the Global Kaleidoscope

The processes of globalisation that are the subject of Sissako's films mirror the processes of narrative transmission and identification that occur in cinema more generally and in classical narrative cinema specifically. Both processes involve communication and transmission (one of goods and services, and the other of the image and the story); both involve the condensing of space and time through technological innovation, as well as the merging of multiple and diffuse realities and viewpoints into a single, linear narrative of development and progress.[3] In classical narrative films, the projection of the filmic image opens up a gap, a space between the spectator and the illusory world of the film. Cinema, through various mechanisms, ranging from continuity editing to the shot/reverse shot structure, to eye-line matches, to the linear structure of filmic narration works to obscure, to hide, this gap and to construct a unified consciousness, that of the film's invisible and absent narrator, and then to force identification between the spectator and this specular subjectivity.[4] This projection of subjectivity, which attempts to force the spectator into the assumption of an outlook or point of view, depends on an illusion of spatial and temporal continuity that is created despite an underlying structure of multiple viewpoints, temporal rupture, and spatial dislocation.

Classical cinema and classical film aesthetics also reflect and transmit the affirmative narrative of global neo-liberalism, because they reflect the Hollywood/American cultural values and ideologies through which they were formed (de Grazia 1989: 77). This transmission and projection is heightened by the 'sensory experience and sensational affect in [classical cinema's] processes of mimetic identification' (Hansen 1999: 70). Films that harness classical aesthetics, wherever produced, are potentially implicated in the transmission and legitimisation of globalisation and the inequalities and inconsistencies of the global capitalist system, even if the content of such films seeks to critique them. Sissako's films, on the other hand, self-consciously reject classical aesthetics, relying on fragmented, multifocal narration and an aesthetics of discontinuity. In this way, Sissako's films reflect not only on globalisation, but on cinema's role in producing and expanding it.

One of the central problems of globalisation, at least for those looking at it from the African continent, is that it has not kept its promises. Whereas the average income in many francophone African nations has increased over time, it has increased less quickly than the incomes in the Global North. In Mali, for example, the average individual annual income in 1900 was $630 and the average individual annual income in 2015 was $1,684, for a net increase, on average, of $1,000. In France the average income in 1900 was $4,314 or approximately seven times the average income in Mali, and in 2015 it was $37,600 or nearly nine times the income in Mali.[5] This is despite the fact that, in francophone Africa in particular, fairly aggressive measures have been undertaken to conform to the officially advocated pathways of global 'development'. Many francophone nations retain close ties with France, for example, following the French lead on economic, labour and trade policy. Many also submitted to World Bank/IMF programs presented as projects of economic development, most notably structural adjustment. Finally, many francophone African nations are members of OHADA (Organisation pour l'harmonisation en Afrique du droit des affaires) and have adopted French-authored laws designed to facilitate international trade.

Film production in francophone Africa has taken note of the dislocations, disruptions and inconsistencies of global capitalism. Even films of the so-called first generation, most notably Ousmane Sembène's *La Noire de . . . / Black Girl* (1966, Senegal/France) and Djibril Diop Mambety's *Touki Bouki* (1973, Senegal), record and reflect on the disruptions of colonial hierarchies and the related dislocations of human and economic relations that the post-independence era produced (Oscherwitz 2014; Diawara 2010: 48). However, Sissako's films constitute one of the most focused and sustained reflections on the effects of globalisation in African cinema, as well as a significant attempt to rework film aesthetics to account for the fragmentation, disruption and parallelism of globalised modernity. Sissako's films record the processes of globalisation while attempting to problematise the discourse of development associated with them, reflecting on what Ngũgĩ wa Thiongo'o has termed *globaletics*, 'the universal interdependence in the reign of industrial capital . . . that has become globalization' (2012: 46). Sissako's films also explore cinema's role in globalisation's 'intensified communication system' (Ngũgĩ 2012: 46), and in doing so they attempt to fragment unifying process of filmic projection and specular identification and to move toward multifaceted processes of diffusion.

Moreover, Sissako's films, both in their content and their pacing, reflect upon questions of movement, mobility and the instabilities of identity that are characteristic of transnationalism (Adesokan 2010: 144). However, arguably the most significant element of Sissako's filmmaking is the creation of a polycentric aesthetics that functions to break down what Gilles Deleuze has termed 'the unity of the filmic image' (1986: 23–31), or the way in which cinema constructs and imposes a particular sense of space and time. It is, therefore, the form of Sissako's films, as much as their subject matter, that gives voice to both the multiplicities and uniformities of the globalised contemporary, while foregrounding and critiquing the hegemony and inequality of the processes that have produced it.

La Vie sur terre: Migration, Circulation and the Millennium

The themes of circulation, migration, multiplicity, and exchange have been central to Sissako's filmmaking from the beginning. His first feature-length film, *La Vie sur terre* (1998), which was made as part of a series of international films reflecting on the millennium, foregrounds the double themes of globalisation and disruption. This is evident from the film's opening sequence, in which Sissako's fictional alter ego, Dramane Bassaro, shops in a Parisian Monoprix supermarket. This opening sequence, which begins without the conventions of cinematic opening – the establishing shots or other elements of exposition – is composed of a series of disconnected shots – a vertical pan up a counter of decorative ceramic geese, a tracking shot along a dairy case featuring an abundance of varieties of butter and cheese, several static shots of Dramane, framed by shelves of shoes and toys, or jewellery and watches, and finally a slow motion backward tracking shot of Dramane ascending on an escalator (see Figure 4.1). The sequence ends with what is structured as an eye-line match that follows Dramane's upwardly turned gaze but that cuts to, not the literal object of his gaze at that moment in the Monoprix, but the object of his internal gaze, the top of a tree in the town of Sokolo, Mali. The cut violates the basic tenets of continuity editing and replaces the illusory unification of the typical filmic eye-line shots with narrative, geographical, and temporal dislocation, as we move from Paris to Sokolo.

As this brief description of the opening sequence suggests, *La Vie sur terre* announces its intention to unstitch the specular identification that classical narrative films create. Where classical narration works to disguise the spatial and temporal dislocations of the filmmaking process to produce

Figure 4.1 Dramane leaves behind the narrative of global prosperity.

an illusory coherence and unified subjectivity, *La Vie sur terre* foregrounds the disjunctures, leaps, and gaps in the filmmaking process, disorienting the spectator and inviting reflection on the hidden incoherence and gaps of film's unified perspective. The opening sequence of the film emphasises this unstitching. What at first seems a highly coherent scene in a specific location is revealed to be a carefully constructed narrative of globalisation built on hidden lapses and illusory coherence, held together by space and time. The signage in the Monoprix, which is nearly always visible in the film's frame in this sequence, embodies this illusory unity, emphasising a certain unified subjectivity – that of a French consumer in a supermarket – at a specific point in time – the millennium. This space symbolises the prosperity of the Global North, even for members of the working classes, who make up the consumer base of a shop like Monoprix. What is carefully edited out of the space of the store is the process by which the array of objects, some of which are made in France, some of which are made in Asia or elsewhere in Europe, has come to be assembled in this specific shop and the processes by which consumers have come to have the resources to purchase these goods.

The shop's narrative of prosperity and upward mobility (as symbolised by Dramane's upward trajectory on the escalator) is disrupted and deconstructed by the disruption of the camera's gaze, consistently blocked and frequently partial, and the editing that ties the shots in this sequence together as well as the unexpected jump that occurs as we move from the escalator in Monoprix to Sokolo, radically reorienting the filmic gaze. Without a certain cultural and geographic orientation – the point of view of a French consumer for example – the ensemble of decorative ceramics, watches, butter, cheese, hats, and the stuffed polar bear Dramane carries with him – makes absolutely no sense. The abrupt shift further fragments the illusory coherence of the Monoprix by contrasting this space with the visibly different Malian town, which shares the same temporality as the Monoprix or as Paris, but not the same prosperity. This in turn suggests a tension 'between Western abundance and an empty African field' (B'béri 2009: 813), which forces the reconsideration of globalisation at the millennium from a number of shifting subjectivities and points of view.

The geospatial shift that occurs is amplified by the film's shifting subjectivities. Upon 'arrival' in Sokolo, the film depicts Dramane's father (Mohammed Sissako) reading a letter sent by his son, and the voice-over narration of the letter introduces Dramane's voice into the film. At the same time, embedded in the letter are a number of quotes from and references to Aimé Césaire's *Cahier d'un retour au pays natal*, which serves as an important intertext to the film and which incorporates 'Césaire's idea of multiple temporalities and spatialities' (B'béri 2009: 814) but also constitutes a 'trenchant modulation of a critique of historical inequalities' (Adesokan 2010: 145). Thus, this second sequence contains at least three subjectivities – that of the father reading the letter, that of Dramane, which has been separated from that of Sissako, and that of Césaire. Each of these subjectivities is associated to a different geographical location – the father to Sokolo, Dramane to Paris, and Césaire to Martinique, as well as to different temporalities – that of the colonial era and that of the contemporary era, and each is associated with a different communicative form – letter, book, film. However, all of these shifting subjectivities and communicative forms meditate on a single point, specifically the prosperity gap between Africa and the Global North and its causes. This multifocal subjectivity reoccurs throughout the film, created by the interplay among the voices and viewpoints of the various inhabitants of Sokolo, as well as the interplay of the film's external camera and the various communicative forms embedded in the film, letters, books, the telephone, the radio, the photographer's camera, advertisements, etc. What is created through the interplay of these various forms is a polyphonic, polycentric, kaleidoscopic space of reflection and representation of the experiences of globalisation. In this way, *La Vie sur terre* unstitches the conventional unified subjectivity of the filmic gaze, capturing the movements and dislocations of globalisation, both physically and through travelling and competing modes of communication. At the same time, and through these shifting geo-temporal and subjective gazes, the film openly interrogates the unfulfilled promise of prosperity that globalisation's dislocations and amplifications was supposed to produce.

If the opening sequences foreground the transnational movement and communication that are the backbone of globalisation, the subsequent sequences emphasise the inconsistencies in mobility and movement that globalisation has produced. The film juxtaposes, for example, Dramane's seamless movement from North to South with the difficulties the residents of Sokolo experience with moving from space to space – whether within the town, between towns, or beyond Mali. Similarly, the film records inconsistencies in communications, in the movement or transmission of the differing viewpoints or perspectives on these realities. Advertisements, images, and radio broadcasts from Britain, France, and Japan are all seen and heard in Sokolo, many of them, the radio broadcast in particular, reinforcing the narrative of prosperity that underpins globalisation. However, the images, products and radio broadcasts that originate from Sokolo, which question such narratives of prosperity, are presumably not seen or heard, or at least not easily, in Paris or elsewhere in the world. This evokes Gayatri Spivak's famous question of whether the subaltern can speak, and reframes that into a question of whether those in positions of structural inequality can be heard *when* they speak (Spivak 1988).

These discrepancies in communication and transportation, circulation and transmission are not, the film reminds us, the result of differences in production capacity or ability, since the film clearly shows products, images, and broadcasts produced in both Sokolo and diverse locations of the Global North. They are rather problems of transmission, the result of the unevenness of the channels and rules governing global distribution and diffusion, which seem to function from North to South, in a linear, often unidirectional way. This is emphasised, for example, in the sequence where Nana (Nana Baby) attempts to make a telephone call from the post office in Sokolo, and where it is explained to her that the rules require connections to be direct, and that unnecessary transfers – which would imply a multiplication of connections and voices – are forbidden by the rules. The sole exception to linear, unidirectional structure of communication and transmission in the film is the film itself, which, as noted, disrupts the typical linear, unidirectional transmission of communication imposed by the telephone transfer rules, and by the rules of classical cinema. The film moves from production in Africa, to transmission across television and movie screens in France and Germany, and then back to Africa. Therefore, the film both models and disrupts the unidirectional pathways of globalisation and posits a substitution for a multi-channeled, multifocal, circulatory network, a network that the film presumably seeks to open.[6]

Transmission, Circulation and Diffusion in *Heremakono*

Circulation and transmission are also dominant structuring mechanisms in Sissako's second feature-length film, *Heremakono* (2002). The film, which is set in the coastal town of Nouadhibou, Mauritania's second largest city, centres on a series of characters, including Abdallah (Mohamed Mahmoud Ould Mohamed), a young man waiting to travel to Europe, Maata (Maata Mohamed Ould Abeid), a former fisherman turned electrician, Khatra (Khatra Ould Abder Kader), his young apprentice, and Nana (Nana Diakité), a grieving mother. The use of Nouadhibou as setting already emphasises movement, migration, and the interconnectivity of transnational commerce and migration. Nouadhibou is, in many ways, a point of transition, both because it is near the sea, and thus a port of entry and exit, and because it is also a key stop on the train route between various Mauritanian towns, including the iron mines of Zouérat. Nouadhibou is also literally a border town, as it is situated very close to the border between Mauritania and Western Sahara, the ultimate no-man's land, as it is not officially recognised by much of the world, and particularly the nations of the Global North.

Nouadhibou's status as a transition point is foregrounded in the film not only by the characters moving in and out of it – one of the film's early sequence features Abdallah's journey into the city by taxi, and one of its final sequences features Khatra attempting to board a train – but also by various images and icons that suggest transnational movement, migration, and exchange. These include the Atlantic Ocean and a blowing tumbleweed, both of which feature prominently in the opening sequence, the veils from Switzerland and China sold by an itinerant merchant, the wares of a Chinese street vendor who sells imported goods, the taxi in which Abdallah travels, and the boats that dot the shoreline in several of the sequences.

These figures and images evoke, like the Monoprix supermarket in *La Vie sur terre*, the circulation of goods and labour in the globalised economy. The nature and quality of these goods, however, is called into question at various places in the film, through references to Taiwanese lightbulbs that do not work, to the taxi that overheats, and particularly through images of the massive ship graveyard in the waters outside the city – ships that have been dumped there from other places in the world. These images of importation are juxtaposed against the implied exportation of labour and raw materials from Nouadhibou that are suggested by the train, and the trajectories, or desired trajectories of those seeking to leave the city. These dual pathways of circulation and transnational exchange embody the circulatory processes of globalisation but also reveal the inequalities inherent in these processes, as Nouadhibou, and places like it in Africa, often lose much more than they gain.

The existence of an uneven or inconsistent global network of circulation is similarly suggested by the electrical current that Maata and Khatra attempt to bring to various residents of the city. The wires through which the electricity travels form a network connecting the houses to one another and to an external source of electricity, and electricity is also a powerful symbol of global modernity, and its availability or non-availability often functions as a measure of economic development and prosperity. The unpredictability of the electrical flow in Nouadhibou, which sometimes works and sometimes does not, is a further suggestion of the unevenness in the flow and distribution of capital, communications, and relations in the global contemporary.

The unevenness is seen in other networks that structure the film, as in the form of the unidirectional television transmission (from France to Africa) or the disparities in transportation capacity, for example. In fact, maritime transportation, embodied by rusting international supertankers and freight ships which are contrasted against the local fishermen's small, wooden boats, constitutes another central network characterised by uneven circulation in Nouadhibou – as we see both the rusting discards of the shipping industry of the Global North in the harbour and the small, locally constructed boats that attempt, largely unsuccessfully, to ferry would-be migrants to Europe, or some stopping point along the way. In this way, the boats embody the inequalities of mobility that separate citizens of the world, a theme reinforced by the contrasting narratives of those moving in and out of the town. For example, the father of Nana's dead child presumably had no difficulty gaining access to Mauritania, but those wishing to leave Mauritania, from Michael to Omar to Abdallah, lack such freedom of movement. Rusting boats and people left behind, therefore, point to the 'leftovers ... the garbage left whose forms have multiplied in the Global South since neocolonialism and globalisation have imposed their orders' (Harrow 2013: 177).

These uneven networks of circulation and exchange are juxtaposed in the film against the various examples of apprenticeship that structure the narrative. Apprenticeship also functions as a network of transmission, in which knowledge and skills pass among persons of different ages and backgrounds. Unlike the uneven networks of transmission critiqued by the film, apprenticeship networks suggest mutuality and equality, in that all parties are sharing and partaking in an economic or cultural system intended to produce substantive or material gain for all parties;

the apprentice in such networks learns from the teacher or expert a trade, a skill, a profession, but the expert or teacher also gains in experience or wisdom in taking on the apprentice, and may potentially gain a helper or assistant who can expand his or her own endeavours.

The apprenticeship networks in the film include Khatra and Maata's relationship, which transmits the modern trade of electrician from one generation to another, but it also includes the relationship between the griotte (Néma Mint Chouik) and her young student (Mamma Mint Lekbeid), which transmits a traditional vocation, and the linguistic apprenticeship that occurs between Abdallah and Khatra, in which Khatra attempts to teach Abdallah Mauritanian Arabic and Abdallah in return teaches Khatra French. All of these apprenticeship networks contain a potential imbalance, like the relationship between Africa and the Global North, in that all of these relationships occur between children and adults. However, unlike the globalised economic and cultural networks of the contemporary era, these apprenticeships are bi-directional, with each party contributing and taking something from the exchange, and with the children teaching the adults as much as the adults teach the children. These apprenticeship networks are, therefore, more egalitarian partnerships than those between the countries of Global North and Global South, and they also cross generational, gender, and national boundaries, as well as the typical barrier between tradition and modernity, as the participants are of both genders, diverse ages and backgrounds, and the skills transmitted belong both to the modern, industrialised spheres and to the traditional, cultural ones. Apprenticeship, as Willeke Wendrich has argued, produces and reinforces communities of practice which allow for the agency of the entire group (2013: 5). These communities and the networks of apprenticeship that structure them, therefore, offer a counter-model to the system of exchange represented by globalisation, one in which there is no presumed hierarchy among the parties connected in a network of exchange, in which nothing is cast off, discarded or wasted in the exchange, and in which everyone who participates stands to gain.

As these apprenticeship networks suggest, *Heremakono*, like *La Vie sur terre*, is focused not only on the depiction of the displacements, exchanges, and disruptions of global modernity, but also on the modes of articulation and representation involved in that depiction. Two of the apprenticeship networks explored in the film, for example – that of the griotte and that of the language instruction, involve modes of communication or representation. The same is true of the future apprenticeship that forms the basis of the narrative, Aballah's impending journey out of Nouadhibou, probably, as the film's autobiographical subtext suggests, to become a filmmaker.

Heremakono, therefore, repeats and expands the multifocality present in *La Vie sur terre*, borrowing several of the first film's emblems of diffusion while increasing the number of narratives and perspectives incorporated into the film. There is a multiplicity of characters from various parts of Africa and other places in the world, a fact foregrounded by the film's diverse languages, including French, Hassaniya, Malinke/Maninka, and Mandarin Chinese, as well as by the emphasis on cross-linguistic transmission and exchange. Moreover, as in *La Vie sur terre*, which referenced Aimé Césaire's poetry as a means of incorporating multiple spaces and temporalities in the reflection on structural inequality, *Heremakono* incorporates the work of Guadaloupean poet Paul Niger in the form of Niger's song 'Petit oiseau'. In place of the French radio broadcasts featured in *La Vie sur terre*, *Heremakono* incorporates the television broadcast of the French game show 'Des Chiffres et des lettres'. As Hélène Tissières has suggested, the film also features direct engagement with the Islamic mystical tradition of representation, such that all things depicted represent not only what is present, but also an unrepresented absence, which produces a type of representational 'radiation' (2011: 246–51). There is also the repeated interplay between the film's external camera and an internal camera, which similarly takes portraits. There is one final emblem in *Heremakono* which stands in, in many ways, for the film itself, or at least a certain aesthetic vision of the function of the film, and that is the kaleidoscope that Khatra finds in Abdallah's room. The kaleidoscope, which embodies the principle of multiple reflection, offers diverse views of a single point. Khatra views both people and objects – specifically a light bulb – through the kaleidoscope, and he can master and manipulate the images of both by manipulating the kaleidoscope. The ideas of light and reflection, as well as the multiplicity of views evoke the work of the filmic camera, which similarly seeks to represent and depict and to capture shifting viewpoints and subjectivities.

Globalisation, Occupation and Violence in *Timbuktu*

At first glance, *Timbuktu* constitutes a radical break from Sissako's previous films. The subject of the film is the occupation of the Malian city by Ansar Dine, a Malian jihadist group affiliated with the Tuareg separatist movement and with Al Qaeda in the Islamic Maghreb (Solomon 2015). This divergence, however, is somewhat illusory, as *Timbuktu* is deeply concerned with globalisation and its consequences, as well as with questions of mobility and communication. Moreover, like the previous films, *Timbuktu* offers multiple points of view on a single focus – in this case, the occupation, as well as the larger issue of Islamism or Jihad, and does so through an array of shifting facets or focal points, producing a kaleidoscopic meditation on a globally recognisable historical moment that in many ways reproduces the image of the light bulb from *Heremakono*.

Timbuktu, as noted, tells the story of the 2012 occupation of the Azawad region and Timbuktu by Ansar Dine, which followed the rebellion in the region against the Malian government orchestrated by the Tuareg-dominated National Movement for the Liberation of Azawad (MNLA). The film contains intertwined narratives about the occupation that detail the experiences of various residents of the city and the greater Azawad region, many of which are drawn from actual occurrences under the occupation. Although not detailed explicitly, the film also references the conflict between the MNLA and Ansar Dine over the implementation of Sharia law, one of the issues that led to Ansar Dine's occupation of the region. Although the film contains several plot lines, the most developed concerns Kidane (Ibrahim Ahmed), a Tuareg livestock herder, and his wife, Satima (Toulou Kiki) and daughter Toya (Layla Walet Mohamed). Kidane gets into a fight with Amadou (Omar Haidara), a neighbouring fisherman who attempts to stop Kidane's cattle from watering in the Niger River. In the process, Amadou kills Kidane's favourite cow, GPS. Kidane, filled with rage over the death of GPS arms himself and confronts Amadou, and the two men fight. During the fight Amadou is killed and Kidane is arrested and tried by the Islamist forces for Amadou's murder and is ultimately sentenced to death.

The Kidane subplot, which is tied to the Jihadist occupation narrative by his trial and conviction, draws attention to the effects of climate change on Mali by symbolically rendering two populations – livestock herders and fishers – whose lives and livelihoods in Mali have been affected by sustained decreases in annual rainfall that are the consequence of climate change. The conflict between Amadou and Kidane over access to water points to the centrality of water for both populations in Mali, and suggests the existence of conflicts over resources such as water that previously did not exist. Water, in the film, is fundamental to the economic and personal mobility of both populations, as both depend upon water for their respective livelihoods and both populations migrate or move in an effort to maintain access to water. The water carrier, who rides a motorcycle to transport water to those who need it, recurs throughout the film and plays a key role in bringing the action to a close, and his presence and mobility suggest the connection between water and the continued flow of existence in the city and in Mali more generally.

Although water appears in the background or foreground of many scenes in the film, there are two key sequences that feature water quite centrally in both visual and narrative terms. In the first sequence, which occurs 32 minutes and 39 seconds into the film (32:39 to 34:38), Issan, the young assistant to Kidane, is watering cattle in the Niger River. Amadou, who is fishing on the opposite bank, warns Issan to keep the animals away from his fishing nets when GPS, Kidane's favourite cow, wanders away from the other animals and moves too near the nets in question. In order to prevent GPS from becoming entangled in his fishing nets, Amadou takes a spear and throws it at GPS, killing her. This action sets up the conflict between the two men, which plays out in a second scene that occurs 44 minutes and 54 seconds into film.

That scene begins with a long tracking shot of Kidane striding across the river from the left bank toward Amadou, on the right. Kidane confronts Amadou about the killing of GPS while asking Amadou whether the river belongs to him or his family. A fight scene ensues between the two men, who are dragged by the conflict into the middle of the river. The fight scene plays out, although two jump cuts prevent the viewer from fully witnessing what transpires during the altercation. Ultimately both men end up lying in the river and, after a few seconds, Kidane gets up and walks back to the left bank from which he came and Amadou attempts to pull himself back to the right. The camera pulls back into a wide, high angle landscape shot that features the river at sunset, and we can see, from a great distance, Kidane as he crosses the river and Amadou as he struggles to reach the bank, but collapses short of it.

The killing of GPS sequence and the conflict between Amadou and Kidane that ensues emphasise both water, as the focus and site of the conflict, and mobility, as suggested by each man's movements. The focus of the scene is the simultaneous and conflicting efforts of both Kidane and Amadou and their families to make a living through their respective, traditional means. The conflict between the two men is made evident through the use of space and the camerawork in the two sequences, and specifically by the use of the river as both a life source for and a barrier between the two men. The use of crosscutting in the first scene effectively means that the scene takes place from Amadou's point of view – when we first see Issan, we are seeing what Amadou sees, even if this fact is initially obscured. This, coupled with the fact that Kidane's narrative is one of the dominant narratives in the film, produces a dual or multifocal point of view (if we consider that of the spectator) on the conflict over the water. This means that, despite some critical assertions to the contrary, the film takes no side in the conflict over water, but rather views the conflict itself as problematic and more importantly as a new conflict that disrupts an existing harmony between the two men and the populations they represent. This is reinforced by the cinematography in the two sequences, which foregrounds the importance of water by figuring it so centrally, and by the positioning of Kidane and Amadou at either side of the frame and on opposite banks. The net result is the presentation of the dispute as the breakdown of such longstanding practices of sharing water, a dispute the film presents from multiple points of view.

The fight between Amadou and Kidane, as noted, features two prominent jump cuts. The result of these jump cuts is that some of what transpires between the two men remains hidden from the spectator. This has consequences on the validity of the judgment rendered by the tribunal later in the film, as it means there are no witnesses to what occurs. Not even the largely omniscient film viewer is a direct witness to the events, because the key event in the conflict – the moment the gun fires – remains off screen. These jump cuts also suggest that no complete understanding of the conflict between the two men is possible without taking into account realities the film does not directly depict. One of the most significant of these issues is the effect of years of sustained drought on Mali and the Sahel region, and the impact that drought – which is the result of industrial production elsewhere in the world – has on local access to water.

Broadly, the conflict between Kidane and Amadou embodies a conflict over water resources between livestock herding populations in Mali and those populations who are traditionally fishers. The fight thus renders symbolically the issues Mali has had over the past two decades with climatic variation due to climate change and decreased rainfall and the problems with access to water these variations have caused. As Morand et al. demonstrated in their 2012 study, tropical inland fishers, such as the character Amadou in *Timbuktu*, are extremely vulnerable to climatic variation and the increased drought and desertification that have accompanied this because the lakes, rivers, marshes, and other waterways these fishermen rely on are extremely vulnerable to changes in climate (2012: 464).

Prior to the sustained drought conditions of the past decades, fishers coexisted in Mali with small share farmers and migratory livestock herders of the type embodied by Kidane. In the past two decades, however, livestock herders have similarly found themselves under pressure from climate change and have, as Turner et al. have noted, also altered their migratory patterns, often becoming less mobile and staying near reliable sources of water (2014: 237). The need to remain near water has restricted the mobility of previously migratory herders, an issue of mobility suggested both by the name of the cow GPS and by the fact that the cow unexpectedly veers from the established path. It is the deviation from the path – the change in migratory pattern over the issue of water – that causes the conflict between Amadou and Kidane, and this is despite the fact that the film suggests very clearly the two know each other quite well and have coexisted for some time.

This disruption of peaceful coexistence is a broader theme in *Timbuktu*, as the film features various visual markers of Mali's internal diversity – city and rural dwellers, Dogon and Tuareg – all of whom are victims of an occupation depicted as a foreign invasion and a consequence of globalisation. Moreover, the dispute between Kidane and Amadou symbolically renders Tuareg concerns about encroachment and loss of their traditional lands and disputes over the validity of communal versus private property rights.[7] The Jihadists who occupy Timbuktu in the film, on the other hand, largely come from elsewhere – France and Libya, for example – locations either in the Global North or places that have experienced disruptions and interventions by the Global North. Thus, the occupation, like climate change, is a disruption with origins far removed from Mali. This linking of climate change and Salafist Jihad is heightened by the fact that access to water was a significant factor in the development of Tuareg rebellions against the Malian government, and the creation of the MNLA, who ultimately laid the groundwork for the foreign occupation.

Ultimately, *Timbuktu* draws attention to the fact that the overall meaning of something as local as the conflict between a fisher and a livestock herder, or as global as Salafist terrorism, is understandable only by broadening one's perspective and taking into account realities that are both local and global, and that may not be immediately apparent in any single context or event. In this way, the film affirms the fundamental interconnectedness of existence in the contemporary world.

Ultimately, the conflicts over mobility and resources in *Timbuktu* occur as the consequence of the disparate levels of mobility in the world. They are, therefore, part of a global pattern of development that affords certain populations the right to move at the expense of other populations. This pattern is not fully readable from a single angle or vantage point. Those driving cars in industrialised nations ignore the consequences of their actions on inhabitants of nations such as Mali. Similarly, residents of places like Timbuktu are unable to perceive all of the causes of the problems they experience much less to intercede to address them.

It is not simply inequalities in global mobility, however, that characterise the events in Timbuktu as the film depicts them. Inequalities in communications are also part of the root of the problem. The Islamist occupiers manipulate and control a number of forms of communication

Figure 4.2 Jihadists make movies: the film within a film in *Timbuktu*.

ranging from megaphones to cell phones to film production and satellite transmission equipment (see Figure 4.2). Kidane, his family and the citizens of Timbuktu also possess various forms of communication technology. However, the occupiers, who have come from elsewhere, have more reliable and more numerous forms of communication and are therefore able to use them to suppress the communicative efforts – from calling on a cell phone to singing – of the city's inhabitants. The occupiers suppress all forms of communication that compete with their own. Their power, therefore, derives as much from their ability to suppress communication as to suppress movement and action, and they are aided in this suppression by the structural inequalities that already govern life in Northern Mali. Therefore, the film suggests, even if all communications technologies are equally available and distributed throughout the world, existing and emerging imbalances in infrastructure, power, and prosperity ensure that not all technologies are equally usable, which in turn expands existing inequalities and creates new ones.

Timbuktu also suggests that power relations and media production in the contemporary era are increasingly decentred and transnational as a result of technological innovation and geographical mobility, which are both cause and consequence of globalisation. This decentred and transnational structure gives previously unheard voices the ability to compete in a marketplace of ideas and to make themselves heard at both local and international levels. Therefore, while transnationalism and, by extension, globalisation are not in and of themselves determinative of an equal distribution of power, resources, or agency, they do provide equalising potential, opening up spaces and methods for communication that were previously blocked. The key question *Timbuktu* seems to ask, in light of this, is whether there is room in any one of the communications, or in the interplay among them, for points of view and realities that are not directly represented by anyone. This point is made most explicitly in the plight of Satima, who tries several times, unsuccessfully, to reach Kidane by telephone, but who can never obtain a cell phone signal. In other words, the film asks whether the disempowered have a voice in a world where the power structures have shifted and expanded, or whether the networks in which we now operate are managed by a newly constituted set of elites who block the voices of the dissident and disempowered.

In asking this question, *Timbuktu*, like all of Sissako's films, relies on an interplay of various forms of communication – some of them internal to the film and some implied by it. However, *Timbuktu*, perhaps more than his previous films, raises the question of which messages circulating in the ever expanding global network are successfully transmitted and ultimately heard. As the film suggests, it is the messages of the Jihadists and messages conflating Salafism with Islam that circulate and predominate in the Global North. All other messages, the songs and cries of the women of Timbuktu, Kidane's testimony, Satima's telephone calls, get lost in the noise. Therefore, the ultimate question *Timbuktu* raises may be one that asks very simply if messages that come from the disempowered, messages that challenge or diverge from dominant narratives, can be successfully transmitted or received in the expanding and interconnected network of global media and communication, or whether they are being broadcast from places and spaces in the world where the signal has quite simply been lost.

Conclusion

Cinema has, from the beginning, been about movement. It was the realisation of the long-held desire to both capture and project movement, and from the very first screened films, *Arrivée d'un train en gare de La Ciotat/Arrival of a Train at La Ciotat* (Auguste and Louis Lumière, 1895, France) and *La sortie des usines Lumière/Workers Leaving the Lumière Factory* (Auguste and Louis Lumière, 1895, France) in particular, it has also been a form that reflects and embodies technological movement, the changes in forms of production and transportation, that we now understand as globalisation. Cinema, in keeping with that original impetus, also moved around the world very quickly, and moved into and out of Africa from nearly the point of origin. The Lumière brothers took their films travelling, into North Africa most notably, in 1896, shortly after their debut in France, and the form came travelling back, and their cameraman Alexandre Promio shot films in North Africa and circulated them back again to France and beyond. The idea of national cinema came later, after the global circulations of films in the silent era and the international co-productions of the interwar era.

Transnational films like those of Abderrahmane Sissako and other producers of cinéma-monde, reprise and reactivate cinema's early tendencies. Like the early films of the Lumière brothers and Alexandre Promio, these films consciously and self-consciously reflect on global movement and on the processes – technological, political, and economic – by which such movement occurs. They also, however, mark an evolution in film form. However far the early silent films travelled, their centre was always Europe and Paris, in particular. Sissako's films, on the other hand, have no centre, no clear anchor point. They reflect the slow unmooring of centres and peripheries that is occurring and arguably accelerating in late globalisation. Moreover, they mark a celebration of that unmooring, a cry against the resurgent nationalisms – in both Africa at independence and the Global North in the twenty-first century – that seek to return the direction of movement to its old, colonial paradigm. The films also re-appropriate and rework older elements of film language – silence and montage – breaking the linear accelerations of continuity in film, those walls of filmic form that guarantee linear development and that lock Africa and other locations in the Global South into the periphery.

Their embrace of free-flowing movement notwithstanding, these films are not naïve validations of the globalised order. They point to persisting inequalities of mobility and access even as they embrace the ideal of diffusion. Sissako's films, in particular, with their images of cell phones and satellites that receive transmissions from France but have difficulty broadcasting from Africa, of overturned fishing boats bound for France, and rusting cargo ships discarded by France, cry injustice in the era of proclaimed mobility. These films are perilously aware of the potential for globalisation to expand the inequalities of the colonial era, in which the north harnessed and arrested the movement of the south, in order to accelerate its own economic ascent. These films, however, are also cognisant of the power of movement, true and unrestricted movement, to correct such imbalances. Their transnational nature permits them to avoid the pitfalls of nationalism, which is critical of globalisation only to the extent that it wishes to restore and reify the hierarchies of a previous era and lock prosperity into northern enclaves protected by trade barriers and physical barriers of concrete and barbed wire.

Sissako's films, and other films of cinéma-monde, are not fully optimistic that the unrestricted movement and collapsed borders promised by globalisation will be fully realised, nor do they accept the nationalist's world of fences and walls. Rather, they aspire, through their own global circulations, to persuade us of the need for open borders, for a world in which human movement produces shared understandings and collective development. They seek, more importantly, to forge the pathway to such a world in light.

Notes

1. Among the novels associated with Afropolitanism are Selasi's *Ghana Must Go* (2005), Teju Cole's *Open City* (2011), Chimanmanda Adichie's *Americanah* (2013), and NoViolet Bulawayo's *We Need New Names* (2013).
2. On this issue see among others Diawara (1992), Dovey (2015), and Genova (2013).
3. The relationship between cinematic form and narratives of progress and development originating in the Global North has been extensively studied. See for example Bordwell et al. (2003), Deleuze (1986, 1989), and Oscherwitz (2010).
4. Writing on subjectivity in cinema is extensive and closely linked to semiotic theories of the cinema and the cinematic apparatus. See for example Oudart (1969), Dayan (1974), Bordwell (1985) and writings by Baudry (1974), Comolli (1971–2), Heath (1976), Metz (1975), Mulvey (1974), and McCabe (1976) in Rosen (1986).
5. As reported by gapminder.org.
6. I am presenting an overarching view of a particular aesthetic and narrative strategy that is common to all of Sissako's films. I am, therefore, dealing with the films rather holistically, as I am discussing several of them. I am not discussing *Bamako*, in part, because I have dealt with it in depth elsewhere (Oscherwitz 2015), and in part because this is the most written about of Sissako's films. For discussions of that film, see Adesokan (2010), Murray Levine (2012), and Maingard (2013) among others.
7. For more on Tuareg separatist movements and land disputes and their relationship to climate change and other policies and practices originating in the Global North, see Benjaminsen (2008), Keenan (2013), and Stern (2007).

Works Cited

Adesokan, Akin (2010), 'Abderrahmane Sissako and the poetics of engaged expatriation', *Screen*, 51:2, pp. 143–60.

Adichie, Chimamanda Ngozi (2014), *Americanah*, New York: Anchor.

Barry, Aminata (2004), 'Pour la grandeur du cinéma africain: une refonte de FESPACO', in *Présence africaine*, 170:2, pp. 93–7.

B'béri, Boulou Ebanda (2009), 'Transgeographical practices of marronage in some African films: Peck, Sissako, and Téno, the new griots of new times?' *Cultural Studies*, 23:5–6, pp. 81030.

Beau, Nicolas (2015), 'Abderrahmane Sissako: une imposture mauritanienne, *MondeAfrique* 20 February 2015, <http://mondafrique.com/abderrahmane-sissako-une-imposture-mauritanienne/> (last accessed 31 August, 2016).
Benjaminsen, Tor A. (2008), 'Does Supply-Induced Scarcity Drive Violent Conflicts in the African Sahel? The Case of the Tuarag Rebellion in Northern Mali', *Journal of Peace Research*, 45:6, pp. 819–36.
Bordwell, David (1985), *Narration in the Fiction Film*, Madison: University of Wisconsin Press.
Bordwell, David et al. (1987)/[1985], *The Classical Hollywood Cinema: Film Style and Mode of Production to 1960*, New York: Columbia University Press.
Bulawayo, NoViolet (2014), *We Need New Names*, Boston: Back Bay Books.
Cessou, Sabine (2014), '"Timbuktu", le film d'Abderrahmane Sissako, loin de la réalité', Rues d'Afrique.
Cole, Téju (2011), *Open City*, New York: Random House.
Dayan, Daniel (1974), 'The Tutor-Code of Classical Cinema', *Film Quarterly*, 28:1, pp. 22–31.
De Grazia, Victoria (1989), 'Mass Culture and Sovereignty: The American challenge to European cinemas, 1920–1960', *The Journal of Modern History*, 61:1, pp. 53–87.
Deleuze, Gilles (1986), *Cinema 1: The Movement Image*, trans. H. Tomlinson and B. Habberjam, Minneapolis: University of Minnesota.
Deleuze, Gilles (1989), *Cinema 2: The Time Image*, trans. H. Tomlinson and B. Habberjam, Minneapolis: University of Minnesota Press.
Diawara, Manthia (1992), *African Cinema: Politics and Culture*, Bloomington and Indianapolis: Indiana University Press.
Diawara, Manthia (2010), *African Films: New Forms of Politics and Aesth*etics, New York and London: Prestel.
Diawara, Manthia (2015), 'Frames of resistance: Manthia Diawara on the films of Abderrahmane Sissako', *Artforum International* 53:5, *Academic OneFile* (last accessed 16 January 2016).
Dovey, Lindiwe.(2015*)*, *Curating Africa in the Age of Film Festivals*, London and New York: Palgrave.
Frankel, Jeffrey (2006), 'What do Economists Mean by Globalization? Implications for Inflationary Monetary Policy,' Academic Consultants Meeting September 28, 2006, for the Board of Governors of the Federal Reserve System, <http://www.hks.harvard.edu/fs/jfrankel/FRB-Globalzn&InflOct4.pdf> (last accessed 10 January 2016).
Genova, James E. (2013), *Cinema and Development in West Africa: Film as a Vehicle for Liberation*, Bloomington: Indiana University Press.
Hall, Stuart (1991), 'The Local and the Global: Globalization and Ethnicity', in Anthony King (ed.) *Culture, Globalisation and the World System*, Basingstoke: Macmillan, pp. 19–40.
Hansen, Miriam Bratu (1999), 'The Mass Production of the Senses: Classical Cinema as Vernacular Modernism', *Modernism/Modernity*, 6:2, pp. 59–77.

Harrow, Kenneth (2007), *Postcolonial African Cinema: From Political Engagement to Postmodernism*. Bloomington: Indiana University Press.
Higbee, Will (2007), 'Beyond the (Trans)national: Towards a Cinema of Transvergence in Postcolonial and Diasporic Francophone Cinema(s)', *Studies in French Cinema*, 7.2, pp. 79–91.
Higgins, Mary Ellen (2012), *Hollywood's Africa After 1994*, Athens: Ohio University Press.
Keenan, Jeremy (2013), *The Dying Sahara: U.S. imperialism and terror in Africa*, London: Pluto Press.
Maingard, Jacqueline (2013), 'African cinema and *Bamako* (2006): notes on epistemology and film theory', *Critical African Studies*, 5:2, pp. 103–13.
Marquart, Michael (2005), 'Globalization: The Pathway to Prosperity, Freedom, and Peace', *Human Resource Development International*, 8:1, pp. 127–9.
Marshall, Bill (2012), 'Cinéma-monde? Towards a concept of Francophone Cinema', *Francospheres*, 1:1, pp. 35–51.
Mbembe, Achille (2007), 'Afropolitanism', in S. Njami and L. Durán (eds), *Africa Remix: Contemporary art of a continent*, Johannesburg: Johannesburg Art Gallery, pp. 26–30.
Morand, P., A. Kodio and N. Andrew et al. (2012), 'Vulnerability and adaptation of African rural populations to hydro-climate change: experience from fishing communities in the Inner Niger Delta (Mali)', *Climatic Change*, 115:3, pp. 463–83.
Murphy, David (2006), 'Africans Filming Africa: Questioning Theories of an Authentic African Cinema', in E. Ezra and T Rowden (eds), *Transnational Cinema: The Film Reader*, London and New York: Routledge, pp. 27–39.
Murray-Levine, Allison J. (2012), 'Words on Trial: Oral Performance in Abderrahmane Sissako's *Bamako*', *Studies in French Cinema*, 12:2, pp. 151–67.
Naficy, Hamid (2001), *An Accented Cinema: Exilic and Diasporic Filmmaking*, Princeton: Princeton University Press.
Oscherwitz, Dayna (2014), 'A Twice-Told Tale: The Postcolonial Allegory of *La Noire de ...* and *Faat Kine*', in L. Vetinde and A Fofana (eds), *Ousmane Sembène and the Politics of Culture*, Lanham: Lexington Books, pp. 51–67.
Oscherwitz, Dayna (2015), 'In the Crossfire: Africa, Cinema, and Violence in Abderrahmane
Sissako's *Bamako* (2006)', in *The Western in the Global South*, M. E. Higgins et al. (eds), London and New York: Routledge, pp. 81–96.
Oudart, Jean-Pierre (1969) 'La Suture', *Cahiers du cinéma*, April, 211, pp. 36–9.
Rosen, Philip (1986), *Narrative, Apparatus, Ideology*, New York: Columbia University Press.
Santana, Stephanie Bosch (2013), 'Exorcizing Afropolitanism: Binyavanga Wainaina explains why "I am a Pan-Africanist, not an Afropolitan"' at ASAUK 2012, <http://africainwords.com/2013/02/08/exorcizing-afropolitanism-binyavanga-wainaina-explains-why-i-am-a-pan-africanist-not-an-afropolitan-at-asauk-2012/> (last accessed 19 January 2016).

Selasi, Taiye (2005), 'Bye-Bye Babar (What is Afropolitanism?)' <http://thelip.robertsharp.co.uk/?p=76> (last accessed 19 January 2016).

Selasi, Taiye (2013), *Ghana Must Go*, New York and London: Penguin.

Solomon, Hussein (2015). *Terrorism and Counter-Terrorism in Africa: Fighting Insurgency from Al-Shabaab, Ansar Dine, and Boko Haram*, London: Palgrave.

Spivak, Gayatry Chakravorty (1988), 'Can the Subaltern Speak?' *Marxism and the Interpretation of Culture*, Cary Nelson and Lawrence Grossber (eds), Urbana: University of Illinois Press, pp. 271–313.

Stern, Nicholas H. (2007), *The Economics of Climate Change: the Stern review*, Cambridge: Cambridge University Press.

Tcheuyap, Alexie (2011), *Postnationalist African Cinema*, Manchester: Manchester University Press.

Thiam, Madina (2015), 'It has become customary to speak of Mali while simultaneously ignoring it', in *Africaisacountry*, December 21 2015, < http://africasacountry.com/?p=94679> (last accessed 31 January 2016).

Tissières, Hélène (2011), 'Heremakono d'Abderrahmane Sissoko: traversée poétique et rayonnment pictural', *Canadian Journal of African Studies*, 44:2, pp. 345–61.

Turner, M. D., J. G. McPeak and A. Ayantunde (2014), 'The role of livestock mobility in the livelihood strategies of rural peoples in semi-arid west africa', *Human Ecology*, 42:2, pp. 231–47.

wa Thiong'o, Ngũgĩ (2012), *Globalectics*, New York: Columbia University Press.

Wendrick, Willeke (ed.) (2013), *Archaeology and Apprenticeship: Body Knowledge, Identities, and Communities of Practice*, Tucson: University of Arizona Press.

CHAPTER 5

The Career of Actress Hafsia Herzi: Crossing Borders, Challenging Barriers
Leslie Kealhofer-Kemp

In 2007, actress Hafsia Herzi broke into the French film industry and gained international attention with her performance in Abdellatif Kechiche's award-winning film *La Graine et le mulet/The Secret of the Grain* (Abdellatif Kechiche, 2009, France), for which she was awarded the Marcello Mastroianni Prize for Most Promising Actress at the Venice Film Festival, as well as the Most Promising Actress César in France. In the film, set in the Mediterranean port city of Sète, Herzi plays Rym, a dynamic young Maghrebi-French woman who is determined to help her mother's aging and recently unemployed partner, Slimane (her stepfather for all intents and purposes), achieve his dream of opening a couscous restaurant and building something to pass on to his children (see Figure 5.1). This was Herzi's first major role in a feature film and the young actress's performance, including the long (and much remarked) belly dance that her character undertakes in the film's final sequence, opened doors for her professionally and effectively launched her career. *La Graine et le mulet* garnered media attention, both in France and internationally, at the time of its release in December 2007 and after the César awards in February 2008, and Herzi appeared on the covers of publications such as *Cahiers du cinéma* and *Les Inrockuptibles*. Shortly after her recognition at the Venice Film Festival, Herzi began receiving increasing numbers of film proposals, and her debut role quickly led to others. Since the release of *La Graine et le mulet*, Herzi has appeared in a diverse corpus of more than twenty feature films, with over half of those in a lead or key supporting role.

Herzi remains best known for her portrayal of Rym, a character whose identity is firmly rooted in the south of France, yet when considered through a broad lens, the actress's films and creative path reflect an overarching desire for mobility and diversity in terms of projects and roles, and this includes a notable global dimension. Geographically, the actress's films are set in various countries in Europe, North Africa, and the Middle East, including France, Belgium, Morocco, Iraq, Tunisia,

Figure 5.1 Hafsia Herzi and Habib Boufares as Rym and her stepfather Slimane in *La Graine et le mulet*.

Algeria, and Israel, and the protagonists in them may also move across borders. In addition, Herzi has worked with directors of diverse origins who hail from Iraq, Israel, Belgium, the United States, Romania, Tunisia, and Germany, amongst other countries. Consideration of Herzi's professional trajectory as an example of a specific cinéma-monde path within the French film industry provides a productive way to think about these and other unique aspects of her career. As this chapter will highlight, the common thread linking Herzi's cinematic output is not the language or national origin of the characters she plays but connections to the French film industry, notably in terms of production and financial backing. This also extends to her reputation and talent as an actress and media coverage of her performances in the French press. Herzi has demonstrated an impressive linguistic ability and range over the course of her relatively short, but prolific, career, as her characters speak a variety of languages and dialects, including French (with regional accents associated with Paris and Marseille), English, Moroccan Arabic, Tunisian Arabic, Palestinian Arabic, and Iraqi Arabic.

There is also a significant French connection that runs through Herzi's career and this is often intertwined with the global elements mentioned above. This French connection does not necessarily hinge on the French language, although she speaks French in many of her films, but rather it exists primarily at the level of production. All but two of her films are either French productions or co-productions,[1] and those that are not are still indirectly linked to France through the characters played by Herzi (they are from countries that were once part of the French colonial empire in North Africa). Thus while Herzi's films may differ in their geographical settings and languages, there is a common denominator that runs through her career, giving it both French and global dimensions. Herzi's cultural output and career thus serve as a useful case study for the present volume's analysis of the cinéma-monde concept, as they invite consideration of how these particular global dimensions exist and function in films produced (or co-produced) from within the French film industry.

When considered as a whole, Herzi's films, while diverse, can be divided into three main categories.[2] The first consists of films set in France, with some of these incorporating an important local dimension, notably with regard to Marseille. The films in question are *La Graine et le mulet*, *Un Homme et son chien/A Man and His Dog* (Francis Huster, 2009, France/Italy), *Le Roi de l'évasion/The King of Escape* (Alain Guiraudie, 2009, France), *Joseph et la fille/Joseph and the Girl* (Xavier de Choudens, 2010, France) *L'Apollonide: souvenirs de la maison close/House of Pleasures* (Bertrand Bonello, 2011, France), *Jimmy Rivière* (Teddy Lussi-Modeste, 2011, France), *Ma compagne de nuit/My Night Companion* (Isabelle Brocard, 2011, France), *La Marche/The Marchers* (Nabil Ben Yadir, 2013, France/Belgium), and *Par accident/By Accident* (Camille Fontaine, 2015, France). In half of these – *La Graine*, *L'Apollonide*, *La Marche*, and *Par accident*, Herzi plays Maghrebi-French (*La Graine*, *La Marche*) or Maghrebi (*L'Apollonide*, *Par accident*) characters. The second category includes films that are set in a transnational context involving a European country and the Maghreb. They all involve young women who were born in Europe (France or Belgium) and are taken by their families, against their will, to a country in the Maghreb (Algeria or Morocco). The films in question are *Française/French Girl* (Souad El Bouhati, 2008, France/Morocco), *Le Sac de farine/The Bag of Flour* (Kadija Leclerc, 2014, France/Belgium/Morocco) and *Certifiée Halal/Certified Halal* (Mahmoud Zemmouri, 2015, France/Algeria). The third category consists of the actress's global roles, which for the present purpose are defined as those in which she plays characters who are detached from the French national context, to borrow Mark Gallagher's terminology (2014). These films are *L'Aube du monde/Dawn of the World* (Abbas Fahdel, 2009, France/Germany), *Les Secrets/Secrets* (Raja Amari, 2010, France/Switzerland/Tunisia), *Héritage/Inheritance* (Hiam Abbass, 2012, France/Israel), *La Source des femmes/The Source* (Radu Mihaileanu, 2011, France/Italy/Belgium/Morocco), *War Story* (Mark Jackson, 2014,

United States), and *Exit Marrakech* (Caroline Link, 2013, Germany). Although these three main categories of films can be distinguished, there are no formal periods to speak of in Herzi's career. In other words, the categories do not develop in chronological order or reflect the development of a specific pattern. At the same time, the absence of any such distinguishable pattern, and the fact that Herzi's roles have varied over time, is itself indicative of the actress's expressed desire, as we shall see, to avoid being branded as a certain type of actress or as an actress only able to play particular kinds of roles, as well as to overcome barriers to her career that have arisen because of her ethnic origins.

The aim of this chapter is to engage with the present volume's discussion of the concept of global cinema in French not via an analysis of the cultural output of a single director, but through consideration of the local, national, transnational, and especially global dimensions of the career of one actress. It will focus in particular on the significance of Hafsia Herzi's global roles. I will argue that these roles have been crucial to the development of her career and have allowed her to build and expand it in significant ways, and notably to overcome the limitations of other roles offered to her – roles set in France or in a transnational context. More specifically, these global opportunities enabled Herzi to begin to break out of – yet not totally reject – a French/Maghrebi framework into which her career could have been limited because of her ethnic origins. In addition, these global roles, and the ways in which they have been treated in the media and discussed by Herzi in interviews, have contributed to the construction of Herzi's identity as a French actress. This is an identity that she firmly defends as well as a label that her career contributes to redefining and broadening. In order to highlight the ways in which the global dimensions of Herzi's career developed and have been integral to her career trajectory, I will begin with a brief overview of her biography and choice of roles early in her career and then will analyse the local (i.e. *marseillais*), national, transnational, and global dimensions of Herzi's films, creative output, and identity as an actress.

Biography and Early Roles

Hafsia Herzi was born in 1987 in Manosque, France, to an Algerian mother and Tunisian father, and was the youngest of six children. Her father died in a workplace accident when she was an infant, and she and her siblings were raised by their single mother in a northern suburb of Marseille. Herzi's identity is firmly attached to this city and, although she has lived in Paris for most of her career, she returns to Marseille on a regular basis to visit her mother and reenergise ('Les 5 dernières minutes' 2009). From a young age, Herzi wanted to be a singer or actress and she enjoyed reciting poems and performing in school ('Graine de star' 2008). At ten, she began working as an extra but she did not take any formal acting classes (Séguret 2007). When she was cast in *La Graine et le mulet* just before her eighteenth birthday, she had only played bit parts in feature films. These parts were very limited in scope and centred on her ethnic origins, and Herzi has expressed frustration about the fact that before *La Graine* her auditions always led to her being offered the part of a specific extra: *la Maghrébine*. According to the actress:

> When I worked as an extra in Marseille, the casting sessions always led to me playing Maghrebi women characters. I had promised myself that if this didn't change, I would write my own roles where I'd be called Charlotte or Juliette! After *La Graine et le mulet*, I met directors who looked at me differently. But I don't deny my origins [. . .] and I think it's great to be able to act in French, Arabic, and, why not, in English. (Quilleriet 2008)

Thus from the earliest points in her career, Herzi was conscious of certain limitations faced by actresses of Maghrebi origin within the French film industry – a challenge that other contemporary Maghrebi-French actresses such as Leïla Bekhti and Rachida Brakni also came up against (Kealhofer-Kemp 2015).[3] After *La Graine et le mulet*, as Herzi received increasing numbers of film proposals, this awareness and concern stemming from her previous experiences influenced the roles that she accepted to play. Although she did not completely avoid films in which she would play Maghrebi-French, Maghrebi, or Arab women – as is evidenced by the lead role that she accepted for her second film, *Française*, discussed below – she refused many other film roles, and in particular those involving portrayals of women that she viewed as clichéd. In 2008, for example, Herzi spoke in detail about her selection (and rejection) of many ethnically marked roles, stating:

> It's not because I speak Arabic that I should be forced to limit myself to Arab films or to roles of the young Maghrebi woman who is beaten up or the victim of a forced marriage. This isn't an exaggeration – it's the reality of the scripts that I have already been offered. I'm sick of this image of the Maghrebi woman. Why not offer me the role of Cinderella? At any rate, I find it very discriminatory to not open castings to all communities. No one talks about it. This has to change! (Lamy 2008)

Herzi's second major project, *Française*, was director El Bouhati's first feature film and it gave the actress her first lead, playing a young Maghrebi-French woman named Sofia. Sofia was born in France to a

Maghrebi-French family and is torn away from her home, friends, and happy childhood at the age of ten because her parents decide to relocate the family to Morocco, the country of origin of her grandparents. The narrative then jumps ahead: Sofia is a young woman who still does not feel at home in Morocco, even after having lived there for several years. Her life goal is to do well in school so that her parents will allow her to return to France. She is energetic, independent, in constant movement, and rebellious (recalling in many ways the characteristics of Rym in *La Graine*), preferring to work outside in the fields with her father than stay in the family home and help her mother, thus rejecting traditional gender norms. She does not accept her parents' expectations for her, notably their desire for her to build a life in Morocco.

According to Herzi, despite the fact that she was wary of accepting another role as a Maghrebi-French woman, she agreed to play this character precisely because, in her view, the film did not cater to stereotypes. For the actress, *Française* '... refuses clichés. Sofia pursues her studies, she has a boyfriend ... She is not locked away in the house. Her parents think that they had good reasons to leave, a kind of unease in France, and they want to protect their daughter' (Quilleriet 2008). This nuance involving the portrayal of Sofia (and her parents) distinguished the film from others that Herzi rejected.

Having played Maghrebi-French women in her first two films, then an Iraqi woman living in a war zone in southern Iraq in *L'Aube du monde*, and a smaller part as a Maghrebi-French maid helping an aging former employer (and dealing with an unintended pregnancy) in *Un Homme et son chien*, Herzi became concerned that she might be pigeonholed playing only Arab women or women of Maghrebi origin – even if the roles were nuanced and avoided clichés. This apprehension led to concrete action on her part with regard to her selection of subsequent roles, and notably the conscious choice to accept an ethnically unmarked role in her fifth film, *Le Roi de l'évasion*. For Herzi: 'I understood that it was an opportunity to play something completely different and to not lock myself into playing clichéd roles and being pigeonholed as the 'token' Arab. In Alain's film, I am a young girl who has a very unusual relationship with a middle-aged man. End of story' (Mandelbaum 2009). In *Le Roi de l'évasion*, Herzi plays Curly, a hardheaded high school student living in a conservative town in southwestern France who rebels against her parents and pursues an unlikely romantic relationship. She is determined to form a couple with Arnaud, a middle-aged tractor salesman who is going through a midlife crisis – and also happens to be homosexual. Curly and Arnaud are in nearly constant movement as they seek to live outside of society's accepted norms and are pursued by the police. Curly's energy, rebellious nature, and desire for mobility are omnipresent in the film, and this role once again recalls the performance style highlighted through Rym in *La Graine* and Sofia in *Française*. Curly escapes from her parents' home to be with Arnaud, traverses the woods with him while on the run from the police, and relentlessly chases Arnaud on foot after he decides to break off their relationship.

The role in Guiraudie's film is significant in that the ethnic origins of Herzi's character do not have an impact on the storyline and are not even mentioned. The film also enabled Herzi to use different dimensions of her acting and to break away from her previous roles in at least two ways: first, it was her first opportunity to participate in a comedic film; and second, her character is involved in fairly graphic sex scenes with some nudity. In the words of Herzi: 'I wanted to go where people did not expect me to' (Desnos 2009). In a similar way, Herzi's global roles provide her with opportunities to add new dimensions to her career, play a greater variety of supporting parts and lead roles, and avoid the risk of being relegated to playing (to borrow Herzi's words, previously cited) the daughter of immigrants or the 'token Arab'. Herzi's global films represent an important – yet, to date, underexamined – part of the actress's filmography. As will be discussed in the following section, in order to understand how the global dimensions of Herzi's career and creative path developed over time, it is necessary to first consider the local origins of her career and identity in the south of France, and Marseille in particular. Herzi's southern roots have played a part in shaping her early career and identity as an actress.

Local Roots: The Marseille Connection

Hafsia Herzi's identity as an actress is anchored in southern France in two regards: first, as previously mentioned, the role for which she is best known, that of Rym in *La Graine et le mulet*, is situated in the port city of Sète, and this character has an accent that is indissociable from that which is often heard in the south of France, including the region surrounding France's second-largest city, Marseille. Rym's regional accent and body language were the subject of media attention after the film's release and were a much discussed part of Herzi's performance. Second, when asked about Marseille in interviews, and particularly early in her career, she expressed her attachment to her home city, its characteristics and way of life, and the qualities shared by its inhabitants. She also commented on various things that in her view distinguish Marseille from Paris, the city that has become her second home. For Herzi: 'I am proud to be *marseillaise*. People from Marseille are very nice, and it's a very beautiful city. They are very generous and have a *joie de vivre* . . . not like in Paris' ('La Grande émission' 2011). The actress has said that it was very difficult for her to move to Paris for professional reasons (soon after filming *La Graine et le mulet*) and that she suffered from a kind of culture shock upon her arrival (Siankowski 2011). When asked about this period of transition years later, in 2013, she spoke about being shocked by the cold weather, the cost of living, the size of apartments, and the stress exhibited by Parisians. In the words of Herzi: 'Now I'm used to it, but it was difficult at the beginning. I'm in between the two now. I can't stay in Paris for too long. Three weeks or a month at most' (Chermont 2013).

Herzi's identity as a *Marseillaise* is expressed not only by her accent; it is something that also extends to certain aspects of her personality. According to the actress: 'In Marseille, girls have personality, they refuse to be pushed around' (Siankowski 2011). These characteristics can be seen to be channelled into many of the roles she has interpreted over the years, and most notably those in which she plays young women who rebel against constraints, limitations, or barriers in their lives (seen in *La Graine et le mulet*, *Française*, *Jimmy Rivière*, *Le Roi de l'évasion*, *Ma compagne de nuit*, *Certifiée Halal* and *Héritage*). Indeed, she was cast in *Héritage* in the (global) role of Hajar, a young Palestinian woman who rebels against the expectations of her family by pursuing a relationship with an Englishman, in part because director Hiam Abbass, alongside whom Herzi had acted in *L'Aube du monde*, had personally observed Herzi's strong personality, a trait that she desired for Hajar. According to Abbass:

> What she [Herzi] is in real life is what I wanted for the character. An 'I don't give a damn' side with an inner sadness, who seems a little out in left field. She has a way of being beyond engagement or non-engagement, of making you feel that she will do what she wants to do, in spite of you! Far from the cliché of the young Palestinian woman who is a victim and rebellious. (Press kit, *Héritage*)

A similar parallel can be drawn between Herzi's personality and that of the character she plays in one of her most recent films, *Certifiée Halal*. She is Kenza, a young feminist from a Parisian *banlieue* whose outspokenness and militant feminism provoke the anger and frustration of her brother, who decides to arrange a marriage between his sister and a cousin in Algeria – unbeknownst to her. Kenza attempts to rebel against this plan and will not accept the marriage. In describing her role, Herzi draws a parallel between certain parts of her own personality and those reflected in Kenza, highlighting the characteristics that she had previously defined as being common to young women from Marseille. In the words of Herzi: 'The character is both close and not close to me. Close in the sense that I'm someone who is [. . .] who won't be pushed around, and who has personality' ('Hafsia Herzi de retour' 2015).

These facets of Herzi's self-defined identity as a *Marseillaise* are recurrent in her performance style throughout her film corpus and have positively impacted her career in several ways, particularly with regard to being offered the roles of energetic and rebellious young women in diverse contexts. However, not all aspects related to her southern background have fuelled her career. Indeed, Herzi had to work to lose her southern accent, made famous in *La Graine*, in order to be cast in a wider range of French-language roles. When she first auditioned for the lead in *Française*, for example, she was not cast as Sofia precisely because of her accent, and it was only when she re-auditioned, after taking classes to help her adopt a Parisian accent, that she was cast in the role. The actress's ability to go back and forth between these accents even became the subject of an episode of Raphaëlle Catteau's Canal+ series *L'Autre émoi* (2009). In it, the *Marseillaise* Hafsia Herzi interviews her Parisian alter ego, and the similarities and differences between the two – notably the accent, speech patterns, and body language, which again echo the character of Rym in *La Graine* – are contrasted for comedic effect.

In addition to being asked by the media to discuss her identity and roots as they relate to Marseille, Herzi has often been questioned about her connection to the Maghreb. The next part of this chapter will examine the transnational, as well as national, dimensions of Herzi's creative output and identity as an actress and will further lay the groundwork for consideration of her global roles.

National and Transnational Frameworks

Although Herzi's *Marseillaise* identity is a recurrent subject of discussion in interviews in the French media, questions directed to her are by no means limited to Herzi's regional French connections. She is routinely asked, even if indirectly, to comment on her identity as it relates to the Maghreb and the countries of origin of her parents (Algeria and Tunisia). This subject is often raised during discussions of films in which Herzi plays a Maghrebi woman (*La Source des femmes*), or characters in transnational contexts (*Française*, *Le Sac de farine*, and *Certifiée Halal*). Close analysis of the actress's responses to these lines of questioning reveals that Herzi views herself as unquestionably French and firmly rooted in France, as opposed to having loyalties split between France and the

Maghreb, as some interviewers automatically assume. Indeed, Herzi voices irritation when interviewers infer from the roles that she plays that she would be anything but French. After the release of *Française*, for example, Herzi expressed frustration about the kinds of questions she received from journalists about her identity and place in France. In the words of Herzi: 'Lately, I was asked about the *banlieues* even though I'm from the Northern neighbourhoods of Marseille. There's no comparison. Or someone wants me to pose in a ghetto style. Most recently, there was a journalist who asked me if I was "fully integrated"! Integrated in what? I'm French' (Mouaatarif 2008). In the same interview, when asked to comment on her connection to Algeria and Tunisia, Herzi clearly distinguishes between her perspective, as someone born and raised in France, and that of her mother, originally from the Maghreb, stating: 'I grew up in France, and I know that, for now, I wouldn't live in Algeria or Tunisia, even if my mother's only desire is to return there. For me, it's impossible. I love going there on vacation, but I don't see myself living there right now.' This distance – and difference in perspective – is again clearly expressed by Herzi in a 2010 television report that was filmed during the production of *La Source des femmes*. Herzi is interviewed in the rural Moroccan village where the film was shot, and although she is still dressed for her role of a Moroccan village woman, complete with the headscarf that goes with the part, her words quickly dispel any possible parallel between herself and the character that she portrays. In briefly discussing the Moroccan women from the village that she has come to know over the course of filming, she says, speaking for herself and presumably the other Maghrebi-French actresses involved in the film, Leïla Bekhti and Sabrina Ouazani: 'We tell ourselves that we're really lucky to live in France and have been born there, because we see the women here . . . even their gazes are different' ('Maroc: le tournage de *La Source des femmes*' 2010). For Herzi, there is a clear distinction between women from the Maghreb and women born and raised in France to families of Maghrebi origin, and this is something that she has regularly voiced (see Figure 5.2).

Elsewhere in the media, Herzi deflects questions that reflect assumptions made about her experiences and identity and presume that there are necessarily parallels between her experiences and those of the characters she plays who are based in the Maghreb. When interviewed about *Française*, for example, she is asked what she would have done if she were in the position of her character, Sofia, who is uprooted from her home (France), lives in Morocco, and dreams of nothing but returning to France. Herzi's response again emphasises the differences between herself and her character, and she even refuses to answer the question,

Figure 5.2 Hafsia Herzi as Loubna/Esméralda in *La Source des femmes*.

stating: 'It is difficult to respond to this question since I was born in France and have never been uprooted' (Lamy 2008). Similarly, at one point during a 2015 television interview on the subject of *Certifiée Halal* (a transnational film set between France and Algeria), the actress is asked to comment on the film *Les Terrasses*, directed by Algerian filmmaker Merzak Allouache – a film in which the actress did not participate. The interviewer asks Herzi if she shares Allouache's opinion that the Algerian capital is 'like an open air prison' ('Hafsia Herzi de retour' 2015). Once again, the actress deflects the question, explaining that she is not in a position to respond to it, given that she was born and raised in France and has limited knowledge of Algeria: 'I don't really know because I was born in France and I grew up in France, and although it's true that I went to Algeria for work or to see family when I was younger, I don't know. I'm not in a good position to . . .' Her response effectively shuts down this particular line of questioning.

In considering the ethnic origins of the characters that Herzi plays in her films that are set in France, as opposed to those with transnational dimensions (*Le Roi de l'évasion*, *Un Homme et son chien*, *Joseph et la fille*, *Ma compagne de nuit*), it is striking to note that in the majority of these films there is either very little or no mention of her characters' ethnic origins within the narrative. If they are defined, as in Bertrand Bonello's *L'Apollonide*, where Herzi plays Samira, an Algerian prostitute, they have little impact on the narrative or the development of the character. In this film, Samira is a woman among others in the turn of the century Parisian *maison close* in which the film is set, and while men are attracted to her 'exotic' appearance, no additional information about her life or connection to Algeria informs the narrative. Alternatively, if the ethnic origins of Herzi's characters are raised in the storyline in her films set in France, as in French-directed *La Graine* and Belgian-directed *La Marche*, the films leave no doubt about the characters' French identity and rootedness in France. In *La Graine*, for example, Rym helps her stepfather to navigate French bureaucracy and speaks out on his behalf. In *La Marche*, Herzi's character, Monia, is a young activist who participates in the 1983 'Marche pour l'égalité et contre le racisme' ('March for Equality and Against Racism'), along with other young people who feel French but are not always treated as such, and she does not abandon the march even after she is the victim of a racist attack.

When considered together, Herzi's interviews, as well as the roles that she plays in films set within national and transnational contexts, point to a conscious effort on the part of the actress to affirm her identity as French and to avoid a focus on her ethnic origins. Herzi has not only sought to avoid clichéd roles relating to Maghrebi or Maghrebi-French characters (notably disempowered women or victims, as previously mentioned), but she has also made a conscious effort to accept roles in which her characters have (in her words) 'French' names such as Marie and Julie and are not immigrants (Jaafar 2009). However, with regard to films set in France, despite the variety of roles that the actress has come to play over her relatively short career, and despite her attempts to avoid films that would potentially hinder her future options, the very parts she continues to be offered remain limited. Herzi has said as recently as 2013 that her film proposals can be grouped to a large extent under the heading of 'the daughter of immigrants.' According to the actress:

> I was lucky that *La Graine et le mulet*, directed by Abdellatif Kechiche, was successful internationally. I receive foreign scripts. I make films with Romanian, German, or American directors. I don't deny my origins, I'm proud of them. I actually have work thanks to them because I speak Arabic. In France, even if the cinema industry is becoming more diverse, I'm still most often offered to play the daughter of immigrants. (Grassin 2013)

This comment sheds light not only on certain barriers that Herzi has faced within the French film industry, but also on how the actress's creative path came to involve a significant global dimension. As will be underscored in the next and final section of this chapter, over the course of Herzi's career, her global films have provided new opportunities for her, as well as a chance to distance herself from the career limitations that she has come up against.

Global Dimensions: Forging a Cinéma-monde Path

Herzi's choice to pursue global roles represents, at least in part, a reaction to barriers that she has faced as an actress of Maghrebi origin within the French film industry. The narratives of the actress's global films exist outside of a French national context or French/Maghrebi dynamic, yet the films themselves may have benefited from French funding and thus are not entirely disconnected from the industry.[4] These films have allowed Herzi to take her career in new directions at various key points and in doing so she has avoided creating a pattern of similar roles that could have imposed further limitations on her acting choices. At the time of writing, Herzi's global films include *L'Aube du Monde*, *Les Secrets*, *Héritage*, *La Source des femmes*, *War Story*, and *Exit Marrakech*. These films represented opportunities for Herzi to expand her acting repertoire and interpret roles in a variety of contexts and languages, playing characters from Iraq, Tunisia, Israel, and Morocco. In speaking about her first global role as an Iraqi woman in Iraqi-French director Abbas Fahdel's *L'Aube du monde*, Herzi emphasised the differences between this film and those (non global) films in which she had previously been involved. According to the actress: 'It's [. . .] completely different from *La Graine*, *Française*, and everything I have done before. I filmed in Egypt, a four-hour drive away from Cairo, and I had to take intensive Arabic classes to play this role. But I'm happy because it's a very beautiful story. The screenplay also won several awards' (Mouaatarif 2008). Unlike her previous roles in *La Graine* and *Française*, in which she plays energetic and determined young women who challenge barriers in their lives through their words and actions, in *L'Aube du Monde* Herzi's performance required a different set of performance tools and also allowed the actress to move away from playing daughters (or granddaughters) of immigrants in France. Her character, Zahra, is an orphan, belongs to the Madans (or Marsh Arabs), which is a persecuted population in Southern Iraq, and lives in a war zone during the time of the First Gulf War. This performance also necessitated significant restraint and subtlety as it involved little physical movement. Zahra remains within the confines of her isolated village and stoically waits for the return of her husband from war in and near her modest lodging. In addition, contrary to Rym and Sofia in *La Graine* and *Française* (and later films such as *Le Roi de l'évasion* and *Jimmy Rivière*), who do not hesitate to speak out and are very vocal, Zahra is a woman of few words. Instead, her emotions are communicated through her facial expressions and gestures. Finally, when Zahra does express herself orally, it is in Iraqi Arabic, a language that Herzi did not speak before accepting this role and had to learn in order to portray Zahra. Herzi's second global film, *Les Secrets*, a psychological drama, is set in an even more enclosed space, an abandoned mansion in rural Tunisia. In this film, Herzi plays an opaque character, a developmentally delayed young woman who is sequestered by her mother and older sister and has had little contact with the outside world. This film offered Herzi the chance to play a less physical role than her early films (as well as ones that she would take on subsequently, such as *Ma Compagne de nuit*, where she plays a caretaker), and also one with greater psychological depth. As was the case in *L'Aube du monde*, this is conveyed through the actress's body language, gestures, and facial expressions. Herzi also learned a new dialect of Arabic (Tunisian) for the film.

The question of language deserves further consideration, as it represents a key component of the global dimension of Herzi's creative output. Although the actress learned Algerian Arabic as a child, in order to play the roles that make up her global corpus she had to learn Iraqi Arabic (*L'Aube du monde*), Tunisian Arabic (*Les Secrets*), Moroccan Arabic (*La Source des femmes*, *Exit Marrakech*), and Palestinian Arabic (*Héritage*), and she also needed to improve her English for *Héritage*, *Exit Marrakech*, and *War Story*. The linguistic differences inherent in these global films reflect a noteworthy aspect of her range as an actress, and one that is not highlighted in her films set in France or in a transnational context. In carrying out these roles, Herzi distinguished herself as an actress with a wide range of linguistic abilities and a commitment to taking on diverse films in which she does not initially speak the language.

The preparation involved in tackling these roles has also become a talking point for Herzi. In interviews relating to her global roles, she has emphasised the intensity of the required linguistic preparation, making clear that playing these global parts was not a given simply because of her family background. For example, in a piece in *L'Express*, Herzi explains that she studied over six hours per day with a language coach in order to learn Iraqi for *L'Aube du monde* (Quilleriet 2008). Her ability to learn this language, and her commitment to the role, also opened new doors for her professionally. According to Herzi, Hiam Abbass cast her in *Héritage* in part because she saw first hand (playing the mother-in-law of Herzi's character in Fahdel's film) that the actress was able to learn Iraqi Arabic, and she was confident that her young co-star could also learn Palestinian (Mazzacurati et al. 2012). In the same interview, Herzi commented on how difficult it was to learn Palestinian, stating: 'Palestinian was a discovery [. . .]. It may as well have been Chinese.' In another interview, Herzi emphasised the fact that she learned Palestinian as part of her preparation for *Héritage*, and in doing so once again subtly noted (as she did vis-à-vis *L'Aube du monde*) that this was not something that she was able to pick up simply because she is of Maghrebi descent and grew up speaking a different dialect of Arabic. According to the actress: 'I had to learn Palestinian for the film, which is really far from my origins and the Arabic language that I spoke in my childhood. I was coached for several months, before and during filming. [. . .] I also needed to improve my English' (Press kit, *Héritage*).

English was also required for her involvement in two additional global films – her two films to date that were not French (co-)productions and that also introduced her to wider audiences. The first was the German film *Exit Marrakech*, directed by Oscar-winning filmmaker Caroline Link, in which Herzi plays a Moroccan woman who works as a prostitute to support her family. The second was the American film *War Story*, in which she is a Tunisian migrant passing through Sicily with the hope of eventually making it to France. Considered together, Herzi's global roles serve to bring to light dimensions of her range and skill as an actress, in particular her work ethic and language skills, which have not been the central focus in her national and transnational films.

While taking on these global roles meant that Herzi worked in international contexts, in languages other than French, and with actors and directors of diverse origins, in the end, these projects did not actually take her on a path that diverged significantly from the French film industry; indeed, on the contrary, they enhanced her place within it in a new way. Although all six of the directors with whom she worked are originally from a country other than France, four of the six (Fahdel, Amari, Mihaileanu, and Abbass) are based in Paris, and they received French funding for the films in which Herzi plays a part. These four films, while co-productions, were majority French in terms of financing, and they also benefited from a release in French theatres, as well as media coverage (some more than others) in French news outlets. *L'Aube du monde* was the subject of six articles in major newspapers in France in 2009, *Les Secrets* was the subject of four articles in 2010, *La Source des femmes* the focus of fifteen articles in 2011 – as well as a selection at the Cannes film festival – and *Héritage* was covered by eleven articles in 2012 (*Ciné-Ressources*). While only *La Source des femmes* had any major impact at the box office (638,824 tickets sold, according to the *Lumière* database) the coverage of these global films contributed to keeping Herzi's name consistently in the media and for a wide variety of roles. Moreover, not only did Herzi have a major role in each of these global films (as opposed to much more minor roles in nationally-based films such as *L'Apollonide* and *Jimmy Rivière* that were released during the same time period), but her respective performances in the films also garnered positive reviews (whereas her 2010 film *Joseph et la fille*, in which she plays a criminal accomplice in a casino robbery, was poorly received).

Herzi's global films and their coverage in the media have had a significant impact on her career in that they have reinforced her identity as a French actress while also serving to expand the parameters of what it means to be a French actress. Herzi is generally not asked to comment on her identity when discussing these films, unlike her experiences in promoting her transnational roles, nor is there any mention of her family's origins. Media coverage of her global roles remains focused on the films in question and her performances.

Conclusion

Hafsia Herzi's global film roles have played a key part in enabling her to broaden her body of work and build her career in the French film industry. In considering specific global dimensions and how they function within films produced in the French film industry, this chapter has highlighted barriers and limitations that have existed throughout the development of Herzi's career, notably because of her ethnic origins. Unlike internationally acclaimed French actresses such as Juliette Binoche and Marion Cotillard, whose success in the national space led to English-language roles, international recognition, and distance from the French film industry (in terms of pursuing opportunities abroad), the global dimensions of Herzi's career have stemmed, at least to a certain degree, from lack of variety with regard to the roles (notably set in a national context) she has been offered. Moreover, contrary to Binoche and Cotillard, whose identity as French actresses has not been called into question over the course of their respective careers, regardless of the roles that they played, at times Herzi has had to defend her identity as a French actress. Revealingly, this has not been the case in discussions about her global films. Instead, these films have allowed for a distancing from barriers and limitations as they have focused attention on her roles and preparation for them, rather than on her identity or identification with the characters she plays based on their ethnic origins. This has provided an opportunity to reconsider what it means to be a French actress as well a concrete example that expands the traditionally limited – and limiting – definition of this concept. Hafsia Herzi represents a new kind of French actress whose professional trajectory, with its local, national, transnational, and especially global dimensions, serves as a model of what a cinéma-monde path within the French film industry can look like.

Notes

1. Nine of them are exclusively French productions.
2. Included in this list are films in which Herzi has the lead or an important secondary role that displays some character development. It thus excludes films such as *Elle s'en va/On My Way* (Emmanuelle Bercot, 2013, France).
3. See Tarr (2015) for further discussion of the careers of Brakni, Bekhti, and Herzi.
4. All but two of Herzi's global films, *War Story* and *Exit Marrakech*, benefited from French funding and a release in France.

Filmography of Hafsia Herzi (Feature Films)

La Graine et le mulet/The Secret of the Grain, Abdellatif Kechiche, 2007, France
Française/French Girl, Souad El Bouhati, 2008, France/Morocco
Un Homme et son chien/A Man and His Dog, Francis Huster, 2009, France/Italy
L'Aube du monde/Dawn of the World, Abbas Fahdel, 2009, France/Germany
Le Roi de l'évasion/The King of Escape, Alain Guiraudie, 2009, France
Les Secrets/Buried Secrets, Raja Amari, 2010, France/Switzerland/Tunisia
Joseph et la fille/Joseph and the Girl, Xavier de Choudens, 2010, France
Jimmy Rivière, Teddy Lussi-Modeste, 2011, France
Ma Compagne de nuit/My Night Companion, Isabelle Brocard, 2011, France
L'Apollonide: Souvenirs de la maison close/House of Pleasures, Bertrand Bonello, 2011, France
La Source des Femmes/The Source, Radu Mihaileanu, 2011, France/Italy/Belgium/Morocco
Héritage/Inheritance, Hiam Abbass, 2012, France/Israel
Elle s'en va/On My Way, Emmanuelle Bercot, 2013, France
Exit Marrakech, Caroline Link, 2013, Germany
La Marche/The Marchers, Nabil Ben Yadir, 2013, France/Belgium
War Story, Mark Jackson, 2014, United States
Le Sac de farine/The Bag of Flour, Kadija Leclerc, 2014, France/Belgium/Morocco
Certifiée Halal/Certified Halal, Mahmoud Zemmouri, 2015, France/Algeria
Par accident/By Accident, Camille Fontaine, 2015, France

Works Cited

Chermont, Stéphanie (2013), 'Hafsia Herzi, la marche à suivre', *Paulette Magazine*, 29 November, <http://www.paulette-magazine.com/fr/article/hafsia-herzi-la-marche-a-suivre/3846> (last accessed 7 July 2017).
Ciné-Ressources, La Cinémathèque française,<www.cineressources.net > (last accessed 7 July 2017).
Desnos, Marie (2009), 'Petite graine devenue star', *Paris Match*, 28 May.

Gallagher, Mark (2014), 'On Javier Bardem's sex appeal', *Transnational Cinemas*, 5:2, pp. 111–26.
Grassin, Sophie (2013), '"La Marche": "le discours xénophone s'amplifie", déclare l'équipe du film', *Le Nouvel Observateur*, 26 November, <http://tempsreel.nouvelobs.com/cinema/20131126.CIN1616/la-marche-le-discours-xenophobe-s-amplifie-declare-l-equipe-du-film.html> (last accessed 7 July 2017).
'Hafsia Herzi de retour dans une comédie, *Certifiée halal*!', *A l'affiche!*, 6 May 2015, France 24 Television, <https://www.youtube.com/watch?v=IUzgFgiSdyg&list=PLXHIA6MCTQWIKvVlMAHsb653r7-oUrZMw&index=1> (last accessed 7 July 2017).
'Hafsia Herzi, Graine de star' (2008), *Le Journal du dimanche*, 24 May, <http://www.lejdd.fr/Culture/Cinema/Actualite/Hafsia-Herzi-Graine-de-Star-92652> (last accessed 7 July 2017).
Jaafar, Ali (2009), 'Hafsia Herzi boards *Campagne*', *Variety*, 10 February, <http://variety.com/2009/film/markets-festivals/hafsia-herzi-boards-campagne-1117999910> (last accessed 7 July 2017).
Kealhofer-Kemp, Leslie (2015), 'Leïla Bekhti, Rachida Brakni, and the New Place of Maghrebi-French Actresses in French Cinema', *Contemporary French Civilization*, 40 :1, pp. 49–70.
'La Grande émission', 4 November 2011, *La Chaîne Marseille*, television, <https://www.youtube.com/watch?v=mAH9ZF0omuI&list=PLXHIA6MCTQWIKvVlMAHsb653r7-oUrZMw&index=14> (last accessed 7 July 2017).
Lamy, Jérôme (2008), 'Hafsia Herzi, à la folie.' *Clin d'oeil*, July. <http://www.clindoeilmagazine.com/articles/La_Une/Hafsia_Herzi.php> (last accessed 7 July 2017).
'Les 5 dernières minutes: Hafsia Herzi', *13h*, 2 February 2009, France 2, television.
Lumière, European Audiovisual Observatory, <http://lumiere.obs.coe.int/web/search> (last accessed 7 July 2017).
Mandelbaum, Jacques (2009), 'Hafsia Herzi: "Ne pas être cantonnée à l'Arabe de service"', *Le Monde*, 15 July, <http://www.lemonde.fr/cinema/article/2009/07/14/hafsia-herzi-ne-pas-etre-cantonnee-a-l-arabe-de-service_1218642_3476.html> (last accessed 7 July 2017).
'Maroc: le tournage de *La source des femmes*,' *19/20 Edition nationale*, 25 November 2010, France 3, television.
Mazzacurati, Iris, Theirry Chèze, and Joséfa Lopez, 'Hafsia Herzi: "Si Hiam Abbass m'avait proposé d'ouvrir une porte, je l'aurais fait"', 13 December 2012, *L'Express*, video. <http://videos.lexpress.fr/culture/cinema/video-hafsia-herzi-si-hiam-abbass-m-avait-propose-d-ouvrir-une-porte-je-l-aurais-fait_1198375.html> (last accessed 7 July 2017).
Mouaatarif, Yasrine (2008), 'Une étoile nommée Hafsia', *L'Atlas*, 16 June, <http://www.lecourrierdelatlas.com/Culture/Une-etoile-Nommee-Hafsia.html> (last accessed 7 July 2017).

Press kit, *Héritage* (2012), interview with Hafsia Herzi.
Press kit, *Héritage* (2012), interview with Hiam Abbass.
Quilleriet, Anne-Laure (2008), 'Hafsia Herzi: La graine d'une grande', *L'Express*, 28 May, <http://www.lexpress.fr/culture/cinema/hafsia-herzi-la-graine-d-une-grande_504850.html> (last accessed 7 July 2017).
Séguret, Olivier (2007), 'Hafsia Herzi, espoir et plus', *Libération*, 12 December, <http://next.liberation.fr/cinema/2007/12/12/hafsia-herzi-espoir-et-plus_108379> (last accessed 7 July 2017).
Siankowski, Pierre (2011), 'Hafsa Herzi: "J'ai la nostalgie de mon quartier à Marseille"', Les Inrocks, 7 May, <http://www.lesinrocks.com/2011/05/07/cinema/hafsia-herzi-jai-la-nostalgie-de-mon-quartier-a-marseille-1115867> (last accessed 7 July 2017).
Tarr, Carrie (2015), 'French Cinema and the Integration of Young Women Actors of Maghrebi Heritage', *Nottingham French Studies*, 54:3, pp. 297–311.

Part II
Voyages, Limits and Borders

CHAPTER 6

Lost at Sea or Charting a New Course? Mapping the Murky Contours of Cinéma-monde in Floating Francophone Films

Michael Gott

This chapter takes to the sea in order to consider the opportunities and limitations of adopting the label of cinéma-monde as a critical framework and follows various vessels as they chart the potential contours of this concept. I will suggest that the aquatic point of entry to cinéma-monde offers a privileged vantage point from which to explore the contemporary parameters of global French-language cultural and linguistic spaces. The itineraries in these films invite consideration of the place of the French language and of France – both by its presence and by its absence – in the world in general and particularly vis-à-vis the nation's former colonies and current neighbours in a tenuously unified contemporary Europe. Floating films work against what Tim Bergfelder terms a 'contained' perspective (2005: 329) that divides national cinemas into discrete discursive categories. They are related to yet also more varied than 'border-crossing films', a category that, as Carrie Tarr theorises, 'call attention to the porosity of national and cultural borders, but in so doing also expose the asymmetrical power relations between hosts and migrants, Western Europe and its others' (2007: 7). The corpus I identify here invites us to think about borders and boundaries differently by decentring our actual and mental maps. More than crossing borders, these films probe at the contours of prevalent lines of demarcation, developing points of contact and calling binaries into question. Absent a clear centre in evident opposition with a periphery or multiple peripheries, borders lose some of their significance as barriers and take on characteristics of 'borderlands' (Balibar 2009) and 'interzones' (Halle 2014).

This chapter analyses five floating films and theorises sea voyages for work, migration and pleasure within the context of contemporary border theories, North-South migration debates, and cinematic production and distribution networks. While my analysis is attuned to the disparate motives and conditions of these sea voyages, I aim to use the liquid contexts that they all share to highlight connections between these productions. I will focus on five floating films: *Diego Star* (Frédérick Pelletier, 2013, Canada/Belgium), *Fidelio, l'odyssée d'Alice/Fidelio* (Lucie Borleteau, 2014, France), *Harragas* (Merzak Alouache, 2009, Algeria/France), *L'iceberg* (Dominique Abel, Fiona Gordon and Bruno Romy, 2005, Belgium) and *La pirogue* (Moussa Touré, 2012, France/Senegal/Germany). Spanning from Quebec to Algiers and from Dakar to the Baltic Sea, these films, in their narratives, production contexts, and web of connections, encompass a wide – if certainly not entirely exhaustive – cross-section of the world where the French language has a significant presence. The French 'linguistic zone' encompassed by these films extends beyond the (post)colonial imprint of *la Francophonie,* pointing to the presence of French in a number of places from Canada to central-Eastern Europe (Wolton 2006: 16).[1] In the course of the cinematic voyages I will consider, characters speak French but also Wolof, Fula, English, Polish, Spanish, Arabic and Inuktitut, an Inuit language spoken in Canada (including Quebec, among other places).

Boundaries and Fluid Linguistic Maps: Seas, Boats and Ports

As outlined in the introduction to this volume, the concept of cinéma-monde should allow us to bring together a variety of film industries and national cinemas, and be inclusive in its definition of 'francophone'. Cinéma-monde expands the geographical limits of what is customarily considered *la Francophonie,* which is depicted as a 'heterolingual' space (Sanaker 2011), and formally recognises an increasing number of films that combine French with many other languages. Floating films, I argue, demonstrate some of the multiple nodes that must be considered in any construction of a meaningful theory of cinéma-monde: production, narrative, economic contexts, and the migration of films, filmmakers and protagonists.

More than a simple assemblage of productions set on boats that traverse or interact with French-speaking zones, the stories told in these films and their production backstories represent the possibilities and potential limitations or barriers to cinéma-monde by constantly engaging with and exploring limits. By limits I have in mind a number of things, but most notably and visibly the recent migrant and refugee crisis and the boundary lines of Fortress Europe (and more broadly the West, including Canada in this context) that bisect zones of cultural affinities and traditions, drawing a line in the water and in ports of call where identities are checked and comings and goings surveilled. Borders cut across linguistic zones, potentially segregating European, North American and African spaces. Francophone zones are also riven with neo-colonial and economic disparities that undermine the significance of linguistic affinities, as we will see in *Diego Star*. This aside, it is worth restating that floating films are not simply concerned with confronting and crossing boundary lines and engaging with the 'Fortress approach' so prevalent in European political and public discourse (Ballesteros 2015: 12). Indeed, one of their salient features is what they say about the complexity of contemporary frontiers, be they French or European.

Ports, the vessels themselves, bodies of water and the so-called 'maritime boundaries' and 'territorial waters' carved onto charts of the seas all represent border spaces in their own right. If territory is fundamentally 'uncertain', as Inge Boer puts it (2006), then 'maritime territories' are even more so. Given that, as Rosalind Galt suggests, European borders have been viewed as 'disconcertingly unstable' (2006: 1) since the early 1990s, films set at sea offer compelling explorations of the potentially flexible contours of those borders. Of course instability is a constant source of angst and unease amongst certain elements of the population in Europe and North America, where working-class communities grapple with the concept that places are not fixed but 'are like ships that move around', as mobility theorist John Urry contends (2007: 42). However, another result of these spatial reconfigurations is the elaboration of new and multiple spaces of potential solidarities. These are not solely 'francophone solidarities'. As Dominique Wolton argues, a shared language is not a sufficient premise for solidarity – one can simply ask immigrant workers in Europe or Harkis, to use his examples – other gestures are necessary (2006: 76).

To a significant extent, the films discussed in subsequent pages consider questions of solidarity and belonging in relation to Europe and its spheres of influence: protagonists travel on European boats, towards the Continent and its external possessions, or from or around Europe. Implicit in many of the narratives – beyond the linguistic questions that frame belonging and identity – is the question of who is European and who is not, or at least who has claim to European space. Within a specifically European context, Étienne Balibar remarks on the potential inherent in border zones 'for hybridity and cultural invention' (2009: 200). In my discussion of these films I consider how floating films expand conceptions of Europe through gestures of solidarity, to encompass a map of interconnected places and zones. While Europe is clearly a limited slice of the wider world that cinéma-monde might encompass, the various intersections with different places represent a useful starting point. Cinéma-monde delineates interwoven spaces and people in a fashion that does not solely rely on linguistic categories and shared use of the French language. Solidarity, then, is a way to measure connections that go beyond mutual comprehension. It is a process tied to language but also independent of it. Globalised *francophonie*, Wolton argues, is no longer simply a leftover from colonialism, but a chance for a future 'cohabitation' founded on cultural diversity (2006: 20). The restrained but flexible parameters of boats and the ports they interact with furnish microcosms of this possible cohabitation.

Rethinking francophone spaces requires reimagining the maps that chart these spaces and places and the mental and cultural geographies behind them. In an essay on what she terms the 'virtual multitudes' of *la Francophonie*, Mireille Rosello points out the limitations of extant 'world Francophone' maps that assign specific hues to particular nation-states: 'the colour code gives us the impression that entire territories share a homogeneous linguistic and cultural practice . . . In fact, those coloured spaces cover (and cover up) extremely fragmented and disjointed usages of what we call "French"' (2009: 49). Rosello suggests that dots on a map are a better way to conceive of links in what she terms a 'post-globalized' (2009: 49) world: 'Rather than homogeneous and circumscribed territories symbolised by blocks of solid colours, global and local Francophone practices form a multitude of dots with various levels of concentration in several continents and cities' (2009: 54). Certainly boats, water and ports could be conceived of as such dots – often mobile and always in transition as people and goods come and go – that make up networks of zones that transcend traditional mapping reflexes.

The floating films on my list are 'francophone', but not exclusively or entirely so. In geographic terms, if with one exception these productions all received some financing from Paris, the capital is entirely absent from their narrative space. Instead the reference points are ports such as Marseille, Lévis (Quebec) and Dakar, and most of the journeys narrated chart courses that do not directly involve France. Thus they exemplify how global production and reception of cinema opens the door to an exploration of the 'relationships among different margins', as Lionnet and Shih theorise 'minor transnationalism' (2005: 1–2). By dint of their funding, these films are also all, to different degrees, European. Or, more precisely, they belong to what Halle describes as a European cultural zone that is not coterminous with the EU, one that extends to Ceuta and Algeria, and arguably beyond. Halle argues convincingly that if 'political union is easy to limit [. . .] cultural union has an ideational quality that is more difficult to control' (2014: 14). Yet 'European' as a static appellation should be qualified here. One of the advantages of taking seas as primary reference point, as conduit rather than barrier, is the potential reframing of spaces and identities along more fluid contours that might subvert the typical fault lines that structure how the world is conceived (Abderrezak 2016: 15–16).

Water in floating films serves as both barrier and conduit, or to use terminology from Klaus Eder, the sea can be a 'hard' or a 'soft' border (2006). In one sense seas facilitate a constellation of possible productive points of contact and connections in cosmopolitan ports and aboard the vessels themselves. In the same vein water also represents the potential for dilution inherent, for example, in broad categorisations such as 'World Cinema'. One central tenant of this chapter is that dilution, or at least diffusion, has positive effects in the realm of French-language cinema. Films set at sea privilege a vantage point that encompasses what Bill Marshall terms a 'multiplication of centres' (2009: 304). Nonetheless in light of the current migration crisis it is impossible to sidestep the question of Europe's frontiers and the binary inside/outside and centre/periphery distinctions evoked by policed borders. Within the current logic of Fortress Europe in particular, water is both a hard border and 'smooth' space of identity renegotiation (Rascaroli 2013: 29), not least due to the continued (welcome or undesired) postcolonial connections it enables. Seas – notably but not exclusively the Mediterranean – facilitate alternative engagements with and perspectives on spaces and boundaries by transcending political frontiers.

The complexities of water might encompass both associations of allure and menace.[2] In one sense the sea decentres cinematic categories and facilitates a constellation of possible productive points of contact and connections in cosmopolitan ports and aboard the vessels themselves. Seas are not entirely borderless and the exchanges they produce are not uniformly positive. In her analysis of *Welcome* (Philippe Lioret, 2009, France), a film set in the port of Calais, with the English Channel as a constant and unavoidable backdrop, Laura Rascaroli turns to the Deleuzian concept of 'striated' space, controlled by the state and riven by enclosures and barriers: 'Even the sea in *Welcome* is striated; each time it is framed, ferries and ships cross the shot. Yet, the sea is also a fluid, 'smooth' space, which suggests the possibility of renegotiating identities, travelling, communicating and starting anew' (2013: 29).

The films under consideration here hardly put forward an entirely utopian notion of travel at sea, which is influenced and/or hindered by both economic and political striation. Some routes are dictated by market fluctuations and economic variables. And for migrants, in a time of Frontex (the EU border policing agency founded in 2004) border security, the 'hard' characteristics of the always potentially perilous sea could not be more evident. Yet there is also an element of what might be called 'positive' (Gott and Schilt 2013) travel in many of these films; particularly but not exclusively when the travelling subject is blessed with a European passport. European protagonists – but also sometimes migrants, who have been described and filmed by French director Boris Lojkine as 'adventurers' (Gott 2016: 156) – engage in a practice that I would label 'touring', albeit of the particularly adventurous variety.[3] 'Touring' is not precisely tourism but a type of voyage in which elements of that often maligned practice overlap with a variety of other modes of travel that include work, study and visiting friends and relatives (Gott 2015a). Migrants faced with hard borders are regularly rubbing shoulders with tourists that epitomise the boundless mobility that has been so central to the European project since the Treaty of Rome in 1957.[4] This has happened most recently in the media on the Greek island of Lesbos, where plastic dinghies full of refugees mingle with yachts. In cinema this confrontation can be seen in some of the films addressed in detail here as well as in *Eden à l'ouest/Eden is West* (Costa-Gavras, 2009, France/Greece/Italy), which opens with a 'clandestine' boat crossing the Aegean Sea towards Greece, where weary migrants will come ashore at a resort full of French and other European tourists.[5] The two groups compete for turf where some of Europe's most appealing holiday real estate doubles as point of arrival for refugees and migrants from the south and the east. The two forms of mobility are bound together and are logical extensions of Europe's internal open border policies, yet are clearly disparate in economic terms, with the claim of the 'traveller' on the space a financial one and that of the migrant a primarily ethical one. Given the mission of this volume to expand the boundaries of 'French' cinema, two other films merit mention here. *Terraferma* (Emanuele Crialese, 2011) is an Italian and French co-production that has no narrative or linguistic connection to France. In the film migrants who are saved from a watery demise by a fisherman mingle with tourists in Sicily. The coalescence of the two groups seems problematic for a number of reasons, but in particular given the potential economic use of the space that the fisherman's family has offered the migrants. Set in the Canary Islands, *Die Farbe des Ozeans/The Color of the Ocean* (Maggie Peren, 2011, Germany/Spain) is an example of a film that has no production connection to a French-speaking nation but which contains French dialogue due to an encounter between Senegalese migrants and a French-speaking German tourist. The economic aspect of the floating equation is a crucial element. Beyond the 'push' and 'pull' factors that motivate migrant voyages (Thomas 2012: 163–165; 170), finances play a role in the voyages of larger ships as well. However, the networks explored and woven in floating films are not simply economic; they are also cultural. The sea in floating films is revealed to be the site of constant wrangling over resources, trade, economics, etc., but it is also a space of human connectivity.

The latter conception tends to be dominant in the imaginary of the Mediterranean world. Pierre Pitiot, co-founder of CINEMED (Festival du cinéma méditerranéen de Montpellier), argues that the Mediterranean delimits a meaningful cultural space that indeed extends beyond its shores while transgressing not only national boundaries but continents and other established geographical boundaries (2009: 13). For Pitiot, cinema is a preeminent force in a recognisable Mediterranean cultural sphere that extends, more or less loosely, from Portugal to the Caucasus (2009: 15); a 'space of physical geography' and a 'world' of human geography (2009: 24). Scholars such as Hakim Abderrezak (2016: 14) and Aine O'Healy (2010: 16) have used the Mediterranean as a cultural and geographic framework and argued that the sea delimits a coherent transnational space of artistic output. Similar conceptions of the Baltic, another enclosed sea that flanks the opposite side of Europe, have recently gained currency since the fall of communism in Eastern Europe, a historical moment that looms large in the spatial consciousness of (at least) one of the films discussed later. Thinking of the Baltic as a coherent cultural space allows for new convergences between the erstwhile 'East' and 'West' of Europe (as mapped in Cold War geopolitical alignments) and comparisons of Nordic, Slavic and Germanic cultures (Šukaitytė 2014: 175).

The Atlantic, the other major body of water in our floating films, has been theorised in a similar fashion. In *The French Atlantic*, Bill Marshall forwards the ocean as a geographic framework for an alternative, decentred cultural and economic history of Frenchness, a 'counter narrative' of the French nation (2009: 8). The American parameters of Marshall's French Atlantic extend from Quebec to New Orleans and on to South America. On the other side of the ocean Marshall's analysis homes in on onetime shipping capitals La Rochelle and Nantes. Both cities are undeniably crucial to the history of French Atlantic trade and exploration but utterly off the radar in the Paris-centric French cultural imaginary and in mental constructions of French postcolonial space. This shift in perspectives exemplifies the dramatically altered outlooks offered when culture is approached from the starting point of the sea in general and floating films in particular. A final theoretical framework that bears mention is Paul Gilroy's influential conception of the 'Black Atlantic'. Gilroy focuses on the British colonial legacy, but is particularly helpful here for its theorisation of ships in motion as a metaphor for diaspora, a chaotic and living entity in 'ceaseless motion' (1993: 122). Gilroy draws on the history of the Atlantic to question the significance of the nation state, suggesting what is a key point to my analysis of floating films: '[N]either political nor economic structures of domination are still simply co-extensive with national borders' (1993: 7). Gilroy's theorisation of sailing vessels is particularly germane to my analysis. The ships that transported slaves to America and goods back to Europe embody in a 'double consciousness', the act of looking '(at least) two ways at once' (1993: 3). These vessels serve as 'conduit of Pan-African communication' (1993: 13) and interface between England's ports and the 'wider world' (1993: 17).

Such states of multiplicity are especially evident in ports, where seas and boats converge with solid land.[6] In floating films, ships dock in a diverse array of ports: Dakar, Gdańsk, Le Havre, Liverpool, Lévis (Quebec) and Marseille. Ports, as Rascaroli contends, transcend binary constructions of borders:

> Arguably, the port is at once a small-scale version of the global melting pot, a microcosmic rendition of the tensions between the north and the south of the world [. . .] the port is a hybrid space in which different logics and laws meet, clash and coexist and in which borders can be negotiated in various ways. (2013: 26)

This conception of ports as existing outside the laws and indeed the typical identity of the nation state calls to mind the description of Marseille as France's 'best back door' in Jamaican-American writer Claude McKay's 1929 novel *Banjo*. In floating films, however, port towns are the front door to what Rosello describes as a 'post-globalized' (2009: 49) world. Sea cinema reframes the port-as-borderland convincingly theorised by Rascaroli as the norm: Marseille is no longer the archetypal example of non-French space, where national identity faces fears of dilution, but the very face of the nation. Thinking about seas and ports as spaces of connectivity and cultural exchange opens the possibility of setting aside political borders, at least provisionally. Films set on boats intrigue in the way they float through the world, constantly interacting with people, goods, foods, music, languages and cultures at ports of call and encountering other objects in movement. Films that chart itinerant courses – whether planned, improvised, or imposed by outside forces – through seas and to ports are a potentially compelling way of thinking about the parameters of French-language spaces and cinemas. It goes without saying that simply drawing boundary lines around places where French is spoken does not accurately reflect the movements and flows involved in culture and language nor the overlapping spaces or Bakhtinian 'contact zones' where French interacts with other languages.

Lévis, Gdańsk, the Canary Islands: Mapping Floating Cinema

I now turn to five specific examples of sea cinema. Given that only a cursory examination of each film is possible here, I will focus on situating the filmic narratives within the contexts outlined above, with a particular focus on language and solidarity as elements that transcend national boundaries and typical mappings of insiders and outsiders. I will then consider the ways in which the production contexts might add to our understanding of floating cinema. The following analysis groups films into sometimes overlapping categories according to the itinerary of the voyage, the type of boat, and the status of the voyagers.

The first two films covered involve voyages on cargo ships. *Diego Star*, a 2013 Canadian-Belgian co-production by Montreal-based director Frédérick Pelletier, opens in the bowels of a Russian ship that is about to suffer a massive engine failure. While the accident is investigated and the boat repaired, the crew is waylaid in a small and frozen shipyard in Lévis, on the Saint Lawrence River near Quebec City. There Traoré (Issaka Sawadogo), an Ivorian engineer whose career has provided for his family while simultaneously keeping him estranged from them, is placed in the home of Fanny (Chloé Bourgeois), a single mother whose work at the dock cafeteria barely covers her bills. Whereas the subsequent productions could all be considered aquatic versions of road cinema, *Diego Star* is focused on a pause in the journey and therefore would best be described as a 'stopover film', a subcategory that reflects a climate of intensified border security in which so many voyagers are left waiting due to their citizenship or financial status (Gott 2015b: 299–300). Although his ship has been rendered immobile, Traoré remains in constant motion in Lévis. The recurring tracking shots of his peregrinations on the frozen, white streets that link the port to Fanny's home highlight on the one hand Traoré's struggle to keep up in a world economy premised on mobility (Viard 2011: 106) and on the other his inability to maintain a solid foothold in one place.

Traoré, however, is not alone in his struggle, and his encounter with Fanny is notable because both are (at least) doubly marginal: as economic subalterns and cultural outsiders in relationship to France as a 'centre' of the French-speaking world. Traoré is also an outsider as an African in a small North American port town, a status underscored by the fashion in which Fanny's mother reacts to his presence in her daughter's home. The ensuing interactions between the denizens of two primarily francophone places enables a number of uneasy linguistic and cultural encounters – the sailor does not know the word used in Quebec for mittens, for example

– that underscore the diversity of *la Francophonie*. The choice of winter attire as point of linguistic misunderstanding also reminds viewers of the disparate and diverse landscapes where French is spoken across the globe. Traoré, it seems, may very well have never needed to know the type of sartorial vocabulary that would be essential in Quebec, where he spends his days traipsing through a frozen city and admiring a snowplough at work, and even if he did he may well have learned a different word for the same item. Despite their differences, their ability to communicate helps to slowly forge a sort of almost solidarity between these two struggling workers from disparate backgrounds. When the boat arrives, Fanny's co-worker jokes that she should invite a Russian sailor home to keep her company; an encounter that likely would have yielded very different results. Although they do make a platonic connection that involves Traoré temporarily taking on the role of household helper and even surrogate father, the limits of their relationship are clearly sketched out. It is not entirely a question of class solidarity or hospitality, for the interaction was at least initially more transaction than invitation. Traoré thanks Fanny for 'welcoming' him into her home, but her tour of the premises focuses on rules and restrictions (he will be fed at the canteen, so no need for him to use the kitchen). Later, despite their emerging affinity, when he is cut off by his company and the bill for his lodging no longer paid, Fanny locks him out, leaving him banned both from his floating home, the Diego Star, and his temporary Canadian domicile.

Beyond this meeting, of interest here is the polyglot nature of life on board the cargo ship, where language is both a point of contact and a symbol of hierarchies. Traoré speaks English with his Russian bosses and French with Timo (whose origins are not identified but is played by Moroccan actor Yassine Fadel) and others who spend their time working below deck. Ultimately the crew members turn on Traoré after he denounces the conditions on board the boat to Canadian authorities, leading the company to freeze all workers' pay in retaliation and to frame the Ivorian engineer for the engine breakdown. When Fanny comes to realise this, she goes to look for him but it is too late, for he has been arrested and will face a deportation hearing. If this sombre film does not find liberation or a happy ending in transnational French-language encounters, it does nevertheless reveal some of the complexities and connections inherent in cinéma-monde narratives and production practices (which I will return to later).

A very different film that nonetheless shares the cargo vessel setting of *Diego Star* is Lucie Borleteau's 2014 French production *Fidelio, l'odyssée d'Alice*. The protagonist Alice (Ariane Labed) is an engineer on a cargo ship based in Marseille and the film is both a love story and the tale of a

Figure 6.1 Alice and shipmates gaze over the Mediterranean.

woman's odyssey through a distinctively masculine world. The geography of *Fidelio*, which opens on the docks of Marseille and plies the waters of the Atlantic off the coast of Africa, is largely responsible for a generally sunnier outlook. The citizenship of the protagonists is also a crucial factor in their approach to sea voyages; the French Alice sails in part for escapist adventure at sea and in port whereas Traoré is compelled to do so to provide for his family. While *Diego Star* highlights stasis – Traoré's stopover takes up virtually all the narrative, and motion is only possible on the snowy streets of Lévis – *Fidelio* follows the movement of the eponymous cargo ship, with the voyage punctuated by numerous brief pauses. The only travelling shots in *Diego Star* take place on land.[7] In contrast, the recurring travelling shots in *Fidelio* highlight the experience of being at sea and the vastness of the (generally) bright blue waters and skies (see Figure 6.1). These shots add to the feeling of adventure and exploration suggested in the title. Sometimes Alice is framed alone looking out towards the passing sea, in a recurring image that seems to reference *Titanic* (James Cameron, 1997, USA), and on other occasions her co-workers join her.

The meandering itinerary (dictated by shifting global market prices) leads first to Dakar – a reversal of the itinerary I will discuss later in *La Pirogue* – back to Marseille, then towards England, Cherbourg, Norway and ultimately Gdańsk, Poland. From postcolonial link to city symbolic of the fall of communism and of the ostensibly united Europe that followed, this film is concerned with exploring spaces as fluid entities without entirely fixed boundaries, to paraphrase cultural geographer Doreen

Massey (1994: 153). By situating the French character and boat – and by extension French cinema and indeed contemporary France as a nation – within this multifarious geographic context, Borleteau's film suggests that the nation is linked to a variety of different economic and cultural spaces intertwined with the post-colony and also to an expanded Europe.

Fidelio is particularly attuned to language aboard the ship and beyond. Whereas *Diego Star* highlights the diversity within the francophone world, Fidelio emphasises the 'heterolingual' (Sanaker 2011) aspect of *la Francophonie*: the voyagers speak French, Romanian, English, Tagalog and Norwegian in the course of their duties on board and their personal lives and occasionally via Skype, a medium that blurs the lines between personal and professional worlds and between voyage and home. The final language heard in the film is Polish from dockworkers in Gdańsk. Unlike in *Diego Star*, where Russian and English are dominant languages on board due to the ship's ownership and management while French is relegated to a subaltern tongue spoken by a handful of subjects from former French colonies, *Fidelio* is a French-run vessel. French predominates amongst the officers, while many of the less advantaged workers speak Tagalog amongst themselves and communicate with the francophone entourage in English. As in *Diego Star*, *la Francophonie* is not presented as a seamless cultural space. Linguistic difficulties emerge most notably between the French and the Senegalese, involving interactions of a clearly neo-colonial variety. When the boat docks in Dakar, a French crewmember claims not to understand the French spoken by a dockworker who serves as the liaison to the ship while in port. Later the crew parties at a nightclub and the captain offers Alice and a male sailor the paid companionship of a local man and woman, respectively, as birthday gifts, further underscoring the economic and power imbalances at play in France-Africa interactions.

Despite such cultural and economic differences, *Fidelio* is also a film about camaraderie and perhaps solidarity. Numerous scenes set around the dinner table provide the best examples of this. Different cultures come together at the captain's table to talk, sing and eat food representing various traditions and ports of call. Yet this is not a utopian film, nor one that overlooks the economic and political fissures that mar the interconnected map drawn by the Fidelio's peregrinations. Romanian and Filipino crewmembers are not on the same level as their French colleagues, as demonstrated by one Romanian engineer's statement – in excellent French – that he is paid much less than his French counterparts and by a scene in which the Filipinos resist but ultimately carry out an order to complete what they see as a dangerous task in the engine room. There is also a sadness in some of the dinner scenes, exemplified by a melancholy song sung by Filipino sailors over Christmas dinner. This episode reminds us that the Filipino sailors are economic 'migrants' in their own right and also face a particular variety of sea crossing that, while less perilous than the migrant voyages discussed later, nonetheless involves the acceptation of personal risk in the hope of achieving economic stability.

L'iceberg, by Brussels-based directing and acting team Dominique Abel (a Belgian) and Fiona Gordon (a Canadian born in Australia) with co-director Bruno Romy, marks a rather dramatic change of pace (and of vessel size) but nonetheless relates to our main themes. At first glance *L'iceberg* would not seem to fit with either the freighter films already covered or those depicting migrant crossings that will be addressed next. If this itinerary is more whimsical and drifting, *L'iceberg* still engages both directly and indirectly with some of the issues in the other films, notably migration and the ethics of solidarity. The sea voyage in this comedic film is prompted by an escapist reflex and premised on an unlikely obsession with frigid things. However, notions of solidarity and otherness lurk just under the surface. *L'iceberg* stages an atypical journey towards the north, in the process underscoring the possibilities and perils of open borders. Among other things, the film offers a particularly unique twist on the existential quest so common in road cinema (Gott 2016: 97–101). *L'iceberg* is of particular interest here because a significant portion of the voyage is undertaken in a sailboat, filmed both in the water and using grainy, retrograde rear-projection images for scenes set below deck that give the film a playfully nostalgic feel. As the title suggests, this trip to escape her stable but mundane existence leads the heroine Fiona (played by Gordon) and later her husband (Abel) to sea, where she chases her dream of encountering a giant frozen mass. The focus on Fiona's ontological odyssey connects to Alice's travels in *Fidelio*.

Given *L'iceberg*'s interest in flexible notions of culture and identity, it seems appropriate that the object of Fiona's quest is itself not spatially fixed, but floats around between different continents and beyond national borders and linguistic zones. This Belgian production is also an interesting linguistic case. Abel and Gordon's reliance on Tatiesque physical comedy leaves little room or need for spoken language in their films such as *La Fée/The Fairy* (2011, France/Belgium), which is set on the docks of Le Havre, and very few French words are uttered in *L'iceberg*. Fiona has a brief but remarkable encounter with clandestine migrants in a scene that suggests that English is the lingua franca of many migrants traversing Europe as well as, frequently, of border policing.[8] Although the quest is Fiona's, the story is narrated from the perspective of the woman who saves the protagonists from a watery demise after their sailboat sinks. The fisherwoman identifies herself in an opening monologue as a speaker of Inuktitut, demonstrating a rather improbable linguistic encounter for an almost accidental Belgian seaward voyage. With its distant conclusion, *L'iceberg* furnishes a reminder that French-language zones encounter and overlap with a variety of other languages in different parts of the world on a regular basis. It also suggests that any map of the francophone world must include spaces where icebergs and the snowy landscapes visible in *Diego Star* proliferate. Yet as noted above, an iceberg is itself errant and therefore fundamentally resistant to mapping endeavours, despite Fiona's attempt to chart her trajectory with simplistic lines pointing towards the object of her quest. It is perhaps difficult to imagine a travel film that does not feature a map, a staple of road cinema that is both practical and symbolic (Gott 2016: 97), and Fiona's indeed serves a particular purpose. Her 'map' becomes a tool of communication, used to visually express her desired travel itinerary to the sailor René (Philippe Martz), who had not uttered a word since a tragic accident many years before.

One portion of Fiona's trek puts her into contact with a group of clandestine migrants. The adventure begins when she climbs into the back of a freezer lorry in order to indulge her obsession with ice. After the door shuts behind her and the vehicle takes off, she (and we) discover that there are others sharing her space. In the symbolically charged darkness of the truck numerous pairs of eyes become visible. The image is a potent reminder that migrants crossing Europe often do so, whether literally or figuratively, in the dark (Gott 2016: 98), whether on land or at sea. In the following scene *L'iceberg* shifts briefly from the representation of a voyage more closely aligned with the adventurous wanderings of Alice in *Fidelio* to undertake a humorously sketched yet overtly political commentary on how European borders are policed. The camera cuts from inside the vehicle to a roadside area where two boxes – labelled 'Yes' and 'No' in English – are sketched on the pavement to demarcate the zones where Fiona and the migrants are assigned by the police conducting an identity check. A large group of African migrants are crowded within the boundaries of the 'No' box while the Belgian resident Fiona is assigned to the relatively spacious 'Yes' square seemingly by herself. However, from behind her gradually emerges a young child she is hiding. In order to protect the boy, Fiona moves in comic lockstep with the police officer who encircles her space. Her ultimately futile gesture of solidarity will be reciprocated at the end of the film when she and her travelling companions are saved from the water by the Inuit fisherwoman. This happy aquatic ending offers a more appealing and flexible response to the enclosed vision of the world expressed by the 'Yes' and 'No' boxes. Framed in long shots against a standard non-place backdrop of power lines and roadside way station, the lines on the pavement create an exclusionary 'map' of sorts. The squares, like the coloured maps of the world discussed earlier, demarcate space according to clear binaries of inside and outside. In contrast, national and linguistic boundaries are insignificant to Fiona's map to the iceberg and to the watery spaces where solidarity proves more meaningful than borders.

The final subcategory of floating films focuses on migrant crossings towards Europe. While some of those making the journey have their sights set on France, the fact that Spain is the immediate destination exemplifies the varied encounters encompassed by cinéma-monde. On the surface, the migrants in search of economic opportunity in these films would seem very different from the travellers in productions I have already discussed. Yet as previously mentioned, not all of those working aboard cargo vessels enjoy a privileged position on board or indeed in the world. Moreover, the characters in migrant crossing films are often filmed in a way that frames their quests in more than simply economic terms; they are 'adventurers' with big – if perhaps hopelessly naïve – aspirations. The clandestine crossings these films narrate stage various linguistic encounters not only between French speakers (on narrative and production levels) but also between French and other languages spoken by voyagers and those who patrol Europe's aquatic frontiers. I will discuss one production that crosses the Mediterranean and another that involves an Atlantic voyage.

La Pirogue, by Senegalese director Moussa Touré, is a co-production of France, Senegal and Germany. Touré is best known for his 1998 film *TGV* (France/Senegal), which narrates a land voyage by collective taxi from Dakar, Senegal to Conakry, Guinea. *La Pirogue* recounts an attempt to reach Spanish territory, or more specifically the Canary Islands – an extra-continental destination that underscores the incongruity of European political borders – in a small, overloaded vessel named the Goor Fitt. Like the freighters in the previously mentioned films, this boat is piloted by a veteran seaman with many years of sailing experience. French is a common language but is not spoken by all, making translation sometimes necessary. On the boat is a mixed crowd from West Africa – Ivoirians, Guineans, Senegalese – of thirty men and one stowaway woman (who, as in *Fidelio*, is alone in a distinctly male setting). The final language we hear uttered in the course of the crossing is Spanish – not because they reach their destination but because the engine goes out and the powerless boat is spotted drifting in the Atlantic by Spanish Red Cross rescuers.

Touré's film spends some time on dry land examining each character's reason for attempting the crossing before turning its attention to the perils of navigating the Atlantic in a vessel charged with migrants. The camera occasionally frames the boat in exterior shots that capture its fluid movements across the water, but generally stays within the vessel in order to capture the claustrophobic experience of such a crossing and the various interactions between characters, who clash, form alliances and talk about their aspirations for Europe. The Goor Fitt's crossing does not go as planned. First the motor goes out, then food and water is lost in a storm as the boat begins to drift and passengers start to die. Such unexpected twists and obstacles, so common if generally less perilous in cinematic travels of all stripes, confront these voyagers at various stages, throwing their journey off course figuratively and literally. The captain worries aloud that the current may take them to Brazil, a reference point that triangulates Atlantic cultural vectors that French comes into contact with and recalls an itinerary that was common during the slave trade era.[9] That South American nation is also evoked in *Diego Star* when the marooned sailors muse that they would rather be stuck somewhere warm such as the Caribbean or Brazil. As scholarly explorations of the Atlantic (Gilroy 1993; Marshall 2009) have noted, the ocean is a historical space of triangular connections. In the case of both films mental maps sketched around the Atlantic privilege links, whether positive or negative, between what are otherwise seen as disparate and distant places: Canada, Africa and Brazil.

The epilogue to *La Pirogue* underscores the director's intent that his work testify to the dangers faced by migrants crossing from Africa to Europe. The text written in French announces that the film is dedicated to the estimated 30,000 people who have tried to cross the Atlantic in the years between 2005 and 2010. Although Europeans are clearly the intended audience for this message, Touré's film also questions the desire to leave Africa and considers the ethical dilemmas facing those who undertake the journey. For example, when the Goor Fitt encounters a stranded boat whose passengers are calling desperately for assistance and water, the captain opts to get as far away as possible. Only a handful of travellers choose solidarity, jumping from the boat momentarily to reach their fellow migrants in danger before being pulled back in. Such a desperate gesture underlines the danger inherent in assisting others in this context. To share water might lead to one's own death. The image of the wayward boat haunts the protagonists and no doubt viewers as well, and this is surely a key objective of the film: to provide images that the European public generally does not see except in sensationalised media accounts.

The final film, *Harragas* (an Arabic term that underscores the desperation of 'clandestine migrants'), is by Merzak Allouache. The director's career and filmography are marked by constant crossings between France and Algeria, both within filmic narratives (as in *Salut cousin*, 1996, France/Algeria/Belgium/Luxembourg) and between different film projects set in one country. The plot follows a group of friends from the port city of Mostaganem who endeavour to reach Spain in a boat piloted by another old seaman ominously dubbed Hassan *mal de mer* (Okacha Touita). With this itinerary *Harragas* contributes to a remapping of the relationship between the Maghreb and France. The destination reflects both the proximity of the Iberian Peninsula to western Algeria and the recent tendency identified by Hakim Abderrezak (2016) for migrants from the region to favour other destinations over the land of their former colonial rulers. As in *La Pirogue*, various problems arise, leading the tiny boat to drift off course, at one point – to the evident dismay of the passengers – towards France (Abderrezak 2016: 164–5). Getting lost is a ubiquitous trope of road cinema and this incidence of disorientation is clearly symbolic. The currents that blow the dinghy off course in a sort of postcolonial autopilot suggest that the old maps of the relationship between Algeria and France still loom large. The lineage of road cinema is also evident visually in *Harragas*. The crossing is filmed with a variety of shots that capture the beauty of the Mediterranean seascape (an extreme long shot of the boat set against a sunrise) and that zoom in on the crowded, tense reality of life on a small boat (medium close-ups that frame unsteady passengers against the backdrop of waves).

In interviews Allouache recounts that he wanted to make this film in Algerian Arabic but funding from the French CNC (Centre national du cinéma et de l'image animée) came with the stipulation that a certain amount of dialogue be in French. In the narrative, language is among other things a question of class and marks distinctions between Algerians from intellectual and working-class backgrounds. The main protagonists speak French whereas the men who ventured 700 kilometres from southern Algeria to make the crossing do not. This stark and important distinction is emphasised when the friends discuss in French the ethics of abandoning the men (who cannot swim) on the dinghy as the latter sit just steps from them. As in *La Pirogue*, the venture to Fortress Europe becomes a case of survival of the fittest, and one of the young companions points out incredulously that the men have set off despite lacking both linguistic and natation skills. Dialogue in French is also incorporated as a symbol of the trio of friends' high hopes for their future in Europe and in general to discuss the voyage ('Je veux partir' – 'I want to leave' – is the first phrase uttered in that language). The impending crossing is discussed in French on various occasions and once they arrive on dry land after fleeing the wallowing dinghy, one of them, Rachid (Nabil Asli), converses in the same language on the phone with an awaiting relative. Thus while French language is a demarcation line between Algerians of different classes, it also represents a link between the protagonists and a wider personal and cultural web of connections.

What transpires on the beach where Rachid lands illustrates how, in the context of migration to Europe, the sea represents the policing of otherness. Being caught at sea or coming out of the water is an evident sign of non-belonging, marking the Mediterranean shore in current political logic as a boundary rather than a space of interconnection and interaction. Once on land Rachid rushes to change, trading his wet crossing outfit for dry, formal clothes in hopes of blending in. The outward importance of clothing as a potential visual cue that demarcates a border between perceived insider and purported outsider is a recurring theme in 'immigration cinema' (Ballesteros 2015: 195). Rachid, however, is still spotted by border guards surveilling the water and beach from a bluff and will ultimately be deported. This scene recalls the opening of Allouache's *Salut cousin*, in which a camera situated on the floor of a train station captures our introduction to the two main characters: one born in France to Algerian parents and the other visiting him there from Algeria. The visitor, Alilo (Gad Elmaleh), is clearly distinguished from his 'city cousin' Mok (Messaoud Hattau) by his worn and unfashionable shoes that mark him as a traveller and outsider. In *Harragas*, Rachid is also planning to be hosted by a cousin in France (in the Mediterranean port of Sète), and the parallel between the two storylines might draw our attention to a dramatic change in the way that the border (physical and juridical) between France and Algeria is conceived and policed. Today Algerians cannot readily make it as far as Alilo, who alighted legally by ferry to Marseille. Instead they come into contact with the fortified outer borders of Europe, which, as *La Pirogue* shows us, may not even be geographically connected to traditional conceptions of Europe at all.

Spanish language again signals controlling political frontiers that divide spaces with shared cultural connections as elaborated in cultural terms by Pitiot or Halle. However, as Abderrezak suggests, the way that Spanish vocabulary is used by the migrants might fit better into such inclusive notions of Mediterranean space. By co-opting the term *bote* (a 'dinghy', which describes a small vessel that would seem hardly suitable for a sea crossing), the voyagers subversively appropriate a word from another language in order to better describe a phenomenon that is still not openly discussed in Algerian society (Abderrezak 2016: 164–5). More broadly such linguistic borrowing suggests that the Mediterranean is a space of cultural contact and exchange. Further encounters are engendered at the detention centre. There, as Rachid's voice-over contends 'we were all mixed, Senegalese, Malians, Moroccans'. This use of the first person plural is highly symbolic in the context of our topic: the first-person plural refers both to detainees from the Global South and also to denizens of non-European French-speaking nations. This unity, albeit based on shared exclusion, does point to the possibility of an opening to a wider world founded on shared language as much as shared migrant experience.

Conclusion: Floating Films and Cinéma-monde's Webs of Production Connections

I will close by shifting the discussion from the narratives to the production contexts of the floating films considered above, each of which involves a web of connections that must be taken into account in any conception of cinéma-monde. The production of *Harragas* involved exchanges and confrontations similar, if decidedly more positive, to those engendered in the detention facility described in Rachid's voice-over. It was inspired by life in Algeria, funded by French sources, and filmed on both shores with a group of Algerian actors. Many of the actors (primarily amateurs) had difficulty obtaining the requisite visas to travel to France for filming. Perhaps appropriately, given Allouache's outlook and stated contempt for the very principle of visas and the barriers they represent, the landing in 'Spain' was in fact filmed in Algeria. The topographical similarity between the two places on the shores of the Mediterranean is but one example of the arbitrary nature of borders. All of the films I have mentioned are the products of countless crossings and there are many other similar production issues and examples of actors and directors with complex trajectories. *La Pirogue* involved collaboration between Senegalese director Touré and French producer and screenwriter Éric Névé. The other examples of cinematic cooperation considered here chart less typical postcolonial courses and probe 'relationships among different margins', to borrow Lionnet and Shih's formulation. Key examples are the Greek-born Ariane Labed, who plays Alice in *Fidelio*, or the filming of that production on a ship as it crossed between Tunis and Marseille. Belgian film editor Marie-Hélène Dozo, who is known for her work with the Belgian Dardenne brothers and the Chadian Mahamat-Saleh Haroun, contributed to *Diego Star*. Issaka Sawadogo, who was born in Burkino Faso and is one of the stars of the latter film, provides another Belgian connection via his role as a migrant in *L'Envahisseur/The Invader* (Nicolas Provost, 2011, Belgium) and brings us back to the Baltic through his professional base in Norway. *Fidelio* also features an actor from that country, Anders Danielsen Lie, who had primarily worked in Norwegian productions before taking on the role as Alice's boyfriend. Not an evident space within the context of the francophone world – as would be the Caribbean, the Atlantic or the Mediterranean, Pacific, or Indian – the Baltic nevertheless demonstrates the broad parameters of cinéma-monde. France and French culture has long been enriched by migrants, notably Polish, from nations bordering the Baltic. Now, these films suggest both through their narratives and their web of productive connections, that the French language is destined to interact with and exist in relationship to any and all of the spaces within or bordering Europe. While such transnational links are certainly not unique to floating films, these productions are quite naturally suited to engage with connections fostered in the making of films within the cinematic narratives.

In assembling this cinematic corpus, I argued that floating films, in their actual itineraries, narratives and production, reflect what cinéma-monde might look like. I could go further and say that 'floating' is also a particularly apt metaphor for cinéma-monde and the cinematic map of the world that such a concept might sketch out. In symbolic terms, cinéma-monde encompasses floating between languages (actors in the same and different films; countries; borderlands). It exemplifies boundary lines that are sometimes imperceptible and that change and revert constantly according to economic and other factors. It is also representative of a certain unmoored quality of being adrift and independent of firm attachments, even if the currents that push them along are often at the mercy of invisible outside forces.

In conclusion, I would like to propose some theoretical comparisons and frameworks for assessing floating films within the context of cinéma-monde. In an upbeat reading, Mediterranean music would seem to be a suitable comparison: 'musical phenomena which cross the sea, which have in their DNA a genetic patrimony that united elements of different cultures' (Magrini 1999: 175). We might also draw on theoretical models such as the rhizome, or the aforementioned theories constructed around bodies of water such as Gilroy's *Black Atlantic*. However what Randall Halle theorises as 'interzones' (2014: 4), post-national zones of 'contact and transfer' that involve complex interactions between highways, rivers, erstwhile bridges, border stops, mental maps and visual media (2014: 8–9), seem to most suitably account for the push and pull between politics and cultures, hard and soft borders, policing and sharing stories around the dinner table found in floating films. Floating films might, at times, involve being 'lost at sea' narratively, but they might also help to chart a new course. This is the case not only for cinema with a link to the French language. Also, more broadly, floating films mark out the boundaries of Europe in a fluid fashion, carving out spaces much like Halle's interzones. If the policing of borders indicates that the political parameters of Europe are inflexible, the narrative sharing of stories and the productive telling of them in different languages demonstrate what Halle calls the ideational and mobile element of Europeanness. In all of the floating films considered in previous pages, these stories address to some degree issues of solidarity and inclusion: who has a right to access European space, whether on solid ground or in its floating extensions, and who should be left astray or set adrift.

Among the films examined here, the connective possibilities of cinéma-monde are most thoroughly on display in *Fidelio*. The stories told on that ship engage with all of the various types of travellers found in floating films: a conversation about the uneven pay received by workers from Romania and France, for example, or the crew's experience with undocumented stowaways. Sometimes, they recount, the *Fidelio* would travel weeks with the clandestine migrants on board, unable to find a European port willing to take them in. Also on the boat, on one end of the spectrum, are workers who are essentially economic migrants from outside Europe and, on the other, the French protagonist for whom every voyage mixes career with adventure. These diverse passengers are clearly not on an equal footing, yet they share an 'interzone' space while aboard the ship. The Fidelio becomes a space of necessary translation, likely accommodation, and potential solidarity at sea. If it is a French production officially, *Fidelio* is best described as a heterolingual French-language film. The final language uttered is not French, but the Polish that accompanies the tracking shot that follows Alice and her colleagues through the shipyard of Gdańsk, where they seem happy to listen to yet another of the diverse tongues they encounter on their voyages. *Fidelio* is also the only film I have discussed that is partly set in France, which is home base for Alice. Yet as in cinéma-monde in general, France is hardly central in this filmic itinerary encompassing multiple seas and continents. There is also space within cinéma-monde for less 'positive' (indeed even deadly) journeys, those that stall or drift off course and in the process facilitate otherwise unlikely encounters such as between Fanny and Traoré in *Diego Star* and between Rachid and his fellow detainees in *Harragas*. Through these encounters, floating films reconfigure mental maps of the French-speaking world, forging possibly less restrictive spaces of contact and overlapping than are found on land.[10]

Notes

1. Other floating films that are not addressed here include Jean-Luc Godard's *Film Socialisme* (2010, Switzerland/France) and Manoel de Oliveira's *Um Filme Falado/A Talking Picture* (2003, Portugal/France/Italy), both set on Mediterranean cruises. Numerous other recent films address migrant voyages, although only a small portion of these focus on the water crossing. Examples include *Harraga Blues* (Moussa Hada, 2013, Algeria), *Eden à l'ouest*, and *Mediterranea* (Jonas Carpignano, 2015, Italy/France/Germany/USA/Qatar). *Clandestins* (Denis Chouinard and Nicolas Wadimoff, 1997, Switzerland/Canada/France/Belgium) is a film about migration set in a shipping container on a vessel much like those in *Diego Star* and *Fidelio*.
2. Water can be dangerous to seabound voyagers, but it is often imagined as a symbolic menace to those on dry land as well. Hakim Abderrezak builds on an analysis by Nancy L. Green in his recent study of migrant crossings in film, literature and music to point out that 'words referring to migration that evoke images of water or fluidity can carry negative connotations' (2016: 13). O'Healy notes the similar use of terms such as 'flood' in Italian media (2010: 3).
3. Lojkine's 2014 film *Hope* (France) ends with a crossing from Morocco towards Spain. While the film documents the travails and perils facing migrants en route for Europe, the director argues that films should not portray them solely as victims.
4. Since the Treaty of Rome, Europe has 'identified itself in terms of four freedoms: the free movement of goods, people, services and capital' (Verstraete 2010: 4).
5. In *L'Envahisseur/The Invader* (Nicolas Provost, 2011, Belgium), this confrontation between seaborne migrants and Europeans lounging on the beach takes place *in media res* as the film opens. The subsequent narrative follows the path of Amadou (Isaka Sawadogo, who will be discussed later in the context of *Diego Star*) in Brussels.
6. Cinéma-monde also encompasses films in which the port is an important extension of the water and the commercial and population flows facilitated by the sea. Examples include Aki Kaurismäki's *Le Havre* (2010, Finland/France/Germany; discussed in Chapter 10), Cédric Klapisch's *Ma part du gâteau* (2011, France) and various Marseille-set films by Robert Guédiguian, particularly *Les Neiges du Kilamandjaro* (2011, France; see the introduction to this volume).
7. A 'travelling shot' has been theorised by David Laderman as a tracking shot intended to convey 'a visceral sense of traveling at a hyper-human, modernized speed' (2002: 15). European road movies' taste for slower modes of conveyance such as walking or public transit demand a new and broader conception of Laderman's travelling shot as a tracking shot that captures at any speed the spirit or the disorientation involved in travel (Gott 2016: 11–12).

8. The prevalence of English as a *lingua franca* in Europe is evident in films tracing voyages such as *Welcome* and touristic or personal voyages in Tony Gatlif's *Transylvania* (2006, France) or Fatih Akin's *Im Juli / In July* (2000, Germany).
9. Moussa Sene Absa's documentary *Yoole: Le sacrifice* (2011, Senegal), based on a similar story of Senegalese migrants who died on a drifting boat that was discovered in the Caribbean, is discussed in Chapter 14.
10. I would like to thank Thibaut Schilt and Gemma King for their feedback on this chapter.

Works Cited

Abderrezak, Hakim (2016), *Ex-Centric Migrations: Europe and the Maghreb in Mediterranean Cinema, Literature, and Music*, Bloomington and Indianapolis: Indiana University Press.
Balibar, É. (2009), 'Europe as borderland', *Society and Space*, 27, pp. 190–215.
Ballesteros, Isolina (2015), *Immigration Cinema in the New Europe*, Bristol: Intellect Press.
Bergfelder, T. (2005), 'National, transnational or supranational cinema: Rethinking European film studies', *Media, Culture & Society*, 27, pp. 315–31.
Boer, Inge E. (2006), Uncertain Territories: Boundaries in Cultural Analysis, Amsterdam: Rodopi.
Eder, K. (2006), 'Europe's Borders: The Narrative Construction of the Boundaries of Europe', *European Journal of Social Theory*, 9:2, pp. 255–71.
Galt, Rosalind (2006), *The New European Cinema: Redrawing the Map*, New York: Columbia University Press.
Gilroy, Paul (1993), *The Black Atlantic: Modernity and Double Consciousness*, Cambridge, MA: Harvard University Press.
Gott, Michael and Thibaut Schilt (eds) (2013), *Open Roads, Closed Borders: The Contemporary French-Language Road Movie*, Bristol: Intellect Press.
Gott, M. (2015a), 'After the Wall: Touring the European Border Space in post-1989 French-language Cinema', *Transnational Cinemas*, 6:2, pp. 183–205.
Gott, M. (2015b), 'The Slow Road to Europe: the Politics and Aesthetics of Stalled Mobility in *Heremakono* and *Morgen*', in *Slow Cinema*, T. de Luca and N. Barradas Jorge (eds), Edinburgh: Edinburgh University Press, pp. 299–311.
Gott, Michael (2016), *French Language Road Cinema: Borders, Diasporas, Migration and 'New Europe'*, Edinburgh: Edinburgh University Press.
Halle, Randall (2014), The Europeanization of Cinema: Interzones and Imaginative Communities, Champaign: University of Illinois Press.
Lionnet, Françoise and Shih, Shu-mei (eds) (2005), *Minor Transnationalism*, Durham, NC: Duke University Press.
Magrini, T. (1999), 'Where Does Mediterranean Music Begin?', *Narodna umjetnost: Croatian Journal of Ethnology and Folklore Research*, 36:1, pp. 173–82.

Marshall, Bill (2009*)*, *The French Atlantic: travels in culture and history*, Liverpool: Liverpool University Press, 2009.
Massey, Doreen (1994), *Space, Place, and Gender*, Minneapolis: University of Minnesota Press, 1994.
O'Healy, A. (2010), 'Mediterranean Passages: Abjection and Belonging in Contemporary Italian Cinema', *California Italian Studies*, 1:1, pp. 1–19.
Palstino, G. (2005), 'Open Textures: One Mediterranean Music', in *The Mediterranean in music: critical perspectives, common concerns, cultural differences*, David Cooper and Kevin Dawe (eds), Lanham: Scarecrow Press, pp. 179–93.
Pitiot, Pierre (2009), *Méditerranée, le génie du cinéma*, Montpellier: Indigène.
Rascaroli, L. 2013. 'On the Eve of the Journey: Tangiers, Tblisi, Calais,' in *Open Roads and Closed Borders: The Contemporary French-language Road Movie*, Michael Gott and Thibaut Schilt (eds), Bristol: Intellect Press, pp. 19–38.
Rosello, M. (2009), 'We, the Virtual Francophone Multitudes? Neo-Barbarisms and Micro-Encounters', in *Empire Lost: France and its Other Worlds*, Elizabeth Mudimbe (ed.), Lanham: Lexington Books, pp. 47–67.
Sanaker, John K. (2011), *La rencontre des languages dans le cinéma francophone: Québec, Afrique subsaharienne, France-Maghreb*, Quebec City: Presses de l'Université Laval.
Šukaitytė R. (2014), 'Lithuania Redirected: The New Connections, Businesses and Lifestyles on the National Screen', in M. Gott and T. Herzog (eds), *East, West and Centre: Reframing post-1989 European Cinema*, Edinburgh: Edinburgh University Press, pp. 175–90.
Tarr, C. (2007), 'The Porosity of the Hexagon: Border Crossings in Contemporary French Cinema', *Studies in European Cinema*, 4:1, pp. 7–20.
Thomas, Dominic (2012), *Africa and France: Postcolonial Cultures, Migration, and Racism*, Bloomington: Indiana University Press.
Urry, John (2007), *Mobilities*, Cambridge: Polity Press.
Viard, Jean (2011), *Nouveau portrait de la France : La société des modes de vie*, Paris: Éditions de L'Aube.
Wolton, Dominique (2006), *Demain la francophonie,* Paris: Flammarion.
Verstraete, Ginette (2010), *Tracking Europe: Mobility, Diaspora, and the Politics of Location*. Durham, NC: Duke University Press

CHAPTER 7

The Beautiful Fantasy: Imaginary Representations of Football in West African Cinema

Vlad Dima

It is a well-known fact that football, the beautiful game, is the most popular sport in the world, and Africa is no exception (Alegi 2010: xi), as football 'is without competitor Africa's game' (Goldblatt 2008: 480).[1] The reasons behind the game's immense popularity are multiple and universal: 'ludic properties, simplicity and lack of expense' (Darby 2002: 26). However, there is perhaps another reason that explains the appeal behind the sociocultural phenomenon that is football in Africa: football has evolved from a mere game to represent the embodiment of the neocolonial[2] fantasy. The traditional neocolonial fantasy of finding a better life in Europe or in America is still widespread in the consciousness of the African people, as evidenced by a few cinematic productions in the new century that will be discussed below. Football holds not only an entertaining value, an escape from boredom, but it also points to the possibility of an actual escape, of striking gold on the old continent by becoming a football star in a European club team. Interestingly, cinematic representations of football propose a doubling of this fantasy: the fantasy of football is mediated by the fantasy on screen, the fantasy that is cinema. This double layer of fantasy physically translates into the fetish object of the football jersey: several secondary characters in West African films wear football jerseys. Starting from this observation this chapter will explore the connections between football, fantasy and cinema in films by three contemporary West African directors, Moussa Touré (Senegal), Abderrahmane Sissako (Mali), and Mahamat Saleh Haroun (Chad). The findings should shed light on the sociopolitical importance of football in West Africa (and its connections with Europe) and its contribution to the concept of cinémamonde. The chapter also aims to begin sketching a psychoanalytical model for neocolonial subjectivity (that is, not European-based) as it emerges from the clutches of fantasy.

Fantasy Veils

It stands to reason that fantasy in the African context must follow a separate set of rules from its European counterpart. Several canonical researchers of African cinema – David Murphy, Kenneth Harrow, and Laura Mulvey, for example – have successfully relied on psychoanalysis to frame their explorations of African cinema. Yet, their studies miss an opportunity to go beyond the limits of European psychoanalysis, to attempt the construction of a properly African model of fantasy.

As one must begin with what is already known, I turn toward a European, Slavoj Zizek, who does not specifically reference Africa in his studies on fantasy, but whose work is crucial to my understanding of the term: fantasy is a type of veil, a protective shield that mediates the subject's relationship with the Real (2008a: 43; 276). In *La Pirogue* (Moussa Touré, 2013, Senegal/France/Germany) the main character, Baye Laye (Souleymane Ndiaye), promises his son an original F.C. Barcelona jersey when Baye sets off for Spain. He never makes it to Europe, though, so on his way home he ends up buying a knockoff jersey from the market in order to keep his promise and explains his decision by claiming that the little one would not know the difference. In essence, the father protects his son from disappointment by offering him a fake 'veil'. Encrypted in this simple, fatherly gesture lies an important question about the neocolonial world: what form does the current fantasy of the neocolonial subject take?

In order to begin formulating an answer, one must explore the (fetish) objects that act as protective shields, in the sense that Zizek proposes: the football jersey, other kinds of clothes, and perhaps even skin itself. The skin is fascinating in that it could refer to both the human skin and the 'skin of celluloid', as it were – the film stock – which is in itself a type of fantasy veil that mediates the relationship of the audience with the Real and with Reality. These veils function as both literal and metaphorical shields that protect the Subject from the horrors of the Real; in the neocolonial world, these shields would protect against the spectre of slavery. So fantasy in the neocolonial context features additional layers: the protective 'skin' of the football jersey – that, problematically, is a fake, a replica jersey, not the 'real' one – and the protective 'skin' of film – also 'fake', an illusion. The effectiveness of the protection relies on the Subject investing belief in the powers of the object, of the veil. In other words, the Subject must believe that it is real; which is why the fake Barcelona jersey is so intriguing: the young boy will mistake it for the real one, while the father will know it to be a replica (and thus not an effective veil). The father unknowingly propagates the fantasy of Europe even though he himself had fruitlessly traversed the fantasy. In other words, his fatherly, kind gesture turns out to be misguided.

In his groundbreaking works on African cinema, *Postcolonial African Cinema: From Political Engagement to Postmodernism*, Kenneth Harrow spends considerable time indulging in psychoanalytical readings of African cinema by focusing on the core idea of misrecognition (visual misrecognition in Lacan's mirror stage, and ideological misrecognition in the case of Althusser's interpellation), which to him is the basis for resisting discussions on authenticity in African cinema and, by extension, notions of hierarchy. Stemming from his musings on misrecognition (2007: 117–18), Harrow goes on to challenge the ways in which we understand limits, what is 'inside' and what is 'outside'. Harrow's binary model connects well with the two 'languages' that this essay attempts to overlap, football and cinema, which essentially erase the borders in and around francophone and neocolonial spaces. In other words, one could speak of both *football-monde* and cinéma-monde, both mediated by the notion of fantasy (and, secondarily, by Lacan's theory of subjectivity) as it surfaces in contemporary African cinema.

In his 2012 article, Bill Marshall calls for increased critical attention to develop the concept of 'francophone film'[3] in both French and Film Studies, 'given the remappings necessary both in relation to the global and transnational turn in analysing film and in rearguard attempts to assert French and other cultural nationalisms that also take place' (2012: 51). Furthermore, this is a cinema that 'dramatically focuses attention on four elements: borders, movement, language, and lateral connections' (2012: 42). A similar series of elements is to be found in the theoretical world of football. Franklin Foer explores the social impact of the sport in the mid-1990s and claims that, 'national borders and national identities had been swept into the dustbin of soccer history' (2010: 3). So borders, movement, languages, connections, identities are all elements that characterise, define, and universalise both football and cinema, leading to the concepts of *football-monde* and cinéma-monde. The latter has merit without the former, of course, as globalism has increasingly erased the qualitative and quantitative perceived differences between First, Second and Third Cinemas. However, as arguably the only game that captivates and unites an entire world, football and *football-monde* can at the very least provide us with one of the most important diegetic pillars of the cinéma-monde.

As mentioned above, the football jersey can be categorised as a fetish, and Murphy and Harrow in particular have often dubbed sub-Saharan cinema as fetishistic, reliant on the magic power of objects. In her analysis of *Xala* (*The Curse*, Ousmane Sembène, 1974, Senegal) Laura Mulvey makes an important connection between the operation of the fetish at the levels of the individual and of the community: both invest meaning and value in the fetish beyond the actual meaning and value of that object, and in doing so willingly surrender knowledge to belief. The mysterious powers attached to this fetish-object hinge on that vulnerable secret and, according to Mulvey, the distortion of the truth from the individual can expand to the collective, which creates a collective fantasy (1994: 520). From the children playing in the dusty roads of Abderhamane Sissako's *Bamako* (2006, France/Mali/USA) and *Timbuktu* (2014, Mauritania/France), Mahamat Saleh Haroun's *Abouna/Our Father* (2002, Chad/France/Netherlands), and back to the conversations around the value of the fake jersey in *La Pirogue*, a collective neocolonial consciousness arises. This idea may be exactly what Frantz Fanon means when he observes that the individual, the neocolonial subject, cannot close himself within his own subjectivity (2002: 49). He (or she) must, instead, contribute to the conception of a collective and public subjectivity. But then another problem emerges: how does one maintain a sense of individuality (read, Subjectivity) within the realm of the collective (Fantasy)?

Like fantasy, subjectivity must flourish in different ways from the cases exposed by Freud and Lacan in the neocolonial world. The neocolonial subject, as we understand him or her, has to deal with another level of reality. It is not just that he or she must become a subject and access the symbolic order through the process of difference and absence generated by his or her countrymen, but also through a mediation with the colonised space. The ego ideal sets him or her on an incorrect path, but one that is required by the political milieu of the colonised space. There are, in fact, two adjacent ego ideal paths and two symbolic orders, and the neocolonial subject must deal with both of them simultaneously. Fantasy in the European context emerges from the traumatic events of the twentieth century (the Gulag, the Holocaust, Vietnam) that have not been dealt with appropriately (Zizek 2008a: 43; 2008b: 51). However, an immediate issue in the neocolonial context is that the subjects do not have such horror to be shielded from; instead, they live(d) in the horror, they lived the trauma of slavery. The fantasy model that must be built for neocolonial Africa, a model that will allow the subjects to continue negotiating their subjectivity and deal with the two symbolic orders, must therefore hinge on a 'thicker' veil, a double veil. The fake jersey – essentially a copy of a copy – perhaps offers that dual layer of protection.

So what is 'fantasy'? Freud himself explains the process of fantasy through a well-known scene that progresses from a sadistic component (the child sees that the father is beating a child who represents a rival) to a masochist phase, and on to the final, impersonal form, 'a child is being beaten'. Constance Penley observes that, in the logic of this fantasy, the girl 'identifies, during [the] three stages with the adult doing the beating, the child being beaten, and with herself as a spectator viewing the beating. She can thus be both subject and object, or identify with the entire scene itself' (1989: 48). In contrast, boys experience a variation in terms of who is doing the beating ('I am being beaten by my father' initially progresses to 'I am being beaten by my mother'), but in the end boys also adopt the sadistic position through an identification with the beating adult in the third stage. Freud's description of the beating fantasy and Penley's subsequent observation show that fantasy invokes multiple identifications, especially in the context of the spectator-film relationship, which also implies an immediate fulfillment of those fantasies. In the case of the neocolonial subject one must include the presence of the colonisers in these sequences and it is not beyond reasonable to assume that the sadistic position is missing – there is no agency acquired by the neocolonial subject. Instead, another intermediate step must be added: 'I am being beaten by my coloniser'. Jumping then to the final step of the neocolonial fantasy, and following through on Fanon's advice about how and why one should use violence in the neocolonial world (that is, to cleanse oneself, to rid oneself of the colonial complex), the fantasy should potentially end with the following possibility: 'I am beating the coloniser'. Naturally, the beating in this instance could take on an actual value (i.e. real violence), but it most certainly functions at a less concrete level as well as a metaphorical one: in the world of football this should translate to 'I am beating my coloniser at his own game'.

According to Lacan, the fulfilment of the fantasy has to be postponed: a fantasy is not a satisfiable need, but an unsatisfiable desire. After the Oedipal trauma – the separation from the body of the mother – the human subject has to constantly search for that eternally lost object (this essentially constitutes the futile search for subjectivity). The perfect embodiment of this search is once again Baye Laye, who fails twice: once in his macro-level quest for a better life and a second time in his promise to deliver an authentic jersey. The reason he is such a textbook example is because fantasy is only meant to sustain the desire, but it is never meant to come to fruition, as Lacan indicates: 'The fantasy is the support of desire, it is not the object that is the support of the desire' (1978: 185).[4] That object is the famed *objet petit a*, the unobtainable object of desire, so the only possible outcome of this search is that the 'subject returns from this journey with "empty hands"'(Silverman 1996: 76).

The father clearly returns home empty handed because the fake jersey is essentially nothing (in psychoanalytical terms), and a new generation of neocolonial subjects (represented by his son) will be fooled into believing in the possibility of the football fantasy. But the F.C. Barcelona knockoff jersey still has a material quality to it, naturally – it is a quintessential *objet petit a*: it is 'not what we desire, what we are after, but, rather, that which sets our desire in motion' (Zizek 2008a: 53). Moreover, the *objet petit a* only becomes apparent when looked at 'from aside', with a distorted look of desire. In other words, the *objet petit a* is always, by definition, perceived in a distorted way, because, outside this distortion, '"in itself" it does not exist [. . .] *Objet petit a* is "objectively" nothing, it is nothing at all, nothing of the desire itself which, viewed from a certain perspective, assumes the shape of "something"' (Zizek 1989: 34). The fake jersey means something only when looked at from the distorted (or deceived) perspective of the young boy. Ultimately, by touting the fake jersey as being real, the father unknowingly delays the traversing of the fantasy by his child.

Football in Africa and African cinema

Football is ever present in the streets of the neocolonial city and village, and since its arrival on the continent it has been a significant criterion for gauging the relationship with the colonial powers throughout Africa. The game was originally 'used by a variety of colonial agencies as a mechanism for creating and maintaining socio-cultural conditions that were favourable for continued European economic penetration' (Darby 2002: 22). According to Laurent Dubois, football played a 'significant role in anticolonial struggles throughout Africa [as it] became a forum for protest and resistance against European rule' (2010: 41). However, as the indigenous infrastructure for African football developed, the game also became a focal point for expressions of solidarity and political protest against Europe (Darby 2002: 26).

Moreover, as it expanded its geographical and social reach, instead of buttressing the colonial values, the game took on characteristics unique to Africa as it began to nurture various playing styles and to incorporate indigenous practices such as magicians and healers, or rituals of spectatorship (Alegi 2010: 15). Still according to Alegi, football spread in francophone Africa slower than in the British areas because of a lack of 'sporting culture comparable to that of Britain' (2010: 4). Instead, the francophone territories focused more on the introduction of physical education programs in the schools, which was in line with the Catholic mission of *mens sana in corpore sano* (a healthy mind in a healthy body) (Alegi 2010: 4).

The Catholic influence played a similarly important part in the spreading of the game toward French Equatorial Africa where missionaries used the game 'to advance the Christian message and provide a moral education' (Darby 2002: 12). Regardless of the slowness or swiftness with which the game spread throughout the continent, it is clear that it acted (and still does) as a unifier of sorts, first within the colonised spaces, and second at an international level.

The international, globalised view on football is immediately clear thanks to the simple fact that the jerseys that appear in the African films are never African[5] (at either club or nation levels), but rather European or South American. It is true that South America and Africa share the colonial experience; however, when it comes to the politics of FIFA and the development of organised football worldwide, South America played a much more important part than Africa in the 'cultivation of Third World political solidarity and the development of a strategy aimed at rectifying the unequal economic relationship with the first world' (Darby 2002: 59). The same could perhaps be said about the role played by Latin America in the theoretical birth of Third Cinema since its original manifesto, *Towards a Third Cinema* (1968), was crafted by Argentinian directors Fernando Getino and Octavio Solanas. This fact, corroborated with the African directors' respect for the history of cinema, could then be equally responsible for the preponderance of Latin American jerseys in African cinema.

There is also a simpler explanation for the prevalence of European and Latin American jerseys: generally speaking, the two continents are considered havens of football (that is, where 'quality' football resides). It is fair, though, to question the lack of support for African clubs and nations in African films. Why has not a famous World Cup victory, such as Senegal over France in 2002, reverberated more in terms of fandom and, in psychoanalytical terms, why has the fantasy not changed since the Senegalese in fact traversed the original fantasy – they actually beat the French? Well, the team that beat France was hardly made up of prototypical neocolonial subjects. Incredibly, according to Dubois 'among the 110 players on five African teams who played in the 2002 World Cup, more than three-quarters played outside of Africa, mostly in Europe. The Senegalese team that defeated France during that tournament included nineteen players who played professionally in France' (2010: 43).

Another reason for the lack of an apparent nationalistic pride could be that some of these players are often very critical of Africa and African habits. Arguably the most celebrated African player of the last decade, Ivorian Yaya Touré, who plays for Manchester City, a wealthy English Premier League football club, has recently voiced his displeasure with not winning the award for African player of the year in the following fashion:

> I think this is what brings shame to Africa, because to act in that way is indecent. But what can we do about it? Us Africans, we don't show that Africa is important in our eyes. We favour more what's abroad than our own continent. That is pathetic. As I've been told many times, you can't take care of Africa too much because Africa will be the first to let you down. (ESPN 2016)[6]

While this should be taken with a pinch of salt (that is, it might be more about Touré's competitiveness than a political statement), it is not an uncommon view among Africans.

The clash between the French and the Senegalese also brought forth the Africans' belief in the power of magic. At the time there was an uproar in the media about the unavailability of France's best player, Zinedine Zidane, who had pulled a hamstring, and which the Senegalese newspapers attributed to the work of marabouts. The African belief in and reliance on magic practices has been well documented by Peter Alegi (2010: 26–29), Michael Schatzberg (2006: 356–366), and David Goldblatt (2008: 658–659). Witchcraft, magic and the supernatural provide us with a way to understand the African collective, but football supersedes them. According to Simon Kuper, 'soccer works as a key to the world' (2006: xviii; 1). Furthermore,

> football is a microcosm through which we may more sharply discern those political, cultural, and economic processes and cognitive structures that are actually important as individuals conduct their daily lives. [. . .] whatever occurs within the metaphoric touch lines of the soccerscape – the small, daily politics of football – will probably reflect the same, or quite similar, tectonic fault lines present in the high politics of the wider society. (Schatzberg 2006: 353)

Arguably, cinema has a similar impact on society and thus it seems there is but a small step to connect football and cinema in terms of their relationship with the world.

Historical Highlights of African Cinema

Neocolonial cinema has generally concerned itself with questions of identity, which takes two crucial shapes: first, an identity regarding the neocolonial subject and his or her place within the world; and second, a cinematic identity – what is African cinema? But this chapter sidesteps the reductive issues of authenticity and originality in African cinema (e.g. to what extent is African cinema influenced by mainstream and auteur cinemas?). African film should not be discussed through oppositions, comparisons and categories, or, as Kenneth Harrow has recently proven, in direct opposition to its pioneers (such as Ousmane Sembène's long shadow). The act of seeing and framing African cinema through oppositions almost necessarily diminishes its intrinsic value and orientalises it. African cinema should simply be Cinema. Here is Harrow's take on the matter: 'The very notion of tradition is a concoction of modernism; the attempt to validate African authenticity, or traditional identity, is a reaction to western domination and is betrayed by its dependence on western epistemological tools, western categories of knowledge' (2007: 27).[7] While one can resist the reductive conversations on authenticity and tradition, one may not be able to ignore another relentless western intrusion: the thrust of globalisation. African cinema has indeed moved toward accepting and even embracing globalisation. It has followed, in many ways, the same trajectory as football.

The first film made by an African is historically considered to be a short by Chemam Chikly from Tunisia, entitled, *La fille de Carthage/ The Girl from Carthage*, dating from 1924. There are also records of films made in Egypt in the late 1920s, but it was only in the 1950s and 1960s that filmmaking started to emerge in Africa, concomitant with the spreading of political independence achieved by most African countries. Many consider Paulin Vieyra and Mamadou Sarr's *Afrique-sur-Seine* (1954, France), which was made in collaboration with a collective of sub-Saharan filmmakers, to be the first African film ever made. However, there has always been some reluctance to even consider the film as 'African' since it was funded and produced only by France. So the model for all of African cinema to pursue was eventually set in 1963 by Ousmane Sembène's short, *Borom Sarret*, followed soon after by the first feature-length African film, Sembène's seminal *La Noire de . . .* (*Black Girl*, 1964, Senegal), which is also the first film to draw attention to the mise-en-scène value of clothes. The main character, Diouana (Mbissine Thérèse Diop), flees Dakar in search of a better life and takes a job as a nanny for a French family. Unfortunately, following months of abuse, she takes her own life. Notions of liberty, emancipation, slavery, and colonial/neocolonial space(s) intersect in this film, and they are all represented by Diouana's careful choices of clothing. People wear history and these clothes symbolise the most personal negotiation of the neocolonial subjects with their surroundings (more so than objects that define the neocolonial space in an obvious manner, like colonial-era buildings). According to Jean Allman, '[f]ashion is [. . .] about status, mobility, and rapid change in a Western, capitalist world' (2004: 2). In other words, '[c]lothing matters and dress is political. [. . .] everyday garments and high fashion, casual clothes and uniforms, voluminous robes and miniskirts, and a host of other styles may be terrains of power' (Martin 2004: 227). The struggle of and for power that has long defined colonial and neocolonial spaces may be embodied, at a much smaller and precise scale, in the choice of clothing that we witness in African cinematic productions.

The cinematic tradition launched by Sembène would continue and develop throughout the next five decades. Clothes, shoes, and headwear generate meaning that resides outside of the main diegesis in order to signal, quite forcefully, that the neocolonial subject decides the type of relationship he or she has with colonial powers. In the case of Diouana, for example, her stripped black and white dress points to the inevitable imprisonment she faces when in France. Furthermore, Diouana initially refuses to take off her fancy dress when working around Madame's apartment. The dress symbolises the elevated status she aspires to, but in the end she is defeated. In the case of football and representations of football in the examples that will follow, the football jerseys we see in the streets of Dakar, Bamako or N'Djamena point to an undeniable fact: imperialism has found a new, more obscure and dangerous shape, as it offers false hope. Darby goes a step further to claim that the way European scouts bring African players (who cannot understand the inner workings of their contracts) to the European top leagues represents a 'modern form of slavery' (2002: 215).[8] This form of slavery takes on a fascinating form in Moussa Touré's film *La Pirogue*.

Moussa Touré's (Football) Fantasy

Touré follows in the footsteps of Sembène for whom he worked as an electrician (Diawara 2010: 316). Like Sembène, Touré seems generally less interested in form and much more in content. His films, beginning with *Toubab Bi* (1991, Senegal/France), which follows two young men's voyage to Europe, explore the social relations between France and its old colony. Space is a key theme and it is always represented as diminished, physically shrinking around the neocolonial subjects who find themselves in metaphorical prisons. For example, in *TGV* (1997, Senegal/France), the filmmaker tracks those relations in the limiting space of a bus, in which he places a heterogeneous group of people. The same logic and theme apply to *La Pirogue*, in which the microcosm of society moves from a bus to a boat.

La Pirogue follows a multinational (Senegalese, Ivorian, and Guinean) group of men (and one woman) who attempt to reach the Spanish Canary

Islands in a large pirogue. Escaping West Africa and the search for the elusive Eldorado are desires still alive and relevant more than fifty years after achieving independence in those countries. In several short episodes Touré gradually reveals the destinations of the passengers (Spain, Paris, Brittany etc.) and their dreams. Most look for money for their families, but there are also specific goals: one man wants a leg replacement, another may attempt to play professional football, and Baye Laye's brother Abou (Malaminé Dramé) hopes to be a musician. Abou refers to Spain as 'Paradise'; another character, Lansana (Laïty Fall) tells the audience in voice-over about searching for 'the money of dreams, the money of happiness'. Both Abou and Lansana essentially underline the idea that the Western world is a sort of fantasy construct, an Eldorado.

Naturally, the quest fails, and the Spanish border police send the two main characters home. Their return to the family, to core values, hints subtly at a positive outlook. But it is just that, a hint. When all is said and done what remains is the little boy's desire – he wanted a Barcelona jersey – so even future generations will have to negotiate their subjectivity through this obstinate European fantasy. Not much seems to have changed since colonial days: it is worth remarking that the pirogue is a vessel that is all too similar metaphorically to the boats that carried slaves to the Caribbean. Many people who attempt to cross over to Europe do not make it alive in the tumultuous waters of the Atlantic, just as they did not in the colonial period. Moreover, this boat harbours the passengers in its hold, its belly, which is the metaphorical place of birth for (contemporary) slaves and manufactured subjectivities – subjectivities that are imposed onto the subject forcefully, just as they were during colonial times. Therefore, the new form of slavery removes the physical presence of the colonisers with the mirage of fantasy and the neocolonial subjects enslave themselves as they seek to reach the shores of Spain.

As already mentioned, while the two brothers walk back home, Baye Laye stops to buy his son a knockoff F.C. Barcelona jersey. The choice of this jersey over any other Spanish or European club is relevant. Barça, as it is affectionately called around the world, is known for a free-flowing style of football, attacking football,[9] and researchers of the game have long attempted to create a link between style of play and personality, whether individual or collective. Renowned Uruguayan journalist Eduardo Galeano appears to believe strongly in this link: 'Tell me how you play and I will tell you who you are' (quoted in Goldblatt 2008: vii). Interestingly, the question of style echoes the question that has long been (wrongfully) asked of African cinema aesthetics – where does it fit? Consider the words of the great Malian player Salif Keita (not to be confused with the eponymous musician who features on the soundtrack of Sissako's *La Vie sur terre/Life on Earth*, 1998, Mali/Mauritania/France), as quoted by Peter Alegi:

> For me, playing for fun, being together joined by the same love for the ball, for the full well-being of body and mind, was amply sufficient to make me happy. [. . .] Also the pleasure of juggling the ball and letting my instincts take the lead. Because in Mali especially, all over Africa actually, technical moves are spontaneous, improvised, not learned through regular training as it is the case in Europe. I must say that at the time I was madly keen on dribbling. Juggling, dribbling, faking, a successful nutmeg [putting the ball through the opponent's legs], there is nothing more natural for the African soccer player! (2010: 33)

The ludic quality of the game clearly stands out as a defining trait. Yet, in this declaration one can hear the echoes of several African filmmakers to whom cinema is about instincts, spontaneity, and ultimately, about happiness. The Barça jersey encompasses all these emotions, and most of all, it embodies the continuing, unrelenting neocolonial fantasy.

Football in the Cinema of Abderrahmane Sissako

Abderrahmane Sissako's films usually deal with questions of identity and exile. *La Vie sur terre* is about returning home, and *Heremakono/Waiting for Happiness* (2002, France/Mauritania) is about a young man saying goodbye to his mother on his way to Europe. *Bamako* shifts the question of identity to a larger scale, from the individual to the collective, as the World Bank is put on trial in a courtyard in Bamako. It is a fictitious trial, of course, a projection and wishful thinking, which are matched cinematically by the usual role played by cinema – both the trial and the film itself tell fabricated stories. While the trial specifies the World Bank as its target, it really signals a more general attack on the Western infrastructure under which one could file the world hierarchy of football, too.

Indeed, there are a few moments in *Bamako* that showcase the everyday presence of football. First, a ball goes up and is seen through one of the character's window without any visible players in the frame. Second, a very young boy tries to kick a ball with a toddler, who does not seem to catch on very quickly. Finally, two jerseys appear: a boy who wears a number 18, red shirt of 'Batistuta', an Argentinian player (although this jersey is from his days with Italian club AS Roma) and a man who wears the yellow number 10 Brazilian[10] national team jersey of 'Kaká'. These visual interventions feel like interruptions from the seriousness of the trial, and they are hard to miss. Their diegetic role is to subtly suggest the reach of globalisation outside of the trial, which is already dealing with Africa's economical position in the world. Moreover, considering that Sissako's four feature-length films constitute an ersatz narrative continuum, I believe that these inclusions are an efficient way to prepare the familiar Sissako spectator for the next cinematic effort in which football takes centre stage.

In *Timbuktu* football similarly provides the characters and the audience with a reprieve from extremely difficult issues. The mixing of commentary on terrorist organisations and football is interesting because there is a violence that surrounds the game, although it is usually an exterior one, a violence that has to do with the fans, with hooligan clashes, heated rivalries etc.[11] Amid the chaotic, violent world of extremism, on one level football functions as a connecting element and on another as a respite (cinematically at least) from the horrors of extremism. There are two key moments in the film that illustrate the significance of football. The first instance is a discussion between two young extremists holding their Kalashnikovs and an elder man, sitting in front of them. The conversation is centred on a comparison between Zinedine Zidane and Lionel Messi. The former is arguably the most famous French player ever, but in this context the men refer to his last club, Real Madrid; the latter is an Argentinian-born player at F.C. Barcelona and is arguably the best football player ever. Real Madrid and F.C. Barcelona have one of the most heated rivalries in the history of the sport and their meetings are pompously dubbed as 'El Clasico'. The older man contends that Zidane has not accomplished as much as Messi (this is not true in terms of team accolades, but certainly true in terms of individual awards and goals scored) and then goes on to critique France's World Cup win by essentially saying that France bought off Brazil by sending them a 'ship loaded with rice, because they [the Brazilians] are poor', and so they allowed France to score three goals on them in the final. The youngsters are in disagreement, arguing that the French team is the only team to 'have beaten everyone'. It is also clear from their reactions that they want nothing to do with a comparison between Real and Barça – it is the latter that they support unconditionally. This seems to be a universal feeling. In spite of their immense following, Real have often been compared to the New York Yankees (that is, they spend ridiculous amounts of money on buying their 'galacticos', as opposed to the Catalan club that grows its own players at their academy – Messi himself has been with the club since his early teens), and therefore have generally attracted more contempt worldwide.

The fascination with Barça, with their players, their playing style, their history (in its search for independence the Catalan region has long been a thorn of sorts in the side of the Spanish government)[12] cannot be missed in Sissako's film when 'Messi' actually makes an appearance in the second important episode connected to football. The terrorist group had banned all forms of entertainment and they had even confiscated the actual playing ball. The youngsters of Timbuktu, though, proceed to play without it! It is a beautiful sequence – a fantasy enacted – scored with symphonic music produced by the soothing violins of the Prague Philharmonic Orchestra (music is globalised, too); in fact, there are no diegetic noises from the kids, the only sound that is heard is the non-diegetic music. This directorial choice removes the visual further from reality – there are no natural sounds – and therefore underlines the phantasmagorical quality of the moment.

The scene begins with a long shot from behind the goal, with a player preparing to kick the invisible ball from the penalty spot. As everyone stands around waiting, a donkey comes into the frame from the left and literally traverses the fantasy. He interrupts the action – a fantasy interruptus, as it were. It is a light-hearted moment that points to the usual daily interruptions that can occur, but also, symbolically, this is thought to be a very stubborn animal. The suggestion here is, perhaps, that art (music) and sport (football) will persevere in the face of oppression. The children run back and forth, with no ball, and the camera tracks them left and right. They all wear colourful T-shirts that stand out in the Sahelian sand, but a few shots into the scene, 'Messi' becomes more visible. The fake Barça jersey is worn by a smaller child, which is rather consistent with reality: Messi himself is an athlete of smaller stature, nicknamed 'the Flea'. Naturally, Messi scores the invisible ball and everyone celebrates. The fake Messi[13] runs away from the goal holding his palms up to make a heart sign.[14] Others run around also celebrating as if they had scored the goal themselves and they mimic the celebrations of other athletes. In this moment, the children and the biggest stars of the world of football coalesce – the *football-monde* is complete.

Mahamat Saleh Haroun's Cinema as Fantasy

In Haroun's first full-length film, *Bye Bye Africa* (1999, France/Chad), a fictional version of the director returns to his native Chad (just as Sissako does in *La Vie sur terre*) to pay respects to his dead mother. The death of the mother functions as a metaphor for the state of cinema, and at the conclusion of the film the director departs for France but not before leaving his camera to a young boy, a passing of the torch as it were: there is hope for the cinema of Chad. Haroun's cinematic effort from 2002, *Abouna*, also features a missing parent,[15] as the two main characters, two boys,

Tamir (Ahidjo Mahamat Moussa) and Amine (Hamza Moctar Aguid), are abandoned by their father and begin to misbehave. They are eventually sent to Koranic school in the countryside by the exasperated mother, where the young one tragically dies, and the older one falls in love with a deaf girl.

There is only one football jersey in this film, worn by a young boy in the city who belongs to Tamir's clique. The blue and black shirt hails from Italian powerhouse Internazionale Milano, colloquially known as 'Inter', a club whose motto reads 'Brothers of the World'. The presence of this particular jersey then suggests brotherhood (the friendship between the boys), as football continues to bridge the gaps between different parts of the world. Beside the Inter jersey, *Abouna* also features football scenes in the countryside that are reminiscent of the end scenes in François Truffaut's *Les 400 coups/The 400 Blows* (1959, France) during which young rascal Antoine uses the distraction provided by a friendly football game to escape. Just as in the French film, Tamir will eventually escape, too. As is obvious from the title – 'our father' – the paternal figure is crucial, and his importance is actually emphasised through lack, through the fact that he is never seen in the film. Metaphorically, the lack of a father represents the sudden disappearance of France as a colonial presence.[16] Tom Conley offers an interesting interpretation concerning a key scene from the aforementioned *400 coups*. When Antoine is in front of the class, a globe is carefully placed next to him in such a manner that the continent of Africa is visible. According to Conley, Antoine's lack of a natural father, combined with Truffaut's own missing father (the film is semi-autobiographical), might translate into a 'missing father' metaphor of the colonial relationship between Africa and France (2007: 149–50). Not only is the father from *Abouna* missing, but he is supposed to referee a football game between the children who play in the street. The metaphor of the colonial missing father is thus extended: when the authority figure is missing, nobody plays anymore. Moreover, the surprising death of Amine (given the mostly lighthearted tone of the film) may also be a troubling continuation of the father metaphor: might the neocolonial independent state head toward death without the help and presence of the colonial father?

The film's phantasmagorical value, though, rests more on the brothers' confusing relationship with cinema, than on the football scenes. During a projection they confuse the character on screen with their real father, as screen and reality mesh to generate confusion, which extends to the audience since we cannot know for sure whether or not the father had disappeared to become an actor. The audience is also able to observe a few eclectic posters around the theatre: *Yaaba/Grandmother* (Idrissa

Ouedraogo, 1989, Burkina Faso/Switzerland/France), *The Kid* (Charlie Chaplin, 1921, USA) and *Stranger Than Paradise* (Jim Jarmusch, 1984, USA). The three posters construct an extra-filmic semiotic world, but that, too, is a world of fantasy, of imagination. As if to fortify the importance of the poster and the reality of a fantasy world, toward the end of the film the missing father sends his children a poster of the ocean – another metaphor for escape. As the children look at the poster on the wall, the film dissolves through the magic of cinema from a shot of the poster into a shot of the 'actual' ocean. However, just as the fake jersey represents a double veil of protection, this second shot of the ocean does not offer us the real ocean, as it remains mediated by the camera, by mimesis – it is but a representation of the ocean. The protective 'skin' of the fake jersey is replaced here by the protective skin of the film itself, of the film stock, which is represented diegetically by the poster. A poster is essentially a still shot, one of the twenty-four frames that generate the impression of movement. So film is stripped to its very core, a singular unit – one frame – which protects the boys from the reality of being trapped in the countryside and teaches them how to desire, as Lacan and Zizek would put it. In other words, like the jersey, the poster is another perfect example of an *objet petit a*.

At another key moment in the film, unsure of whether or not they had seen their real father, the two brothers steal a film wheel, which they roll down the street as children usually do with tyres. The *déroulement/* unrolling of the film wheel (and later, of the film roll itself as the children search through the frames), as well as that of the very film we are watching, is therefore doubled in this scene and points to the fact that cinema is a playground. Like the ball children kick around, the film roll can also supply endless amounts of fun, as a literal wheel, but also during its regular unrolling on the projector. The film also provides the audience with a clear understanding of Tamir's fantasy, which materialises toward the end when he sees himself playing football with his little brother on the beach. It is the same beach toward which the camera had penetrated through the poster of the sea. The fantasy shot is filmed silently and could point to Tamir's new perspective on life (his new girlfriend is mute), but more likely, just as it was the case with Sissako's football fantasy scored with symphonic music, the silence underlines the lack of reality, of diegetic sounds, and further engages the audience in the cinematic world of fantasy.

Conclusion

The game of football is so irresistibly appealing that even the stoic founders of the Negritude movement, Césaire, Damas and Senghor, started a team, suggestively named 'The Good Hope' (Dubois 2010: 52). As the optimistic name implies, football is a game meant to bring people together, but it is also a game that gives way to unthinkable clashes of violence (rivalries and hooligans) and racism (still rampant across Europe, with several recent cases of abuse from the stands in Spain and Eastern Europe). Africa's fascination with the game is matched elsewhere in the world – this is truly the one sport popular worldwide, a veritable *football-monde*. Cinema, a universal phenomenon in its own right, portrays football within its diegetic borders, but it also helps point to the game's incredible phantasmagorical quality. In doing so, African cinema universalises a common fantasy in the neocolonial world. In a typical psychoanalytical reversal, it is also thanks to the presence of football within its diegetic borders that cinema boosts its own phantasmagorical quality and further reaches for universality itself. In fact, interestingly, if one were to consider the varied countries, African and European, involved in the production of the films discussed above, one would have to conclude that the goal of universality may have already been reached, allowing African cinema to become, or contribute rather, to a burgeoning, veritable cinéma-monde.

Notes

1. I opt for the British term 'football, as opposed to the American 'soccer', because it is the more common terminology throughout the world. However, if the original quote from a secondary source uses 'soccer', I have kept it unchanged.
2. As opposed to the term 'postcolonial', which may be wrongly applied to contexts from which colonialism has never really disappeared, the term 'neocolonial' seems more appropriate for my current argument. According to Ella Shohat, 'The "neocolonial", like the "postcolonial", also suggests continuities and discontinuities, but its emphasis is on the new modes and forms of the old colonialist practices, not on a "beyond"' (2006: 241).
3. For a discussion on the ambiguity of the term 'francophonie' see the introduction to *Post-colonial Cultures in France* by Alec Hargreaves and Mark McKinney (1997: 3–6, 11–13).
4. Zizek agrees with this assessment: 'A fantasy constitutes our desire, provides its co-ordinates; that is, it literally "teaches us how to desire"' (2008a: 7).
5. Jean-Pierre Bekolo provides us with a glaring counter-example in his mockumentary *Le Président/The President* (2013, Cameroun/Germany). Both the introductory scenes and one of the main characters showcase the national jersey for the Indomitable Lions. Given the revolutionary tenor of the film, the presence of these jerseys enhances the sense of national pride that the director sought to project.

6. Touré has won four straight awards. He lost to Pierre-Emerick Aubameyang from Gabon (and Borussia Dortmund as a club). For more please see the full ESPN article (no assigned author) from 8 January, 2016, <http://www.espnfc.us/african-nations-cup/story/2782452/yaya-toure-says-losing-player-of-year-a-shame-to-africa> (last accessed 7 July 2017).
7. That said, the work previously done by trailblazers such as Manthia Diawara (1992: 141–64) and Teshome Gabriel (1989: 45–52), and their initial categories of African cinema remains important as it represents the necessary beginning of this discussion.
8. In Benoît Mariage's *Les Rayures du zèbre/Scouting for Zebras* (2014, Belgium/France), Belgian scout José Stockman (Benoît Poelvoorde) recruits young Ivorian Yaya Koné (Marc Zinga) to play for Sporting Club of Charleroi. The film reinforces two issues relevant to this essay. First, José attempts to debunk the Eldorado myth by speaking reproachfully of the fact that 'Africans think the streets are paved with money in Europe'. Second, José's scout friend refers to Yaya as 'perle noire' (black pearl). This is a pejorative qualifier that points to the monetary value of the athlete or, in other words, to the modern slave.
9. In part developed by manager Pep Guardiola, the 'tiki-taka' style – moving the ball constantly with short, fast passes – made Barça into one of the most successful clubs ever and defined the first decade of the new century.
10. In the aforementioned *Les Rayures du zèbre* when José first meets Yaya Koné, the latter wears a practice T-shirt of the Brazil national team.
11. For more on violence in the sport, see Foer 2010: 13–15; 35–40.
12. Simon Kuper discovers that Barça is a big enough symbol for the Catalans that it supersedes the need for sovereign state (2006: 110).
13. There is a thin line between the boy pretending to be Messi (by copying his moves) and the boy imagining what it is like to be Messi. So he could easily be 'fantasy Messi'.
14. This is a gesture used in the celebration of many football stars, but it was first popularised by Welsh and Real Madrid player, Gareth Bale.
15. Family is not the director's sole thematic concern. He also uses the Civil War in Chad as a backdrop to both *Daratt/Dry Season* (2006, Chad/France/Belgium/Austria) and *Un homme qui crie/A Screaming Man* (2010, Chad/France/Belgium). Completely unique and somewhat of a thematic departure, his latest, *Grigris* (2013, Chad/France) is a tale about a man with a paralysed leg who wants to be a dancer.
16. Problematically, white man José of *Les Rayures du zèbre*, calls himself Yaya's father.

Works Cited

Alegi, Peter (2010), *African Soccerscapes: How a Continent Changed the World's Game*, Athens: Ohio University Press.

Allman, Jean (2004), 'Fashioning Africa: Power and the Politics of Dress', *Fashioning Africa*, Jean Allman (ed.), Bloomington: Indiana University Press, pp. 1–9.
Conley, Tom (2007), *Cartographic Cinema*, Minneapolis: University of Minnesota Press.
Darby, Paul (2002), *Africa, Football and FIFA: Politics, Colonialism and Resistance*, London: Frank Cass Books.
Diawara, Manthia (1992), *African Cinema. Politics & Culture*, Bloomington and Indianapolis: Indiana University Press.
Dubois, Laurent (2010), *Soccer Empire: The World Cup and the Future of France*, Berkeley: University of California Press.
ESPN (2016), 'Yaya Toure says his losing player of the year "brings shame to Africa,"' first accessed January 8th, 2016, <http://www.espnfc.us/african-nations-cup/story/2782452/yaya-toure-says-losing-player-of-year-a-shame-to-africa> (last accessed 7 July 2017).
Fanon, Franz (2002), *Les damnés de la terre*, Paris: La Découverte/Poche.
Foer, Franklin (2010), *How Soccer Explains the World: An Unlikely Theory of Globalization*, New York: Harper.
Freud, Sigmund (1952), *The Major Works*, London: Encyclopedia Britannica, William Benton Publisher.
Gabriel, Teshome (1989), 'Towards a critical theory of Third World Films', *Questions of Third Cinema*, Jim Pines and Paul Willemen (eds), London: British Film Institute, pp. 30–52.
Goldblatt, David (2008), *The Ball Is Round. A Global History of Soccer*, New York: Riverhead Books.
Hargreaves, Alec and M. McKinney (eds) (1997), *Post-colonial Cultures in France*, London: Routledge.
Harrow, Kenneth (2007), *Postcolonial African Cinema: From Political Engagement to Postmodernism*, Bloomington: University of Indiana Press.
Kuper, Simon (2006), *Soccer Against the Enemy: How the World's Most Popular Sport Starts and Fuels Revolutions and Keeps Dictators in Power*, New York: Nation Books.
Lacan, Jacques (1978), *The Seminar of Jacques Lacan, Book XI: Four Fundamental Concepts of Psycho-Analysis*, trans. Alan Sheridan, New York: Norton.
Marshall, Bill (2012), 'Cinéma-monde? Towards a concept of Francophone cinema', *Francospheres*, 1:1, pp. 35–51.
Martin, M. Phyllis (2004), 'Afterword', *Fashioning Africa*, Jean Allman (ed.), Bloomington: Indiana University Press, pp. 227–31.
Mulvey, Laura (1994), '*Xala*, Ousmane Sembene: the Carapace that Failed', *Colonial Discourse and Post-Colonial Theory: A Reader*, Patrick Williams and Laura Chrisman (eds), New York: Columbia University Press, pp. 517–34.
Murphy, David (2001), *Sembene: Imagining Alternatives in Film & Fiction*, Trenton: Africa World Press.

Penley, Constance (1989), *The Future of an Illusion,* Minneapolis: University of Minnesota Press.

Schatzberg, Michael (2006), 'Soccer, Science, and Sorcery: Causation and African Football', *Africa Spectrum*, 41:3, pp. 351–69.

Shohat, Ella (2006), *Taboo Memories, Diasporic Voices.* Durham, NC: Duke University Press.

Silverman, Kaja (1996), *The Threshold of the Visible World*, New York: Routledge.

Žižek, Slavoj (1989), 'Looking Awry', *October*, 50, pp. 30–55.

Žižek, Slavoj (2008a), *The Plague of Fantasies*, London: Verso.

Žižek, Slavoj (2008b), *The Sublime Object of Ideology*, London: Verso.

CHAPTER 8

Merry Christmas in No Man's Land: European Borders, Language Barriers and Front Lines in Christian Carion's *Joyeux Noël*

Gemma King

A geographic and symbolic space characterised by borders and barriers, Europe is the site of plural cultural identities and complex multilingual interactions. Through massive events like the First and Second World Wars, the establishment of the European Union and the tense border negotiations surrounding the contemporary refugee and migrant crisis, the porosity of the European continent, the placement of its borders and the significance of its shared cultural space have evolved dramatically over the past century. Despite being a mostly unbroken land mass, continental Europe is dissected by a series of lines that have ranged from borders on a map to trenches in the ground. What constitutes the European continent, who belongs within it and who should possess the mobility to travel across it are questions that have cropped up throughout the twentieth and early twenty-first centuries. Such questions have been most intensely scrutinised during wartime, and are frequently broached in cinema.

Around the centenary of World War I, a number of French films have appeared which offer new frameworks for investigating the concept of Europe. These films investigate the front lines, national borders and language barriers that carved up the continent during the Great War, evoking Mireille Rosello's notion of 'mosaic Europe' (2012: 15). Films such as Jean-Pierre Jeunet's *Un long dimanche de fiançailles/A Very Long Engagement* (2004, France/USA) examine the brutality and tragedy of trench warfare. In Jeunet's film, warring armies fight to redraw the dividing lines between territories, and to wrest land from enemy groups. In such a context, the space between these lines, commonly known as no man's land, is an ontological void. No man's land is less identifiable as national territory and more suited to Marc Augé's concept of the *non-lieu*, or non-place. According to Augé, 'if a place can be defined as relational, historical and concerned with identity, then a space which cannot be defined as relational, or historical, or concerned with identity will be a non-place' (1995: 77–8). The result is a space that cannot be inhabited and is characterised by a certain emptiness. In most films about trench warfare, no man's land is inherently devoid of identity and closed to constructive interaction between groups.

Yet in one 2005 film, Christian Carion's quadrilingual *Joyeux Noël/ Merry Christmas* (France/Germany/UK/Belgium/Romania/Norway/ Japan), this *non-lieu* and its hostile borders are radically redefined. Based on the true story of the 1914 Christmas truce, the film recasts the *non-lieu* in an optimistic light: home to no one, no man's land becomes a common ground for transnational interaction. On this new terrain, language appears as what Chris Wahl calls 'a common ground and a strange world' (2005: 3), and offers a neutral playing field for multicultural communication. In this way, *Joyeux Noël* proposes pacifist frameworks for understanding the European space and for treating its visitors and inhabitants. Critical of cultural separatism, the film sees border crossing and transgression as central to a constructive European experience, and investigates 'the play of external borders and internal boundaries' (Marshall 2012: 50). Such a conception of the European space provides a useful means of understanding cinéma-monde, both in terms of the film's transnational production and its border crossing, multilingual narrative.

The Great War in French Cinema

Given its lingering impact on the French cultural consciousness, it is perhaps unsurprising that World War II is the most frequently depicted war on French screens. Over the past few years, numerous films have explored little-known events in France between 1939 and 1945. Rachid Bouchareb's 2006 *Indigènes/Days of Glory* (France/Algeria/Morocco/ Belgium) explores the plight of Algerian soldiers enlisted to fight for France in World War II. *Diplomatie/Diplomacy* (Volker Schlöndorff, 2014, France/Germany) relates how the Swedish consul-general to Paris, Raoul Nordling (André Dussollier) skilfully convinced the Nazi military general, Dietrich von Choltitz (Niels Arestrup) to disobey orders to destroy Paris in 1944. The Resistance has long been a point of French cultural fascination, yet French complicity in the Occupation has also been the focus of a number of recent films. In particular, 2010's *La Rafle/The Round Up* (Rose Bosch, France/Germany/Hungary) and *Elle s'appelait Sarah/Sarah's Key* (Gilles Paquet-Brenner, France), detail the events of the 1942 Vel d'Hiver roundup. Named after the 15th-arrondissement velodrome which was used as a temporary internment camp, the Rafle du Vel d'Hiv, whereby French police agreed to the roundup of foreign-born Paris Jews in return for the protection of French-born ones, was long neglected in historical and public discourse before the release of these films. In similar ways, stories of the Algerian War have also appeared in contemporary French-language cinema, such as in Bouchareb's film about the Front de Libération Nationale (FLN), *Hors la loi/Outside the Law* (2010, France/Algeria/Belgium/Tunisia/Italy). Exploring another key twentieth-century war, in 2009 *Joyeux Noël*'s director Christian Carion released *L'affaire Farewell/Farewell* (France), which examines the interplay of multilingualism and politics in the Cold War and covers a little-known tale of Franco-Russian espionage. However, as its centenary has approached, the Great War of 1914–18 has become a more prominent focus of concern for French filmmakers.

Throughout the inter-war period of the 1930s, World War I was of particular fascination to filmmakers such as Jean Renoir and Georg Wilhelm Pabst. These directors used the war as a narrative device to promote pacifist perspectives in films such as Renoir's *La Grande Illusion/Grand Illusion* (1937, France) and Pabst's *La tragédie de la mine/Comradeship* (1931, Germany/France). Around the same time, films like the American *All Quiet on the Western Front* (Lewis Milestone, 1930, USA) and the German *Niemandsland/Hell on Earth* (Victor Trivas, 1931, Germany) espoused the same ideals. After the 1930s the war faded as an object of cinematic focus until the contemporary age, which has seen a sizeable resurgence in World War I films. In addition to *Un long dimanche de fiançailles*, French productions on the topic include François Dupeyron's *La chambre des officiers/The Officer's Ward*, of 2001, Gabriel Le Bomin's *Les fragments d'Antonin/Fragments of Antonin* (2005), Yves Angelo's *Les âmes grises/Grey Souls* (2005) and Serge Bozon's *La France* (2007). In addition, a range of television films have also appeared in the twenty-first century, such as Jean-Louis Lorenzi's *La tranchée des espoirs/Trench of Hope* (2003) and Philippe Triboit's *Les fusillés* (2015). Amongst these, *Joyeux Noël* stands out as one of the most noteworthy, circulated, awarded and analysed films of recent years on the Great War. It also shares key similarities with the quintessential World War I film *La Grande Illusion* in its depiction of Franco-German fraternisation, the introduction of humour into the wartime experience, and an overarching pacifist message. Commercially well received, with almost two million ticket sales in France alone, *Joyeux Noël* was also screened at the Festival de Cannes in 2005 and nominated for six César awards and for Best Foreign Language Film Oscar at the 2006 Academy Awards.

The film relates a remarkable moment in European history. On Christmas Eve of 1914, in trenches outside a village along the Western Front, German, French and Scottish lieutenants instructed their troops to lay down their weapons, stepped onto no man's land and agreed upon an unofficial Christmas truce. On the anonymous stretch of earth between the trenches, the men and their soldiers gathered to share in a midnight mass and celebrate the holiday with food, games and conversation. The following day, when the truce was supposed to end, each side allowed the other to shelter in their trenches as air forces bombed each enemy in turn. Along with multiple other groups around France who had also participated in Christmas truces, all involved were gravely reprimanded for fraternising with the enemy, and their units disbanded. Yet despite the condemnation of their actions by each of their superiors, the characters' truce offered a premonitory vision of the European model that was to appear thirty years later. For the spatial and symbolic mapping of the truce, in which multiple cultural and national groups crossed once-uncrossable lines to gather on common ground, embodies the ideal of the European Union. In this ideal, cultural differences are to be appreciated, and while borders are not erased, movement across these lines is fluid and results in a pan-European solidarity that transcends the national. In this space, multilingual dialogue is crucial to the border crossing that defines the film and its portrait of Europe. Once a *non-lieu*, no man's land is thus transformed into what Mary-Louise Pratt calls a 'contact zone': a 'social space where cultures meet, clash, and grapple with each other' (1991: 34), in which multilingualism is an intrinsic part of successful cross-cultural exchange.

Lines, Borders and Barriers

Militarily, physically, linguistically and culturally, barriers define the space that the characters of *Joyeux Noël* occupy. The clearest example of this is the mapping of the German, French and British trenches (in this battle, occupied by Scottish soldiers) that carve up the countryside. As each army advances or retreats, these lines are redrawn. Trench warfare involves the micro-negotiation of borders, and thus the continual re-identification of space. The front line is, by definition, not static but shifting, and the battlefield is a terrain upon which violent political expansion is played out. Yet the lines themselves are not simply borders on a map, but inhabited furrows in the earth. The lived spaces of the battlefield, therefore, are not so much the expanses of land between the lines, but the lines themselves. The trenches come to represent an intense, lived example of physical and cultural separation. This mapping of battleground lines and territories can also be scaled up and applied to the European continent. Continental Europe is essentially a uniform stretch of land occupied by distinct cultural entities. The result is a geographical space upon which arbitrary lines are drawn and space is divided up, and trench warfare is a paradoxical act of imposing difference upon a single land mass. The battleground is cohabited by different groups, and is an inherently plural space. Yet the divisionary mapping of the front line, the interminable void of no man's land, curtails and even forbids exchange between these groups.

This divisiveness is intensified by the way in which we are first introduced to no man's land in *Joyeux Noël*. Early in the film, the French troops attempt to cross the snowy expanse of earth and storm the German side. Yet the mission is futile and the men are instantly attacked; bodies are riddled with bullets, shells explode and obscure the screen with flame and deafening crashes dominate the soundtrack as the men die in their dozens. The cinematography in this scene is frenzied; the use of close-ups and smoke-obscured shots creates a chaotic fracturing of space. The initial depiction of no man's land is as a site of hostility and destruction, a space that can be neither occupied nor traversed.

In both real and metaphorical terms, the linguistic landscape of the front line is also illustrative of this divisive mapping. For the German, French and Scottish characters at the beginning of *Joyeux Noël*, language is symbolic of cultural difference, singularity and identity. The language barriers between the different armies are representative of the other insurmountable barriers that separate the groups. Even the naming of the trenches as German, French and English-language streets ('Friedrichstraße', 'rue de Vanves' and 'King Street') conveys the cultural distance separating the armies despite their physical proximity. Monolingualism theory helps explain the isolating effects of language barriers, and the ways in which they can ossify rifts between groups. For Claire Kramsch, for example, 'monolingualism is the name not only for a linguistic handicap but for a dangerously monolithic traffic in meaning' (2007: 102). To be monolingual in a multilingual space is to be enclosed within one's own group and shut off from those beyond it. Conversely, to be multilingual is to be more socially competent, to be an active participant in the transgression of barriers. And as these barriers are broken down for the truce in *Joyeux Noël*, multilingualism reveals itself as a valuable border-crossing tool.

Boundary Breaking and Border Crossing

Despite the predominance of barriers in the film's early scenes, *Joyeux Noël*'s primary focus is not on the divisiveness of borders, but on the possibilities presented by border crossing. Such border crossing occurs in multiple ways in the film. First, the groups initiate a dialogue through Christmas music played from each of their trenches. Next, they undertake a physical crossing of borders between territories. Finally, they share in a series of mutual cultural practices, including eating, celebrating mass, playing football and ultimately burying their dead together. Throughout these acts of transgression, the characters must also cross back and forth between languages, offering up their own language, stepping into the other's native tongue and using Latin and music as symbolic bridging codes. Such physical and linguistic acts unite rather than divide the different groups, the use of Latin in particular underlining their shared heritage. The act of forging the Christmas truce, while failing to erase the existence of the lines that criss-cross the battlefield, offers an alternative means of interacting within such a space. In this context, no man's land takes on an unprecedented symbolism, as a space 'with only the most tentative connections to territory, [allowing the characters] to step out of their respective linguistic houses' (Smith 2012: 79). During the truce, the anonymity of no man's land allows it to take on a transnational identity.

The initial barrier breaking is both a linguistic and musical one. As the sun sets over the battlefield and the soldiers begin to reflect on the significance of the 24 December date, the Scots break into song. Though they are initially only singing for one another, the sound carries over the battlefield. Accustomed to hearing only enemy fire, the German troops are taken aback by the sounds of their enemies' voices. In response, one of their men, Sprink (Benno Fürmann), a famed opera singer, responds with a German-language rendition of *Silent Night, Stille Nacht*. In turn, the Scots begin to accompany the familiar tune with bagpipes, creating a transcultural carol. No face-to-face contact occurs in this scene, as each army offers up their variation on Christmas music from the safety of the trenches. Yet it is a powerful gesture which simultaneously showcases the armies' differences and similarities.

After this initial foray into shared experience, the fraternisation extends to physical movement. An initial bond cemented, Sprink steps out of the German trench and heads towards the centre of no man's land, carrying an illuminated Christmas tree and singing as he walks. Then, signalling to their men to lay down their weapons, the French, German and British lieutenants, Audebert (Guillaume Canet), Horstmayer (Daniel Brühl) and Gordon (Alex Ferns), climb out of their respective trenches and join Sprink. In the heart of the battlefield, the three meet for an unlikely discussion. Audebert arrives just after Horstmayer, Gordon and Sprink have begun to talk.

Lieutenant Gordon: [English] Good evening. Do you speak English?
Lieutenant Audebert: Yes, a little.
Lieutenant Gordon: Wonderful. We were talking about the possibility of a truce; just for Christmas Eve.

This conversation allows the characters to feel out which languages they share; just as no man's land must become a shared territory for the truce to succeed, so too must they find a linguistic common ground on which to meet. Though certain characters are bilingual in both French and German, it is determined that English is a language shared by almost all the characters. The *lingua franca* instantly takes on a key diplomatic role.

Once the representatives of each group have physically crossed the front lines and shaken hands on the truce, their troops follow suit, exiting their respective camps and meeting their counterparts on neutral territory. The move is a risky one. But as they leave behind the relative safety of the trenches, so too do they leave behind the role relations of trench warfare. The drastic shift in dynamic from mortal enemies to Christmastime compatriots is a jarring one for most of the film's characters, and the initial conversations are stilted and uncertain. Yet the boundary crossing has only just begun, and through a number of language-centred exchanges that follow, the characters 'cross [a] linguistic threshold' (Smith 2012) and are thus able to meet on even terrain. After some initial multilingual greetings, in which almost equal combinations of French, English and German circulate, the men lapse into casual conversation, exchange photographs of their sweethearts and share rations. As a group of French and German soldiers sit down together, a rogue cat wanders through the group. At the same moment, a German soldier, Jörg (Frank Witter), and a French one, Ponchel (French star Dany Boon), each call to the cat:

Jörg: [German] Felix! Where have you been? Felix.
Ponchel: [French] No, his name is not Felix. It's Nestor.
Jörg: It's Felix.
Ponchel: No. Nestor. It's the cat from the Delsaux farm. No, I know better than you.
Jörg: [*picks up the cat*] Felix.
Ponchel: [*takes the cat back*] No, it's Nestor. It's Nestor.
Jörg: Felix.
Ponchel: [*calls to cat*] See? Nestor. It's Nestor. See? It's Nestor.
Jörg: Felix. [*the cat wanders off*]

The cat has multiple names, and thus multiple perceived identities, for the different armies. But the weight of this brief scene lies in its microcosmic parallels between the cat, the battleground, and Europe at large. The soldiers may try to assign Felix/Nestor different names and different alliances yet, ultimately, it is irrelevant which language is used to name him, for each language is being used to name the same thing. This dynamic parallels many other moments in the film, such as the lieutenants' wishes to one another over a glass of champagne; 'Merry Christmas', 'Fröhliche Weihnachten' and 'Joyeux Noël'. Indeed, while very different on the surface, parallels can be drawn between the Felix/Nestor scene and the opening shots of the film. In these first scenes, three children recite poems about the region of Alsace during World War I. Reflecting the identities of the three armies to follow, a German child recites his poem in German, a French child in French and a British child in English. Each stands at the front of a classroom, against the backdrop of a map of Europe. While each child's poem reveals a culturally situated standpoint that casts their own country in a favourable light, and while each child's poem is delivered in a different language, the scenes ultimately treat the same material. They may be telling it differently, yet each child is telling the same story. Shared cultural and historical experience, despite linguistic difference, thus becomes a recurring motif in the film.

In light of this motif, it is significant that the children's poems are centred on Alsace, a region claimed over the ages by both France and Germany. Alsace's borders have been incessantly redrawn, its locations renamed, its official languages changed. It has been identified and re-identified throughout the centuries. Yet Alsace is not a place which oscillates neatly between two separate identities; it does not shift from being entirely French to being entirely German and back again, according to lines on a map. Instead, the region is culturally plural and its people are largely multilingual. Even today, despite Alsace-Lorraine being an official part of France, German language and culture holds an important place in the region, especially in cosmopolitan areas such as Strasbourg. *Joyeux Noël* is set outside the town of Lens, near the Belgian border, rather than in Alsace-Lorraine. Yet the trilingual references to Alsace in the opening sequence are symbolic. Much like the film's ultimate vision of Europe, borders do not define Alsace; rather it is the inherent hybridity of the region that characterises its cultural identity and linguistic practices.

As midnight approaches, the three groups congregate for Christmas mass, led by a priest, Father Palmer (Gary Lewis), who is also a stretcher bearer from the Scottish side. While the other Scottish priest represented in the film delivers his sermon in English, Palmer holds his mass in Latin. A common language for church services at the time, especially in France,

Latin is familiar to all of the characters, though few would understand it fluently. Certainly, Latin could not be used as a language for casual conversation between the men, yet the use of Latin in the mass is not exclusionary. Instead, it functions as a symbolic code that is both mutually incomprehensible and mutually familiar to all present. Instead of being intended to convey semantic meaning, the language is used to enact a shared cultural custom and evoke a common religious background. Thus, much like the space of no man's land, upon which all the characters stand but which none of the characters own, Latin is a significant language for all present, but a native language for none. Both linguistically and spatially, the terrain upon which the characters meet is equally known and unknown to all. To recall Wahl's reading, it is 'a common ground and a strange world' (2005: 3). To return to Smith's, it is 'a space "on the doorstep" in which a tentative cultural meeting can be initiated on equal terms and without commitment to the dangerous crossing into that place where the other is at home' (Smith 2012: 75–6). The result is a linguistic and physical space that (if only temporarily) places those within it on an equal footing and encourages communication.

In most contemporary multilingual French films, cross-cultural interaction occurs between French and migrant (or other non-European) populations. Key examples include the films of Jacques Audiard (*Un prophète/A Prophet*, 2009, France/Italy and *Dheepan*, 2015, France), Rachid Bouchareb (*Hors la loi* and *London River*, 2009, UK/France/Algeria; see Chapter 2), and Abdellatif Kechiche (*La faute à Voltaire/Poetical Refugee*, 2000, France and *La graine et le mulet/The Secret of the Grain*, 2007, France), among multiple others (King 2017). By contrast, in *Joyeux Noël*, the different groups involved are all Western European. The representation of the Christian religion and the Latin language in this context, therefore, is inclusive rather than imperialistic. In fact, even the non-Christian characters in the film experience the Latin-language mass as an inclusive act. As the groups prepare to return to their respective trenches, Horstmayer confesses to Audebert, 'I'm Jewish. Christmas means nothing to me. But I will always remember what happened tonight'. Thus the symbolism of the mass transcends the specifics of religion to become a powerful social moment.

Horstmayer's words highlight how Europe is not only composed of different nationalities, but of a plethora of religious, cultural and social identities. This message reappears at many points throughout the film. For example, the British troops are quick to underline their Scottish identity as distinct from the English; when the Germans cry out 'good evening, Englishmen!' they reply, 'good evening, Germans! But we're not

English, we're Scottish!' The characters who disagree over the cat's name, Jörg and Ponchel, quickly become friendly despite sharing no language, apparently because of a shared mild intellectual disability. During the mass, a German soldier who has dropped back from the crowd strikes up a conversation with a nearby Scottish character, Jonathan, presuming him to be an atheist like himself. However, Horstmayer is the most striking example of plural identity in the film, and of the ironic arbitrariness of nationality and barriers. Horstmayer's case problematises the lines that identify certain people as belonging to a group, and others as being excluded from it. In 1914, Horstmayer is a respected German lieutenant. However, for the film's audience, the revelation that he is also Jewish casts a shadow over what is to come. If he is to survive this war, the next one will not see him granted the same professional and social status. He will be re-identified as a target for the German army, rather than a leader within it. In addition, Horstmayer's final revelation further complicates his position:

> **Audebert:** [French] Your French is much better than my German.
> **Horstmayer:** I have an unfair advantage. Your wife is not German.

Horstmayer's marriage to a French woman means his German-born children will not only be Jewish, but half-French. Horstmayer is initially cast as the most nationalistic and militant character in the film, yet this complex figure, with his German, French and Jewish identity and his fluent multilingualism in German, French and English, embodies the film's ultimate message, which posits Europe as an inherently mixed space and problematises its borders.

Upon completion of the mass, the soldiers listen to a performance of *Ave Maria* by the Danish opera singer Anna (Diane Kruger [singing voice: Natalie Dessay]), who has been visiting Sprink, her partner, in the German trenches. The hymn is once more sung in Latin, allowing all three armies to enjoy it on the same footing. The symbolism of this shared experience is heightened by Anna's nationality. Throughout World War I, Denmark maintained a precarious but neutral position between the warring forces. The northern nation therefore shares a European history with the three armies, but is not an active participant in their conflict. Anna herself is perhaps the most linguistically proficient character in the film, speaking each of the film's languages seamlessly. She is also the only main character who is not enlisted in any army. In these ways, Anna's performance, along with her multilingualism and her Danish identity, further elevates the battleground to a transcendental setting.

Even the conditions under which the film was produced reflect a pan-European identity that extends the concerns of cinéma-monde from the diegetic to external production contexts. A complex co-production, *Joyeux Noël* was funded not just by France, Germany and the UK, but also by Belgium, Romania, Norway and even Japan. Likewise, when writing the film, Carion refused to settle for a monolingual French-language script, despite suggestions that French-only dialogue would render the production process simpler and more cost effective. In an interview, Carion remarked 'J'ai raconté l'histoire comme je l'entendais . . . je voulais aussi respecter les langues, c'est un souci de vérité' ('I told the story as I heard it . . . I also wanted to respect the languages, out of respect for the truth'; Carion and Jeamart 2005). The reality of shooting in several languages rendered English (a language Carion is not fluent in) the *lingua franca* on set, rather than his native French. Yet despite this personal challenge, Carion insisted that multilingualism was essential to the film's themes. Such an arrangement reveals the complex web of cultural and linguistic components that comprises contemporary cinéma-monde. As Alison Smith writes, *Joyeux Noël* is a strong example of how '"the cinema industry", in whole or in part, should be considered as a complex "language contact zone" '[in which multilingualism is] a boundary-levelling or boundary-maintaining strategy, which contributes, as a result, to the definitions of role and role relationships' (2010: 39–40). As a result, *Joyeux Noël*'s portrayal of a multilingual, unified Europe crosses yet another border: from the film's internal narrative to its external production context.

To cross a border from one's country is to enter a territory that is not one's own. In such a territory, one will usually encounter another for whom the territory is home, creating an inherent power imbalance. Yet in rare cases, such as no man's land in *Joyeux Noël*, a territory may be home to no one; a site rendered a *non-lieu* by its location on a border or in a contested space. In *Joyeux Noël*, no man's land is transformed from a battleground into a common ground, where multilingualism and shared codes allow for constructive 'communication [within] an intermediate linguistic space that neither "owns"' (Smith 2012: 76). The space functions much like the Latin language in the film, as a resource 'accessible to two speakers but home to neither, as a means of establishing communication without demanding assimilation' (81). In this environment, space and language take on a parallel significance. It is not simply the sharing of one's own language, nor even the use of the other's language, but the act of stepping into a mutually foreign-yet-familiar language, that makes the truce possible.

Interlude or Premonition?

Joyeux Noël is situated in a historical moment during which relations between European nationalities were at their most hostile. Yet the film proposes an alternative means of navigating barriers, and presents the simultaneously contested-yet-neutral space of no man's land as a solution for transcending them. While lines, barriers and borders continue to exist in *Joyeux Noël*, the film's narrative arc centres on the traversal of such borders, and on the establishment of meaningful cultural exchange between groups. From well-known Christmas carols to the traditions of midnight mass to jovial multilingual conversation, the border crossing and pacifist transgression at the heart of *Joyeux Noël*'s storyline hinges on language. Such language need not even be intelligible, as in the Latin-language delivery of the mass, to be a unifying force. In this context, the ability to converse in multiple languages is a powerful skill and a valuable asset. Not only is the German and French officers' ability to speak English a practical requirement in order to coordinate the truce, but a symbolic display of 'establish[ing] common territory' (Smith 2012: 84). Horstmayer's fluency in French and knowledge of France forges an additional link between himself and Audebert. The well-meaning disagreement on the naming of the village cat ostensibly centres on linguistic division – much like the opening classroom scenes – yet the exchange ultimately shows that linguistic differences do not equate to ontological ones (Harrod 2012).

A pessimistic view of the film's events would be to consider this border-crossing transgression as temporary and unsustainable. Indeed, the truce cannot be reasonably held beyond a few hours: the participants must return to battle and face punishment for their actions. The war at large will continue for another three years, and be followed by an even more destructive conflict mere decades later. Yet to view this film from a more optimistic viewpoint and on a grander scale, the truce can be seen not as an interlude, but a premonition. The characters' decision to ignore what would otherwise be impenetrable barriers offers a vision of multicultural interaction out of place in its 1914 setting, but reflective of the European Union to come.

Like *Joyeux Noël*, a number of other contemporary French-language films have problematised the arbitrary nature of drawing borders, stressing the reductive consequences of defining individuals according to the limiting concept of national identity. In films such as Rie Rasmussen's *Human Zoo* (2009, France), which features dialogue in French, English, Albanian and Serbo-Croatian, national identity gives way to a murkier, but more operable, notion of Europeanness. Early in the film, the Eastern European protagonist Adria's American boyfriend poses her an outmoded question about national identity. In English, the *lingua franca* the two always speak together and a language detached from European identity, he asks 'what' she is: is she 'Serbian? Kosovar? Albanian?' In response, Adria (Rasmussen) shrugs. She points to the map spread out before them, swirling her finger across the borders of a number of Balkan states. The borders are manmade, arbitrary, and cut across a unified land mass. They divide nation states that essentially speak the same language, and impose different labels on groups and spaces that had not hitherto been clearly demarcated. The map has clear lines, but the regions it delineates are confused, contested and resistant to borders. 'All', she says, her finger crisscrossing the lines between countries, 'Nothing. I guess I am the product of imaginary lines, around failed states. Where are Czechoslovakians? Yugoslavians? Ottomans?' Adria's father was Albanian of Yugoslavian background, her mother Serbian-born. She now lives in France, with an Anglophone partner. For Adria, the distinction between countries is not useful to understanding self. Her rejection of borders as defining identity factors recalls Bill Marshall's view of cinéma-monde, in which 'borders are as much about non-identity as identity, internal limits as well as external boundaries' (2012: 47). In *Human Zoo*, Adria does not feel she belongs to one specific nation or culture, but locates herself across many. Her identity could thus be seen as European, pan-national, regional, global. Adria's conception of identity does not erase cultural specificities, but rather questions the value of drawing lines between them. Tim Bergfelder targets the same problem when he writes that '"European" functions less as the signifier of a specific culture, and more as an abstractly supra-national, and quasi-ethical framework of cultural practice' (2005: 317). Much like the characters of *Joyeux Noël*, Adria locates identity *across* lines, rather than within them.

In films like *Human Zoo* and *Joyeux Noël*, along with multiple other contemporary French-language films,[1] it is in the in-between spaces – between front lines, across national borders and among languages – that characters are able to tease out the problematics of identity, and establish a workable European space. Such films' representation of Europe is as a diverse yet generally unified realm. Mireille Rosello conceptualises this as a 'mosaic Europe' in which language difference is key: 'a fragmented and often chaotic mosaic of linguistic encounters, the Europe [that these films] help us imagine is made up of micro-encounters between individuals for whom languages are both a challenge and an opportunity to invent new modes of communication' (2012: 215). This mosaic of difference and similarity is crystallised in one of *Joyeux Noël*'s final scenes, in which German, Scottish and French soldiers play an improvised game of football. From battleground to common ground to football ground, no man's land becomes a playing field that encourages difference (there can be no game without separate teams), but also promotes friendly interaction. From a *non-lieu*, no man's land becomes a place of intercultural communication; and when it is ultimately repurposed as a burial ground, it is transformed from a land of 'no man', to a land of many men.

Conclusion

Today, the conception of the European continent as a sealed and definable entity is once again in crisis, and Europe is the site of shifting tensions between concepts of self and other. The European Union, as an ideological concept, is inclusive, designed to forge links between cultures, facilitate movement between nation states and foster peace and security. Yet as a physical zone, it is frequently exclusive and restrictive. As the contemporary refugee crisis has further revealed, freedom of movement across borders is only open to internal inhabitants of Europe, and borders are mostly closed against refugees fleeing conflict in states such as Syria and Eritrea. Such a dynamic has led scholars such as Higbee (2014), Thomas (2014) and Loshitzky (2014) to write of 'Fortress Europe'; a space that is open to some, but closed to others, often in inhumane ways. The exclusionary concept of the fortress, so evocative of the trenches of World War I, can also be applied to the failed *banlieue* housing projects in France, which strand disenfranchised populations of international origins in isolated spaces severed from the French urban centre.

The dichotomy between insider and outsider is also eroded by the reluctance shown by many Western states towards populations migrating from within the EU; the hostile reception of Polish workers in the UK, Brexit, and attempts to expel Roma communities from France are some of the most prominent examples. Perhaps the most contentious European relationship is that between the EU and the far eastern state of Turkey, which has been attempting to enter the Eurozone since 2005. At the time of writing, negotiations are still underway, but Turkey's accession into the Union appears unlikely amidst the stresses of the economic and refugee crises and the so-called war on terror. Contemporary debates surrounding the definition and role of the European Union, therefore, centre on deciding who is and isn't European, and thus who deserves to benefit from the border-erasing mobility of the Schengen Zone. According to Carrie Tarr, films have an important role to play in this environment, in that 'their representations of spatial and bodily border crossings call attention to the porosity of national and cultural borders, but in so doing also expose the asymmetrical power relations between hosts and migrants, Western Europe and its others' (2007: 7). Indeed, cinema is a key means through which to investigate and articulate the role of contemporary Europe, and cinéma-monde in particular offers alternative means of conceptualising the region. As Higbee suggests:

> At a moment in time when the very idea of Europe as geopolitical entity, ideological project, cultural identity, liberal democracy, and common market is being simultaneously defended and redefined, protected and rejected, European cinema has emerged as one of the crucial sites of cultural and political engagement and a sphere in which concerns about immigration, neoliberal globalization, and national and transnational identity formation are expressed, imagined, and contested. (2014: 28)

Of course, films such as *Joyeux Noël*, with their early twentieth-century World War I settings, largely avoid the need to consider a Europe composed of members of non-Western European origins. Yet the film's mapping of Europe as a plural space is nonetheless significant. The European Union may be plagued by contemporary identity issues, yet the Christmas truce portrayed in *Joyeux Noël* was not simply a moment of distraction, an interlude lost in time. Instead, the film presents a microcosmic image of the European mission. Official discourse on contemporary Europe supports a mosaic-like structure; maintaining cultural specificities, preserving individual languages and celebrating differences, while also encouraging multilingual exchange. *Joyeux Noël*, like the EU, promotes the concept of a heterogeneous, yet unified, European community. Both acknowledge the complexity of the map on which its players stand. Neither attempts to deny the existence of lines on such maps, yet both promote the crossing of such lines and the fostering of a continental identity that is more than the sum of its parts.

The multilingual Christmas truce portrayed in *Joyeux Noël* proposes a contemporary frame for envisioning multiculturalism. Though the film is not required to confront the modern challenges of today's more diverse Europe, it nonetheless proposes an optimistic outlook on the possibilities of European unity and identity. Carion's film is less concerned with drawing lines between nations than with exploring the power of language to traverse, redefine and even erase them. Diverse yet connected, separate yet unified, the film's microcosmic Europe features borders and barriers, but also shared spaces and mobility. Despite its historical setting, *Joyeux Noël* reflects the ideals of the contemporary European Union far more than the socio-political separatism of the Great War. Through the traversal of physical, cultural and linguistic lines, *Joyeux Noël* proposes a reading of Europe as a simultaneously heterogeneous yet ultimately unified region, in which borders exist to be crossed. This presents a progressive, if overly optimistic, mapping of the contemporary European space into which the film was released.

Note

1. See examples such as *Eden à l'ouest/Eden is West* (Costa-Gavras, 2008, France/Greece/Italy), *Le Grand Voyage/The Great Journey* (Ismaël Ferroukhi, 2004, France/Morocco/Bulgaria/Turkey), *Dheepan* and *L'affaire Farewell* (King 2017).

Works Cited

Augé, Marc (1992), *Non-lieux: introduction à une anthropologie de la surmodernité*, Paris: Seuil.
Augé, Marc (1995), *Non-Places: Introduction to an Anthropology of Supermodernity*, London: Verso.
Bergfelder, T. (2005), 'National, Transnational or Supranational Cinema? Rethinking European Film Studies', *Media, Culture & Society*, 27:3, pp. 315–31.
Carion, C. and A. Jeamart (2005), 'Christian Carion pour la sortie de son film *Joyeux Noël*', *Critikat*, 15 November, <http://www.critikat.com/actualite-cine/entretien/christian-carion.html> (last accessed 16 July 2017).
Ďurovičová, N. and K. Newman (eds) (2010), *World Cinemas, Transnational Perspectives*, New York: Routledge.
Harrod, M. (2012), 'Linguistic Difference as Ontological Sameness in *Bienvenue chez les Ch'tis* (2008)', *Studies in French Cinema*, 12:1, pp. 75–86.
Higbee, W. (2014), 'Hope and Indignation in Fortress Europe: Immigration and Neoliberal Globalization in Contemporary French Cinema', *SubStance*, 43:1, pp. 26–43.
King, G. (2017), *Decentring France: Multilingualism and Power in Contemporary French Cinema*, Manchester: Manchester University Press.
Kramsch, C. (2007), 'The Traffic in Meaning', *Asia Pacific Journal of Education*, 26:1, pp. 99–104.
Loshitzy, Y. (2014), 'Screening Strangers in Fortress Europe and Beyond', *Crossings: Journal of Migration and Culture*, 5:2/3, pp. 187–99.
Marshall, B. (2012), 'Cinéma-monde? Towards a concept of Francophone cinema', *Francosphères*, 1.1, pp. 35–51.
Pratt, M.-L. (1991), 'Arts of the Contact Zone', *Profession*, pp. 33–40.
Rosello, M. (2012), 'Plurilingual Europeans in a Multilingual Europe: Incomplete and Imperfect Communication Tactics', *European Studies*, 29, pp. 215–33.
Smith, A. (2010), 'All Quiet on the Filmic Front? Codeswitching and the

Representation of Multilingual Europe in *La Grande Illusion* (Jean Renoir, 1937) and *Joyeux Noël* (Christian Carion, 2005),' *Journal of Romance Studies*, 10:2, pp. 37–52.

Smith, A. (2012), 'Crossing the Linguistic Threshold: Language, Hospitality and Linguistic Exchange', in Philippe Lioret's *Welcome* and Rachid Bouchareb's *London River, Studies in French Cinema*, 4:1, pp. 75–90.

Tarr, C. (2007), 'The Porosity of the Hexagon: Border Crossings in Contemporary French Cinema', *Studies in European Cinema*, 4:1, pp. 7–21.

Thomas, D. (2014), 'Fortress Europe: Identity, Race and Surveillance', *International Journal of Francophone Studies*, 17:3/4, pp. 445–68.

Wahl, C. (2005), 'Discovering a Genre: The Polyglot Film', *Cinemascope*, 1, pp. 1–8.

CHAPTER 9

An Ostrich, a Backhoe and a few Ski-Doos: Tracking the Road Movie in Quebec and Beyond

Thibaut Schilt

The Quebec film industry has gained significant momentum in the past three decades, in part thanks to the international recognition of the films of Deny Arcand and a handful of others. Despite obstacles, Quebec cinema is now increasingly recognised as a successful example of North American, French-language resistance to the hegemony of Hollywood (Jean 2005: 11). Since the 1990s films produced in the province have arguably been less visibly preoccupied with defining Québécois identity, as opposed to films made during both the Quiet Revolution in the 1960s and the sovereignty debates in the 1970s and 1980s. Instead, contemporary directors from Quebec have been more inclined to devise crowd-pleasing opuses of various genres that thrive locally and, with ever more frequency, on the international scene. These productions, which comprise both commercial blockbusters and smaller budget, so-called auteur films, have revealed new directing talents such as Denis Villeneuve, Jean-Marc Vallée, Philippe Falardeau, and Kim Nguyen, whose feature film *Rebelle/War Witch* (2012), a French- and Lingala-language Canadian film shot in the Democratic Republic of Congo, received multiple Jutra prizes (Quebec's own French-language film awards) and Genie awards (Canada's national film prizes) in the year of its release.[1] As in most national film industries besides (perhaps) France, female directors are still largely underrepresented in Quebec fiction cinema, though women have slowly been making their mark on the industry. These contributions include the films of pioneer feminist filmmaker Anne Claire Poirier, who started directing in the 1960s, of the Swiss-born Léa Pool, who began her career in the late 1970s, and a newer and hopefully growing wave that includes Catherine Martin, Lyne Charlebois, Manon Briand and Louise Archambault.[2]

Twenty-first century films also attest to the tremendous diversity of the filmmaking industry in Quebec, which releases, in addition to its especially popular comedies (*La grande séduction/Seducing Doctor Lewis*, Jean-François Pouliot, 2003; and *Bon Cop Bad Cop*, Erik Canuel, 2006) and numerous literary adaptations in costume (*Séraphin: Un homme et son péché*, Charles Binamé, 2002), bona fide genre films, from the horror flick (*5150 rue des Ormes*, Eric Tessier, 2009) to the crime drama (*Polytechnique*, Denis Villeneuve, 2009) and the suspense thriller (*Détour*, Sylvain Guy, 2009) (Beaulieu 2002: 56–7).[3] To that, we may add an increasing number of queer-themed works such as *Mambo Italiano* (Émile Gaudreault, 2003), *C.R.A.Z.Y.* (Jean-Marc Vallée, 2005), and much of the filmography of Cannes Film Festival favourite Xavier Dolan, who directed an impressive six critically acclaimed feature films between 2009 and 2016. Additionally, several Canadian reviewers have used the term 'nouvelle vague québécoise' (Lavallée 2011: 41) and 'Quebec New Wave' to refer to a certain tendency of auteur cinema made in Quebec in the past decade (since 2004–5, they argue), especially as they describe small-budget, anti-commercial, anti-nostalgic, dark-humoured films that focus on 'suburban ennui, substance abuse, and suicide' (Bailey 2010). Critics cite Sébastien Pilote, Raphaël Ouellet, Denis Côté, Maxime Giroux, and Stéphane Lafleur as contributors to this trend. Finally, the road movie, which will be the focus of this chapter, is an ever more prevalent genre in Quebec cinema, and like other road films produced in other regions of the world (notably, the United States, South America, Europe, and Africa), they often combine several genres (comedy, drama, thriller) in addition to their 'road' component.

Despite this richness and the occasional attention from non-Canadian film magazines and the international festival circuit, Quebec-produced films are seldom prominently featured in either anglophone or francophone academic scholarship (whether produced in Europe, North America, or elsewhere) on French-language cinema. This limited interest (on the part of international scholars and non-Québécois spectators alike) may be partially explained by what Bill Marshall has described as the culturally and geographically peripheral position of Quebec cinema, as well as its relative inexportability, if one excludes the international triumphs of a select few (2010: 122).[4] However, I want to suggest that Montreal, home of the Quebec film industry, is a legitimate, vibrant, and self-sufficient hub of cinéma-monde where 'Quebec films . . . always now surpass those from France' (Marshall 2012: 38) at the local box office. This chapter aims to rectify, however modestly, the relative lack of attention accorded to this industry, in contrast to other areas of cinéma-monde, and proposes to discuss Quebec films through a lens (the road movie) that has been reserved mostly for films in other geographical contexts.

Travel cinema, another way to describe films with characters who take to the road, has historically received some scholarly scrutiny, but had been initially limited to English-language, North American cinema. In the past decade, however, increasing numbers of scholars have written about the genre from a perspective that surpasses its Hollywood boundaries and recognises its worldwide presence – indeed, going as far back as the advent of cinema in the 1890s, starting with the Lumière brothers. In the francophone context, scholarship on travel cinema has focused on films produced in French-speaking Europe, the Maghreb and sub-Saharan Africa, but little on Quebec (see Archer 2013; Gott 2016; Gott and Schilt 2013). Yet the province's majestic wide open spaces, its famous harsh, snowy winters, and the ubiquitous presence of the Saint Lawrence River in the life of its citizens make for propitious and particularly cinegenic opportunities to explore mobility within the region. And indeed, a number of Québécois filmmakers have borrowed tropes from the road movie genre (American and otherwise) in their work, as we shall see. With a literary precedent in Jacques Poulin's 1984 Kerouac-esque road novel *Volkswagen Blues*, which chronicles the transformative journey from Gaspé to San Francisco of a white French-Canadian man and a Métis woman, and an even older filmic antecedent in the 1960s documentaries of the cinéma direct, these contemporary fiction films often reflect in unique ways on the place and face(s) of today's Quebec. Because of these various influences, contemporary road films look simultaneously *inward*, offering a window into the lives of Quebec's current inhabitants within its borders, and *outward*, borrowing from a now international genre on the one hand, and pondering how twenty-first century global human movements may shape the future of the francophone province on the other.

In this chapter, I discuss what I consider to be an eclectic yet representative sample of road movies produced and directed in Quebec since the beginning of the twenty-first century, the genre's most fruitful period.[5] I have elected to discuss three films in particular: Stéphane Lafleur's *En terrains connus/Familiar Grounds* (2011), Denis Chouinard's *L'ange de goudron/Tar Angel* (2001), and Philippe Falardeau's *Congorama* (2006, Canada/Belgium/France). With the exception of *Congorama*, which straddles three continents (but was actually shot only in two), these films are set exclusively within the frontiers of the province, and all offer the spectator windows into its cultural specificities. They also bear witness to the thematic and stylistic features of Quebec's filmmaking and its complex dialogue(s) with other national cinemas. In rather typical North American road movie fashion, the three films under consideration favour the automobile as the preferred mode of transportation; though, as the title of this chapter underscores, the Ski-Doo, named after a popular brand of Canadian-made snowmobiles, makes a number of special guest appearances in all of the films. As I have noted elsewhere with reference to numerous French-language European films featuring protagonists in search of their real or perceived 'roots', the 'return to "origins"' thematic component is a common subgenre of the road movie (Gott and Schilt 2013: 5–6). In the three films, the protagonists embark on a voyage back to their family lineage, or on a quest for a missing relative. After tracing in a preliminary section the cinematic antecedents of Quebec's contemporary road movies, I will consider each film separately. The intent is to highlight some of the unique contours and distinct cinematic viewpoints of the francophone province, and to assess the varying degrees to which the films' *Québécité* (in other words, their specific Québécois identity) takes centre stage. In keeping with the cinéma-monde theme common to all chapters in this volume, I also ponder, whether directly or indirectly, the films' position within the current trend of travel films produced around the world, particularly as it relates to its French-language cousins in both continental Europe and francophone Africa.

Mapping Out Quebec Cinema

Six minutes into Gilles Groulx's first fiction film *Le chat dans le sac/Cat in the Sack* (1964), the main female character Barbara (Barbara Ulrich), a twenty-year-old anglophone Jewish aspiring actress, studies with acute intensity the map of Quebec that she finds hanging on her boyfriend's wall. After noting how minuscule Montreal appears within such a vast territory (she uses the terms *espace*/space, then *pays*/land or country, to describe Quebec) she points to the map and, as her index finger moves up the Saint Lawrence river towards the Côte-Nord region and further north still, alongside the coast of Labrador and ending in the direction of Nunavik, Barbara indicates her desire to travel to all of these places. She states her firm intention to 'see things' and her deep interest in 'these lives, these inhabitants, Eskimos, all these peoples, various ethnic groups'.[6] The first half of Barbara's hypothetical journey, in which she aims to sail just north of Anticosti Island across the Jacques Cartier Strait and the Strait of Belle Isle, is none other than the route Cartier took during his first exploratory trip to the region in 1534. By indirectly evoking the journey of the legendary French navigator, who, along with Samuel de Champlain, is indelibly engraved in the memory of the province and its French-speaking inhabitants, and by concomitantly acknowledging the existence of and fascination for ethnic groups that predate European presence in the area, *Le chat dans le sac* cultivates the myth of nonurban, northern Quebec as a captivating land still partially unexplored.[7]

It is a place in which, not unlike the American West of yesteryear, new acquaintances can be made and new lessons may still be learned.[8] During the opening credits of the same film, Barbara's twenty-three-year-old boyfriend and would-be journalist Jacques (Jacques Godbout) announces categorically: 'I am French Canadian, therefore I am in search of myself'. Unlike Barbara, Jacques leans more towards introspection than exploration (he admits to searching for what he calls 'certain truths' not around but within himself), yet like Barbara, he too feels the need to escape urban living and (eventually) travels northbound in the snowy midwinter for a self-exploratory hermitage.

The idea that Québécois identity is somehow linked to a personal exploration of the territories that constitute the province, including those far away from the more populated south, has become common in Quebec cinema, especially in films with a 'road' component. Four decades after the release of *Le chat dans le sac*, a secondary character in Denis Côté's first feature film *Les états nordiques/Drifting States* (2003) tells an unseen interviewer that all Quebecers ought to visit the remote James Bay region, particularly the area around the locality of Radisson, where a series of hydroelectric power stations were built in the mid-1970s. This pilgrimage must be done in order to understand, in his words, 'where we [Quebecers] come from', which according to him is the only way to know 'where we are going'. He considers the creation of the power stations and the arduous work of its builders to be a particularly momentous event in recent history and compares them to other pioneer working men elsewhere in the province, from the first farmers of Abitibi to the first woodcutters of northern Mauricie.

The desire to understand one's identity (whether individual or collective) through travel, then, is underscored in both Groulx's and Côté's films. More generally, this desire also recalls the project of the seminal documentary and occasionally fictional cinematic trend known as cinéma direct, which revolutionised the Quebec film industry in the late 1950s and early 1960s, and whose influence is still palpable today, as Côté's film attests. In the words of Gilles Marsolais, this trend developed as a group of generally untrained filmmakers, among whom Groulx, Michel Brault, Pierre Perrault and Arthur Lamothe, 'attempted to restore an accurate image of the Québécois people, that is, an image that is not distorted by the eye of the "other"' (2011: 11). With precursors in the silent cinema of Robert Flaherty and Dziga Vertov and parallel traditions in the United States' Direct Cinema and France's cinéma vérité, these Québécois filmmakers used lightweight cameras and direct sound to film their subjects in their natural context, with as much precision, and as unmediated (as directly) as possible. This often involved travelling to remote, rural locations to shoot. Two famous examples of this tradition are Lamothe's *Bûcherons de la Manouane* (1962), a raw account of lumberjacks working in the Lanaudière region, and Perrault's and Brault's *Pour la suite du monde / Of Whales, the Moon and Men* (1965), in which locals revive the ancestral tradition of beluga fishing on the Île-aux-Coudres, an island in the middle of the Saint Lawrence River. Some of these filmmakers also turned their cameras to members of Quebec's First Nations, the most ambitious project being Lamothe's thirteen-film series *Chronique des Indiens du nord-est du Québec* (1974–83). These three examples, as well as many others produced during the cinéma direct era and the following decades, fulfil Barbara's previously mentioned dream to travel and to discover, in this case via the silver screen, an elsewhere that is perhaps unfamiliar to urbanites yet fully part of the fabric of Quebec's identity.[9]

Quebec's unique geographical and linguistic position within North America, its longstanding cultural ties to and dialogue with the francophone European (and especially Metropolitan French) film industry, and the previously evoked blossoming into a robust national cinema and notable paradigm of cinéma-monde, are especially noteworthy in the context of twenty-first century travel cinema. I would like to propose that fictional road movies as well as travel documentaries recently produced in the province, in addition to showcasing Quebec's own post-referenda specificities,[10] show influences that emanate from three distinct yet interconnected cinematic sources. First, tropes borrowed from the Hollywood strain of the fictional road movie, which generally involves extensive car trips, casual encounters with women along the way, and the subsequent self-discovery or redemption of its (often male) protagonists, are found in the Quebec-produced *Yellowknife* (Rodrigue Jean, 2002), *Route 132* (Louis Bélanger, 2010), *Camion* (Rafaël Ouellet, 2012), and to a lesser extent *Québec-Montréal* (Ricardo Trogi, 2002) and *La chasse au Godard d'Abbittibbi* (Éric Morin, 2013). Second, the ethnographic interest of cinéma direct filmmaking is apparent in Alanis Obomsawin's *Kanehsatake: 270 Years of Resistance* (1993), a documentary about a case of land dispute between the Mohawk people and the Quebec town of Oka; in Elisapie Isaac's autobiographical documentary *Si le temps le permet / If the Weather Permits* (2003), which explores the Inuk side of the singer/ director's identity; and in Mélanie Carrier and Olivier Higgins' *Rencontre* (2011) and *Québékoisie* (2014), two accounts of the complex relationships between aboriginal and non-aboriginal people in Quebec.[11] And lastly, one may detect in Denis Chouinard and Nicolas Wadimoff's *Clandestins* (1997, Switzerland/Canada/France/Belgium) and in Frédérick Pelletier's *Diego*

Star (2013, Canada/Belgium; see Chapter 6) the influence of the European and African varieties of road movies, which have been especially concerned with (often illegal) human migration and the policing of European borders against non-European, non-white intruders. The latter films tend to be international co-productions, as opposed to most other Quebec films, which are typically produced by Canada only. In order to examine in greater depth these three influences, I will now turn to an analysis of the three aforementioned films that constitute, in my opinion, a representative sample of fictional travel films that have come out of Quebec in the past fifteen years. Each film displays characteristics from one or more of the three aforementioned categories of travel films.

Static Journeys and Northbound Return to Origins:
En terrains connus

Stéphane Lafleur's (tragi-)comedy *En terrains connus* unfolds in the bleak midwinter, 'a season that belongs to us [the Québécois people]', according to the director (Delgado 2011: 271). Although a proper road movie in the film's second half, the journey in *En terrains connus* begins in earnest after a deliberately immobile first half. The snowy landscapes featured in *En terrains connus* are familiar to its people and also logically tend to dominate its film history. And while Lafleur acknowledges the influence of Gilles Carle's cinema, especially his wintry but cheery 1965 classic *La vie heureuse de Léopold Z* (Tremblay 2011), which follows a snowplough driver working for the city of Montreal, the landscapes in the less urban *En terrains connus* are more reminiscent of those showcased in its cinematic antecedent and fellow road movie *Mon oncle Antoine*, Claude Jutra's 1971 masterpiece. Only this time, the horse-drawn sled that Antoine and his nephew Benoît use for transportation in Jutra's opus has been replaced by a capricious Ski-Doo (piloted by another character named Benoît) and, as we shall see, a series of other, generally inoperable, wheeled vehicles.

The obsession with machines, the noises they produce, and their occasional inadequacies, already pervasive in Lafleur's quirky and powerful first feature *Continental, un film sans fusil/Continental, a Film Without Guns* (2007) is apparent from the onset of *En terrains connus*.[12] The film opens to a sequence during which the unemployed, childlike – but fully grown – Benoît (Francis La Haye), armed with a metal detector that emits strange cosmic sounds, unearths from a snow-covered yard an inexpensive miniature toy car, an item that suggests the character's immaturity and anticipates the automobile journey upon which Benoît will eventually embark. Meanwhile, Benoît's sister Maryse (Fanny Mallette), a factory worker, is desperate to get rid of the backhoe that has been sitting unused in her front yard for many months, but her husband Alain (Sylvain Marcel), a loving but dull bike-racing aficionado, is unable to find an interested buyer. Benoît, who still lives with his ailing father André (Michel Daigle) but entertains the futile hope to move in with a single mother named Nathalie (Suzanne Lemoine), meets a car salesman (Denis Houle) who claims to have visited the not too distant future – he only travelled temporarily to the following month of September, before returning to the present. The man's straightforward announcement of Maryse's imminent death in a car crash, combined with the same woman's determination to haul the backhoe off her property and Benoît's concomitant resolution to accompany her in order to prevent his sister's forecast demise, take the two siblings on a road trip to their parents' lakeside vacation house.

The first part of the film was shot in distant suburbs west of Montreal, and the journey to the family cabin transports us to the rural, mountainous Laurentides region. In the process it conjures memories of Quebec's cinematic past filled with characters who, as I mentioned earlier, travel northbound, away from the urban landscape to find themselves and gain a better understanding of their relationship to others. The story, which unfolds within a relatively short time period, is structured around three 'accidents', a common trope in road movies. Depending on the circumstances, these accidents either propel the narrative, or temporarily stall it. Three different machines provoke the three accidents, which are announced numerically, in advance of their occurrence, via onscreen titles against a black background. The first one, announced five minutes into the narrative, happens minutes later in Maryse's factory, and causes one of her coworkers to lose his arm; the second, announced at the fourteenth minute, is less of an accident and more of a breakdown of the father's snowmobile while the machine is in Benoît's possession; the third, announced forty-six minutes in, is the automobile accident involving Maryse and her brother, and happens as Benoît drives home from the cabin. In contrast to the man of the Future's prediction, however, it leaves both characters unharmed. Besides the car, which bestows upon the film its most recognisable road movie qualities, other modes of transportation and machines of all types are featured, but they are shown as either dangerous, static, or largely inadequate: the factory machine has the capacity to sever limbs; the backhoe, whose presence on the front yard remains unexplained until the end, is useless to the couple and everyone else; the aforementioned Ski-Doo is in poor mechanical shape and can only be jump-started by the father (pointing to Benoît's incapacities); and the furnace at the lake house appears defective and only turns on when Maryse and Benoît are ready to leave the premises. Additionally, the father's main occupation is to repair broken bicycles, which are lined up, inoperable, against his house walls. Finally, Alain's main hobby consists of competing virtually in the Tour de France on a stationary bicycle positioned in front of the television in his living room. The idea that modern machines are harmful to humans, and actually prevent proper communication between individuals, pervades the narrative beyond the three main accidents; it also aligns Lafleur's cinema with that of French director Jacques Tati, particularly *Playtime* (1967, France/Italy). Maryse is the character that most evidently feels this anxiety towards mechanical apparatuses: she is deeply perturbed by the factory tragedy, and this new state of mind causes her to reject both her loving husband (who worships virtual bicycles) and what she sees as the invasive, and altogether traumatising (because of what it indirectly represents) presence of the backhoe.

In terms of genre, the strong presence of other modes of transportation besides the automobile distinguishes *En terrains connus* from its North American road movie peers. The defectiveness or overall motionlessness of the bicycles, Ski-Doo, and backhoe, underscores the immobility of the film's first half (a metaphor for the characters' own perpetual state of apathy), and further dramatises the actual mobility of the second half, which leads to a pivotal breakthrough in the relationship between Maryse and Benoît. Lafleur calls the first (static) half of *En terrains connus* – a pun that when read aloud in French suggests one thing (terrains connus/familiar grounds) and its exact opposite (terres inconnues/unfamiliar places) – the 'mise en situation', or a lengthy but crucial prologue that sets the stage for the second half of the film: the 'road movie' proper (Tremblay 2011). The film's assumed genre explicitly appears in the French-language synopsis of the film, printed on the jacket of the Canadian DVD, and announces the fate of the siblings in the following fashion: 'une série d'incidents fortuits [. . .] plongeront frère et soeur au coeur d'une sorte de road-movie qui changera leur destinée'.[13] What is striking about this description is the fact that the road movie quality of *En terrains connus* is announced here not as an extra-filmic piece of information *about* the film, but as a something that veritably penetrates its diegetic realm. Whether deliberate or not, this generic intrusion into the description of the narrative arguably suggests that as Maryse and Benoît set off on their northward voyage, the fictional world of the brother and sister in the story's first part becomes something else in the second part, an exercise in meta-cinema, a reflection on the road movie genre itself. Such self-reflexivity can be (at least partially) explained by the fact that, as I have argued earlier in this chapter, *En terrains connus*, like other films produced in Quebec since the post-cinéma direct period, aligns itself with a cinematic past that accords great importance to travel and travel narratives as means to explore one's personal, but especially collective, identity.

There is certainly something astonishing, and even amusing about the fact that, with the exception of Maryse's driving instructor husband, who possesses an automobile for professional reasons but prefers his stationary bike, none of the other characters in the film are car owners. This makes *En terrains connus* a recalcitrant road movie, one whose main two characters are peculiar, inexperienced travellers unaccustomed to traversing (at least without their parents) the wide open spaces between their suburban homes and their lakefront destination.[14] The sole admitted purpose of the car trip is to retrieve the father's trailer that will facilitate the permanent removal of the invasive backhoe. But the film has a secret, revealed in the even harsher winter of the northern cabin: like *Congorama*, and to a certain degree *L'ange de goudron*, which I will discuss next, the siblings' journey in *En terrains connus* is also an inadvertent return to 'origins', a journey back to a time when the family was united by the presence of the mother.[15] Tongues become untied during the journey and as the two protagonists reach their destination, it is revealed that the death of the mother had tragic consequences for the remaining family members: it severed all meaningful ties and effective modes of communication between them. Before Maryse and Benoît actually begin conversing in earnest, albeit with few words, irritating noises of machines and inanimate objects inundate the soundtrack (the beeping metal detector, kitchen utensils rattling in a drawer, whirring stationary bikes, deafening factory noises, bowling balls loudly knocking over pins). These invasive sounds, which often stall communication, are an aural representation of the barriers between the characters.

But it is another machine (a mostly silent one, this time, significantly) that provides the siblings with a sense of peace, and ties them back, temporarily but powerfully, to their deceased mother (see Figure 9.1). Just before leaving the cabin, they sit in front of a device made of bright neon bulbs that the father had built years before to chase away the mother's winter blues caused by the scarcity of light during the coldest Quebec months. This 'light machine' differs from other machines in the film in that it is homemade (as opposed to factory produced); it also serves a useful function and was designed as an act of love.

Yet, at first glance the profound ennui that seems to emanate from their faces at that particular moment echoes other moments in the film where characters aimlessly and silently stare into the distance, and initially confirms claims from critics that the films of Lafleur and other so-called

Figure 9.1 Benoît and Maryse sit in front of their mother's light machine in *En terrains connus*.

Quebec New Wave directors are profoundly pessimistic about contemporary life in the province. The remainder of the film, however, negates or at the very least complicates such an assumption. First, this comforting, makeshift spa experience clearly brings the two siblings together, physically and emotionally, and this newfound connection extends into the following day, on their return, southbound journey. Second, the healing, almost supernatural powers of the light contraption arguably save their lives: although the car accident that the Man of the Future had predicted does indeed happen, it kills neither Maryse nor her brother. Instead, the spectator is left with the dramatic, and for once harmonious, soundtrack of a performance by the famous Red Army Choir (*Les cloches de la nuit*), coupled visually with the smiling (practically for the first time) faces of the two unharmed protagonists, and Benoît's authoritative, resolutely incongruous yet profoundly hopeful affirmation that 'on va avoir un bel été, de la belle température!' (this summer will be beautiful and warm!). This offbeat optimism could easily conclude the film, but Lafleur prefers to end his narrative more enigmatically with a succession of shots of a gesticulating blue AirDancer tube man, a recurring figure in the film that resides outside the car dealership owned by the Man of the Future. The incessant, jerky movements of the inflatable man are undoubtedly amusing to the spectator, and confirm Lafleur's preference for a happy ending, however unorthodox it may appear. Like the characters in the story, the blue dancer is firmly anchored in a sleepy suburban town that it may not have otherwise chosen. Like Maryse and Benoît, it belongs there;

and its upbeat demeanour at the film's close suggests that the siblings' homecoming may coincide with the end of their longstanding torpor.

Immigration, Integration and Rebellion: *L'ange de goudron*

The remaining two films to be discussed deviate thematically from *En terrains connus* in that they feature characters who grew up outside of Quebec (Algeria in one; Belgium in the other), and either migrate to or temporarily visit the region as adults. Yet like *En terrains connus*, the trips that take place in both *L'ange de goudron* and *Congorama* are northbound, happen within Quebec, and involve a search for or reconnection with a family member. With *L'ange de goudron*, by far the most politically engaged film of this corpus, Montreal-born Denis Chouinard further explores the subjects of exile and immigration that he had approached in his powerful first full-length feature *Clandestins* (co-directed with the Swiss Nicolas Wadimoff, 1997, Switzerland/Canada/France/Belgium), two themes commonly tackled in contemporary French and Belgian cinema that remain surprisingly rare in Quebec filmmaking.

L'ange de goudron concerns a family of four who fled the violence of the Algerian civil war in the late 1990s and has been living in Montreal's working-class Parc-Extension neighbourhood for three years. When the film commences, Ahmed Kasmi (Zinedine Soualem), a roofer, his pregnant stay-at-home wife Naïma (Hiam Abbass), their nineteen-year-old son Hafid (Raba Aït Ouyahhia) and teenage daughter Djamila (Kenza Abiabdillah) are about to obtain their Canadian citizenship. Rather than conforming to his parents' wishes of stability and integration, Hafid engages in radical political activism alongside a left-wing, alter-globalist underground Québécois group named Crisco (short for 'les compagnons de la crise') determined to stop the deportation of African refugees, which Hafid and his fellow-activists consider inhumane. When Ahmed finds out about the activities of his now fugitive son, activities that could compromise the entire family's ability to settle in Canada, he sets off on a quest to find him and stop future militant actions; first on the snowy streets of Montreal, and then, alongside Hamid's girlfriend Huguette (Catherine Trudeau), in Quebec's wintry mountainous north.

Straddling multiples genres (family/social drama, political thriller, road movie), the point of view in *L'ange de goudron* is predominantly that of Ahmed, an outsider who discovers various facets of Quebec (both geographical and ideological) as his quest progresses.[16] The gradual discovery of a land and its culture(s) is reinforced extra-filmically in that it is the first film made on Canadian soil for both Zinedine Soualem, a well-known

Maghrebi-French actor, and Hiam Abbass, an actress and film director of Palestinian descent and Soualem's real-life partner at the time of filming.[17] Thematically, the film owes much to European political thrillers from the 1970s. In fact, Chouinard met Costa-Gavras while he was writing the script for *L'ange de goudron*, and the Greek-French *Z* (1969, France/Algeria) director introduced the Québécois filmmaker to the Algerian screenwriter Salem Brahimi, who helped him refine and finalise the script. Closer to Chouinard's home but still originating in the same cinematic era, the leftist political engagement present in the 2001 movie recalls the political films of Jean-Claude Lord such as *Bingo* (1974), inspired by Quebec's October Crisis of 1970, and the environmental thriller *Panique* (1977) (Jean 2005: 65/114).

Throughout Ahmed's search for his missing son, *L'ange de goudron* playfully exposes its main protagonist to an assortment of cultural codes and practices that are unfamiliar to him: tattoo culture, alcohol consumption, university culture, political activism, Ski-Doo driving (more on that later). This fish-out-of-water narrative strategy, which is deliberately comical at various points of the story, is commonly employed in cinema, especially in films that chronicle the trials and tribulations of travellers or newly arrived immigrants.[18] Although at ease with his profession as a construction worker specialised in spreading tar on flat roofs, Ahmed epitomises the hard-working immigrant who works too much to have time to learn about his host country; unlike his more culturally savvy wife and children. Ahmed is the tar angel of the title, and as Chouinard explains on the director's commentary track of the DVD, the roof, from which he is forced to come down to search for his son, metaphorically represents Ahmed's heretofore detachment from Quebec's quotidian reality.

There are two phases to Ahmed's mission to find Hafid (and concomitant discovery of his new home country). The first is an urban search within Montreal's city limits, during which he ventures into new neighbourhoods, penetrates inside unfamiliar buildings (the Cégep de Saint-Laurent, where Hafid goes to school, as Chouinard did before him; abandoned factories, where Crisco secretly meets), and navigates unknown streets, dirt paths and alleyways. Throughout this phase, which occurs roughly during the first half of the narrative, an abundance of tunnels, footbridges, and overpasses appear on screen, some even as artwork inside private apartments.[19] In a tension-building episode, Ahmed stands on a bridge overlooking a busy highway (*autoroute métropolitaine*), and the spectator wonders whether he is about to jump in despair until a concerned policeman advises him to go home. Ahmed's inner-city movements and the accompanying symbols of mobility (bridges, cars and other means of transportation) evoke a subcategory of travel cinema that critics have referred to as the 'urban road movie'.[20] These movements, although shorter in length, also anticipate the 'traditional' road movie portion of the film, which begins in earnest forty-seven minutes into the narrative, as Ahmed and Huguette leave the city behind to look for Hafid and dissuade him from participating in a dangerous anti-deportation mission led by Crisco.

Once the odd couple hits the road and navigates through a mountainous area many miles from their departure point (the film's second half was shot in the Lanaudière region, about two hours north of Montreal), Chouinard deploys all the tricks of the road movie trade. At the level of the narrative, we recognise many attributes of the North American strain of the genre: two people are forced to travel together for a common cause; they lose their way, fight and make up; occasionally engage in illicit activities (such as theft) to achieve their goal; their vehicles break down or fail to start; they almost run out of money; and a policeman pulls them over for speeding. Visually, the film delights us with overhead (helicopter) shots of the travellers' truck winding around roads surrounded by snow-capped mountains; lateral tracking shots of frozen lakes, valleys and rare human-made structures; and extreme long shots of wide open spaces.

While the way *L'ange de goudron* depicts Ahmed and Huguette's regional adventures may appear formulaic from the above description, the film also revels in the culturally specific mystique of the Quebec winter. Once Hafid's whereabouts become clearer, they settle in a town where a snowmobile convention is being held, and Huguette quickly realises that a Ski-Doo will be a much more appropriate means of transportation than their current truck (see Figure 9.2).

A sequence follows during which Ahmed clumsily but successfully steers the strange, stolen machine to a house where they eventually find Hafid and his fellow-activists. Beyond the story that unfolds in the present, however, there is a palpable need, typical of contemporary Quebec cinema, as I have already argued, to pay homage to Quebec's cinematic legacy, and in this case particularly that of cinéma direct filmmaker Michel Brault: first, Chouinard choses for his protagonists to stay in the same inn (La Glacière) in Saint-Zénon as the East-Montreal characters who travel north to go on a hunting trip in Francis Mankiewcz's *Le temps d'une chasse* (1972; Brault was the film's cinematographer); second, there is a sequence in the room of the same hotel during which Huguette watches a famous, lyrical scene from Brault's 1967 *Entre la mer et l'eau douce/ Between Sweet and Salt Water* that depicts a couple riding a snowmobile; and third, Chouinard employed as his cinematographer Guy Dufaux, who

Figure 9.2 Ahmed prepares to ride a Ski-Doo for the first time in *L'ange de goudron*.

at the beginning of his career worked as an assistant on the set of *Entre la mer et l'eau douce* and was present during the filming of the very same snowmobile sequence.[21]

If the film populates its present with the pleasant ghosts of Quebec's past, it also douses the spectator with an equally pleasant, non-diegetic musical soundtrack that is closely associated with the experiences of Ahmed's character, and juxtaposes images of Quebec with North African and Middle Eastern melodies: the strains of Montreal-based Iranian setar player Siamak Nasr, the Arabic lyrics of Moroccan singer Samy El Maghribi, the compositions of the Moroccan-French musician Armand Amar, and of the French-Armenian duduk player Lévon Minassian.[22] This repeated attempt to blend Ahmed's original culture with his new surroundings is reinforced by Chouinard's decision to shoot in the winter because of the visual connection the director sees between Quebec's snowy open spaces and the topography of Algeria's Sahara desert (quoted in Ramond 2008).

As with many a road movie, the visual, and in this case melodic, beauty of time spent on the road abruptly comes to an end when travellers reach their destination. The film concludes with the success of Crisco's anti-deportation mission at a regional airport, but also with the tragic death of Hafid at the hands (and kicking feet) of the Québécois authorities, a dark side of the Kasmis' new land that Ahmed (and some viewers) perhaps did not suspect. Chouinard's desire to expose the brutal and heartless treatment of refugees by some western governments is further evidenced in the film's final dedication to Semira Adamu, a twenty-year-old Nigerian asylum seeker who was suffocated to death in 1999 by two Belgian police officers who attempted to calm her during her expulsion. The second dedication goes to the Québécois poet and politician Gérald Godin, who served as *Ministre des communautés culturelles et de l'immigration* in the 1980s and in that capacity worked to facilitate the assimilation of new immigrant communities. These two homages further refine the film's political alter-globalist stance, particularly as it relates to the protection of minority cultures within the so-called developed world.

Positioning Quebec in the Age of Globalisation: *Congorama*

Philippe Falardeau's *Congorama*, although much different in scope and content, also engages in a reflection on the relationship between the Global North and Africa. Out of the three road movies under discussion here, Falardeau's is the one that articulates most clearly its 'quest' element. *Congorama* received funding from Belgium, Canada, and France, and adheres to a subcategory of road movies that I have termed elsewhere 'return to "origins"' and defined in the following way: 'The slippery concept of "origins" [in road cinema] at times references a genealogical link to a nation, or else may be interpreted less literally as a voyage/quest into family or personal history, either of the protagonists or the director' (Gott and Schilt 2013: 5). This definition fits the present film rather well. The intricate story follows Michel Roy (Olivier Gourmet), the Belgian son of the wheelchair-bound writer Hervé Roy (Jean-Pierre Cassel), the husband of Alice, a Congolese refugee (Claudia Tagbo), and the father of Jules (Arnaud Mouithys), an aspiring tennis champion. Michel is an avid inventor misunderstood by his employer. At age 41, he learns unexpectedly that he was born secretly in a barn in the province of Quebec, in the town of Sainte-Cécile-de-Masham, north of Gatineau, and given up for adoption shortly afterward. In the summer of 2000, Michel travels there in search of his biological roots and finds a predictably unfamiliar small town.[23] While there, he meets a man, Louis Legros (Paul Ahmarani) who drives a car with a technologically advanced hybrid engine. As the two men drive back together to Montreal, an accident changes their lives forever, and what is uncovered will have a strong impact on the automotive industry.

Congorama is a complex, ambitious, multilayered film that spans a few years, evokes past historical events from various periods and locales, and travels across three continents. Inspired by the interconnected narratives in Alejandro Iñarritu's *Amores perros* (2000, Mexico) and Woody

Allen's *Match Point* (2005, UK/Russia/Ireland/Luxembourg/USA), the story is separated into two sections of roughly the same length. We first witness the point of view of Michel, and secondly, that of Louis. In addition to being about the 'origins' of Michel, who was unaware he was adopted until his father reveals it suddenly, it is a tale of multilocal filiation: Michel's grandfather resided in the (then Belgian) Congo, his father lives in Belgium, and his son is half Congolese. I must reveal that Michel turns out to be Louis' biological brother, and that Michel also meets, without realising it, his biological mother while in Sainte-Cécile. But beyond the individual stories, the film is also about racial and national identity as well as the effects and aftereffects of colonisation. Particularly, it is a commentary on the postcolonial contours of today's Belgium. At various points of the film, we are shown archival images of Brussels' Atomium, of the Brussels World's Fair 'Expo 58', with a special focus on Congolese people who visited the Belgian capital for the occasion. We also see Congo's pavilion, and part of the sound and light show justifying the film's title named 'Congorama', a spectacle highlighting the benefits of 'civilisation' in the Congo, a country that became independent from the Belgian kingdom two years after the fair, in 1960. Finally, there is a mention of the illegal Congolese diamond trade (also linked to the diamond city of Antwerp), which, we find out, precipitated Alice's forced migration to Belgium. As the film progresses, it becomes clear that the spectator is expected to see Michel's individual (hi)story, as well as that of his family members, through the prism of these collective historical events.

In light of the above description, it is not immediately clear how the province of Quebec fits into this amalgam beyond the director's national origins. Yet, in many ways the Quebec component is what sets *Congorama* apart from a significant number of (European-produced) films engaging in a binational dialogue between one European and one African country (in the Belgian context, one can think of Dominique Standaert's 2002 *Hop*, about a Burundian father/son pair living in Brussels illegally), and turns it into a transnational film, perhaps most representative of the complex exchanges occurring within cinéma-monde, about the interconnectedness of nations beyond the former coloniser/colonised dialectic.[24] One Québécois critic sees Falardeau's film as a positive political and artistic move for the province's film industry: 'By universalizing the story, the director places Quebec and its cinema in the age of what should be a globalization of culture' (Castiel 2006: 30). Falardeau, who was born in Hull, Quebec, opted to set the majority of his film in Belgium, and not in France (which, as already mentioned, co-produced the film) for very specific reasons. As the filmmaker explains in an interview: 'Why choose Belgium to tell a story of transmission of origins? Surely, because like Quebec, the political discourse in Belgium revolves around the notion of bilingualism, and of sharing a territory. There is also a Nordic Latinness [*une latinité nordique*] in both countries, from which emerges a particular kind of humour' (Castiel 2006: 30). Falardeau also denounces the linguistic intolerance of the French film industry, which forces Belgian and Québécois actors and actresses working in France to conceal or modify their accent (he uses the term 'travestir leur accent'), which he finds absolutely intolerable.[25] Going back to Falardeau's above comment, the film does play with the multilingualism of both regions. Twice Michel affirms, while inebriated, 'Ich bin ein Quebecker', referring to John F. Kennedy's famous 'Ich bin ein Berliner' speech from a presidential visit to Germany in 1963, but also speaking one of the three official languages of Belgium. Michel also resorts to speaking English when French does not work while in Quebec ('there was an accident, call the gendarmes', he yells as he bangs on the door of a nearby house); and later on, Louis introduces himself to Michel in Dutch, a phrase he had prepared for an upcoming trip to Antwerp.

These incessant shifts in *Congorama*, be they linguistic, historical, or geographical, are reflected metaphorically in the many modes of transportation that appear in the film. River barges, bikes, planes, solar-powered lawnmowers, and of course, cars, particularly of the hybrid variety, appear on the screen. And this is particularly meaningful for our discussion of the place of Québécois identity in the film, given that Falardeau also aimed to pay homage to the Québécois inventor Raymond Deshaies, who in 1966 crafted a hybrid engine designed for city buses and who inspired the character of Louis' father (a lengthier, more explicit homage is paid to Dehaies in an extra feature on the North American DVD of *Congorama*).

While this postcolonial, global road movie clearly treads beyond 'the road' and the car as principal mode of transportation, being closer in spirit to transnational road films made in Europe and Africa, *Congorama* does pay homage to the North American 'origins' of the genre in the accident scene caused, astonishingly, by an ostrich. The interrupted journey occurs as Louis reluctantly agrees to drive Michel to Montreal, at a time when neither character yet knows that they are blood-related. As the car trip commences, the song 'Jean du sud' by the legendary Québécois singer Gilles Vigneault comes on the radio, to Michel's delight. The song anticipates the upcoming crash, as it chronicles the voyages of a valiant sailor from Quebec who ends up dying after his boat capsizes. The conversation moves from local music to diamonds; Louis' knowledge of them, as well as Alice's unfortunate and inadvertent connection to the diamond trade in the Congo. After the travelling pair makes a stop and Louis discovers his father's notebooks about hybrid engine building, Michel questions a reticent Louis about the notes, through which Michel also surreptitiously glanced. The accident occurs as the two argue and fail to see the two-legged bird standing in the middle of the road. The violent clash almost causes Louis' death, and enables Michel to steal from Louis' car, in a desperate and arguably unethical attempt to reclaim his own origins, the secret of the hybrid engine.

The presence of the ostrich, as both I and Michel have been wrongly calling it, may seem bizarre in the Quebec countryside, and indeed, on one of the film's official posters the juxtaposition of the bird with a Canadian road sign warning motorists against the presence of snowmobiles (another Ski-Doo sighting) appears (deliberately) incongruous. It actually is less surprising than one may think, because the emu (an Australian bird, as opposed to the African ostrich) is widely raised in Quebec, where it is sold for its edible meat, and used to produce emu oil. So here, as elsewhere in the film, we are presented with various symbols of multiple cultures that appear at odds with one another, but that actually turn out not to be. Because these symbols are so manifold, and the narrative as ambitious as it is multidimensional, some, especially non-Québécois reviewers have criticised *Congorama* for its excessive complexity (see Henderson 2007), while others have praised its inventiveness and originality (see Castiel 2006). Whatever one's opinion of the film's intricacies, *Congorama* deliberately demarginalises traditionally off-centred regions of French-language cinema, and productively interrogates our individual and collective place within the postcolonial world.

Conclusion

En terrains connus, L'ange de goudron, and *Congorama* are three fictional films produced in Quebec and directed by Québécois filmmakers in the past fifteen years. All of them borrow liberally from the vocabulary of the road movie genre, a category particularly in tune with this volume's overarching concept of cinéma-monde. Because of this genre's distinct ability to explore concepts of space, mobility and (trans)national identity in a postcolonial, interconnected world, its cinematic presence has become increasingly pervasive, in all regions of the world, over the last twenty-five years. Given Quebec's distinct situation within both the North American continent and the francophone world, a point of view that often transpires in its cinematic output, we note that the three films borrow from the subgenres I mentioned in the introduction to this chapter: the Hollywood strain with characters travelling in automobiles in search of themselves; films that share the ethnographic interest of the cinéma direct; and 'global' road movies. They also exhibit various degrees of *Québécité*, whether in their tendency to pay tribute to the province's cinematic past or, more generally, their commitment to reaffirm the cultural distinctions of this francophone region and its North American locale. It is significant that both *Congorama* and *En terrains connus* feature songs by classic Québécois singers Gilles Vigneault and Willie Lamothe in the former, and Lamothe again in the latter. *L'ange de goudron*'s *Québécité* transpires not in its soundtrack (for thematic reasons highlighted in my discussion of the film) but in its active engagement with Quebec's film history, and in the tender glorification of its landscape. At the same time, the film is concerned with the difficulties of human migration in our global economy, like many of its European and African counterparts.

The three films' quests all have a genealogical or filial link, which may be seen as metaphorical for a questioning of Québec's increasingly complex contemporary identity. Because of the crucial presence of characters from Europe and Africa, *L'ange de goudron* and *Congorama* most closely resemble their transatlantic cinematic counterparts in the way they explore the meaning and implications of human migration in the postcolonial era (from the 'South' to the 'North', from the 'Old' to the 'New' World), either complicating traditional notions of kinship in Falardeau's case, or denouncing current models of society as uncompassionate and outmoded in Chouinard's film.[26] Quebec travel cinema, then, is, like the province itself in its relationship to the outside world, a unique paradigm within cinéma-monde. It is a microcosm of francophone world cinema that looks both inward, questioning its own evolving identity as a culturally distinct region (and self-sufficient cinematic hub) of the world, and outward, as global influences (filmic and otherwise) inexorably affect its present and reshape its future.[27]

Notes

1. Most films discussed in this chapter are Canadian-only productions. Therefore, I will only mention countries of production after I mention a film for the first time in two cases: if Canada is not the sole country of production (a rather rare occurrence); and for non-Canadian films. In addition, given that a number of the films discussed were not released in the English-speaking world, or were released under their original French titles (such as *Mon oncle Antoine*, for example), I will provide equivalent English film titles only if they officially exist.

2. Many films directed by women in Québec are documentaries (see Jean 2005: 72–80 and Marshall 2001: 208–38 for more information on women's filmmaking in the province).
3. *Séraphin* was described, because of its tremendous popular success, as 'Quebec's *Titanic*' (Marshall 2010: 122).
4. The 'inexportability' of certain Quebec films may concern comedies (or other genres) that are too culturally specific, or films with dialogue in a heavily accented Québécois French, something to which Metropolitan French audiences are notoriously unwilling to become accustomed.
5. Denis Villeneuve's *Un 32 août sur terre/August 32nd on Earth* (1998) is a late twentieth century precursor to the contemporary strain of Québécois road films.
6. Unless otherwise noted, all translations from the original French are my own.
7. The Quebec landscape's suitability for road cinema is highlighted by its adoption for foreign-produced films such as *Je suis mort mais j'ai des amis/I'm Dead but I Have Friends* (Guillaume and Stéphane Malandrin, 2015, France/Belgium).
8. Robert J. Flaherty's legendary ethnographic documentary *Nanook of the North* (1922, USA/France), which follows the life of an Inuk man and his family, takes place on the Ungava peninsula in Northern Quebec, which is roughly the end point of Barbara's hypothetical journey in *Le chat dans le sac*.
9. Other 'travel films' made by directors associated with cinéma direct include Brault's *Entre la mer et l'eau douce/Between Sea and Salt Water* (1967), a fiction film that chronicles a young singer-songwriter's journey from the Côte-Nord to Montreal, and the protagonist's subsequent fame; Perrault's *Un pays sans bon sens!* (1970), a documentary that explores the concept of national identity via three different groups: francophone Québécois, members of Quebec's first nations, and Bretons; Perrault's trilogy about the (failed) colonisation of the Abitibi region: *Un royaume vous attend* (1976), *Le retour à la terre* (1976), and *Gens d'Abitibi* (1980); and Bernard Gosselin's *L'anticoste* (1986), a documentary dedicated to the beauty of Anticosti Island, in the Gulf of Saint Lawrence.
10. I am referring to the two failed referenda for Quebec's independence, which occurred in 1980 and 1995. The 'no' vote received 59% in the former, and 50.58% in the latter.
11. See Karine Bertrand's article (2003) for further information on Inuit cinema, and a close reading of a specific, woman-directed film.
12. See Nicolas Gendron's extensive interview with Stéphane Lafleur for further comparisons between the two films.
13. The English version of the synopsis, which appears on the same DVD cover, reads: 'a strange series of coincidences [. . .] launch Maryse and Benoit on a life-changing road trip'. Unlike the French version, the term 'road movie' is not used here. See the bibliography for further details about the DVD.

14. In this regard, Maryse and Benoît recall the offbeat, inexperienced travelling characters in Finish director Aki Kaurismäki's dark comedy/road movie hybrids, a famous example of which is *Leningrad Cowboys Go America* (1989, Finland/Sweden).
15. Maryse and Benoît's inadvertent return to 'origins' are reminiscent of similar voyages – often as side trips or stops on the way – into family history, which are staples of European road cinema going back to *Smultronstället/Wild Strawberries* (Ingmar Bergman, 1957, Sweden) and *Il Sorpasso* (Dino Risi, 1962, Italy).
16. Of course, Chouinard, who penned the screenplay and directed the film, is an insider to Quebec culture, and was raised in the Roman Catholic tradition, as he points out in the director's commentary track. He also mentions having done extensive research on the alter-globalist movement, attending meetings of such groups in London and Montreal, and witnessing the intensive training group members undergo. In order to portray Algerian customs as accurately as possible, he solicited the help of Algerian screenwriter Salem Brahimi.
17. The fact that the real-life Soualem/Abbass couple has two children together, as do their characters in *L'ange de goudron*, brings an autobiographical dimension to the film that creates spontaneity and, as other elements in the film, winks at cinéma direct.
18. In the French context, Yamina Benguigui's *Inch'Allah dimanche* (2001, France/Algeria), which was released the same year as *L'ange de goudron* and also stars Zinedine Soualem in the role of family patriarch, comes to mind.
19. Chouinard's recurring use of bridges in the film is deliberate, as he explains on the DVD's commentary track. For him, these bridges (which he calls *passerelles*) metaphorically represent connections that he wishes happened more between the Québécois people and new immigrants of various cultures and religions.
20. Martin Scorcese's *Taxi Driver* (1976, USA) is an example of the urban road movie subgenre. For a definition of the urban road movie and a case study, see David Laderman's analysis of the Dardenne brothers' *La promesse* (1996, Belgium/France/Luxembourg/Tunisia) in Gott and Schilt's *Open Roads, Closed Borders: The Contemporary French-Language Road Movie* (2013).
21. Dufaux is not officially credited as assistant cinematographer in Brault's 1967 film, but Chouinard reveals this information on the DVD's commentary track. See Manon Dumais' 2001 review of *L'ange de goudron* for further parallels between the film and Quebec's cinéma direct.
22. See John Kristian Sanaker's analysis of the film *L'ange de goudron* for a discussion of the subtle presence of the Arabic language in the film (Sanaker 2010: 87–89).
23. Philippe Lioret's latest film *Le fils de Jean* (2016, France/Canada) is another transatlantic return to 'origins' tale. It follows a young Frenchman's journey from Paris to Montreal, then rural Quebec, as he searches for the body of his

dead Québécois father he never knew existed. Like *L'ange de goudron*, the film was partially shot in Saint-Zénon.
24. Another such transnational film includes the return to 'origins' road movie *La fille de Keltoum/Daughter of Keltoum* (Mehdi Charef, 2001, France/Belgium/Tunisia), about a young woman of Algerian ancestry adopted by a Swiss family who returns to Algeria to find her biological mother.
25. This type of 'accented cinema' is neither 'diasporic' not 'exilic', so it is different from, yet reminiscent of, that articulated by Naficy (2001).
26. The films *Hop* (Dominique Standaert, 2002, Belgium), *Welcome* (Philippe Lioret, 2009, France), and *Illégal* (Masset-Depasse, 2010, Belgium/Luxembourg/France) are all openly critical of the inadequate treatment of refugees in France and Belgium. The African-made road movies (and 'boat movies' or 'floating films') *Frontières/Borders* (Mostefa Djadjam, 2001, Algeria/France), *Harragas* (Merzak Allouache, 2009, Algeria/France), and *La pirogue* (Moussa Touré, 2012, France/Senegal/Germany) directly chronicle the difficult, dangerous, and often unsuccessful attempts of African refugees to migrate to Europe.
27. I thank Leslie Kealhofer-Kemp and Michael Gott for their invaluable feedback on this chapter.

Works Cited

Archer, Neil (2013), *The French Road Movie: Space, Mobility, Identity*, New York: Berghahn Books.
Bailey, Patricia (2010), 'A New Generation of Quebec Filmmakers Captures a Culture Adrift', *This*, 6 July, < https://this.org/2010/07/06/quebec-film/> (last accessed 18 January 2016).
Bertrand, Karine (2003), 'Cinéma inuit et postcolonialisme: La revendication de la parole des femmes dans le film *Le jour avant le lendemain* (2008) de Marie-Hélène Cousineau et Madeleine Ivalu', *Studies in French Cinema*, 13:3, pp. 197–213.
Beaulieu, Julie (2002), 'Québec-Montréal de Ricardo Trogi', *Ciné-Bulles*, 20:4, pp. 56–7.
Cartier, Jacques (1843), *Voyages de découverte au Canada entre les années 1534 et 1542*, Quebec: William Cowan and sons.
Castiel, Elie (2006), '*Congorama*: Dualité génétique', *Séquences* 245, pp. 30–1.
Delgado, Jérôme (2011), 'Stéphane Lafleur: "J'ai essayé de raconter une histoire"', *Séquences*, 271, pp. 42–3.
Dumais, Manon (2001), '*L'ange de goudron*: De l'exil et d'autres réalités', *Séquences*, 215, pp. 38–9.
En terrains connus/Familiar Ground, film, directed by Stéphane Lafleur, Les Films Séville, 2011.
Gendron, Nicolas (2011), 'Stéphane Lafleur, scénariste et réalisateur d'*En terrains connus*', *Ciné-Bulles*, 29 :2, Spring, pp. 18–24.

Gott, Michael (2016), *French-language Road Cinema: Borders, Diasporas, Migration and 'New Europe'*, Edinburgh: Edinburgh University Press.
Gott, Michael and Thibaut Schilt (2013), *Open Roads, Closed Borders: The Contemporary French-Language Road Movie*, Bristol: Intellect Press.
Henderson, Eric (2007), 'Film Review: *Congorama*', *Slant Magazine*, 8 March, <http://www.slantmagazine.com/film/review/congorama> (last accessed 18 January 2016).
Jean, Marcel (2005), *Le cinéma québécois*, Montréal: Boréal.
Lavallée, Sylvain (2011), '*En terrains connus*: Un titre éloquent', *Séquences*, 271, March/April, p. 271.
Marshall, Bill (2012), 'Cinéma-monde? Towards a Concept of Francophone Cinema', *Francosphères* 1:1, pp. 35–51.
Marshall, Bill (2010), 'New Spaces of Empire: Quebec Cinema's Centers and Peripheries', *Cinema at the Periphery*, Detroit: Wayne State University Press, pp. 119–33.
Marshall, Bill (2001), *Quebec National Cinema*, Montreal: McGill-Queen's University Press.
Marsolais, Gilles (2011), *Cinéma québécois: De l'artisanat à l'industrie*, Montreal: Triptyque.
Naficy, Hamid (2001), *An Accented Cinema: Exilic and Diasporic Filmmaking*, Princeton: Princeton University Press.
Poulin, Jacques (1988), *Volkswagen Blues*, Montréal: Babel.
Ramond, Charles-Henri (2008), '*L'ange de goudron*, film de Louis Chouinard', *Films du Québec*, 27 December, <http://www.filmsquebec.com/films/ange-de-goudron-denis-chouinard/> (last accessed 18 January 2016).
Sanaker, John Kristian (2010), *La rencontre des langues dans le cinéma francophone: Québec, Afrique subsaharienne, France-Maghreb*, Quebec: Presse de l'Université Laval.
Tremblay, Odile (2011), 'Rendez-vous en terrains connus ...', *Le Devoir*, 12 February, <http://www.ledevoir.com/culture/cinema/316613/rendez-vous-en-terrains-connus> (last accessed 18 January 2016).

CHAPTER 10

Accented Mappings of France in a Globalised World: *Le Havre* (2011) and *Samba* (2014) through the Lens of Cinéma-monde

Leïla Ennaïli

The ongoing changes fuelled by the many facets of globalisation have been extensively recorded by cinema. The evolution of communication, working practices and mobility are three major themes through which this impact can be assessed. Cinéma-monde, understood as a concept favouring a decentred approach, invites us to evaluate the ways in which films in French capture these evolving realities of globalisation. Emphasising relationality and a global perspective, cinéma-monde is emancipated from the national framework without overlooking the realities of the national paradigm. One way, in cinema, of decentring the perspective is to focus on what is commonly called the margin, a term that immediately implies its opposite, centre, thereby reinforcing the national framework hierarchy. However, the conceptual logic underlying cinéma-monde, understood as a theory and a practice, implies that the nation is not an all-encompassing level of analysis and that a more global perspective highlighting connections with the rest of the world, at various levels, be they national or of a different nature, reveals a different picture worthy of being exposed.

The following analysis examines two recent films, *Le Havre* (Aki Kaurismäki, 2011, Finland/France/Germany) and *Samba* (Olivier Nakache and Éric Toledano, 2014, France), about illegal immigration to or through France. In *Le Havre*, by Finnish director Kaurismäki, shoe-shine man Marcel Marx (André Wilms) helps the young Idrissa (Blondin Miguel) cross the border from Le Havre, where the container in which he was hiding was mistakenly unloaded, to England in order to be reunited with his mother. In *Samba*, the eponymous character (Omar Sy) has been living in Paris for ten years when he is notified by the French authorities that he has to leave French territory. He instead hides, struggles to stay employed, and develops a relationship with Alice (Charlotte Gainsbourg), a single woman who volunteers for a migrant assistance organisation as part of her therapy to recovery from her occupational burnout.

The marginal position of migrants in France can be exposed in cinema in a variety of ways depending on the degree of emphasis put on the characters of migrants and on the degree of reliance on features of mainstream cinema. *Samba* and *Le Havre* frame this wide spectrum suggested by these two variables within which *Welcome* (Philippe Lioret, 2009, France) has become a benchmark. *Welcome* explores the theme of illegal immigration by focusing on the *délit de solidarité* (the illegal act of helping a migrant) perpetrated by a Frenchman (Vincent Lindon) who helps the young illegal migrant (Firat Ayverdi). The film, built on two love stories and conventional cinematography, was a blockbuster that successfully brought attention to the issue of illegal immigration, albeit through a dominant perspective. In addition to the theme of illegal immigration and the filmic treatment of this subject, the situatedness of the director as well as the production and wide circulation of the film are other defining traits. Thus, *Welcome* is not part of what Hamid Naficy calls 'accented cinema' principally because Lioret did not operate within the interstices of the cinema industry and his film was widely distributed. The disconnect existing between Lioret's identity and the life and fate of illegal immigrants is another parameter preventing the film from fitting the category of accented cinema as understood by Naficy. In other words, Lioret's film is by no means 'a performance of its author's identity' (Naficy 2001: 6).

Naficy's concept of accented cinema has been invaluable to understanding a crucial part of the corpus of films devoted to issues of immigration by emphasising the role of authorship and the direct tie that he posits – somewhat problematically – between the filmmakers' identities and the themes developed in their films. Today, accented cinema has come to refer to the filmic production by exilic and diasporic filmmakers about their exilic and diasporic position in the world. Yet this use of the phrase 'accented cinema' is limiting for it was originally understood by Naficy as a synonym for 'alternative cinema'. Thus, a film can be characterised by a variety of accents – a term understood here metaphorically and literally – that distinguishes it from mainstream 'dominant' cinema, which relies on formulaic features that allow it to be easily consumed across borders. Naficy's book title, *An Accented Cinema: Exilic and Diasporic Filmmaking*, reminds us that his argument applies only to the scope of accented cinema pertaining to 'exilic and diasporic filmmaking'. I wish, in the following analysis, to restore the broader meaning to Naficy's concept: 'all alternative cinemas are accented, but each is accented in certain specific ways that distinguish it. [. . .] Consequently, not all accented films are exilic and diasporic, but all exilic and diasporic films are accented' (Naficy 2001: 23). The linguistics-related adjective 'accented' captures more accurately than the term 'alternative' the situatedness characterising these films while avoiding the limiting binary opposition dominant or mainstream/alternative. It also suggests a wide variety of accents whereas 'alternative' tends to homogenise a diverse corpus. Although authorship is key to understanding Naficy's sub-group of exilic and diasporic accented cinema, in the broader corpus of accented cinema not limited to exilic and diasporic films that I am referring to, authorship does not necessarily play a central role. Thus, it is possible to avoid confining filmmakers and their films to the limits of their identities.

Kaurismäki's film *Le Havre* can be understood as an example of accented cinema in the less confined sense defined above. It qualifies as such for several reasons. First, Kaurismäki is a Finnish *auteur* whose films have had a deliberately limited circulation. He is also a 'cosmopolitan filmmaker' who has made films outside of Finland – in France and the USA – but always with a few Finnish actors included in the local cast. Finally, his overall aesthetics go against mainstream cinema conventions. One could say that, within accented cinema, Kaurismäki is a major figure. *Samba*, however, does not fit the accented cinema category. Nakache and Toledano are French directors whose films operate in the mainstream film industry, particularly since the success of *Intouchables/The Untouchables* (2011, France) through which both directors have attained international stature. Relying heavily on cross-cultural operability, Nakache and Toledano's films, including *Samba*, are easily translatable and understood in many countries.

The concept of cinéma-monde facilitates a dialogue between these two films – one with a discernible accent, the other without – by promoting a wider perspective that invites us to take one step further and transcend this opposition between accented and mainstream films. This creates a levelled field that puts in perspective all accents be they standard or marginal, keeping in mind that '[e]ven though from a linguistic point of view all accents are equally important, all accents are not of equal value socially and politically' (Naficy 2001: 23). The following comparison of *Samba* and *Le Havre* follows Marshall's point that 'the Francophone cultural and linguistic world is interesting only when all its accents, contexts, and mixings are made audible' (Marshall 2012: 45). Cinéma-monde allows me to make 'lateral connections' (Marshall 2012: 45) between *Samba* and *Le Havre*, two films linked by the theme of illegal immigration to France. They each offer substantially different yet valuable mappings of France's global situation. I will examine issues of languages and accents, working practices, and mobility in both films to orient the analysis. Before examining both films closely, I will first map the concept of cinéma-monde in relation to the adjacent concepts of francophone, transnational, and world cinemas.

A Conceptual Mapping of Cinéma-monde

Scholars have outlined the shortcomings of categories such as transnational, world and francophone cinemas and they have sought to recast these concepts by highlighting their pitfalls. Transnational cinema has the potential power to 'obscure the question of the imbalances of power' (Higbee and Lim 2010: 9); world cinema can become 'this all-inclusive approach [that] dilutes concepts of difference and distinctiveness' (Hayward 2013: 435); and francophone cinema perpetuates the hierarchical dichotomy between France and the rest of francophone world (Marshall 2012). These scholars have each recommended emphasising interconnectedness and polycentrism while remaining acutely aware of political specificity and power relations. 'Francophone cinema,' 'transnational cinema,' and 'world cinema' are concepts that have emerged in reaction to the limits of the national framework.[1] The concept of cinéma-monde incorporates Marshall's ideas about a recast concept of francophone cinema as well as some of the key features of transnational and world cinemas, chief among which is 'the interconnection of cinematic practices beyond the national boundary' (Dennison and Lim 2006: 10).

In the same way that the terms world cinema, transnational cinema, and francophone cinema have been developed to describe a particular balance or imbalance between the universal and the specific, between the global and the local, between inclusion and exclusion, cinéma-monde is a conceptual tool that seeks to capture these two ends of the spectrum. Because the phrase is formulated in French and not destined to be translated, it indicates a certain situatedness that seeks to be polycentric within the French language world. Emphasising interconnectedness can run the risk of glossing over specificities and implied power relations, whereas focusing on specificity can limit the scope and not account for the effect of globalisation at various levels. On top of seeking to navigate these two pitfalls, cinéma-monde is irremediably parasitised by the controversies related to the *littérature-monde* manifesto and the ensuing scholarly debates,[2] and, as a direct translation of 'world cinema,' by this concept's pitfalls. The potential shortcomings of the concept of cinéma-monde laid out above do not preclude its use and it remains possible to ensure, at this early stage, an adequate use of the concept.

First, at the very least, the category of cinéma-monde constitutes a salutary effort at decentring French cinema studies. Cinéma-monde puts forward a valuable framework emancipated from the national reference but within which the nation can remain an object of study in a global context. The strength of this concept lies in the hyphen linking the two nouns, a link that is at once central and open-ended. Additionally, contrary to the *littérature-monde*, the concept of cinéma-monde is not followed by the epithetic phrase *en français*, which rids it of the centrality of the French language. I argue that studying films centred on issues of migration is an effective way to assess the potentiality of the cinéma-monde scope in that these films stage cross-cultural encounters, border crossing and identity issues. The category of cinéma-monde allows these films to be decompartmentalised from too often marginalised, interstitial positions in the film industry. The positioning of foreigners and illegal immigrants reveals alternative mappings of France in the world that cinéma-monde ambitiously seeks to chart.

Samba and *Le Havre* create a different representation of the position occupied by France in the world. With *Samba*, Paris is filmed as a globalised city whose underside – the exploitation of illegal foreign labour – is highlighted. In *Le Havre*, Kaurismäki dramatises the tensions between, on the one hand, a France from the past – *populaire, solidaire* and inclusive – and on the other hand, class tensions and the lack of empathy and humanity of the state. These two films offer mappings of contemporary France from the centre, Paris, or from the periphery, Le Havre; from the point of view of French directors, Nakache and Toledano, or from the vantage point of a Finnish director, Kaurismäki. Both movies differ significantly in budget ($20 million for *Samba* and $4.5 million for *Le Havre*) and in their box office impact in France ($24 million for *Samba* and $3.5 million for *Le Havre*).[3] Regarding the representation of illegal migrants, Samba is the main character in the story, whereas in *Le Havre*, Idrissa, the young migrant from Gabon, remains for the most part in the background, even though his presence functions as the main narrative engine. The different mappings of France in the world emerging from these films are particularly noticeable in the fashion by which each treats accents and languages in relation to the theme of identity. Referring to Naficy's concept of accented films, it is possible to see the realistic use of faked accents by characters and actors alike in *Samba* as a feature contributing to the overall standard accent of the film itself. In *Le Havre*, the unexpected portrayals of French characters by foreign actors who speak French with strong foreign accents endow the film with its alternative accent. As mentioned earlier, the concept of cinéma-monde allows us to put all these accents, be they faked or not, part of the diegesis or not, in dialogue.

Accents, Languages and Identity

In Nakache and Toledano's film, French-born actor Omar Sy plays an undocumented Senegalese immigrant named Samba, a role for which he worked on perfecting a Senegalese accent. Tahar Rahim, another French-born actor, plays a young undocumented Algerian immigrant who pretends to be Brazilian in France and goes by the name of Wilson. He speaks French with a Brazilian accent, mixed with occasional Portuguese words. He then evolves to speak French without any noticeable North-African accent when his real identity is uncovered by Samba. In this film, accents are faked but sound believable and are part of one of the main themes of the film, namely that identities are performed.

In *Samba*, the foreignness of both illegal immigrants is toned down by the fact that these two characters are non-threatening, likeable, and hard-working, and that they are both played by French-born actors who are familiar to the public in the French cinematographic landscape. In some ways, Samba is the inverted image of Driss from *Intouchables*, a character who tries to collect unemployment benefits by doing the bare minimum. Samba, on the contrary, does not spare any effort to find jobs. The representation of foreigners in this film intersects with the very familiar faces of young French men of immigrant descent. The blurring of the lines between the categories of immigrants and individuals of immigrant descent – and therefore the very borders of the French national community – is a major dimension in the narrative and this potential confusion is enabled by the identity of the actors and some of the roles they have played previously, namely the characters of Driss from *Intouchables* (Sy) and Malik (Rahim) from *Un prophète/A Prophet* (Jacques Audiard, 2009, France).

Adopting a Brazilian accent enables Wilson to avoid the heavy postcolonial baggage and appear more exotic. Lucid about the loaded past between France and Algeria, he opts for a Brazilian identity as part of a survival strategy: 'Everything is simpler when you say you are Brazilian'.[4] This laconic yet telling explanation provided by the character foregrounds the discrimination of Algerian men in France today, and more broadly of Muslims and Arabs. Wilson maintains his lie far along in the story and manages to seduce Manu (Izïa Higelin) who confesses to Alice that she loves South American men. It is during a high-tension scene in which Wilson and Samba run from the police who raid a building site where they are illegally employed, that Wilson reveals his North African identity by speaking Arabic to a maid, asking her to let them in an apartment in an attempt to slip away from the authorities. Wilson, although a very likeable character, is also depicted as duplicitous, never telling Manu who he really is. Similarly, Samba is not devoid of flaws. In spite of his overall loyal and candid attitude, he betrays Jonas (Isaka Sawadogo), a man he met at the retention centre, by having an affair with his girlfriend.

This interplay of faked accents makes the postcolonial subtext of the film more audible. The two illegal immigrants from former French colonies, Senegal and Algeria, never explicitly articulate any reference to history, yet it remains latent through accents and other narrative details. Samba's past and motivation for going to France are exposed at the beginning of the film when he is brought before a court. Perpetuating colonial power relations, Samba never tells the judges of his past and instead his appointed French lawyer, who is not seen prior to or after this scene, speaks for him. His migration, resulting from economic necessity rather than from violent political situations easily linked to the legacy of colonialism, is a more oblique way of tackling the postcolonial subtext.[5] His status as an economic migrant is contrasted with the case of his friend Jonas, who is a political migrant from the Republic of the Congo fleeing a war and seeking refugee status. Underlying references to the *fracture coloniale* can be construed from Wilson's concise justification for his fake Brazilian identity and from the scars on Samba's back that appear on two occasions in the film but are never discussed.[6] Like accents on his body signifying his situatedness in France, these scars function as a metaphor for a brutal colonial past that endures through the fate of illegal immigrants whose labour is exploited on the black market.

Both films disconnect accents from national identity. In *Samba*, a North African character fakes a Brazilian accent. In *Le Havre*, the action takes place in Normandy, yet all of the accents align with the country of origin of the actors, not with the fictional origin of the characters. Accents are used to disrupt any stable and normative conception of identity. Idrissa, the main character of the foreigner in the film, does not speak French with any evident African accent. Similarly, another illegal immigrant that Marcel, the main character, meets in Calais, speaks French without a discernible accent. This interplay of accents and identities contributes to the questioning of categories such as 'foreigner' and 'national'.

Le Havre does not merely invert codes, it disrupts them altogether. Thus, Claire, the French owner of the bar *La Moderne* that Marcel patronises, is played by Finnish actress Elina Salo who speaks French with a very strong foreign accent. Arletty, Marcel's wife, is also played by a Finnish actress, Kati Outinen, who in the story is a foreigner whose origin remains undisclosed. Her name, Arletty, adds another layer of complexity inasmuch as it refers to an iconic French actress and singer of the 1930s with whom Outinen bears very little resemblance. The French characters in the film may or may not have a foreign accent and similarly, the foreigners may or may not have a foreign accent when they speak French. The seeming lack of verisimilitude does not undermine the film insofar as it is only one of the many dimensions that go against typical realist cinematographic conventions. The deadpan humour, the acting stripped of any dramatisation, and the unique mix of present and an idealised past are all part of Kaurismäki's cinema as a whole.[7]

Similarly to Samba and Wilson in *Samba*, one character in *Le Havre* has assumed a different identity in order to stay in France. Chang (Quoc Dung Nguyen), his fake name, is a shoeshine man like Marcel who is originally from Vietnam but decided to embrace an assumed Chinese identity and papers because they have allowed him to live legally in France. However, Chang also feels like he does not truly exist. When Marcel asks him for his opinion on the government's destruction of the Jungle in Calais, he comments: 'In the Mediterranean, birth certificates are more common than fish because it is difficult to deport an anonymous man'. Reading between the lines of this laconic remark, one understands that destroying a shanty town will not make migrants disappear because their lack of papers –and by extension verifiable points of origin – undermines the deportation process.

Chang's fake identity document is of good quality, it is 'everywhere in the databases' and allows him to benefit from several rights, including voting and access to social security. Samba and Wilson however, are forced to buy second-rate fake *titres de séjour*. The temporary job agency employee even refuses to offer Samba a job because of the low quality of the document. At this point, Samba's uncle gives him his own (authentic) identity card so that he can continue to work, but this generous gift only allows Samba to work for a short period of time, until the authorities confiscate the card after the police raid of a construction site where he works. Both films emphasise how much illegal immigration is a constituent part of a global economic system and not an unintended consequence.

The last identity that Samba assumes differs from all the previous ones in that it results from a conscious choice indicating a problematic shift in the character's personality that the ending resolves in a somewhat simplistic manner. Samba, on the advice of Alice, decides to take on the identity of Jonas who died in a canal after a fight with him over his betrayal. Although he is at first reluctant to exploit this opportunity – Jonas had been officially granted refugee status and his residence permit fortuitously ended up in Samba's possession – Samba ultimately accepts this new identity. The ease with which Samba manages to make Jonas' refugee status his own contributes to the critique of a system in which illegal immigrants are interchangeable. In the last sequence of the film, Samba is preparing food in a large kitchen when a man in a *gendarme* uniform asks him who wrote the menu for the day. The description of the meal, written by Samba in comically elaborate jargon mimicking the language of haute cuisine, points to the progress made by Samba professionally and socially. The officer then asks him his name to which Samba replies with a smile 'Mon prénom à moi?' This scene is part of a series distilled throughout the film in which Samba is called by different individuals by his fake names – successively Modibo Diallo and Lamouna Saw – and responds each time after a few seconds, betraying his difficulty to perform other identities than his own. The last scene is cut without including his answer, leaving his identity suspended. The film ends with a slow-motion sequence alternating between Samba leaving the building in which he works, the headquarters of the *Garde Républicaine*, a symbol of the French Republic, and a fully confident Alice, back at her corporate job and leading a meeting. Samba pets a horse on his way out – a habit of Alice's during the film when stress overwhelms her – while Alice is conspicuously wearing Samba's lucky green Senegal soccer jersey under her sweater, in stark contrast with the black and white clothes that her clone-like co-workers are wearing. Diegetic sounds are muted during the sequence and the song 'To know you is to love you' by Stevie Wonder and Syreeta Wright is heard for the second time in the film, indicating that the answer to the officer's last question lies in Samba's new life and in his relationship with Alice, who knows who he truly is.

Just like Chang, Samba decides to exploit a loophole in the system to his advantage, although in his case, at a great ethical price that seemingly does not weigh on his mind, as evidenced by his smile and serene face in the final sequence. Whereas Chang remains on the margins of society, Samba has moved up and is symbolically positioned at the heart of power. While Chang is clearly aware of the deeper consequence of living under a false identity, the end of *Samba* emphasises that the main character, now officially the war refugee chef of the *Garde Républicaine*, has embraced his contradictions in an opportunistic manner. Issues of accents and languages in both films contribute to situate the films themselves and the representation of France that they offer. In *Samba*, a postcolonial subtext orients the representation; in *Le Havre*, it is firmly multicultural and elusive. In both films, the national paradigm does not contain or control identities. Instead, other factors such as luck, work, and market value (Samba's fake ID costs less than Wilson's) play a substantial role in the process of delineating identities.

Local and Global Working Practices in the City

A cinéma–monde approach invites us to reflect on what connects individuals to create a *monde* – a collective of individuals and their environment – and on the forces that disrupt these connections. Examining the working world within the space of the city as represented in *Samba* and *Le Havre* allows us to identify the processes at play. The Samba/Alice couple, beyond the development of their relationship, is the narrative device through which a criticism of work is articulated in *Samba*. On the one hand, Alice becomes a successful workaholic in the corporate world and she ends up feeling like an invisible cog. On the other hand, Samba's labour is exploited and a blind eye is turned to his illegal status. Nakache and Toledano represent illegal labour as an integral part of the capitalist system. Samba, in this sense, is also invisible in the job market. In the opening sequence of the film, the unimpeded choreographed and synchronised movements of dancers at a lavish 1930s-themed wedding reception are put in parallel with the mechanic and confined gestures of Samba wiping the remaining food off plates in a corner at the back of the kitchen. The film visually catalogues the sectors in which illegal labour is used. Samba is successively a dishwasher in a luxury hotel, a night security guard in a mall, a high-rise window washer, a construction worker, a recycling centre worker and a road maintenance worker. Reinforcing Abdelmalek Sayad's idea that the figure of the immigrant is problematically perceived exclusively in relation to his role as a worker, Samba is rarely seen in private spaces, first because he actually does not have his own private space in his uncle's cramped apartment, and second because he cannot afford to be idle (Sayad 2006: 45). As Tarr comments regarding other films about immigrants, 'their constant displacements suggest that they are not truly "settled"' (Tarr 2007b: 70).

In *Samba*, positions of power are architecturally coded. First, the depiction of a traditionally rich French bourgeoisie is symbolically represented by Haussmannian buildings next to which Samba and Wilson often work and from one of which they escape from the police. Second, high-rises in the La Défense district where Samba and Wilson wash windows represent the powerful sphere affiliated with the globalised corporate world. It is on the suspended platform on one of these high-rises that Wilson playfully acts out a Coca-Cola TV advertisement and starts a striptease in front of an office full of female employees who play along with Wilson's reference (see Figure 10.1). The scene, comical because of Samba's fear of heights and shocked reaction to Wilson's act, also dramatises the level to which

Figure 10.1 Wilson playfully acts out a TV advertisement on a suspended platform as Samba looks on.

advertising and corporate discourse has penetrated all social strata across national borders.

Toledano summarises the main arc of the film in an interview: 'Actually, the one and only theme is the relationship to work from the lowest to the highest rung on the social ladder' (Gaumont 2014). One could find the comparison between the alienated condition of an insider like Alice and the invisible and marginal position of an illegal immigrant like Samba – both victims of the globalised capitalist system – to be problematic. Yet, the film addresses the extent of the gap between these two positions. The character of Alice is constructed around a few sequences in which obvious communication gaps reveal her advantaged position and her inability to grasp Samba's and other illegal immigrants' reality. While Samba is in a retention centre, she shamelessly eats the macarons his uncle carefully packed for him. During her shift at the volunteer organisation, she compares her current problems with the water heater in her comfortable apartment with the story of a man recounting the traumatic circumstances in which he was detained in an Islamist camp in Algeria without running water. She then carelessly interrupts that meeting to go see Samba to explain to him that he cannot initiate any formal procedure to become legal in France for at least one year. Samba is angry and panicked at the idea of waiting so long and Alice, attempting to give the situation a positive spin, tells him: 'It can be a good thing to have a transitional period', a remark that betrays how much her job in a major recruiting firm frames her analysis of Samba's situation. Of course, Samba is in no position to have a period of professional transition because his whole family relies on him for financial support and his status as an illegal migrant is not conducive to working on a career plan. Finally, later in the film when Alice confides in Samba the circumstances of her occupational burnout, she likens her long working days to a form of slavery. Socially awkward, with an inability to relate to the fate of illegal immigrants, Alice's empathy seems limited.

These personality traits are at odds with her professional profile as a recruiting specialist who is expected to exhibit confidence and strong communication skills. Outside of her relationship with Samba, to whom she is quickly attracted, Alice does not show any genuine interest in illegal immigrants, or anyone for that matter. We understand towards the end that her involvement with the organisation was a means for her to recover from her burnout. Along with petting horses, volunteering to help illegal immigrants is part of a therapy seeking to *raccrocher* (to re-anchor, the verb used by Alice) individuals who have lost their bearing in life. *Samba* depicts through the character of Alice the alienating force of the corporate world as well as the deeply individualistic behaviour it fosters. Interestingly enough, Alice goes back to her job at the end of the film, voluntarily subjecting herself to the system that created her burnout. Samba's final position as the chef of the *Garde Républicaine* points to an alternative image of success. He embodies a certain idea of Frenchness through his relationship with food, his use of the French language to describe the food he makes, and the nature of the building he now works in. A redefined concept of *identité nationale* opened to illegal immigrants like Samba contrasts with the image of a parallel corporate world. Ultimately, Nakache and Toledano's film dramatises the ways in which the nation, France, positions itself in relation to the flux created by the forces of globalisation.

In *Le Havre*, capitalism does not take the form of the corporate system seen in *Samba* but corresponds rather to a capitalism from an earlier era.[8] Once, while Marcel eats his dinner in the kitchen with Arletty, they listen to a show on a radio station called *Radio réelle* discussing the difficulties of choosing a dishwasher. The host's comments on planned obsolescence are in stark contrast with the bare interior of Marcel and Arletty's house. Likewise, Marcel's job as a shoeshine man is at odds with contemporary fashion. Marcel and Chang have a reflex of looking down at people's shoes to identify potential customers but these shots of the shoes worn by passersby reveal that most of them are wearing sports shoes not designed to be polished. The jobs of other characters in *Le Havre*, from small shopkeeper to baker to bar owner, are all at odds with today's consumer society. If the film does not offer this dated picture as a plausible alternative, it at least points to the human factor that has been lost through mass production and distribution. The solidarity in Marcel's community contrasts with Alice's individualism and her inability to relate to others. Cinéma-monde articulates a reminder that the human dimension is threatened by neoliberal economics and connections between people weakened.

The city of Le Havre has a significant cinematic history, which Kauriskmäki's film engages with on many levels. A network of connections can be outlined by linking *Le Havre* with *L'Atalante* (Jean Vigo, 1934, France), *Le Quai des brumes* (Marcel Carné, 1938, France) and *La bête humaine* (Jean Renoir, 1938, France), all classic 1930s films shot in the French port city. The French actors cast in Kaurismäki's film, Jean-Pierre Léaud, Jean-Pierre Darroussin and André Wilms, and the reference to Arletty (the name of Marcel's wife) also establish links with French cinema. Other ties are also thematic in nature and include, among others, an emphasis on the working class, an evocation of travels to and from distant lands, and crimes.

Samba takes place in Paris but the title of the film evokes other territories, be it Brazil or African countries where the name is common. The directors represent the city of light not as a museum city, a common cinematic trope, but rather as a hub of the global economy. Skyscrapers, illuminated buildings at night, non-places (metro stations, an airport, a gas station), and crowded streets are some of the recurring elements in the film. Paris is, of course, also a major cinematic city, but in *Samba* connections with this subtext are not made explicit. The story could well have taken place in New York or London. The contrast between *Le Havre* and *Samba* in their treatment of urban space allows us to further define the scope of cinéma-monde.

Compared to Paris in *Samba*, *Le Havre* offers an altogether different mapping of urban space. Laura Rascaroli in her cogent analysis of the film adopts a European scope and chooses Kaurismäki's film for its self-reflexive and metaphoric power to address the endangered situation of European art cinema (Rascaroli 2013: 326). For her, '*Le Havre* is an example of a certain tendency of twenty-first-century European art cinema to speak about the entire continent from a specific location' (Rascaroli 2013: 328). The film, according to her, maps Le Havre as part of 'globalized Europe' (Rascaroli 2013: 328). Yet, Kauriskmäki's film manages to do so without emphatically referring either to Europe or to the nation – in this case France. Rascaroli evokes a larger scale when she explains that 'Kaurismäki's *Le Havre* may be a port of the European cultural imagination, but it is also a contemporary city inserted in a precise socioeconomic tissue which is transnational and, indeed, global' (Rascaroli

2013: 336). I suggest that beyond the European framework on which Rascaroli insists, *Le Havre* stages the multiplicity of connections tying the world to the French port city. *Le Havre* exemplifies ties between local and global without the intermediary levels of the nation or Europe.

The narrative conspicuously avoids representing strong ties to the nation in which the story develops. Of course, the title of the film already locates the story but the characters are not defined by being French. Instead, local identity is a more potent factor. Thus, the opening scene of the film in which Marcel and Chang are standing in the train station, waiting for passengers to request their services, signals clearly – an actual sign located behind Marcel on the wall indicates the name of the city – the local lens through which the story will be told. The location in the station and the sound of trains on the railway immediately present Le Havre as a connected space. It is even connected to globalised crime during this opening scene: a passenger whose briefcase is handcuffed to his wrist sits momentarily to have his shoes polished. After that, the man, who is being threateningly observed by two others, interrupts Marcel with the word 'Basta' – presumably identifying him as a foreigner, and more specifically as a member of the Italian mafia – pays and leaves. The sounds of gunshots, squealing tires, and screeching women indicate that the client, now off-screen in front of Marcel and Chang and behind the camera facing them, has been killed.

The local-global network is also emphasised by the press in the film. On two occasions, local newspapers frame the news. The first newspaper seen in the film belongs to one of Marcel's customers who reads it while Marcel shines his shoes. The frame cuts off the title of the publication but the word Havre appears in the title, clearly identifying the newspaper as local. A point-of-view shot shows the first page of the newspaper that Marcel reads while accomplishing his task. The formatting of the main headline on the page suggests an editorial line whose goal is to feed the readership's fears. The first line, 'Ties with al-Qaeda?' is in a red font followed by 'One of the refugees from the container on the run', with the last two words in italics for emphasis. The final line of the title reads 'Armed and dangerous? Extensive search in progress!!', with the word 'search' in bold. By employing key words emphasised in multiple ways and excessive punctuation – nothing less than two question marks and two exclamation points – the title attempts to connect a local event to the broader theme of global terrorism. The non-threatening nature of the subject seen in the photo accompanying the title, which shows paramedics helping women and children found in the container, does not align with the anxiety-inducing headline. Kaurismäki is contributing to a trend in cinema that

Figure 10.2 A close-up of a sensationalist headline in *Le Havre*.

seeks to counter the dominant media representation of foreigners. In a recent book Ipek A. Celik discusses other films that 'reveal and challenge the limited and often generic frames of visibility imposed on Europe's Others in the media's histrionic approach' (2015: 4).

The second newspaper appears later in the film at the bar *La Moderne* where Chang, Claire, Marcel and another customer watch a newscast on television about the destruction of the Jungle in Calais. Claire conspicuously turns off the television when the report transitions to the *Ministre de l'immigration*'s speech in which he justifies the State's action: 'This operation does not target the migrants themselves'. The camera then switches to a close-up of the first page of *Havre libre* with the following headline: 'Twenty refugees discovered in container at Atlantic Terminal. Young boy on the run' (see Figure 10.2). The montage connects visually the events in Le Havre with the destruction of the Jungle in Calais. The prominent presence of activists from the European No Border network in the news footage presents the story in a global light. The newspaper found in *La Moderne* has adopted a substantially different editorial line than that of the newspaper read by Marcel's client. In *Havre Libre*, the headline is descriptive and does not suggest any link with terrorism. The mentality of *La Moderne*'s clientele is made evident by their choice of reading material in stark contrast with that of Marcel's upper-class customer. Marcel and those around him do not respond to the rhetoric of fear and anti-immigrant sentiment.

Regional identity intervenes also in the bar, where a few customers are shown discussing different regional characteristics. The tension between

Normandy and Brittany is crystallised in the conversation about the historical identity of Mont Saint-Michel, which has been claimed by both regions over time. The conversation also revolves around the concept of culture and whereas one man insists that Brittany is more than a region and that it has indeed its own culture of which Mont Saint-Michel is a part, another group argues the contrary. The camera then moves to another table where one man claims that in his region of Alsace ducks are very good, a claim dismissed by his interlocutors. Kaurismäki allows ample time for these casual conversations to develop in the film, emphasising that they are not merely part of the background. Finally, the character of Little Bob – an actual musician from Le Havre who plays himself in the film – functions as another element anchoring the narrative at a local level conceived as always tied to the global. Little Bob, embodying the world culture of rock and roll, is intrinsically tied to the port city. The local scale does not imply that the city is uniform or unified. It is instead riddled with tensions mainly presented as class-based and it includes individuals who are not rooted locally. The robot-like CRS (national police) and policemen embody the State as well as the figure of the *Préfet* whose face remains unseen. Inspector Monet, the local officer in charge of finding Idrissa, is, however, rooted in the city. When he first appears on the screen, he introduces himself to port workers and CRS agents as 'inspecteur Monet, Le Havre.' As the film unfolds, it becomes clear that he shares values similar to Marcel's.

Kaurismäki's films have often been described as problematising the national framework. Discussing Kaurismäki's film *I Hired a Contract Killer* (1990, Finland/France/Germany/Sweden/United Kingdom), Kääpä comments that the protagonists 'exist beyond national identification, where their common bond is one of outsiderness, a beyondness of national existence, where identification with the national is no longer required' (2004: 91). This remark can easily be applied to *Le Havre* where characters have in common their marginal position in society and where national identity is not part of the debate. As Nestingen points out:

> Kaurismäki's films bristle with global elements that cannot be understood as national: global circulation of capital and people pervade his films, time and space are shaped by transnational interconnections and exchanges, and the films cue the viewer to attend to their transnational sources and hybrid forms. These elements intersect with the historical moment in which the films are set. (Nestingen 2004: 96)

Le Havre is no exception in Kaurismäki's work. The circulation of money is at the heart of the plot with close-ups on hands holding money, reminiscent of Robert Bresson's *Pickpocket* (1959, France). Similarly, the circulation of Marcel through and beyond the city to work, to visit his wife at the hospital, and to find a solution for Idrissa to be reunited with his mother in London, evokes networks that are not limited to the national space. Transnational connections are also established through the use of music from a variety of traditions. The soundtrack of the film includes artists such as Damia, the famous French singer from the 1920s, Finnish singer Hasse Walli, classical music by Bach, and the aforementioned Little Bob, a French rock and roll singer of Italian descent.

Whereas Alice's behaviour in *Samba* is imbued with individualism, the cross-cultural encounter in *Le Havre* is based on mutual respect and selfless, uncelebrated solidarity. Marcel's assistance to Idrissa is not a topic of discussion for the characters, and instead, the minimalist dialogues present Marcel's actions as common sense. Rosello defines hospitality as

> always caught between two ideals; on the one hand, we can imagine it as an infinite, unconditional, selfless, and endless gift (of your time, of your space, of your resources) or, on the other hand, it can be conceptualized as a well-balanced exchange of mutual services. (Rosello 2002: 177)

Marcel gives Idrissa his time during a difficult period in his life (his wife is at the hospital); he gives him money although he does earn much; finally, he gives the young boy food and shelter, although his resources are rather limited. After he meets Idrissa for the first time, Marcel leaves his own lunch along with a bill in a bag destined for the young boy. The foreigner is not ungrateful. Idrissa gives Marcel the bill back, washes dishes, and polishes Marcel's shoes. The 'exchange' is not well-balanced but the effort of the young illegal migrant is nonetheless meaningful.

Similarly, the help Marcel receives from his community is spontaneous and does not require any discussion or negotiations. In opposition to this one-dimensional silent solidarity, the official discourse of the state appears all the more ambivalent. Illegal immigrants are caught between humanitarian and security discourses. The sequence in which the container where they are hiding is opened by the authorities dramatises this double and contradictory discourse. The camera frames the scene to capture the visual juxtaposition of nine CRS agents with their military arms in front of four Red Cross paramedics. The policemen are wearing blue uniforms on the left, the paramedics red jackets on the right, both groups separated by a white gurney. The ambiguous national discourse that the illegal immigrants are about to be acquainted with is visually evoked through a composition emphasising the *tricolour*. 'State hospitality' is undermined by the presence of the police (Rosello 2002: 176).

The filmic language – the accent – developed in both films, although fundamentally different, allows them to resonate with audiences across borders due to their reliance on or subversion of what Rascaroli names the 'majoritarian language' of cinema. A comparison of similar scenes in which migrants are fleeing from the police can make this point evident. In *Le Havre*, Idrissa comes out of the container and unrealistically manages to run away from the armed CRS. Rascaroli studies this scene in detail, in which she sees 'a subversion of linguistic proficiency.' (2013: 329–331). This 'deliberately defective articulation of the basic components of a major filmic language' (331) – which characterises the scene – contrasts with the formulaic way a similar scene is filmed in *Samba*. Wilson and Samba are working atop building-site scaffolding when the police arrive. Both men climb up the scaffolding into a balcony from which they enter an apartment. They come out of the apartment into a corridor, unfold an attic ladder, and end up on the roof of the building. The camera follows the movement of the running characters creating a sense of urgency that is precisely undermined in *Le Havre*. The scene, as unrealistic as the one in *Le Havre*, conforms nonetheless to the 'major filmic language' of dominant cinema. In fundamentally different ways, *Samba* and *Le Havre*, as films, can easily cross borders and be exported. The first one, because it relies on a formulaic style widely recognisable, and the second because it undermines and questions such a style. Kaurismäki's films, with 'this mixture of universality and the transcription of cultural specificity [. . .] transcend and gain relevance beyond the national context' (Kääpä 2004: 88).

Nakache and Toledano's film, even though it fits the conventions of dominant cinema, is not devoid of ambivalence. It is anchored in French cinema with sequences like the one discussed above that parodies *Peur sur la ville/ Fear over the City* (Henri Verneuil, 1975, France), in which Jean-Paul Belmondo chases gangsters with great agility on the roofs of Paris. Within the economy of the narrative, this sequence echoes a previous scene in which Samba and Wilson are washing the windows of a high-rise in La Défense. Wilson performs his fake Brazilian identity on the platform, in front of the women in their office, in the most commodified way possible, through a reference to a powerful corporation's product. In the other sequence, Wilson's lie is uncovered and he reveals his true identity to Samba. An establishing shot sets both characters on a roof facing the Eiffel Tower in the distance. During the discussion, a series of over-the-shoulder shots emphasise the connection between Wilson and Samba, who now knows his friend's real name. The Grande Arche de la Défense, symbolising modern economic power, in the Coca-Cola scene is replaced in the escape scene by the Eiffel Tower, indexing a traditional representation of the city. The city, just like the illegal immigrants, has several facets.

Conclusion: Towards a *Cinémappemonde*

Dudley Andrew proposes in one of his writings to create 'an atlas of world cinema' (2006:19). Referring to Franco Moretti's work, he invites us to think of cinema in terms of '"waves" which roll through adjacent cultures whose proximity to one another promotes propagation that not even triangulation can adequately measure' (21–2). Cinéma-monde offers just that, a way to 'examine the film as map – cognitive map – while placing the film on the map' (24). Filmmaker and anthropologist Jean Rouch in a 1981 article published in *Le Monde* chronicles his *rencontre* with cinema, from his childhood favourites to the multiple screenings of films he attended in Africa. Rouch remembers the magic of cinema, how it permeates reality, and the ways in which films connect with each other. For him, films opened up new worlds, new 'cognitive maps'. Keeping the ties between each film of its corpus loose and elusive, cinéma-monde can become one way of charting the *cinémappemonde* that Jean Rouch evoked over thirty years ago (Rouch, 1981).

I mentioned at the beginning of this chapter that the main strength of cinéma-monde resides in its hyphen and the plurality of relations in the world that cinema can reveal. This hyphen can be put between *Le Havre* and *Samba* in that they both offer mappings of France in a globalised world. The theoretical framework of cinéma-monde also reveals the multiplicity of cognitive maps that emanate from each film. The city of Le Havre is now part of a cognitive map of Finnish cinema and connections between Finnish and French cinema are also created through Kaurismäki's film. On this map, Le Havre is not just a French city, it is portrayed as transnationally connected through the flux of immigration and cultures. *Le Havre* maps a city in which a partly romanticised notion of local solidarity counters the dehumanising forces of globalisation. In *Samba*, the waves from mainstream American comedy and American music colour references to French cinema and the national colonial subtext. Nakache and Toledano's film maps Paris as part of the global neoliberal corporate network in which survival requires individualistic and opportunistic behaviours. It is significant that neither film presents Europe as an alternative cognitive map to the one of globalisation. This blind spot can be interpreted as signifying that Europe is fully dissolved in the globalised system. Cinema and comparative cinema studies have a role to play in defining and defending a renewed and strengthened European project and a sense of Europeanness by providing and analysing multifold trans-European cognitive maps in films.

Notes

1. Regarding the limits of the transnational perspective on cinema, see Tarr 2007a.
2. For a detailed analysis of the controversies see Migraine-George (2013).
3. Numbers are retrieved from www.boxofficemojo.com.
4. All translations in this chapter are the author's.
5. Poor economic conditions in former colonies can also result from the legacy of colonialism but *Samba* does not render this link explicit.
6. The phrase *fracture coloniale* corresponds to the title of a book in which the authors contend that contemporary France is heavily shaped by the country's colonial experience (Bancel, Blanchard and Lemaire (2005).
7. For a detailed analysis of Kaurismaki's cinema see Nestingen (2013).
8. See Kääpä (2010) and Rascaroli (2013) for an analysis of 'the collision of the past and the present' (Kääpä 2010: 187).

Works Cited

Andrew, D. (2006), 'An atlas of world cinema', in Stephanie Dennison and Song Hwee Lim (eds) *Remapping World Cinema. Identity, Culture and Politics in Film*, London and New York: Wallflower Press, pp. 19–29.

Bancel, Nicolas, Pascal Blanchard and Sandrine Lemaire (2005), *La fracture coloniale*, Paris: La Découverte.

Celik, Ipek A. (2015), *In Permanent Crisis. Ethnicity in Contemporary European Media and Cinema*, Ann Arbor: University of Michigan Press.

Dennison, S. and S. H. Lim (2006), 'Situating world cinema as a theoretical problem', in Stephanie Dennison and Song Hwee Lim (eds) *Remapping World Cinema: Identity, Culture and Politics in Film*, London and New York: Wallflower Press, pp. 1–15.

Gaumont (2014), Press kit: *Samba*, <http://medias.unifrance.org/medias/29/255/130845/presse/samba-dossier-de-presse-francais.pdf > (last accessed 11 January 2017).

Hayward, S. (2013), 'World cinemas/world cinema/third world cinema', in *Cinema Studies: The key concepts*, Abingdon: Routledge, 428–500.

Higbee, W. and S. H. Lim (2010), 'Concepts of transnational cinema: towards a critical transnationalism in film studies', *Transnational Cinemas*, 1:1, pp. 7–21.

Kääpä, P. (2004), 'The working-class has no fatherland': Aki Kaurismäki's films and the transcending of national specificity', *Journal of Finnish Studies*, 8:2, pp. 77–95.

Kääpä, Pietari (2010), *The National and beyond: The Globalization of Finnish Cinema in the Films of Aki and Mika Kaurismäki*, Oxford: Peter Lang.

Marshall, B. (2012), 'Cinéma-monde? Towards a concept of Francophone cinema', *Francosphères*, 1:1, pp. 35–51.

Migraine-George, Thérèse (2013), *From Francophonie to World Literature in French: ethics, poetics, and politics*, Lincoln: University of Nebraska Press.

Naficy, Hamid (2001), *An Accented Cinema: Exilic and Diasporic Filmmaking*, Princeton: Princeton University Press.

Nestingen, Andrew (2013), *The Cinema of Aki Kaurismäki: Contrarian Stories*, London, New York: Wallflower Press.

Nestingen, Andrew (2004), 'Leaving home: global circulation and Aki Kaurismäki's *Ariel*', *Journal of Finnish Studies*, 8:2, pp. 96–115.

Rascaroli, L. (2013) 'Becoming-minor in a sustainable Europe: the contemporary European art film and Aki Kaurismäki's *Le Havre*', *Screen* 54:3, pp. 323–41.

Rosello, M. (2002), 'European hospitality without a Home', *Studies in 20th-Century Literature*, 26:1, pp. 172–93.

Rouch, J. (1981), 'Cinémappemonde', *Le Monde*, 9 November.

Sayad, Abdelmalek (2006), *L'immigration ou les paradoxes de l'altérité: 1*, Paris: Raison d'agir.

Tarr, C. (2007a), 'French Cinema: Transnational Cinema?', *Modern and Contemporary France* 15:1, pp. 3–7.

Tarr, C. (2007b), 'Transnational identities, transnational spaces: West Africans in Paris in contemporary French cinema', *Modern and Contemporary France* 15:1, pp. 65–76.

Welcome, film, directed by Philippe Lioret, Warner Home video, France, 2009.

Part III

Hubs and Spheres of Production

CHAPTER 11

Activist Cinéma-monde in Paris: Filming Foreigners in the French Capital

Alison Rice

Since 2000, a growing number of films set in Paris have focused an empathic lens on the experiences of those with foreign origins in the French capital city. These cinematic works have highlighted in various ways the diversity of cultures, beliefs and languages that come together in this location, often resulting in misunderstandings and occasionally leading to violence. Four full-length feature films in particular embrace an activist stance in their portrayal of Paris as a location where individuals from elsewhere often suffer due to their perceived differences. Whether it is a question of the intersecting fates of Malian or Romanian immigrants in the French capital in Michael Haneke's *Code inconnu: Récit incomplet de divers voyages/Code Unknown: Incomplete Tales of Several Journeys* (2000, France/Germany/Romania), the life-or-death situation of an Algerian immigrant who has been forced into prostitution in Coline Serreau's *Chaos* (2001, France), the purposely hilarious socio-political activism of a young woman whose father is an immigrant from Algeria and whose newfound love is of Jewish descent in Michel Leclerc's *Le nom des gens/The Names of Love* (2010, France), or the spontaneous kindness a witness to a fatal hit-and-run accident shows to the Moldavian victim's wife in Catherine Corsini's *Trois mondes/Three Worlds* (2012, France), it is evident that these filmmakers have turned an attentive eye in their recent movies to the injustices that mark the experiences of those from beyond French borders whose trajectories have brought them to the City of Light.

It may be unsurprising that the Austrian filmmaker Haneke chose to bring immigrant populations into the limelight in his first French film, a work that integrated no fewer than seven languages into its composition. But it is significant that the other three films in my corpus are French-only productions by French-born directors, all of which focus on foreigners in multilingual cinematic works conceived and produced in France. My conception of 'activist cinéma-monde' can be seen in relation to a larger movement that Martin O'Shaughnessy identifies as a 're-emergence of commitment' characterising many French films after 1995 (2007: 5). While O'Shaughnessy is concerned primarily with the political messages of directors who underscore class differences in their cinematic creations, I am interested in the ways these four selected films portray possible activist responses to problematic situations that protagonists from outside France face in the capital. These cinematic representations not only heighten the viewer's sensitivity to the plight of those from other locations, but they also feature characters who are transformed through their interaction with foreigners, individuals who cannot help but become activists when confronted with injustice. These films bring awareness to the diversity of worlds that coincide in this unique city that is often perceived to be the very centre of France, the quintessence of all things French, and they point to the clashes that occasionally occur in this metropolis when individuals fail to take others into account with sensitivity and respect.

In my interview with Bessora, the writer born in Belgium to a Gabonese father and a Swiss mother, she asserts that people of diverse cultural and ethnic backgrounds have not long been included in French films: 'When you watch movies from 15 or 20 years ago, you see that scenes in the metro are filled with white people' (Rice 2007). She doesn't think that the directors were racist; in her interpretation, they simply hadn't taken into consideration the fact that there are 'blacks or Arabs or Chinese in France'. If filmmakers overlooked this important reality, it is because of what Bessora terms 'mental structures', modes of thinking that 'have been elaborated this way for a long time' and that preclude truly seeing and hearing others. Fortunately, Bessora believes that 'things are changing', but she nonetheless points to a longstanding tradition that is not unique to filmmaking: people of foreign origin are often ignored in the French capital. As Algerian-born French writer Hélène Cixous laments, 'if there is an experience missing from French culture, it is hospitality' (2008: 52). Films that participate in what I call 'activist cinéma-monde' attempt to correct this failure to welcome others not only by including individuals of different origins from outside France in the screenplay, but also by bringing characters of diverse backgrounds into prominent positions, placing them in front of the camera in a gesture that allows the viewer to see them and hear their stories in an unprecedented manner. In addition, these directors draw attention to the filming process itself in highly conscious ways that ultimately involve the spectator in the process of making meaning. As a result, learning to look at and listen to a variety of others hailing from a multiplicity of worlds is an indispensable part of watching works of cinéma-monde set in Paris.

Watching Out for Others: *Code inconnu*

A ten-minute sequence shot at the beginning of *Code inconnu* sets the tone for a film that continually questions what it means to live side-by-side in Paris, to share the pavements and the modes of transportation, and to live within earshot of each other in buildings that allow some in and keep others out, through the use of codes. This introductory scene begins with a lost-looking teenager named Jean (Alexandre Hamidi) who has fled the family farm to join his older brother in the city, only to find that the code to the building's entrance has changed and he is stuck outside. Fortunately for Jean, his brother's girlfriend Anne (Juliette Binoche) emerges onto the street and provides him with the new code and a morning pastry before heading to an appointment. When Jean hastily tosses his wrapper onto the lap of a begging woman (Luminita Gheorghiu), another young man (Ona Lu Yenke) touches his shoulder and implores him to apologise for humiliating this individual. Jean objects, shaking off the hands and the words of his unexpected interlocutor, and when policemen quickly arrive on the scene, it is not Jean but rather the well-intentioned young man who is handcuffed and taken to the station while the woman whose dignity he had hoped to restore is subjected to a dreaded identity check. This sequence demonstrates the skill of an expert filmmaker who captures everything in a single, seamless travelling shot on a parallel plane on the streets of Paris, in order to reveal how all who walk these streets are precisely not on the same plane, but occupy entirely different spheres of perception and prejudice, and therefore are treated very differently not only by the individuals they encounter, but also by the societal institutions that are firmly in place in this location.

The film later makes it clear that the young man seeking to inspire remorse in Jean for his thoughtless action is a French citizen of Malian descent named Amadou who was hit and humiliated in the police station after his arrest; Maria, the woman asking for money on the busy Parisian street, is an undocumented immigrant from Romania who is deported following the altercation. Their treatment bolsters Dominique Wolton's argument that 'in spite of all of the immigrant populations that have lived and continue to live in France, French racism persists' (2006: 266). Achille Mbembe concurs that 'it is no longer enough to be a French citizen to be considered completely French – and European – and treated as such' (2010: 94–5). Indeed, the skirmish between Jean and Amadou reveals longstanding racial dynamics in France, a 'heritage' of a particular 'ethno-racial vision' that dates back to the colonial era, and that must be transformed into an expansive definition of 'citizenship' (Wolton 2006:

266). Even though Amadou possesses the right to remain in the city of their meeting, he is nonetheless taken to the police station while Jean is allowed to depart without further questioning; Maria, who lacks the proper papers, is expelled to her native country by force.

What is so interesting in this compelling scene from *Code inconnu* is that it brings these very different individuals together in a way that is rare, both in cinema and in general, even though we might expect to see migrants and their offspring, regardless of their places of origin, occupying the same spaces in Paris. Indeed, Sylvie Durmelat and Vinay Swamy affirm that groups of different backgrounds have movements and places in common: 'North Africans in France share social and cultural trajectories with migrants of other origins' (2011: 7). But the coming together of Amadou and Maria is nonetheless an unusual convergence, according to Paula Geyh: 'The characters of *Code inconnu* face one another across a series of cultural divides that separate them from each other and fragment the city' (2011: 106). Migrants of diverse backgrounds are confronted with what Durmelat and Swamy astutely term 'urban segregation', and they consequently 'face similar obstacles to making their voices heard' (2011: 8). This is salient when Amadou seeks to explain himself calmly to the policemen who arrive on the scene, but is repeatedly interrupted by these impatient officers who must move quickly, who do not have time to listen.

A later scene, shot entirely in a metro car, features a young man who raises his voice at length to harass a woman. He and a friend initially stand at the far end of the car, where she is sitting with her back to the camera. His words are harmless enough, as he asks her if she is a top model, but his tone is harsh and vindictive, and his movements are menacing. He creeps closer, standing above and leaning over her, then taking a seat next to her before chiding: 'You don't speak to scum [*la racaille*]?!' When the young man pronounces this loaded term, his friend snickers loudly and gestures from the corner where he remains standing, occupying a privileged position of spectatorship from which he is obviously taking great pleasure. An older woman seated closer to the camera turns her head upon hearing these raucous bursts of laughter, but all of the other passengers appear to ignore the entire performance. After the young man asks her how she can possibly be so beautiful and arrogant at once, the woman stands and walks toward the camera, situated at the opposite end of the metro car. This is the moment when the spectator, who has probably picked up on the clues revealing this woman's identity, no longer has a doubt: Anne takes a seat right in front of the camera, and the young man yells out, 'What am I going to do, all alone, in this great big, mean city?' While these words are sputtered facetiously, they are not without import; in fact, they likely hold a great deal of meaning for this young man who is acting out with such vehemence toward someone who appears to represent everything he has been denied. He undoubtedly guesses she was born into privilege, with the looks and the wealth necessary to achieve success in the vocation of her choice, presumably a profession of prestige.

This scene feels excruciatingly long because of the tense moments of silence, and it is not nearly over when Anne takes the greatest distance possible from her unwelcome assailant. He stealthily moves in her direction, interrogating other passengers along the way, until he comes to a stop in front of Anne. The camera angle allows us to see her face clearly, but only part of the body of the young man who towers above her; these impartial views imitate those of the fellow passengers on the metro. In fact, the filmmaker has transformed the spectator into just another person in this car, inevitably confronted with the question of what to do in the face of such behaviour. The aggressor addresses Anne with the informal 'tu' as he taunts her: 'What are you going to do now? Are you going to take off, for another car?' He seems fascinated with his power. It is almost as if he were alone with this woman, who comes from a higher social class, but who cannot escape his presence in the confined space of this form of public transportation. He benefits from the absence of any authority figure, and seems certain that the people around them will fail to intervene in any way. This enclosed space allows him to move closer than he ever could outside the metro, to penetrate a world that has heretofore been out of reach. He emphasises his usual social exclusion with these words: 'I am just a little Arab [*beur*] who is only asking for a bit of affection. Like everybody'.

When the train finally screeches to a stop, the young man spits in Anne's face before jumping to exit the car, but an older man suddenly trips him. The young man immediately returns, placing himself in front of the older man and vociferating, 'Are you a jerk [*con*], or what?' The older man carefully removes his glasses, hands them to Anne, and stands up to meet the young aggressor face-to-face. All that is visible to the spectator at this point is their bodies (see Figure 11.1). The older man spouts: 'And you, you're not a jerk?' And then he changes linguistic codes, forcefully uttering a word in Arabic, a term of reproach that indicates that they share a background, that they know the same tradition, and that this younger individual has caused the older one to feel shame. Even without subtitles, the viewer could grasp the meaning of this admonition. This verbal expression silences the voluble young man who is subdued until the next station, where he jumps with a shout before running off. Anne is visibly

Figure 11.1 Anne looks on as a fellow passenger stands up to her aggressor on the metro.

shaken by this encounter, but she is also touched by the gesture of the man who ultimately came to her defence, who demonstrated his solidarity with her, as a fellow traveller deeply bothered by the intrusive manner and message of the young man. She is able to pronounce a word of gratitude before bursting into tears. It is evident that the final gag was the last straw for her composure; her nerves cannot take the tension anymore, and her body heaves with emotion as she struggles to regain control.

This scene in the metro toward the end of *Code inconnu* serves as a fascinating counterpoint to the sequence on the sidewalk from the beginning of the film. The older man whose utterance in Arabic indicates that he shares a background with the younger man intervenes in a manner meant to restore dignity to the victim of aggression in his midst. In the earlier scene, a young man also intervenes in a way meant to honour the victim of a highly discourteous gesture. Taken together, these scenes pose the crucial questions of *who* is positioned to take action, and how effective these attempts to help turn out to be. When must a witness of injustice move to act, in an effort to combat the wrong, in the hope of making a difference, out of a desire to truly effect beneficial change?

Several of the fragmentary scenes that make up *Code inconnu* reveal a dilemma that Anne faces when she overhears some cries from a neighbouring apartment and then receives a note under her door signed with the words, 'A poor, defenceless child'. Anne does not know how to react when confronted with a reality that remains uncertain since she has not personally witnessed any abuse but suspects that a girl living very close by might be terribly mistreated by her own parents. Anne seeks the advice of her boyfriend Georges (Thierry Neuvic) as they walk through a supermarket in another sequence shot that flows from one aisle to another. He seems disengaged from the conversation as Anne tries to figure out what she should do, and she accuses him of not caring. His response is that he does care, but she received the letter; it was not intended for him. He argues that he cannot decide in her stead, but she counters with great agitation that he could at least help, that it is too easy for him to wash his hands of the matter. He maintains that he has never heard this child cry: 'This doesn't concern me!' The scene ends abruptly, in mid-conversation, but a later scene is set in a cemetery; the child has died. In a film that displays various scenarios in which individuals attempt to help others, this tragic ending to a young life makes it clear that even if acting on behalf of someone else does not always work out perfectly, it is preferable to inaction. Neglecting to watch out for others altogether can prove fatal. If only Anne had adopted the appropriate course of action, if only she had intervened in an effective way, if only she had known the right code, perhaps her young neighbour would have lived.

In his analysis of political cinema, Martin O'Shaughnessy proposes that 'an ethics is characterised above all by one's responsibility before the other' (2007: 52). It is possible that Anne has not acted responsibly with respect to the child next door. But it is admittedly difficult to assume responsibility for the other who remains elusive, and it is often daunting to find an applicable code for unclear situations, as Catherine Wheatley underscores in her study of 'ethical reflexivity' in Haneke's films (2009: 1). As the filmmaker himself repeatedly emphasises, Haneke's work is intended to inspire spectators to reflect, rather than provide them with facile responses containing the illusion that complex issues have been resolved: 'I despise films that have a political agenda. Their attempt is always to manipulate, to convince the viewer of their respective ideologies' (Zielinski 2014). Haneke insists that he has no desire whatsoever to impose his own perspective on others. In Jonathan Ervine's analysis, the long sequence shots in *Code Inconnu* are integral to Haneke's 'careful and self-reflexive use of techniques' designed to 'minimise' 'cinematic manipulation' and ultimately allow the public to participate in the process of interpretation, far from the 'simplistic negative stereotypes' that the media and politicians project in order to further their agenda (2013: 22). According to this understanding, viewers of 'activist cinéma-monde' are compelled to become activists themselves, as they engage in difficult reflections and assume responsibility for their own reactions.

Running the Risk of Responsibility: From *Chaos* to *Le nom des gens*

If a reluctance to get involved characterises Georges's attitude when he learns of the possible abuse of the neighbour girl in *Code inconnu*, an even more striking refusal to become implicated in preventing obvious wrongdoing is present at the opening of *Chaos*. Paul (Vincent Lindon) and Hélène (Catherine Frot) make up a well-dressed married couple headed to an evening event when a bloodied young woman (Rachida Brakni) flails toward their car, screaming for help. Even though the desperate victim is pursued by men who intend to harm her, Paul locks the car doors and focuses on getting away from the scene as quickly as possible. When his wife indicates her desire to call emergency services, he responds, 'Are you crazy? Didn't you see the traces of blood on my windshield?' She immediately asks, 'And the girl?', and he answers, baffled, 'What girl?' This brief exchange is followed by the image of the couple sitting in their car, going through a carwash, in an attempt orchestrated by Paul to remove all signs of this unexpected encounter with an undesirable other, with this forgettable being whose path has crossed theirs for just a moment. Paul's sole goal is to put this moment behind him. But Hélène cannot stop thinking about the young woman who was violently beaten just after they failed to come to her rescue, and the next day she goes to the hospital instead of heading to the firm where she works as a lawyer.

Paul's apparent inability to see the victim with whom he came face-to-face during her panicked flight illustrates a situation that Mbembe describes as follows: 'For the moment, a too-large mass of citizens, obscure and invisible, are literally related to foreigners in the imaginary of the public' (2010: 116). Paul's mental suppression of the very existence of the woman who came into contact with his car – evidenced by his shocking question, 'What girl?' – is partly attributable to this invisibility that likely exists on an unconscious level for him. He is concerned that he will personally be accused of a crime, and while he did not contribute directly to hurting the woman, he is guilty (under French law) of not coming to the aid of a person in danger. But Hélène puts her finger on his greater worry later on when she informs him that she has been to the hospital to check on the victim. He is livid: 'Do you know what we risk?' She responds calmly to his incensed words, assuring him that her involvement in the victim's recovery will not entail any inconvenience for him. For, in the end, he simply does not want to be bothered.

But Hélène's devotion to the victim means long hours in the hospital, and when she is not in their beautiful Parisian apartment to prepare his meals and iron his shirts, Paul quickly falls apart. Then, when she misses a dinner at their friends' home, he leaves her an impassioned voice message: 'Behave like a responsible person, that's all!' While he berates her for not being the reliable wife and mother she always has been, Paul does not realise that the adjective he has chosen to emphasise in this recording may be precisely the right descriptor for Hélène's recent conduct. She is no longer focused on the petty problems of her own small sphere of familial and social duties, but that does not mean she has become irresponsible as a human being. Instead, Hélène has assumed another form of responsibility, by devoting herself to an unknown other. She feels an obligation to this individual, not because she owes her something, though she clearly believes that her presence at the scene of the crime carries a commitment to see the victim through her coma and convalescence, but because they share a common humanity: their meeting on a Parisian street means that they are in this together. Hélène takes a vacation from work for the first time in twenty years in order to focus on this young woman who apparently has no family around her, who has no one to care for her, in any sense of the expression.

Hélène finds herself taking a number of risks in the days that follow, but these actions are nothing compared to the many harrowing experiences that have characterised the trajectory of the young woman she has befriended. After the latter regains consciousness and control of her faculties, she looks right into the camera and recounts her life story. While she is obviously telling Hélène about who she is, she is also informing a larger audience of the circumstances that have brought her to this moment in her life, and the director's choice to have her gaze head-on into the camera calls attention to the filming itself. The spectator is now face-to-face with the individual who heretofore was merely a subject of a work of fiction, and suddenly her life takes on new meaning. This is a moment of unprecedented intimacy in a film that is shot entirely with a small, lightweight digital video (DV) camera, a relatively rare technique at the time this film was made, one that can provide moviegoers with a sense of closeness with the characters. Malika's personal story is one of tremendous loss and terrible violence, as she was removed from her mother's home in Algeria to lead a miserable life in a small apartment in France with her father and stepfamily. When she realised at the age of sixteen that her father was sending her back to her native country to be married by force, she ran for her life, only to wind up in a prostitution ring with no visible way out.

It is well into her story that this principal protagonist reveals her true name, Malika, which she has wisely kept secret from the men who have controlled her for years, who have drugged her and raped her in order to keep her in line, but who have not managed to prevent her from using her intellect to make an enormous amount of money. In order to recover these sums and turn these menacing men over to the French police, Malika requires the help of Hélène, whose unsuspicious appearance as a typical Frenchwoman is indispensable to the Algerian immigrant's plan. These women work together beautifully, leading to a gripping finale in which they watch the trapping of the thugs with riveted attention, along with the film's spectators, from a vantage point in the Lutèce Hotel that overlooks a Parisian park next to the metro entrance beneath them.

In her study of *Chaos*, Françoise Lionnet mentions the 'multiple sites of encounter in which differences are not blurred but become the ground on which solidarity can be conceived' (2006: 109). Hélène adopts an activist stance when she works hand-in-hand with Malika; she does not do so with an attitude of condescension, but instead treats her as an equal. There is never a hint of superiority in her exchanges with Malika. To the contrary, Hélène appears to be filled with respect for this other person, and their interactions reveal what Lionnet calls an 'ethics of relationality' (2006: 109). The selflessness and openness that have been an indispensable part of their friendship can also be described as an 'ethics of meeting', to take up Mbembe's term, in which different individuals do not seek to efface what makes the other unique, but instead focus on the 'sharing of singularities' (2010: 119).

Coline Serreau's film itself constitutes what Mbembe calls an 'ethical event', which must begin with the 'rediscovery of the body and the face of others inasmuch as they represent not only the spoken traces of their existence, but in that they make this person my *fellow human*, if not my *neighbour*' (2010: 119, emphasis in the original). The filmmaker has done something important by placing Malika front and centre before the camera and allowing her to relate in her own terms the 'traces of her existence'. She has accorded a consequential place to the foreign-born individual who has a lot to say, and who just needs an opportunity to make her voice heard.

It is clear in the context of this film that Hélène is making an exceptional departure from the usual behaviour of the indifferent Paris dweller whom her husband Paul represents so well. As Greek-born francophone writer Vassilis Alexakis maintains, Parisians are not known for going out of their way to help others:

> When you are in need of comfort in Paris, it is better to turn to institutions than individuals. Turn to hospitals, town halls, fire stations, Catholic Relief Services. I know social workers who are very attentive and nurses who are absolutely charming.

If there are so many humanitarian associations, it is possibly in order to make up for the indifference of private people. (2015: 329)

But even institutions that are specifically intended to help those with needs are often disappointing, as *Chaos* reveals. A desperate Malika arrives in the office of SOS Racisme to explain that she is in danger of losing her life to the men who have enslaved her, only to meet with a rebuke of her reprehensible actions: the man behind the desk vehemently instructs her that 'he is there to help victims of racism, not women who have wronged Islam'. In response to a question about this aspect of her film, Serreau condemns the sexist attitudes that such institutions embrace: 'Have these activists ever once attacked forced marriage, sexism in the *cités*, excision or polygamy? Those who defend human rights have very selective indignations' (2001). She goes on to establish this striking distinction: 'When a man is a victim of torture or mistreatment, it's a crime. When a woman is, it's tradition' (2001). In the film, Malika does not hope to change the system; what she does so effectively is work the system, using her position of victimhood to eventually gain the upper hand, and transform her future. She isn't vindictive toward her family. She realises that her brothers have been hopelessly indoctrinated to behave in accordance with what they have been taught, and she therefore buys them off with a pair of motorcycles, in order to distract them from her larger goal of saving her younger sister from the fate that could have been hers. Then, when Hélène's husband Paul becomes a potential obstacle toward the end of the film, Malika is forced to use her powers of seduction to throw him off their trail. She is successful, and he falls for her charms, until the moment when she reveals her identity as the person he chose to ignore when it mattered most, on a pivotal night when her life was on the line, underscoring that her invisibility at that moment was only relative, shocking him with this revelation: 'You knew me already, for a long time'.

Mbembe argues for the dissolution of 'the darkness that surrounds the presence' in France of 'citizens who are made invisible by' 'forms of exclusion' whose only justification is that of 'race' (2010: 116). He maintains that it will no longer be possible in the near future to live 'in an anonymous mode'; instead, individuals will find themselves 'condemned to learn to *live exposed to each other*' (2010: 116, original emphasis). If Mbembe is correct that one of the meanings of 'democracy' is '*the possibility of identification with the Other*' (2010: 117, original emphasis), Malika's movements in *Chaos* have opened up a variety of such possibilities. It is important to note that although the film grapples with serious issues, it often does so in a humorous manner. While it may tell a sobering story, it does so within a funny framework and in this respect it is similar to *Le nom des gens*, a film that stages the militant meanderings of a young woman fully committed to denouncing harmful stereotypes and promoting the advancement of foreigners in France in whatever way possible; nothing can distract her from these tandem goals. Co-written by Michel Leclerc and Baya Kasmi, this film unabashedly addresses difficult historical questions with implications in France, specifically the Holocaust and the Algerian War, alongside the present prevalence of xenophobic attitudes.

From the outset, the two central characters of the film voice their stories, looking straight into the camera in close-up shots that are reminiscent of the one in *Chaos* when Malika is given the opportunity to speak. These meta-fictional moments do not detract from the impact of the work of fiction but instead provide the characters with additional opportunities to express themselves and give the viewer insight into their idiosyncrasies. These protagonists begin by providing background information on their names, Bahia Benmahmoud (Sara Forestier) and Arthur Martin (Jacques Gamblin), appellations that have significance when it comes to their family histories, their personal identities, and their treatment in France. They also give descriptions of their parents, and Bahia's voice-over accompanies her mother's footsteps on a Parisian sidewalk in the 1970s:

> My mother Cécile Délivet is a hippy. She was born into a rich French family but she hates the French and the rich, as well as fine food, vulgar jokes, consumerist society, [. . .] the French national anthem, [. . .] the smug West [. . .]. But one day, she discovers she hates someone more than all the rest.

The woman who has been walking with a certain degree of confidence up to this point looks into a distorted mirror as her daughter pronounces these final words, and gazes with scrutiny at her own image as it is reflected back at her. After this view of herself, the young woman is no longer content to criticise the world she lives in, but must take action in order to change it. Shortly thereafter, she is collecting signatures for a political petition and meets Mohamed: 'When my father arrives in France, he is an immigrant, a penniless war victim and an illegal alien. And that, for my mother, is so cool!' The woman is delighted to exchange her very French name for his Algerian one, they quickly have children, and their Parisian lifestyle includes taking homeless people into their abode as often as possible – and encouraging as many false weddings as possible. The film features one of these *mariages blancs*, apparently the third that Bahia has engaged in, to provide young men from other lands with the legal status necessary to remain in France.

Figure 11.2 Bahia (Sara Forestier) exudes compassion as she helps an elderly couple into a metro car.

It is evident that Bahia is following in her mother's footsteps, devoting her entire being to improving the world she inhabits, as evidenced in a delightful scene in a metro station when she sees that an elderly couple will not be able to board the train in time; she jumps up from her seat and forces the doors open, yelling at the conductor to wait until these two individuals have been able to get in. She takes the woman's arm and helps her up, and they laugh as they step into the car together. This joyful moment of solidarity in the metro stands out in stark contrast to the immense tensions that characterise the metro scene in *Code inconnu*. When a man eventually takes action in Haneke's film, he does so with deep dismay, harshly admonishing the young man who has been harassing Anne. In *Le nom des gens*, the daughter of an immigrant adopts an entirely different role in the space of the metro, one that entails helping others in need, and she is overjoyed when her efforts meet with success. After watching her perform this gesture of solidarity, Arthur gazes approvingly at Bahia and kisses her passionately. At this point, she who proudly speaks of her Algerian heritage does not know that her lover has Jewish roots. When she finds out, she celebrates their differences, indicating that together, 'we are all of France!', and pointing ahead to their joyful decision to name the child who is born of their union at the close of the film 'Chong Martin-Benmahmoud', in a challenge to ethnic and racial stereotypes. The film's co-writer Baya Kasmi contends in an interview that this gregarious protagonist 'is someone who simplifies things out of necessity. The world today is so complex that in order to be an activist, you have to hold to a tight set of interpretations' (Kasmi and Leclerc 2010). This emphasis on the character's need to resort to simplification in order to take action is interesting, for the film as a whole, along with other films that participate in 'activist cinéma-monde', highlight instead the immense complexity that makes activism so profoundly challenging.

The central characters of *Chaos* and *Le nom des gens* indicate through various forms of activism that they are willing participants in a society that is changing in positive ways, in an urban space that is less and less divided and more open to movements of solidarity both in the metro and beyond, in accordance with Mbembe's reflections:

> the *democracy to come* will depend on the response we give to the questions *who is my neighbour, how should I treat the enemy*, and *what should I do with the foreigner*. The 'new question of the Other' in all forms – or that of the presence of others among us, the appearance of the *third* – is at the heart of the contemporary problematic of the human world, of a politic of the world [*d'une politique du monde*]. (2010: 118; original emphasis)

What the creators of these two recent works of cinéma-monde do so well is to 'invent ever-new forms of human coexistence' (119) that provide glimpses of a bright future that Mbembe anticipates with careful formulations: 'the responsibility for others, taking into account the past, will become the orbit that serves as the starting point for putting into motion a discourse on justice and democracy' (120). The storylines of *Chaos* and *Le nom des gens* are inspiring, especially as they depict individuals who are willing to run the risks of responsibility, in the finest sense of this term.

Selfless Seeking: Involvement and Investment in *Trois mondes*

Catherine Corsini's *Trois mondes* contains a pivotal early scene that bears a faint resemblance to the opening sequence of *Chaos*, in which a victim comes into contact with a car at night, a man is eager to escape any connection to the crime, and a woman cannot help but act in response to what she has witnessed. The circumstances are vastly different in this more recent cinematic work, however, for the Frenchwoman who witnesses a hit-and-run accident from her Parisian apartment is a stranger to the Frenchman behind the wheel whose misconduct has put an innocent man into a coma. Juliette (Clotilde Hesme) rushes to the scene of the crime, speaking to and holding the hand of the victim until the ambulance arrives. The following day, she finds herself unable to concentrate in her medical school course, so she leaves for the hospital. She engages in some investigative work to find out the man's name and discovers that he has been illegally employed in insalubrious conditions. In the days that follow, as the victim's life hangs in the balance, Juliette befriends Vera (Arta Dobroshi), the victim's wife, an undocumented Moldavian immigrant who came to France to escape poverty.

Trois mondes takes great care to paint a well-rounded portrait not only of Vera and Juliette, but also of Al (Raphaël Personnaz), the driver who unlawfully departed from the scene of the crime, a young man who is poised to marry his boss's daughter and become a manager of the car dealership where he has slowly worked his way up. Juliette saw this man well enough from her apartment window the night of the accident to identify him and she goes to meet with him when the financial burden of the hospital stay becomes overwhelming. Since Vera's husband has no official pay slips from his years of illegal employment, he is not eligible for health insurance and she must pay for his medical care. Juliette explains to Al that the financial circumstances of the victim's family are dire, and he promises to pay. He opens up to her about his personal life and expresses his curiosity about why she hasn't turned him in to the authorities. Juliette responds that she was unable to. Since she has taken the time to get to know the two of them, since she has listened to the stories of those on the opposing sides of this unfortunate occurrence, she possesses compassion and understanding for both the perpetrator of this unintentional crime and the wife of the victim. Unfortunately, Juliette has come to occupy the untenable position of mediator, and when the Moldavian man dies from his injuries, tensions become unbearable.

The well-intentioned witness is now convinced that she shouldn't have gotten mixed up in this affair, that her involvement has been a mistake. Indeed, this is a question that emerges throughout the film, and Juliette's Parisian interlocutors remain dumbfounded by her behaviour. During a conversation, a friend expresses her inability to understand the empathy that Juliette feels for the man who committed such a heartless crime: 'Why do you always want to help everyone like that?' A similar reproach can be found in the speech of her boyfriend, who was with her in the apartment when the accident occurred, but who is not motivated to become engaged in the way Juliette is. In fact, he admonishes her harshly: 'What are you seeking? You get involved. Without thinking. You get hurt. It's narcissistic to want to fix people's lives. It's pretentious'.

Up until the man's death, Juliette serves as a friend and ally to Vera, whose command of French allows her to express all that she needs with clarity in this foreign tongue, but who is painfully aware that her undocumented status means that she has very little power in this system. Juliette's presence and support are a comfort to Vera, who doesn't appear to have any other French friends. But the death changes things. An especially powerful scene consists of Vera's discussion with medical personnel regarding the possible donation of her husband's organs. They are encouraging her to authorise this gift, but she demands financial compensation, imploring them: 'How much for his body?' When they respond that French law does not allow for payment in exchange for organs, Vera retorts that she and her husband have worked on French soil for five years and that she deserves something in return: 'What am I going to receive? What have they given us? Nothing! That's France. They kill my husband and take his body parts for free.' In her view, France has taken advantage of her beloved, sucking the very life out of him, without recognising him in any way. The French have refused to see him as a human being; they have only viewed him as a means to make a profit.

All three principal protagonists are present at the funeral, which is the final scene of *Trois mondes*. Juliette and Al have obviously been deeply affected by this man's loss of life. They share a profound sense of involvement, investment and responsibility. If Al's every move prior to this fatal event was calculated in order to climb the social ladder, he has changed. He arguably did not possess a moral or ethical code before the accident and habitually closed his eyes to his boss's illegal dealings. But after he found himself obliged to do the same underhanded things to obtain money for the victim of his crime, he came to realise how sordid this way of life is. The film suggests that French society is similarly guilty of focusing on its own rise, its own status, its own standing. It has used immigrants as nameless, faceless participants in a whole range of projects. Despite their work, the nation has excluded them from the system, denying them the benefits they deserve and forcing them to lead a precarious existence. Just as Al failed to see the pedestrian in the crosswalk, so the French in general have turned a blind eye to so many who are making crucial contributions to their country.

The activism of this film proposes a change in perspective, a transformation that is not easy, but that is irreversible. Once she has begun to care for the others in her midst, Juliette realises that there is no going back. She is shunned for her efforts; she is criticised heavily from both sides of the conflict. But she is engaged, truly compassionate, and she is seeking solutions – not easy solutions, but complex meetings among those on either side of the divide who are tempted to see things in stark terms. She is aware that there is no clear distinction between right and wrong in this instance, and comes to discover that the pain of this accident affects them all: the bereaved wife, the drunken driver, and the witness. Juliette forces us to consider what it really means to be present at an unfortunate event, what the many implications are of having seen a crime take place. Juliette is compelled to follow up, to help. This is an inconvenience, an imposition, and it places her in a position that proves to be nearly impossible.

But she is anything but presumptuous, no matter the accusations of her boyfriend. She is driven to activism, but her intervention is private, and it eschews the official channels. She seems to embody the forgiveness that Al begs for when he finally meets Vera in person and struggles with her, face-to-face, in bodily combat. While the widow does not grant him this pardon he requests so fervently, their encounter does lead them in the direction of a certain form of reconciliation. This begins with three gestures: an acknowledgment of the wrong; intense empathy; recognition of the other, of their name and their face.

The tension among these different individuals will likely remain, but it might be attenuated by this movement, by the proximity and the intimacy of these avowals, these exchanges, these mutual expressions of pain. The death of the foreigner in Paris has not entirely been in vain. As Al articulates it with such emotion, this unthinkable event 'is engraved in the depths of his being'. It has marked him for life. And it has changed him for good. Their coming together at the ceremony commemorating this innocent victim's life means that these three individuals, although they may hail from different worlds, are nonetheless united. As David Sorfa writes with respect to *Code inconnu*, 'Haneke implies that everyone is by necessity connected to everyone else and that there is no position of non-complicity: everyone must share the blame' (2006: 99). Paris may well continue to be characterised by difference and division, as the title of Corsini's film indicates, but its varied inhabitants cannot afford any longer to avoid the questions that these activist films pose with aplomb. By '[p]lacing us within this divided city', such cinematic works force us to consider the following: 'what do we owe to others? To our relatives and friends and neighbours? To passersby and foreigners in our midst? To our former colonial subjects? To those who seek refuge among us?' (Geyh 2011: 106). Works that contribute to 'activist cinéma-monde' play a significant role in prodding viewers to ponder these pressing questions and to recognise the crucial presence in Paris of foreign-born individuals from around the world whose lives and stories have often been overlooked, to the detriment of French society at large. Like the character Juliette, all those in the capital city must become wholly involved, truly invested, in selfless seeking of the others among them, at any price.

Works Cited

Alexakis, Vassilis (2015), *La clarinette*, Paris: Seuil.
Cixous H. (2008), 'Celle qui ne se ferme pas', *Derrida à Alger: Un regard sur le monde*, Arles: Actes Sud, pp. 45–58.

Durmelat, Sylvie, and Vinay Swamy (eds) (2011), 'Introduction', *Screening Integration: Recasting Maghrebi Immigration in Contemporary France*, Lincoln: University of Nebraska Press, pp. 1–24.

Ervine, Jonathan (2013), *Cinema and the Republic: Filming on the Margins in Contemporary France*, Cardiff: University of Wales Press.

Geyh, P. E. (2011), 'Cosmopolitan Exteriors and Cosmopolitan Interiors: The City and Hospitality in Haneke's *Code Unknown*', *The Cinema of Michael Haneke*, Ben McCann and David Sorfa (eds), New York: Columbia University Press, pp. 105–16.

Kasmi, B., and M. Leclerc (2010), 'Interview for *The Names of Love*', <http://www.cinemotions.com/interview/117280> (last accessed 13 July 2017).

Lionnet, F. (2006), 'Cultivating mere gardens? Comparative Francophonies, Postcolonial Studies, and Transnational Feminisms', *Comparative Literature in an Age of Globalization*, Haun Saussy (ed.), Baltimore: Johns Hopkins University Press, pp. 100–13.

Mbembe, Achille (2010), *Sortir de la grande nuit: Essai sur l'Afrique décolonisée*, Paris: La Découverte [Édition de poche, 2013].

O'Shaughnessy, Martin (2007), *The New Face of Political Cinema: Commitment in French Film since 1995*, New York: Berghahn Books.

Rice, A. (2007), filmed interview with Bessora, Paris, <http://francophonemetronomes.com/bessora> (last accessed 13 July 2017).

Serreau, C. (2001), 'L'esclavage des femmes, ça suffit!', Interview for *Chaos* with Jacqueline Remy, *L'Express*, 4 October 2001, <http://www.lexpress.fr/actualite/societe/justice/l-esclavage-des-femmes-ca-suffit_491836.html> (last accessed 13 July 2017).

Sorfa, D. (2006), 'Uneasy domesticity in the films of Michael Haneke', *Studies in European Cinema*, 3:2, pp. 93–104.

Wheatley, Catherine (2009), *Michael Haneke's Cinema: The Ethic of the Image*, New York: Berghahn Books.

Wolton, D. (2006), 'Des stéréotypes coloniaux aux regards post-coloniaux: L'indispensable évolution des imaginaires', *Culture post-coloniale 1961–2006: Traces et mémoires coloniales en France*, Pascal Blanchard and Nicolas Bancel (eds), Paris: Autrement, pp. 255–67.

Zielinski, L. (2014), 'Interview: Michael Haneke, The Art of Screenwriting No. 5', *The Paris Review* 211, <http://www.theparisreview.org/interviews/6354/the-art-of-screenwriting-no-5-michael-haneke> (last accessed 13 July 2017).

CHAPTER 12

Cinema Made in Liège: A 'Hub' of Francophone Belgian Filmmaking

Jamie Steele

In an interview with Philippe Reynaert, the head of Wallimage, stated in an interview that 'Brussels has always been the centre [of film production], but in recent years, an impetus in Walloon filmmaking has been imposed on Liège, the homeland of the Dardenne brothers, like a real *Pôle de l'Image*' (Reynaert 2011). Although Reynaert's comment was ludic in tone, it highlighted the emerging tendency for filmmaking in Wallonia to coalesce around the city of Liège. In *Sight and Sound*, Goodfellow first recognised the emergence of Liège as an important filmmaking centre in Belgium and Wallonia, signposting the work of the Dardenne brothers, Thierry Michel, and Bénédicte Liénard's *Une part du ciel/A Piece of Sky* (2002, Belgium/Luxembourg/France) (2003: 26). This article, however, foreshadowed the development of economic incentives and film production facilities that have since encouraged film projects to the city, with the creation of the regional film fund Wallimage in 2001, the Tax Shelter in 2003 (revised in 2014) and Pôle Image de Liège (PIL) in 2006. It is important to note that the discourse adopted in the aforementioned film institutions and fund accounts, summaries and initiatives is not confined to the film sector, instead being inclusive of the audiovisual sector and increasing moves towards 'trans-media'. Against this backdrop of favourable financial conditions for feature filmmaking, Liège has been given the moniker 'Hollywood-sur-Meuse' (Gillet 2010). The 2014 Cannes film festival proved a key point for the visibility and valorisation of film production in Liège with five films, *Deux jours, Une nuit/Two Days, One Night* (Jean-Pierre and Luc Dardenne, 2014, Belgium/France/Italy), *Grace of Monaco* (Olivier Dahan, 2014, Switzerland/France/Belgium/Italy/USA), *Jimmy's Hall* (Ken Loach, 2014, UK/Ireland/France), *Alléluia* (Fabrice du Welz, 2014, Belgium/France) and *P'tit Quinquin/Li'l Quinquin* (Bruno Dumont, 2014, France), selected for screening. This cross-section of films neatly epitomises current trends in *Liégeois* filmmaking with regional and 'national' films operating seamlessly alongside international co-productions. Moreover, the Dardenne brothers remain a significant feature in the city's filmmaking heritage – in part a shorthand for *Liègeois* filmmaking – from a nascent period in the 1970s through to the current 'economic' turn.

The city of Liège is located in southeast Belgium in the French-speaking region of Wallonia. In terms of the overall Belgian urban hierarchy, Luik/Liège is positioned third behind the capital region of Brussels/Bruxelles and the Flemish city of Antwerp/Anvers (Loopmans et al. 2007: 86). The number of inhabitants in Liège is approximately 380,174 (OECD 2016), whereas the overall population number for the Liège arrondissement (the metropolitan area) was approximately 740,000 in 2014 (OECD 2016). In Wallonia, the creation of a regional 'centre' or 'capital' is rather convoluted since there is no recognisable dominant city. Namur is the governmental capital of Wallonia, Charleroi is the most populous municipal area, Mons was the joint European capital of culture in 2015 and is seen as the cultural capital of Wallonia, and Liège has the largest metropolitan area. This perceived weakness in recognising a regional centre in Wallonia is partly attributed to 'the lack of a medieval urban tradition, comparable to that of Flanders' (Thomas 1990: 47). The rapid development of the region's cities and towns occurred instead during the period of industrialisation in the nineteenth century, which has created an intrinsically urban industrial character.

Klinkenberg proffers that Liège has adopted a position as a 'centre-périphérique' in Belgium (2010: 39–40). This interpretation is primarily linked to the city's cultural context in the 1970s. For Klinkenberg, Liège functions as a 'centre' or a 'capital' in terms of socio-political and cultural debates and the production of avant-garde work (2010: 39). Presently, the city is perceived as the unofficial capital of culture in Wallonia, which speaks to its reputation for developing innovative and creative talent. As we will see in this chapter, this 'centre-périphérique' dynamic is particularly suggestive of Liège's position in Belgium, as a potential regional centre in a country that is geographically and linguistically divided into three regions, and as decentred in terms of Belgium's association with *la Francophonie*. For Murphy, *la Francophonie* introduces debates that align with a French 'centre' and a francophone 'periphery' since France eschews membership (2002: 173). This is furthered by Spaas's (2000) survey of francophone cinema, which overlooks France in the discussion dedicated to European *francophonie*. To this end, francophone Belgian cinema is conceptualised as decentred in relation to France, operating in a marginal and peripheral position. Spaas's survey also includes references to only two (technically, three) filmmakers based in the *Liégeois* region in Wallonia, Jean-Jacques Andrien and the Dardenne brothers. Spaas's overview from the 1930s through to the late 1990s coalesces around filmmakers whose films represent a 'struggle for identity' (2000: 9), such as filmmakers that bridged the Flemish/French-speaking cultural and linguistic divide (Charles Dekeukeliere, Henri Storck, André Delvaux, and more recently Jaco Van Dormael), diasporic filmmakers (Chantal Akerman, Boris Lehman, Michel Khleifi) and filmmakers with work produced in Brussels (Van Dormael, Chantal Akerman). This foregrounds the economic shift in Belgian cinema towards the south and the region of Wallonia since 2001 that has since witnessed the emergence of a new group of young filmmakers. Klinkenberg's (2010) premise of Liège operating as both a 'centre' and a 'periphery' represents an apposite means of highlighting the city's importance to developing and enhancing film production in the French-speaking regions of the country.

Clusters, Cities and Audiovisual Hubs

For Porter, clusters encourage a fresh and renewed interpretation of national, state, and local economies in which companies, government and institutions (such as universities and trade associations) come together to foster a greater sense of collaboration, competition and innovation (1998: 77–9). This collaboration and competition is enhanced by proximity between the relevant firms. As Porter concludes '[p]roximity in geographic, cultural, and institutional terms allows special access, special relationships, better information, powerful incentives, and other advantages in productivity and productivity growth that are difficult to tap from a distance' (90). This sense of proximity is particularly instructive for providing a detailed study of the city's audiovisual sector. First, we can identify the concentration of film production companies and Tax Shelter incentives, second the number of specialist audiovisual companies and technical providers, and thirdly film projects drawing on these opportunities and facilities from France. In this sense, proximity is not merely geographic, since there is an emphasis on linguistic and cultural mutual intelligibility that stretches across national and regional borders. In Belgium, audiovisual 'clusters' operate on three separate levels: first city-based; second regional (Wallimage and Screen Flanders); and third supranational (Ciné-regio). This chapter will concentrate on the city, with references to how decision-making at a regional and national level supports audiovisual practices. The city-based audiovisual cluster is a relatively new phenomenon in Belgium, with the creation of PIL in 2006 and Bruxellimage (now Screen.Brussels and 'Cinema made in Brussels') opening in 2009.

In a cinematic context, the city represents a centre point for film and media production, bringing together film production companies, film institutions, funding agencies, distributors and film festivals (as a market place). From this premise, Tremblay and Cecilli (2009) offer an interpretation of Montreal as a 'North American hub for film and audiovisual production', emphasising the 'relational proximity' of film firms and companies that has engendered competition and innovation. Alternatively, television historian Curtin proposes the concept of 'media capitals' that portray cities, such as Hong Kong and Chicago, as 'sites of mediation, locations where complex forces and flows interact' (2003: 205). In this sense, a 'media capital' moves away from the national and regional paradigm, instead encouraging an interpretation of audiovisual production through a transnational lens. These flows are not limited to 'capital' as a purely economic term, since it also posits a 'centre of activity' and 'a concentration of resources, reputation and talent.' (205) This concept chimes with Porter's (1998; 2000) approach to 'clusters'. As part of this network of flows, the city is also described as a 'node' (Curtin 2003), which takes into account the city as an area of mobility. This mobility arises in the form of businesses, finance, films, television and radio programmes, and people (such as film technicians, actors, directors and producers) that intersect in a particular city. Bill Marshall similarly places mobility and different 'mobile forms', whether they may be related to language, film talent and personnel, films and finance, at the forefront of the cinéma-monde concept (2012). It is within this paradigm that 'plateaus', predicated more on artistic and personal exchanges and connections, intersect (2012: 51). From this premise, a (French-speaking) city can enable a period of filmmaking activity, operating freely outside the nation and within a French-speaking context, due to flows of people and finance.

In terms of regional policy, the Walloon government funded the T.W.I.S.T scheme (Technologies Wallonnes de l'Image, du Son et du Texte), which actively promotes cluster building in the audiovisual and digital media sectors. This turn towards cluster building in Wallonia was encouraged as part of a wider policy by the Walloon government to rejuvenate the business sector against the backdrop of declining heavy and metallurgic industries in the region. The shift to business clusters in January 2000 – a priority measure for the regional government – was included as part of the phasing out of the Objective 1 and 2 programmes from the European Structural Funds (Clusters.wallonie.be 2015).[1] The European Structural Fund Objectives 1 and 2 intended to develop regions that were considered to be 'lagging behind' and actively supported 'the economic conversion of declining industrial areas' (Evans and Foord 1999: 63). The initial identified areas were Hainaut (Objective 1) and the urban and rural areas of Liège, Namur and Luxembourg (Objective 2) (Clusters.wallonie. be 2015). To this end, Liège (15) has the largest number of T.W.I.S.T members registered with the scheme, followed by Mons (11), Namur (4) and Charleroi (1). In the Hainaut region, Mons and Marcinelle specialise in the development of broadcasting and multimedia technologies, with, for instance, Virtualis based in the area. There are developments designed to diversify audiovisual practices further with the creation of a 'pole' outside Charleroi (Peeters 2013: 18). However, this is not to say that the European Structural Fund Objectives are not still salient in the context of the audiovisual sector in Wallonia, and in particular in Liège. Meusinvest, a public partner of both Pôle Image de Liège and Films de la Drève S.C.R.L, is part-financed through Innodem 2 S.A, which adheres to Objective 2 of the European Regional Development Funds. In doing so, Meusinvest supports primarily local concerns. This is imbued in the fund's name, which references the river that runs through the heart of the city of Liège.

A Filmmaking Eco-history of Liège

Let us first take a step back to better understand how this increasingly developed site of film and audiovisual production in Belgium emerged. In terms of film production, Liège has risen from a marginal and peripheral position, with the city first noted for its 'militant' and 'socially conscious' form of video and filmmaking in the 1970s (Jean-Pierre and Luc Dardenne 1981: 69; Mosley 2001: 156; Mélon 2010: 127). The traditions and filmmakers that emerged in this period are salient to the development of feature-length film production in the 1990s and 2000s. Prior to this development in videomaking, there was little Belgian film culture in the city, beyond the viewing of imported films through distribution firms based in Brussels (Mélon 2010: 120). The 'militant edge' emerges from the heritage of creative video art and video documentaries that were developed in the 1970s and 1980s for the programme *Vidéographie* in association with the television company RTBF (Radio Télévision Belge Francophone). In the 1970s, RTBF opted to decentralise its television production, installing facilities and centres across the region in Charleroi, Liège, Mons and Namur (Roekens 2009: 195). Robert Stéphane – the director of RTBF Liège – highlighted how the channel intended to create programmes that differentiated it from televisual output produced in

Brussels (Cartes sur Cables 1986: 5). *Vidéographie*, created by Jean-Paul Tréfois in 1976, commenced with a series of six episodes dedicated to American video, showcasing the work of Nam Jun Paik and John Jonas, before supporting Belgian talent in the form of *Marcher, ou la fin des temps modernes* (Boris Lehman and Michèle Blondeel, 1979). This video documentary was the first to be produced at the studios of RTBF Liège. The show ran for a period of ten years – to 1986 – after being under review annually for de-commissioning. However, it is this regular airing of video shorts and documentaries that helped to foster creativity and support emerging young filmmakers in Wallonia. As Luc Dardenne notes,

> [t]his type of collaboration is evidently ideal, not only from a financial perspective but also in terms of the availability of technology. If we were able to produce films by benefitting from RTBF-Liège's image editing equipment, we could work a lot more on working on the image than on the moment captured. (Begon and Van Cauwenberge n.d: 9)

The creation of this programming opened up opportunities for aspiring independent filmmakers to disseminate their work as well as providing access to key facilities. This productive relationship was interpreted as a 'movement to debureaucratise modes of production' (Begon and Van Cauwenberge n.d: 9). The availability of new analogue technologies, such as video, democratised the camera and enabled a new generation of filmmakers to learn their craft. As Mosley crucially observes, the 'non-institutional' status of video production provided freer access for female filmmakers in particular to develop their output (2001: 157). In this period, Liège was represented not only by Jean-Pierre and Luc Dardenne, but also by Jean-Claude Riga, Rob Rombout, André Roumas, Thierry Michel, Manu Bonmariage,[2] Eddy Luyckx, Anne-François Perin, Marie-France Collard and Nicole Widart (Mélon 2010: 135).[3]

Sojcher observes that, at the end of the 1970s and start of the 1980s, subsidised production companies and funding mechanisms were formed after the implementation of an 'avance sur recettes' style system (1999: 257–8). These subsidised *ateliers* (workshops) by the Fédération Wallonie-Bruxelles (CFWB) are divided into three distinct lines; first, the film schools; second, production companies (for example Dérives); and third, regional workshops. The documentary-focused audiovisual structures Wallonie Image Production (W.I.P.) and a parallel structure Centre de l'Audiovisuel à Bruxelles (C.B.A), based in Brussels, fall into the third category. As a result, W.I.P. was required to produce at least 40% of films by first-time filmmakers in order to adhere to the *Arrêté de l'Exécutif du 26 juillet 1990* (CCA 2010: 97).

W.I.P. was founded in 1982 in Liège with support from the Minister of Culture for the French-speaking Community, Philippe Moureaux. The production centre was set up with an initial budget of approximately 4 million Belgian francs, and it was designed to support projects that 'privilege original and personal film projects, capturing the uniqueness of a culture in order to roam though the imaginary [arpenter l'imaginaire] and open it up to the world' (Neys 1989). From this premise, W.I.P. proposed to fund and produce video documentaries and experimental projects that engage with cultural concerns. For instance, *Regarde Jonathan, Jean Louvet, son oeuvre/Look at Jonathan, Jean Louvet, his work* (Jean-Pierre and Luc Dardenne, 1983, Belgium) was provided with 350,000 Belgian francs and was first broadcast on *Vidéographie* in October 1983. The video documentary is experimental in terms of its form and editing, with interpolated sequences from Jean Louvet's three plays *Le train du bon Dieu*, *Conversations en Wallonie*, and *L'homme qui avait le soleil dans sa poche*. These sequences highlight the difficulty in living in 1980s Wallonia – particularly for the young, working-class male – against the backdrop of both an active and inactive industrial landscape (Fraipont 1983).[4] W.I.P. also aimed to 'open up' these works to an international audience, reaching beyond the region and the local TV stations, to receive valorisation at film festivals. For instance, *Regarde Jonathan* achieved a special screening at the Festival de Montbéliard, the festival where the Dardenne brothers' earlier work *Lorsque le bateau de Léon M. descendit la Meuse pour la première fois/When Léon M's boat went down the Meuse for the first time* (1979, Belgium) was 'discovered' by *Cahiers du Cinéma* (Fargier 1982). Nicole Widart's *Paysage imaginaire* (1983, Belgium) and *Fin de carrière* (1985, Belgium) were screened at the San Sebastian film festival (B.D. 1984: 53). This premise of international distribution and dissemination still remains, with W.I.P.'s website offering DVD copies (as of 2016) of the audiovisual works back to 1982. Moreover, the *atelier* remains as a key point of call for producing documentaries in Wallonia, supporting works by both established and emerging filmmaking talent, such as *D'arbres et de charbon/About Trees and Coal* (Bénédicte Lienard, 2012, Belgium), *Haïti, la terre/Haiti* (Jean-Claude Riga, 2013, Belgium/Haiti), *L'homme qui répare les femmes: La colère d'Hippocrate/The man who mends women: The wrath of Hippocrates* (Thierry Michel and Colette Braeckman, 2014, Belgium/Congo/USA) and *Eurovillage* (François Pirot, 2015, Belgium). Since 2006, its premises have been housed in the building developed by Pôle Image de Liège.

Moreover, new, subsidised production companies were created and run by talent from the region, such as the Dardenne brothers forming the Dérives Collective ASBL (association sans but lucratif) in 1977 and the Fleur Maigre co-operative set up by Christine Pireaux and the filmmaker Thierry Michel. The co-operative is no longer operating with the two founding figures currently working for Les Films de la Passerelle (also based in Liège). Dérives, however, remains extant even after the Dardenne brothers' turn to feature films and the creation of Les Films du Fleuve in the same office block in 1994. The creation of a financing support system and subsidised production companies highlighted a turn to an organised and developed audiovisual sector. The Dérives Collective initially benefitted from funds provided by the *Ministère de la Culture française* to produce videos that focused on the workers' movements in the *Liégeois* region (Jean-Pierre and Luc Dardenne 1981: 69–70). As a consequence, the production company was positioned in the 'interstices of the institutional system' (Begon n.d: 23), drawing on state subsidies whilst using an affordable and flexible medium in the form of video. Initially, the Collective drew on non-professional videomaking equipment, such as half-inch videotape, due to the expense of 16mm film stock and trade union regulations that came with professionalisation (23). At this point, video and film production was low budget and predicated on local and community-based mechanisms providing support, as well as the filmmakers drawing on personal funds for the projects. The films deal with local articulations and socio-political issues latent in the recorded images. The Dardenne brothers, in particular, draw on the memories of workers to recount the workers' strikes in Seraing and Liège, as opposed to creating a pro-filmic event to re-stage and re-present the action. Subsequent productions, such as *R . . . ne répond plus/R . . . No longer responds* (Jean-Pierre and Luc Dardenne, 1981, Belgium), used U-matic video stock, which required the use of editing equipment available at the RTBF studios and Médiaform Production in Liège (Jean-Pierre and Luc Dardenne 1981: 70). The Dérives Collective still operates with these established connections, purchasing material with the W.I.P. and collaborating with RTBF for the distribution and exhibition of the documentaries in Belgium (Verhaeghe 2004).

Filmmakers, such as the Dardenne brothers, Jean-Jacques Andrien and Jean-Claude Riga, to name but a few, still play a crucial role in the filmmaking ecosystem in Liège and across Wallonia since the 1990s. To this end, these filmmakers have played a role in the reform and the development of cinema and filmmaking practices on both an economic and cultural level. The Dardenne brothers are a crucial case in point, remaining a shorthand for filmmaking on a national, regional and local level due to their involvement in the documentary and feature film sectors as both producers and creators.

1990s–2000s: The Economic and Institutional Turn in Liégeois Filmmaking

At the Namur film festival in 1998, Jean-Jacques Andrien foregrounded the discernable absence of filmmaking activity in Wallonia, recognising the leftovers from the documentary era, such as W.I.P., as the few financial supporters of cinema in Wallonia. Andrien (1998) offers a criticism of Belgian film production as particularly prohibitive for 'regional' modes of filmmaking, with the need to disseminate film funds more widely to develop production beyond the 'centre' of Brussels. This position is derived from Andrien's experiential understanding of the industry, after moving his production company, Les Films de la Drève, from Brussels to Liège in the 1970s. As a result, Cinéma Wallonie was created in July 1997 in Liège, with the aim of grouping together modes of production, distribution and exhibition in the region. Membership for Cinéma Wallonie was not reserved for only filmmakers, but involved writers, editors, producers, journalists, distributors and exhibitors. Key members were Jean-Claude Riga, Marie-France Collard, Yasmine Kassari and Paul Meyer, amongst others. One notable absence from an involvement in Cinéma Wallonie was Jean-Pierre and Luc Dardenne, who largely sought international finance, primarily from France, to produce their films based in Liège. With reference to cinéma-monde, Marshall observes the fluidity of the 'national' paradigm due to the preponderance of co-productions in a francophone cinematic context, placing emphasis on the figure of the auteur in these interactions (2012: 39). The local – in this case Liège operates as the starting point – and the international intersect at a point of funding and production that bypasses the 'national'. This is compounded by the auteur-centred nature of the production centres and methods in the francophone Belgian context, eschewing 'national' structures in favour of regional and international modes of production.

This represents a stepping away from a Brussels-centred or even 'national' Belgian film industry – incorporating Flemish, *Bruxellois* and Walloon cinemas – with the active development of an industry along regional lines. As previously outlined in this chapter, the range of funding bodies and production facilities increased in the early to mid-2000s in Wallonia, after the intervention of Cinéma Wallonie. From this premise, we can now see the move towards the creation of a new 'pole' or 'node' (in economic terms), which is particularly borne out by the name of the audiovisual hub Pôle Image de Liège. This evolution is primarily economic in terms of its remit and focus. Young and emerging filmmaking talent in the French-speaking regions of Belgium have developed their filmmaking style through support from production companies investing in their short films. This turn will be addressed in the final section of this chapter.

The Walloon government initially implemented Wallimage as a resource designed to support the production of feature-length films, TV series and animated films in the French-speaking region. In this period, documentaries and short films have not received financial support from the economic-focused funds in Wallonia. After the closure of Cinéma Wallonie, Jean-Jacques Andrien's role in the economic development of the Walloon film industry continued through to the subsequent institution Wallimage, where he worked on the selection committee alongside Hubert Toint, Robert Reuchamps, Jean-Pierre Dardenne, Benoît Mariage, and Patrick Quinet. The economic turn of filmmaking in the French-speaking region is predicated on restrictions within which the Walloon government operates. As Reynaert outlines,

> [t]he Walloon government has no cultural authority, so we concentrated on the economic aspect [...] We wanted to create new businesses in the film industry on a long-term basis, and decided to pump money into local projects. The only commitment film producers had to make was to reinvest the money in the local economy. (Peeters 2013: 17)

The 'cultural authority' of francophone Belgian filmmaking lies to the north of Wallonia in the Capital-region of Brussels and with the *Centre du Cinéma et de l'Audiovisuel* (CCA). The CCA was formed in 1995 to administer film production and project selection in French-speaking regions in Belgium, Brussels and Wallonia. As the CCA grants selective aid, film projects are assessed against 'cultural project tests'. Conversely, the economic remit of the Brussels-based film industry is not as developed as in the South of the country, with Bruxellimage functioning as a subsidiary to Wallimage. This has since shifted with Brussels film professionals rebranding, and separating the film fund, to distance it from its former Walloon partner.

The institutionalisation of film funding in Wallonia was created through two 'lines', first Sowalim (renamed Wallimage Coproductions), followed by Inwa (now Wallimage Entreprises) in 2008. SofiPôle, a subsidiary of SRIW (Société régionale d'Investissement de Wallonie), currently funds the Entreprise line and Wallimage Coproductions. The intention is therefore to intervene in the economic development of the region and the film industry, following the model already established with the Länder across the border in Germany. In order to qualify for the aforementioned funds, film production and post-production companies must be based in Wallonia and independent of the television sector. As a result, the line contributes financially to a range of activities, such as production companies, new technologies, facilities and Tax Shelter intermediary companies. For instance, Wallimage Entreprise provided a capital investment of 833,090 Euros to PIL in 2010 (Wallimage Entreprises 2013: 20), four years after its opening.

In terms of 'national' funding mechanisms, the Tax Shelter, established in 2003 and revised in 2014, offers a tax-based incentive to private companies to facilitate inward investment to the film industry.[5] By offering tax incentives to locate a film project in Belgium, screen policies, formed at the level of national government, are able to entice film productions to the nation or linguistically similar regions. The city of Liège has become home to several film production funds that tap into the Tax Shelter system, such as Cinéfinance (in operation since 2012 and currently integrated into Casa Kafka), Invers Invest (2005) and Fast Forward (2003). In 2009, the Festival international du film policier de Liège launched a film market dedicated to enhancing francophone Belgian filmmakers' and producers' knowledge of the Tax Shelter and how it operates.

The intermediary company Cinéfinance has gained a certain visibility and valorisation in this sector by virtue of its association with the Dardenne brothers and the inclusion of their production company, Les Films du Fleuve, in its framework. The Dardenne brothers' production companies – Dérives, and Les Films du Fleuve – both have a long tradition of working on projects as international co-production partners. This coheres with the pooling of finance from numerous international sources, such as France, Italy, Luxembourg and Tunisia, to produce their early feature-length films, *La promesse/The Promise* (1996, Belgium/France/Luxembourg/Tunisia) and *Rosetta* (1999, Belgium/France). In the 1990s, the Dardenne brothers co-produced the Luxembourgish film *Three shake-a-leg-steps to Heaven* (Andy Bausch, 1993) and the French-Tunisian co-production *Les siestes grenadine/Grenadine siestas* (Mahmoud ben Mahmoud, 1999) as a form of 'reciprocity' (Duculot 2003b: 47). To this end, the arrangement with the Tax Shelter system to co-produce film projects represents a logical step forward for Les Films du Fleuve. The idea of creating an intermediary company that operates between three production companies within the framework of the Tax Shelter was initially discussed between Les Films du Fleuve and Versus Productions in 2006 (Duculot 2006b: 62). As Jean-Pierre Dardenne notes, the filmmakers' tendency to work as co-producers, and regularly pool funding for their own projects through co-production partners, recalls their collaborative work when creating documentaries (du Jaunet 2015a: 32). This highlights the significance of collective filmmaking that has been inculcated in (francophone) Belgian, Walloon and Liège-based filmmakers since (at least) the 1970s.

Cinéfinance brings together three production companies (Tarantula and FraKas) alongside the Pôle Image de Liège (PIL). From this premise, the film fund once more highlights the significance of proximity in Porter's (1998; 2000) work on 'clusters' in the context of creative production on a local level, with production companies in a certain location working together to develop innovative film projects. As Reynaert (Siritzky 2015: 22) observes, since the increase of tax credit for film projects, Wallimage has witnessed more 'mid-range' film productions in terms of their budget, which, in essence, translates to 'auteur' films. This is neatly captured in the film output of production companies Les Films du Fleuve and Tarantula (founded in 1996), which have co-produced films by established auteurs such as *Visage/Face* (Tsai Ming-Liang, 2009, France/Taiwan/Belgium/Netherlands), *La bataille dans le ciel/Battle in Heaven* (Carlo Reygadas, 2005, Mexico/Belgium/France/Germany/Netherlands), *Au delà des collines/Beyond the Hills* (Cristian Mungiu, 2012, Romania/France/Belgium) and *The Angel's Share* (Ken Loach, 2012, UK/France Belgium/Italy). This cross-section of co-productions imbricates two of Hjort's (2009: 15–30) typologies of cinematic transnationalism, as either 'opportunistic' or 'auteurist' forms.[6] For instance, *Au delà des collines* represents an 'ad hoc' (Hjort 2009: 23) arrangement with the Dardenne brothers, after the francophone Belgian filmmakers actively encouraged a Cristian Mungiu retrospective at the Cinémathèque Royale in 2012.[7]

At this point, the shift in economic conditions in the audiovisual sector has facilitated the growth of Wallonia as a means of funding local, regional, national or international film projects. Film producers are able to collaborate with Belgian intermediary companies and production companies in order to supplement a project's budget. However, this does not account for technical expertise, the presence of technical providers, and post-production facilities available in Wallonia, and in particular Liège, to drive film projects to Belgium.

Local Clustering: 'Walliwood' and Pôle Image de Liège

In 2005, Reynaert posited that Liège presented the region with an opportunity to create a 'Walliwood' (Law 2005). This idea concerned the creation of a concentrated centre of film and audiovisual production, which could become a byword for francophone Belgian – or more precisely – Walloon filmmaking. The initial premise for the creation of a 'Walliwood' in Liège was suggested after the Minister for Economics and Employment in Wallonia visited the Västra Göteland site in Sweden (Lorfèvre 2006). The launch of PIL coincided with the creation of CLAP in the same year, which provided producers with a first port of call to find technicians and actors in the area and gain permissions for location shooting. These services further geared the area towards generating a greater administration and management of creative production. For instance, CLAP provides financial and technical support, such as shooting locations and horeca (catering), to projects on a local level in the area of Liège. In terms of film location centres, Wallonia is arranged into three areas; the Walloon Brabant region, the Liège, Namur and Luxembourg provinces, and the Hainaut region.

Since the formation of PIL and CLAP in 2006, there has been a dramatic increase in feature films drawing on the facilities in the area, from six films in 2006, to twenty films in 2007 and finally thirty-four projects in 2013 (CLAP 2013: 10).[8] In terms of feature films commissioned in the same period by the CCA (francophone) Belgian film production stands at twenty in 2006, twenty-one in 2007 and twenty-eight in 2013 (CCA 2014: 223). Since 2007 the number of film projects using Liège and its facilities as a production centre has surpassed the total number of minority and majority francophone Belgian co-produced films supported by the CCA. Between 2010 and 2015, investment in film projects in Liège exceeded funds provided to films across the region of Wallonia, with 13 million Euros provided to projects in Liège and 11.5 million Euros across the rest of Wallonia (Wallimage, 2016).

Moreover, among the majority of films produced in Liège are international co-productions, primarily with France. For instance, in 2009 six majority French co-productions were produced in the city, four of which featured Belgium as a minority partner.[9] Four films were produced as either 100% Belgian or Belgian majority co-productions in the same period. By 2013, the co-production patterns are more complex with a greater diversification of film projects from the Netherlands, Germany, Canada and the USA coming to the region. However, the 'affinitive' (Hjort 2009: 17–18) and co-operative relationship with France remained discernably present, with ten majority co-productions from France and ten majority Belgian co-productions. This coheres with the regional statistics, which state that 52% of films produced in Wallonia are international co-productions ('Wallimage puts on a show' 2014).

In *Écran Total*'s issue dedicated to Belgian cinema, Pascal Diot, the director of Pôle Image de Liège, outlines the intentions to develop Liège as a 'vrai hub créatif' [a true creative hub] (du Jaunet 2015b: 19). As a

Figure 12.1 The PIL facility in Liège, with slag heaps in the background, highlighting the city's coal-mining heritage.

result, PIL was set up to stimulate audiovisual production in and around the city. The decision to form the local cluster was initiated by corporate partners, namely IMG (Invest Minguet Gestion SA), in order to bring the advantages of an economy of scale to the small and medium enterprises (SMEs) in the audiovisual field. Their economic interest in audiovisual and broadcasting technologies have been established since 1994 with the development of EVS broadcasting equipment. Public partners concerned with local investment, such as Meusinvest, later joined the funding of the local cluster.

Within the PIL facility there are approximately forty companies working in content production (film and television), digital media, and broadcasting (du Jaunet 2014: 7) (see Figure 12.1). There are two key strands to PIL as a film organisation: (1) film finance through the Tax Shelter (such as through the aforementioned Cinéfinance); and (2) a home to professional associations. As Iland (2016) outlines, the last five years (since approximately 2010) have witnessed a growth of technical providers in the region. This is particularly the case in terms of digital and special effects companies, which, according to Reynaert, have enabled the region to become more 'competitive' (Brébant 2013: 53).

In light of the changing film funding ecosystem in Belgium, production companies and post-production facilities have either (re-)located or diversified from their country of origin and opened a Belgian arm. For instance, post-production facilities HoverLord, Digital Graphics, and Wallonie

Effets Visuels (FX), a subsidiary of the French company Mikros Images, have tapped into these available resources.[10] French technical provider Mikros Images and equipment provider TSF.be moved to Liège in 2008 and 2010, with loans of 300,000 Euros made by Wallimage Entreprises to their development in 2014 and 2013 respectively (Wallimage Entreprises 2013: 35).[11] The technical provider has worked on approximately 350 feature films in their three locations in France (since 1985), Belgium (2008) and Canada (2011), with *De rouille et d'os/Rust and Bone* (Jacques Audiard, 2012) presently being valorised in an event dedicated to the company (Cinémathèque.fr 2016).

The French majority, Belgian minority co-production *De rouille et d'os* highlights the role played by minority co-productions in the *Liégeois* filmmaking ecosystem. The Dardenne brothers, and their production company Les Films du Fleuve, operated as the Belgian partner on the project. The film also drew on the expertise offered by Mikros Images in post-production for special effects, dividing the work on 200 shots equally between the bases in Paris and Liège (Frei 2012). For this work, the two post-production bases worked autonomously on the project (Ibid.). According to Reynaert (2012), Belgium contributed only 12% of the film's budget of 15.5 million Euros. In terms of regional finance, Wallimage contributed the most significant sum and, as a consequence, recorded audiovisual expenditure of 930,290 Euros (338% of funding provided) (Ibid.). At this time, Wallimage was operating with a territoriality clause attached to the finance, and this required a project to spend no more than 80% of the budget in the region (Wallimage 2009: 13). The revised European Cinema Communication (2013) has since lower these territoriality requirements to around 160% of finance provided to an audiovisual project. The importance of attracting the minority co-productions to Wallonia, and to Liège, is heightened by the sizeable budget of these productions in comparison to (francophone) Belgian filmmaking, which has an average budget of approximately 3 million Euros (Engelen 2015).

PIL's current emphasis is on enhancing its international scope, supplementing the developed ties with its linguistic neighbour and frequent co-producer France and 'national' film production. As Diot notes,

> [t]he new Tax Shelter rules and regulations will be more favourable to non-European production companies. We must open ourselves (Belgium) up more to the non-francophone world, even if there are already things in development with Quebec. (Fabes 2014)

As a result of Belgian tax reform, co-production connections and links across Europe and the globe have been formed beyond the established and co-operative relationships with France. Reynaert foregrounds the geographical proximity of Germany to Liège as a potential factor for enhancing co-production links between the two countries (Peeters 2013: 19).

As previously outlined, the 2013 accounts published by CLAP evince this increased diversification of film projects drawing on the facilities on offer in the region. This is also borne out by representatives from Wallonia – and Liège – lobbying in the USA (Brébant 2013: 54–5) and embarking on trips to England, Germany and Canada (Iland 2016) in order to foster and develops greater relations. For instance, 2013 records show four majority and minority co-productions developed with Canada, such as the majority Belgian co-productions *Hors les murs/Beyond the Walls* (David Lambert, 2012, Belgium/France/Canada), *Moroccan Gigolos* (Ismaël Saidi, 2013, Belgium/Canada), *Tokyo Fiancé* (Stéphane Liberski, 2014, Belgium/France/Canada) and *Je suis à toi/All yours* (David Lambert, 2014, Belgium/Canada). These examples evince an extension of the 'affinitive' (Hjort 2009: 17–18) connections beyond France to other members of *la Francophonie*. This is a particularly salient evolution to consider in the current context, with financial incentives to (re-)locate a film and audiovisual project to Wallonia, and the technical providers available in PIL, paramount to the sector's development. Moreover, presently, Iland (2016) notes that there has been a substantial increase in funds to the Tax Shelter since the reform (from around 12 million Euros to around 25 million Euros), which has led to PIL searching for additional film projects with greater level of finance available in the sector.

'New Francophone Belgian Cinema': The Emergence of Film Talent and Short Filmmaking

In the mid-1990s to the early 2000s, production companies (such as Versus Productions and Latitudes Productions in Liège, and Need Productions in Brussels) and the CCA invested in cultivating film talent. This policy was designed to favour films by first- and second-time directors. The CCA, supported by the Fédération Wallonie-Bruxelles (CFWB), functions as a selective aid and cultural subsidiary, opting for film projects that adhere to its set of cultural criteria. These cultural criteria are primarily concerned with the articulation of the film project in French, the location of the film in Belgium, and the use of studio and technical facilities in Belgium (Gyroy 2000). Decision-making processes for short filmmaking have remained the responsibility of the 'national' film institution (that is, the institution for the linguistic community). According to Herold (2014), the European Commission uses cultural project tests increasingly as a means of preventing large, big budget productions from entering into a given country's film industry. The regional funding mechanism of Wallimage overlooks short filmmaking, instead focusing its intentions on developing feature-length films and majority and minority co-productions. This is evinced by the fund's economic remit and its focus on economic fallout and expenditure in the region. As a result, we can map the creation of short films in a select few locations, primarily large cities with adequate filmmaking funds and facilities available.

In 1995, short filmmaking constituted 11% of the CCA's total production budget with progressive increases to 23% in 2000 (CCA 2004: 217–218). At this time, production companies invested in the medium were concentrated in the Capital region of Brussels. The first short film based in Liège to receive production support was *Mort à Vignole* (Olivier Smolders, 1999, Belgium). From this premise, 1999 proved a turning point in short film production, with Latitudes Productions (set up by Jean-Claude Riga in 1992 and closed in 1999), Dérives and Versus Productions supporting projects by young, emerging film talent. Prior to its closure, Latitudes Productions supported Lanners' first entry into filmmaking in the form of the 17-minute short *Travellinckx* (Bouli Lanners, 1999, Belgium) and Micha Wald's first 12-minute short *La nuit tous les chats sont gris* (1999, Belgium). This line of production adheres to the requirements of the *Arrêté de l'Exécutif du 26 juillet 1990* and the *Décret relatif au soutien au cinéma et à la création audiovisuelle* (2011 and modified in 2013), which place an emphasis on subsidising audiovisual works – with public funds – for a filmmaker's first- and second-time work.

In 2002, the annual journal dedicated to Belgian cinema – *Cinéma Belge* – recognised a turn to short filmmaking as part of a 'shifting landscape' in which young filmmaking talent was provided with the opportunity to create their first films ('Paysage en mutation' 2002: 64–65). Cultivating talent via the short film form is a proven route to successful feature-length filmmaking, particularly in and around the city of Liège. Héliot (2008: 88–89) identifies the work of Versus Productions and its intention to develop short filmmaking talent to feature-length filmmakers as a key contributor to the 'effervescence' of francophone Belgian cinema in the mid-2000s. For instance, Versus Productions had a significant presence at the 2004 Locarno film festival, with two filmmakers nominated for the 'Leopards of Tomorrow' competition (for short-film filmmakers who had not yet made a long film) in the form of *Alice et moi* (Micha Wald, 2004, Belgium) and *Dans l'ombre/In the Dark* (Olivier Masset-Depasse, 2004, Belgium). Masset-Depasse's film was awarded the highest prize in that competition – the second time the filmmaker had won the award – and Wald's short received the *Petit Rail d'or* at the Cannes film festival in the same year (Dupagne 2004).[12] As a result, these filmmakers developed and honed their own style of filmmaking, and in turn this has been recognised and valorised at international film festivals from a nascent point in their filmmaking careers.

Versus Productions, created by Jean-Henri Bronckart and Olivier Bronckart in 1999, turned to developing relationships with aspiring filmmakers as they produced their first films outside the film school environment (Feuillère and Vlaeminckx 2006).[13] The film company was formed with capital of only 7,500 Euros (Jean-Henri Bronckart, in Morel 2011: 22), and subsequently the initial production policy was focused on short films and documentaries in the early 2000s (Duculot 2006a: 21). Four of these filmmakers, Olivier Masset-Depasse, Bouli Lanners, Joachim Lafosse and Micha Wald, have been considered part of the 'new' generation of contemporary francophone Belgian filmmakers that extends beyond the Dardenne brothers' corpus of work. These calculated 'gambles' have been interpreted as one of the primary reasons for the production company's success, alongside co-productions through the aforementioned Wallimage system (Duculot 2003a: 45; Duculot 2006a: 21). Versus Productions has since focused on building relationships with this emerging talent, transitioning from short film production through to their first and second feature-length films. This is combined with the aforementioned turn to regional mechanisms, such as Wallimage, and co-production financing, primarily with France, in order to secure funding for the films. This is particularly the case for Bouli Lanners (*Ultranova* [2005, Belgium], *Eldorado* [2008, Belgium/France]), Micha Wald (*Voleurs de chevaux/In the Arms of the Enemy* [2007, Belgium/France/Canada]), and Olivier Masset-Depasse (*Cages* [2006, France/Belgium] and *Illégal/Illegal* [2011, Belgium/Luxembourg/France]). *Voleurs de chevaux* was the first film to receive financial and logistical support from the newly created CLAP bureau. The film highlighted the potential that the region offered in terms of its studio facilities, technical expertise and variety of landscapes (Lorfèvre 2007). It was also packaged as part of the first 'Cinema Made in Wallonia' DVD series and drawn upon as a boon for Walloon filmmaking in promotional material (UWE 2007: 18). In doing so, the majority Belgian co-production, with Canada in this case, shifts the debate back around to the economic turn in Walloon filmmaking.

The legislation put in place by the CCA, encouraging the cultivation of first- and second-time filmmakers in the francophone regions of Belgium, has led to the development of producers that have built up relationships with talent from the many film schools across the country. Consequently, both established and emerging producers in the city have a certain production 'knowledge' on a local level. This concerns both knowledge of locations of significance and interest and filmmaking talent emerging from the region. The concentration of such producers in Liège is linked to the fiscal incentives in Wallonia and territoriality clauses, particularly since the creation of Wallimage in 2001, and the Walloon government's active intention to foster a filmmaking centre in Liège.

Conclusion

This chapter has outlined the progressive development of film and video culture in and around the city of Liège from (at least) the 1970s through to its current incarnation as a 'pole' or 'node' of filmmaking that extends beyond the local and the region. Drawing on Wallimage, the Tax Shelter and PIL, the film sector has adopted a primarily economic turn in which there is an emphasis placed on audiovisual expenditure, economic impact and territoriality clauses. In light of the changing filmmaking and financial conditions in the region, there has been an increasing turn to international co-productions to draw on the post-production facilities and technical providers present in the area. These conditions have rendered the region, and the city of Liège with its developed facilities, a viable and favourable co-production partner, whether that may be as a majority or minority partner. The significant levels of international co-productions in Liège are also representative of wider trends in francophone Belgian filmmaking. The final section of this chapter shifts the debate to the 'cultural' and the contribution production companies in the city of Liège have made to cultivating and supporting young talent from short films through to first-time feature-length filmmaking. It is this turn, supplemented by the development of economic factors such as Wallimage and the Tax Shelter, which has witnessed the development of a 'new francophone Belgian cinema' that extends *Liégeois* and francophone Belgian filmmaking beyond the work of the Dardenne brothers. Drawing on the cinéma-monde concept, the city of Liège can be described as operating as a 'hub' and centre of activity for the production of primarily French-language films where flows of finance and personnel from French-speaking countries intersect. As a result, this filmmaking activity bypasses the 'national' paradigm (in this case Belgium), operating on a scalar level that floats between the local and a francophone-specific understanding of the transnational.

Notes

1. For the period 2013 to 2016, T.W.I.S.T was granted a little over 2 million Euros as part of the European Union's FP7 line for Regions of Knowledge as the lead on the Eurotransmedia project (Cordis 2016). This project represents a shift to create a transnational cluster in the digital and audiovisual sector. From this premise, innovative projects are created in order to extend the region's competitiveness.
2. Bonmariage's film *Malaises* (1984, Belgium) was funded by W.I.P. and set in the wider *Liégeois* basin, the industrial suburbs of Seraing. Sojcher (1999: 259–263) also outlines the extent to which Bonmariage's films drew on C.B.A. funding in the 1980s as part of a period that he describes as 'un nouveau cinéma du réel'.
3. Nicole Widart, Rob Rombout and Jean-Claude Riga also directed episodes for a ten-part series for Canal Emploi that focused on socio-economic issues, unemployment and the workers of the *Liégeois* region (Widart 1987: 53). This community-orientated television channel increased funding opportunities for young filmmakers from 1979 to 1986.
4. Mai (2010: 20–24) and Mosley (2013: 52–55) provide detailed analyses of this video documentary, particularly concerning how the work articulates cultural and social concerns in Wallonia.
5. See Steele (2015) for a more detailed breakdown of 'national' and regional film funds in Belgium and for an analysis of the Belgian Tax Shelter system on a transnational and regional scale. In 2015 the Tax Shelter system underwent a reform, which led to the opening up of support for projects beyond the audiovisual sector. It is now able to support theatre and live performance acts, for instance.
6. In interviews conducted during research for this chapter, the term 'opportunistic' is not viewed as an adequate and complete means of describing co-production relationships that have been built up over the long-term to support film projects.
7. The Cinémathèque Royale arranged a Cristian Mungiu retrospective at the behest of the Dardenne brothers in 2012 ('Cristian Mungiu' 2012: 5). This included the screening of his short films *Mîna lui Paulista/The Hand of Paulista* (1998, Romania), *Zapping* (2000, Romania) and *Izgubljeno Nadeno/Lost and Found* (2005, Bosnia and Herzegovenia/Serbia and Montenegro/Bulgaria/Germany/Hungary/Romania) and his feature films *Occident* (2002, Romania), *4 luni, 3 saptamâni si 2 zile/4 Months, 3 weeks and 2 days* (2007, Romania/Belgium) and *Amintiri din epoca de aur/Tales from a Golden Age* (2009, Romania/France).
8. The statistics produced by CLAP include the provinces of Namur, Liège and Luxembourg.
9. One of these film projects, *Fatwa* (Mahmoud ben Mahmoud, 2014), was initially supported in 2009 with Les Films du Fleuve as the co-production

partner, but it did not receive further funding in Belgium until 2013. The Tunisian-born filmmaker has an established relationship with filmmaking in Belgium, since he graduated from the Brussels-based film school INSAS in the 1970s.
10. In 2001, the production company Saga films re-located from Brussels to nearby Namur.
11. Wallimage Entreprises also provided TSF.be with a capital injection of 250,009 Euros in 2013 (Wallimage Entreprises 2013: 35).
12. It is salient to note that Masset-Depasse's film *Dans l'ombre* is set and filmed in the filmmaker's hometown of Charleroi in the Hainaut region. The film, however, was produced by Versus in Liège.
13. Belgium has a much-celebrated film school system that has trained both Belgian and international filmmakers since they were founded. The notable film schools are l'INSAS (Brussels), l'IAD (Ottignies-Louvain-la-Neuve), and la Cambre (Brussels). However, none of these schools are based in the city of Liège. La Cambre specialises in animation.

Works Cited

Andrien, J.-J. (1998), 'Présentation de l'Association Cinéma Wallonie pour le *Journal Le Matin/Festival de Namur 98*', *Cinéma Wallonie*, 14 September 1998 <www.cinemawallonie.be> (last accessed 14 January 2016).

B. D. (1984), 'La vidéo-création belge se porte bien', *La Libre Belgique*, 30 November, p. 53.

Begon, R. (n.d.), 'Notes de fin de parcours', *À propos de 'Lorsque le bateau de Léon M. descendit La Meuse pour la première fois'*, pp. 21–3.

Begon, R. and Van Cauwenberge, G. (n.d.), 'Entretien 1 Vidéo independente: conditions matérielles de production et de diffusion', *À propos de « Lorsque le bateau de Léon M. descendit La Meuse pour la première fois*, pp. 7–10.

Brébant, F. (2013), 'Quand le "Made in Belgium" fait son cinéma', *Trends.be*, 20 June, pp. 52–5.

Cartes sur Cables (1986), 'Entretien avec Jean-Paul Tréfois: Producteur de l'émission "Vidéographie" de la RTBf Liège', *Cartes sur Cables*, 9, pp. 4–13.

CCA (2004), 'bilan, Le: production, promotion et diffusion cinématographiques et audiovisuelles', *Centre du cinéma et de l'audiovisuel*, <http://www.audiovisuel.cfwb.be/index.php?id=6225> (last accessed 21 January 2016).

CCA (2010), 'Volume 2: Le cadre réglementaire', *Centre du cinéma et de l'audiovisuel*, <http://www.audiovisuel.cfwb.be/index.php?id=9008> (last accessed 21 January 2016).

CCA (2014), 'bilan, Le: production, promotion et diffusion cinématographiques et audiovisuelles' *Centre du cinéma et de l'audiovisuel*, <http://www.audiovisuel.cfwb.be/index.php?id=avm_bilancca> (last accessed 22 January 2016).

'Cristian Mungiu' (2012), *Cinematek*, 23, p. 5.

Cinémathèque.fr (2016), 'Mikros, Trente années d'images de synthèse;

Conférence de Edouard Valton' < http://www.cinematheque.fr/intervention/844.html> (last accessed 14 February 2016).

CLAP (2013), 'Bilan des activités 2013: Analyse statistique des retombées économiques de 27 films entre 2009 et 2013', Liège: CLAP Wallonie.

Clusters.wallonie.be (2015), 'Walloon Clusters: The Clustering Policy – Detailed History', <http://clusters.wallonie.be/federateur-en/detailed-history.html?IDC=342> (last accessed 18 December 2015).

Cordis (Community Research and Development Information Service) (2016), 'Eurotransmedia', <http://cordis.europa.eu/project/rcn/109532_en.html> (last accessed 14 Februrary 2016).

CNC (2016), 'The Tax Rebate for International Productions (TRIP)', <http://www.cnc.fr/web/en/tax-rebate> (last accessed 6 February 2016).

Curtin, M. (2003), 'Media Capital: Towards the study of spatial flows', *International Journal of Cultural Studies*, 6:2, pp. 202–28.

Dardenne, J.-P. and Dardenne, L. (1981), 'Dérives: images de nos guerres', *Revue 'Pointilles'*, 11 May 1981, pp. 69–71.

du Jaunet, O. (2014), 'Pascal Diot devient DG du PIL', *Écran Total*, 1019, 19 November 2014, p. 7.

du Jaunet, O. (2015a), 'Jean-Pierre Dardenne: "La réflexion n'exclut nullement le plaisir"', *Écran Total*, 1030, 4 February 2015, p. 32.

du Jaunet, O. (2015b), 'Le nouveau tax shelter tombe à PIL', *Écran Total*, 1037, 25 March 2015, p. 19.

Duculot, P. (2003a), 'Versus Productions', 104, May 2003, p. 45.

Duculot, P. (2003b), 'Les Films du Fleuve augmentent le débit', *Cinéma Belge*, 104, May 2003, p. 47.

Duculot, P. (2006a), 'Versus Productions: Le bel essor d'un producteur Liégeois', *Cinéma Belge*, 107, May 2006, p. 21.

Duculot, P. (2006b), 'Wallimage: 5 ans au service du cinéma de la region wallonne', *Cinéma Belge*, 107, May 2006, pp. 61–3.

Dupagne, M.-F. (2004), 'Présence belge au 57ème Festival International du Film de Locarno', *Cinergie*, 1st September 2004 <http://www.cinergie.be/webzine/presence_belge_au_57eme_festival_international_du_film_de_locarno> (last accessed 24 January 2016).

EAO (European Audiovisual Observatory) (2016), *Lumière Database* <http://lumiere.obs.coe.int> (last accessed 17 January 2016).

Engelen, A. (2015), 'Le cinéma belge, un sectur d'activité ultra dynamique, mais menacé!', *Union des producteurs francophones de films*, <https://upff.wordpress.com/2015/03/24/le-cinema-belge-un-secteur-dactivite-ultra-dynamique-mais-menace/> (last accessed 20 November 2015).

European Commission (2013), 'Communication from the Commission on State aid for films and other audiovisual works', *Official Journal of the European Union*, 2013/C 332/01.

Evans, G. and J. Foord (1999), 'European funding of culture: Promoting common culture or regional growth?', *Cultural Trends*, 36:9, pp. 53–87.

Fabes, O. (2014), 'Le Pôle Image de Liège mise sur l'international pour grandir', *Le Soir*, 8 December, <http://www.lesoir.be/728293/article/economie/entrepreneuriat/2014-12-08/pole-image-liege-mise-sur-l-international-pour-grandir> (last accessed 5 January 2016).
Fargier, J.-P. (1982), 'Vidéodoc', *Les Cahiers du Cinéma*, February.
Feuillère, A. and J.-M. Vlaeminckx (2006), 'Jacques-Henri Bronckart', *Cinergie*, 1 January, <http://www.cinergie.be/webzine/jacques_henri_bronckart_20150108165806> (last accessed 10 January 2016).
Fraipont, C. (1983), 'Jean Louvet, un homme, une oeuvre, une région', *Videodoc*, September.
Frei, V. (2012), 'Rust and Bone: Cedric Fayolle – VFX Supervisor – Mikros Images', *Art of FX*, < http://www.artofvfx.com/de-rouille-et-dos-cedric-fayolle-superviseur-vfx-mikros-image/> (last accessed 2 February 2016).
Gillet, J. (2010), 'Hollywood-sur-Meuse?' *La Libre*, 17 July, <http://www.lalibre.be/regions/liege/hollywood-sur-meuse-51b8c04fe4b0de6db9bc7448> (last accessed 22 June 2015).
Goodfellow, M. (2003), 'Liège standards', *Sight and Sound*, 13:4, p. 26.
Gyroy, M. (2000), 'Making and Distributing Films in Europe', *European Audiovisual Observatory*, <http://www.obs.coe.int/oea_publ/eurocine/index.html> (last accessed 14 August 2010).
Héliot, L. (2008), 'L'effervescence du cinéma belge francophone', *Festival international du film de la Rochelle*, pp. 88–107.
Herold, A. (2014), 'Film Policy and Economic Law: Marriage or Misalliance', paper presented to CinEcoSa, Université Sorbonne Nouvelle – Paris 3, 18 November.
Hjort, Mette (2010), 'On the plurality of cinematic transnationalism', in *World Cinemas, Transnational Perspectives*, N. Durovicová and K. Newman (eds), New York: Routledge, pp. 12–33.
Iland, Cédric (2016), *Telephone Interview with Dr. Jamie Steele*, 2 February.
Klinkenberg, J.-M. (2010), 'Savoirs et contre-pouvoirs', N. Delhalle, J. Dubois and J.-M. Klinkenberg (eds), *Les tournant des années 1970: Liège en effervescence*, Brussels: Les Impressions Nouvelles, pp. 23–40.
Law, P. H. (2005), 'Fast Forward, l'argent du Tax Shelter', *Lalibre*, 7 October. <http://www.lalibre.be/economie/actualite/fast-forward-l-agent-du-tax-shelter-51b88bdae4b0de6db9acccb3> (last accessed 7 January 2016).
Loopmans, M., S. Luyten and C. Kesteloot (2007), 'Urban policies in Belgium: A puff-pastry with a bittersweet aftertaste', in L. Van ben Berg, E. Braun and J. Van der Meer (eds), *National policy responses to urban challenges in Europe*, Aldershot: Ashgate, pp. 79–102.
Lorfèvre, A. (2006), 'Les "Moteur! " wallons s'emballent', *La Libre*, 15 May, <http://www.lalibre.be/economie/libre-entreprise/les-moteur-wallons-s-em ballent-51b88e93e4b0de6db9adf28c> (last accessed 24 January 2016).
Lorfèvre, Alain (2007), 'Le cinéma belge un peu plus à l'Est', *La Libre*, 21 May, <http://www.lalibre.be/culture/cinema/le-cinema-belge-un-peu-plus-a-l-est-51b8934fe4b0de6db9afbd7b> (last accessed 4 February 2016).

Mai, Joseph (2010), *Jean-Pierre and Luc Dardenne*, Urbana: University of Illinois Press.
Marshall, B. (2012), 'Cinéma-monde? Towards a Concept of Francophone Cinema', *Francopshères*, 1 :1, pp. 35–51.
Mélon, M.-E. (2010), 'Cinéma et video: Utopie et réalité', N. Delhalle, J. Dubois and J.-M. Klinkenberg (eds), *Les tournant des années 1970: Liège en effervescence*, Brussels: Les Impressions Nouvelles, pp. 117–38.
Morel, P. (2011), 'Les autres frères du ciné liégeois', *Le Soir*, 11 May, p. 22.
Mosley, Philip (2001), *Split Screen: Belgian Cinema and Cultural Identity*, Albany: State University of New York Press.
Mosley, Philip (2013), *The cinema of the Dardenne brothers: responsible realism*, New York: Wallflower Press.
Murphy, D. (2002), 'De-centring French studies: towards a postcolonial theory of Francophone cultures', *French Cultural Studies*, 13 (165), pp. 165–85.
Neys, R. (1989), 'Le WIP: ainsi s'envole le cinéma wallon', *La revue toudi*. <http://www.larevuetoudi.org/fr/story/le-wip-ainsi-senvole-le-cinéma-wallon> (last accessed 7 January 2016).
OECD (Organisation for Economic Co-operation and Development) (2016), 'Metropolitan Areas', <http://stats.oecd.org> (last accessed 2 January 2016).
'Paysage en mutation' (2002), *Cinema Belge*, No. 103. May 2002, pp. 64–5.
Peeters, T. (2013), 'Wallonia's Film Industry', *Wallonia and Brussels Magazine*, Winter 2013/2014, pp. 16–19.
Porter, M. (1998), 'Clusters and the new economics of competitiveness', *Havard Business Review*, December, pp. 77–90
Porter, M. (2000), 'Location, competition and economic development: local clusters in a global economy', *Economic Development Quarterly*, 14, pp. 15–34.
Reynaert, P. (2011), *FW: Interview*, email to Jamie Steele (js271@ex.ac.uk), 20 April.
Reynaert, P. (2012), 'National vs Regional', *Medici – The Film Funding Journey* <http://www.focal.ch/medici-training/reports/index.html> (last accessed 12 October 2014).
Roekens, Anne (2009), *Mon bel écran, dis-moi qui est encore belge ... La RTB(F) face au débat identitaire wallon (1962–2000)*, Namur: Presses Universitaires de Namur.
Siritzky, S. (2015), 'Philippe Raynaert', *Écran Total*, 1037:25, March, p. 22.
Spaas, Lieve (2000), *The Francophone film: A Struggle for Identity*, Manchester: Manchester University Press.
Sojcher, Frédéric (1999), *La Kermesse héroïque du cinéma belge II: Le miroir déformant des identités culturelles 1965–1988*, Paris: L'Harmattan.
Steele, J. (2015), 'Towards a "transnational regional" cinema: the francophone Belgian case study', *Transnational Cinemas*, doi: 10.1080/20403526.2016.1108112.
Thomas, P. (1990), 'Belgium's North-South divide and the Walloon regional problem', *Geography*, 75:1, pp. 36–50.
Tremblay, D.-G. and Cecilli, E. (2009), 'The Film and Audiovisual Production

in Montreal: Challenges of Relational Proximity for the Development of a Creative Cluster', *The Journal of Arts Management, Law and Society*, 39:3, pp. 156–86.

UWE (Union Wallonne des Entreprises) (2007), 'Liège fait son cinéma', *Wallon dynamism*, No. 202, February.

Verhaeghe, M. (2004), 'Dossier Ateliers: Dérives asbl', *Cinergie*, 1 January, <http://www.cinergie.be/webzine/dossier_ateliers_derives_asbl> (last accessed 12 January 2016).

Wallimage (2009), *Wallimage Coproductions: Réglement*, Mons: Wallimage.be.

Wallimage (2016), *Cinéma made in Liège: Le bilan des activités, Dr. J. Steele*, 23 February.

Wallimage Entreprises (2013), *Wallimage Entreprises: Invest sectorial des technologies su net et de l'audiovisuel*, Mons: Wallimage.be.

'Wallimage puts on a show' (2014), *Wallonia.be.*, 4 June, <http://www.wallonia.be/en/news/wallimage-puts-show> (last accessed 9 February 2016).

Widart, N. (1987), 'En images et en sons', *Études de communication* [En ligne], No. 8 <http://edc.revues.org/3007> (last accessed 1 January 2016).

CHAPTER 13

'Images of Diversity': Film Policy and the State Struggle for the Representation of Difference in French Cinema

Michelle Stewart

The climax of *Beur sur la ville* (Djamel Bensalah, 2011)[1] features a squad of policemen dressed in full burqas at a mosque during prayer hours, laying in wait for a killer who may just have a burqa fetish(see Figure 13.1). The ensuing slapstick draws its laughs from the men's voices emerging from behind the veil and from the Keystone cop-style chase, impeded by the long gowns. This very broad comedy might be taken as a kind of burqa-farce, a minstrelsy that lampoons the culture of the performers (the directors, the actors). Given that the film's comedy depends almost entirely upon widely circulating stereotypes about Maghrebi-French and other ethnic minorities, it might be puzzling to some to learn that the film benefitted from a government film fund meant to promote diversity, the '*Images de la diversité*' ('Images of Diversity') fund.[2]

Figure 13.1 Still from the climax of *Beur sur la ville*.[3]

In the wake of the political unrest that shook France in 2005,[4] the government sought creative measures for the recognition and promotion of France's minority communities. Aiming for a 'better representation of cultural diversity and the promotion of equal opportunity in France,' the National Agency for Social Cohesion (ACSÉ, *L'Agence nationale pour la cohésion sociale*)[5] and the National Film and Moving Image Centre (CNC, *Centre national de la cinématographie et l'image animée*) jointly launched *Images de la diversité*.[6] The initiative sought to fund projects that contribute to:

1) the construction of a common history of the values of the Republic;
2) an understanding of the realities of the 'priority neighbourhoods of France's Urban Policy'[7] and their inhabitants; an understanding of the realities and expression immigrant populations or those with immigration histories and their integration, as well as the populations of the overseas departments, regions, and collectivities, as well as the valorisation of their memory, history, and cultural patrimony and their ties to France;
3) the visibility of the ensemble of populations that make up French society today; and
4) the struggle against discrimination on the basis of one's origins or belonging to an ethnic group, a nation, a race, or a chosen religion.
(CNC(b), *author's translation*)

The *Images de la diversité* Commission began reviewing proposals and granting funds by the end of 2007.[8] Disbursing between 1 million and almost 4 million Euros each year, the *Images de la diversité* fund has offered the potential of significant support for minority directors, without being reserved specifically for underrepresented artists. Rather than frame the support offered by *Images de la diversité* as increasing minority participation in the generation of the image repertoire of cultural heritage, ACSÉ and the CNC have left the criteria open to support any production encouraging images of diversity in terms of subject matter. To reserve funds for one cultural group over another would have been considered a form of *discrimination positive* (affirmative action) in France, which is a controversial policy. Alec Hargreaves (2007) has described at length the extent to which both the politics of multiculturalism (British and American style), as well as affirmative action policies have been resisted in France for fear of engendering *communautarisme*, 'American-style' identity politics, generally viewed in a negative light. Nonetheless, the support, available for all stages of production (up to 50,000 Euros per year per project with an average around 27,000 Euros per project), including the early stages of scenario development and extending through to exhibition and distribution in theatres and by DVD has proven to be particularly important in terms of gaining exposure for films falling outside the common circuits for either art films or blockbusters.[9]

With its link to the CNC, the commission/fund might have signalled a more centralised and auteurist notion of images as representation – a product over process approach to the role of images in supporting minority identity.[10] Clearly, the mandate of *Images de la diversité* has meant that the funds tend to promote professionalised and aestheticised audiovisual production, with the aim of subsidising public works that would be seen via standard channels of distribution and consumption. In the review process, the commission has the power to determine the meaning of diversity and the kinds of images that support 'equal chances'.

The commission is led by Alexandre Michelin, a former programming director at the TV network France 5. Like other masked attempts at affirmative action in French social policy – for example, in housing and education, with *zones urbaines prioritaires* (urban priority zones) – geography often stands in for ethnic inequality. *Images de la diversité* takes a slightly different, yet equally oblique, approach: rather than award grants directly to minority filmmakers – filmmakers who are members of prominent ethnic groups in France – it awards any filmmaker who treats films touching upon the theme of diversity.[11] By focusing on the themes of the films, the policy straddles the question of representation – giving some support to minority directors among others (increasing the numeric representation of minority directors in production), whose thematic focus might increase discussion of the topic of cultural diversity on national screens/airwaves. Thus the policy could either be seen as suffering from a blurry interpretation of the meaning of representation (and what constitutes meaningful representation) and a veiled double purposing – as it has succeeded in giving some access and support to minority directors. From 2007–16, the fund has managed to support some controversial and serious films as well as more mainstream and popular fare. One could argue, however, that even lesser films have succeeded to the extent that they afforded acting and industry jobs to ethnic minorities.

Official policies for diversity aim to increase the visibility of ethnic minorities. However, Nadia Kiwan points to a contradiction at the heart of such initiatives,

> the schizophrenic nature of a government which wants to increase colour visibility of minorities on the one hand (by increasing representation of non-white yet culturally

indistinguishable individuals in the workplace and the media) yet curb cultural or religious visibility and distinction on the other. (2007: 170)

Over the last few years, France's changing demographics have received much media attention, especially during repeated public debates about the wearing of the veil in public schools and about *laïcité*, the assumption that the fundamental character of the French nation (and citizenship) is both neutral (colour-blind) and secular. The mainstream media in France has at times fuelled these debates by painting a self-evident divide between European communities (read as democratic, secular, and 'culturally' Christian) and its immigrant, largely French Arab communities (read as Muslim, religiously conservative, and culturally closed).

An examination of *Images de la diversité* chronicles an official effort to reflect, acknowledge and promote the internal diversity of Frenchness, of the multicultural fact of post-colonial France. Considering the extent to which French cinema has constituted France's 'cultural exception' in international trade policy, the recognition of diversity at the heart of national cinema signifies an important transformation in cultural policy.[12] As such, this chapter heeds Bill Marshall's call for a theoretical conception of 'cinéma-monde', 'a mapping of the history and geography of cinema [. . .] in a period in which it is more blindingly obvious than ever that this cultural form and industry needs to be understood in its global articulations' (2012: 36). To this end, this chapter explores the construction of a notion of diversity from within the CNC – the government agency responsible for the defence of 'French cinema' – with particular attention to how Maghrebi-French and French-African filmmakers have envisioned a contemporary French identity with diversity and transnationality at the heart of 'Frenchness'. These filmmakers, using popular and familiar genres, fulfill the *Images de la diversité* fund's mandate to challenge a version of the secular Republic that would suppress cultural diversity.

Film Policy and Diversity as State Struggle

At a roundtable entitled 'Mediterranean Cinema and Cultural Diversity' held in Montpellier in October 2009 at the Festival of Mediterranean Cinema, Alexandre Michelin, the president of the *Images de la diversité* committee, addressed the question of what constitutes meaningful representation and how to foster images of diversity. In his view, the mission of a fund such as *Images de la diversité* is to help combat the sensationalistic media discourse of Samuel Huntington's thesis that equates diversity with war.[13] During the discussion, Michelin attacked the notion of 'social cohesion' as a veiled form of coercion encouraging assimilation. Instead, he suggested that diversity ought to play a larger role in the 'picture' of French national identity. He thus embraced his participation on the commission for Images of Diversity, indicating that the complicated mandate of the fund meant that, finally, 'cultural diversity had become a *state struggle* and an *official institution*'.

Also participating in the round table, film critic Pierre Murat championed the promotion of diversity afforded by the fund, though he worried about the problem of getting tokenist films rather than artistically accomplished cinema. He argued that *Telerama*,[14] for example, tends to promote three or four films that might be called 'diversity' films each year. With loose terms for diversity, the results were rather poor in terms of both quality and social critique, in Murat's opinion. Where, he asks, is the public that demands better, more diverse films? Murat detected a general social lassitude on this front, arguing that the French are just now starting to understand what 'tokenism' is. Thus, a film like *Neuilly sa mère/ Neuilly Yo Mama* (Gabriel Julien-Laferrière, 2009), supported by *Images de la diversité*, is, in Murat's view, a 'dumb, popular film' that promotes a certain kind of tokenism.[15] And indeed, this 'fish out of water' teen comedy features a kid from the poor suburbs moving in with his aunt and her rich white husband's family in the most upmarket of Parisian suburbs. Murat is right to question the value of supporting lowbrow comedies as 'images of diversity' given that the 'fish out of water' formula thrives on exaggerated and predictable stereotypes to which few in mainstream or minority culture wholly subscribe. Moreover, one notes a tendency to represent ethnic divisions in geographic terms. Despite a charming lead and some successful lampooning of the *nouveau-riche*, the film ends by reconciling all, leaving a watered down sense of cultural difference and encouraging the audience to applaud its own openness and savvy at being 'in' on the joke and completely against these broad comic versions of the other: the audience leaves secure in its magnanimity and social tolerance.

Neuilly sa mère was produced by Djamel Bensalah, who also directed *Beur sur la ville*. The film opens with an act of tokenism: our 'hero', Khalid Belkacem (played by Booder), a bumbling French-Algerian cop, is promoted because the Prefect needs more people of colour in the city's employ to placate critical journalists. His mother (played by Biyouna) rejoices, 'That's France! She gives everyone a chance!' Though Belkacem's incompetence constantly threatens to derail the investigation, he also lends his intimate knowledge of the *banlieues* and minority culture to the investigation, for example, his knowledge of Muslim prayer times. As the film progresses, it remains ambiguous whether the performance of these stereotypes 'for laughs' merely recycles them, caricatures them, or perhaps both at once. Indeed, in his discussion of the rise of a *cinéma des producteurs*,[16] a more mainstream box-office-oriented category of film that draws on global genres (if not formulae) for its success, Will Higbee identifies the 'significant role' of 'Maghrebi-French and North African émigré directors' [...] 'in this recent revival of popular or mainstream French cinema' (2013: 29).[17] Identifying three general categories of Maghrebi-French and North African émigré filmmaking, Higbee argues that the first two categories, the low-budget social realist drama or comedy and the middle-budget auteurist film that aspires to 'crossover over to a more substantial audience',[18] have been joined by a third trend. This trend, beginning in the 2000s, marks the rise of a number of Maghrebi-French and North African émigré filmmakers to mainstream recognition and success via popular comedies. As Higbee also notes, the films of Djamel Bensalah figure prominently in this move towards mainstream recognition and box office success. *Images de la diversité* has consistently funded all three kinds of filmmaking outlined by Higbee, low-budget social realist dramas and comedies, middle-budget art films by Maghrebi-French directors, and bigger budget, rather broad, ethnic comedies.

Though critics, such as Murat, worried about the social utility and artistic failings of the lowbrow films aided by the fund, Michelin defended them, arguing that the role of the commission is 'not to determine quality, but rather to support the fund'. 'It takes all to make a world – we need a lot of diverse films', Michelin insisted, adding '[t]he success of American cinema, in this regard, is the search for the banal and quotidian, the dimensions of diversity that make people laugh.' Michelin's framework raises an important question: has diversity become an official discourse or a banal exoticism? Michelin defends a comedy like *Neuilly sa mère* first because, despite its popular approach, the director had considerable trouble getting it made. As long as discrimination remains a problem in the industry, Michelin felt that the fund should support all minority productions: 'We need to see that lowbrow popular films, art films, and documentaries get made that address these issues' (Michelin).[19]

While *Neuilly sa mère* comically reverses the phenomenon of social exclusion by postal code in France, *Beur sur la ville* foregrounds the question of representation and tokenism throughout. Michael Billig's theory of 'banal nationalism' points to the role of 'the routine and familiar forms' in fuelling nationalist sentiment (1995: 9). Billig sees national identity as built upon 'unnoticed' symbolism and 'the embodied habits of social life. Such habits include those of thinking and using language' (1995: 8–9). Popular film plays a significant role in propagating the symbols and language that circulate in daily life. Michelin's interpretation of diversity as a state struggle, as entailing an audiovisual policy that disseminates a diversity of images in a diversity of cultural idioms, outlines a model of casual multiculturalism as an antidote to banal nationalism. If diversity is a 'state struggle' ('une lutte menée par l'état'), in his terms, then the multiplication of minority actors, minority directors, and diversity-themed production across France's airwaves can only contribute to a subtle shift in those unnoticed influences on national sentiment. The diversification of French screens means the diversification of the 'look' and sound of 'Frenchness'; it means making visible and audible the great variety of French speakers, of French accents and dialects. In this sense, the *Images de la diversité* fund serves as a counterweight to what Bill Marshall identified as 'the demographic imbalance of France being the largest Francophone territory', a demographic imbalance that had worked against the possibility of establishing a 'notion of cinéma-monde' (2012: 37–8). Following this logic, the diversification of images of French culture promoted by Images of Diversity has installed a richer notion of francophone cinema from within the CNC.

In terms of film policy, Michelin addressed the difficulty of creating specific forms of aid to promote internal cultural diversity and to fight discrimination, a larger socio-political struggle. He acknowledged that the auteurist model of the CNC and its standard national granting criteria promote a kind of artistic, and thus tacit, social conservatism. For example, Michelin defended the support offered by *Images de la diversité* to *Entre les murs/The Class* (Laurent Cantet, 2008), a difficult film to shoot given its improvisational and intimate style. Michelin argued that with its daring approach and controversial subject matter, the director might not have been able to obtain funds from the usual channels.[20] As funding for white directors like Laurent Cantet and Philippe Faucon makes clear, the fund has followed through on its promise to award grants on the basis of themes as opposed to the director's social belonging. However, as the largest ethnic group in France, Maghrebi-French directors have benefited from the existence of the fund nonetheless.

Diverse Images for Diverse Audiences

With the aim of reaching the largest audience, the fund has contributed to the production of a diverse array of films, from higher-brow art films to middlebrow family comedies, and to popular contemporary urban dramas. In the discussion that follows, I will pay particular attention to those films receiving less critical attention, the middlebrow television comedies and the films of urban popular culture. I will track how contemporary Maghrebi-French and French-African filmmaking responds to the questions posed by the creation of a fund like *Images de la diversité*. Does a focus on the theme of diversity rather than a direct programme of affirmative action for minority directors foster diverse images of contemporary French society? Does the production of middlebrow and lowbrow films, in addition to serious art films, spur meaningful debate regarding equality of access and cultural recognition?

As mentioned earlier, the commission has awarded funds to well-known directors of artistically daring fare. The fund has demonstrated a strong preference for works by minority directors offering an alternate vision of French history, particularly of French empire and decolonisation, in addition to minority experiences of World War II. It is in this echelon that *Images de la diversité* has sponsored the production of more highbrow art films. Films such as Robert Guédiguian's *L'Armée du crime/ Army of Crime* (2009), Ismaël Ferroukhi's *Les Hommes libres/Free Men* (2011), Tony Gatlif's *Korkoro/Freedom* (2009), Rachid Bouchareb's *Hors-la-loi/Outside the Law* (2009, France/Algeria/Belgium/Tunisia/Italy), and Mehdi Charef's *Cartouches gauloises/Summer of '62* (2007, France/ Algeria) embed diversity in the remembrance of major historical events or directly counter official histories. In so doing, these films participate in the production of what Michael Rothberg has called multi-directional memory, a form of remembrance that is 'subject to ongoing negotiation, cross-referencing, and borrowing, as productive not privative . . . This interaction of different historical memories illustrates the productive, intercultural dynamic that I call multidirectional memory' (Rothberg 2009: 3). In addition to reinscribing diversity into the history of World War II, reminding viewers of the toll of deportations, collaboration, and minority persecution, but also unsung alliances in resistance to the Nazis, these films have 'the potential to create new forms of solidarity and new visions of justice' (Rothberg 2009: 5).

The historical films funded by *Images de la diversité* have also contributed to significant debate regarding empire, decolonisation, and the Algerian war. *Hors-la-loi* participates in the retelling of the toll of French decolonisation by dramatising the history of the massacre at Sétif in 1945.[21] Michelin often points to the need for *Images de la diversité* in noting that it took Rachid Bouchareb 25 years to make his last historical epic, *Indigènes/Days of Glory* (2006, Algeria/France/Morocco/Belgium), without the help of a 'blind' fund, like *Images de la diversité*. In aiding established directors to address contested chapters in French history, the artistic and social value of the diversity fund is rather clear. Yet the *Images de la diversité* commission has not shied away from contemporary social issues and it has held to Michelin's policy of contributing to all levels of filmmaking.

The Republican Melodrama: A New *Cinéma de Banlieue*?

A survey of the films receiving *Images de la diversité* aid over the last decade demonstrates that the fund subsidised sentimental, made-for-television dramas, as well as genre films (comedy and crime) aimed at a wider audience. Amongst these, the fund underwrote the emergence of a new kind of *banlieue* film[22] – *Chronique d'une cour de récré/Chronicle of a Playground* (Brahim Fritah, 2013), *Tête de turc/Scapegoat* (Pascal Elbé, 2010), *Aïcha* (Yamina Benguigui, 2008–2011), *Qu'Allah bénisse la France!/May Allah Bless France!* (Abd al Malik, 2014), *Fracture* (Alain Tasma, 2010), *Des Apaches/The Apaches* (Nassim Amaouche, 2015), and *Geronimo* (Tony Gatlif, 2015). In addition to the numerous documentaries about the *banlieue* sponsored by the fund, these features portray the multiethnic landscape of France's urban periphery.[23] These films directly address the failures of French Republicanism, racism, and the presence of Islam within France. While Higbee underscores the extent to which contemporary Maghrebi-French directors have tried to shake free of the 'ghettoization' of the labels of *beur* and *banlieue* cinema, the *banlieue* and the *cité* (housing projects) remain prominent in both setting and thematic focus. Contemporary urban dramas highlight increasing despair and segregation experienced by urban youth and young adults. In so doing, they do not reject Republicanism, but hope to encourage multicultural acceptance and tolerance against the policy of a colour-blind secularism (*laïcité*) that refuses to address discrimination.

Across these films, there is deliberate attention to the geography of ethnic divide. The towers of the *cités* (the HLMs [Habitations à loyer modéré]) of the *banlieues* populate a skyline far from the familiar landmarks of central Paris. And yet, for some directors, there is nostalgia and a will to see beyond the media frenzy painting the urban periphery as a wasteland of murderous machismo, nihilism and radicalisation. In *Chronique d'une cour de récré*, director Brahim Fritah casts a nostalgic look at his adolescence in a *banlieue* that was to him a place of multiethnic solidarity and not a battleground. *Tête de turc* attempts to humanise adolescents of the *banlieues* by showing the complex roots of violence. Based on an actual incident that took place in the northern suburbs of Marseille in October 2006, *Tête de turc* weaves together the stories of a cop (Roschdy Zem), his brother the doctor (Pascal Elbé), a Turkish adolescent (Samir Makhlouf), and several other characters brought together by their connection to place. In an effort to contravene easy assumptions, the film attempts to show the interconnected fates of this cast of characters with pathos. The story links the actions of each character to constellations of social factors: family, friendship, class and ethnicity. Most significantly, we come to understand the motivations of the adolescent boy, who sets the events of the film in motion when, encouraged by his friends, he lobs a Molotov cocktail at the doctor's car. The boy, having second thoughts, rescues the doctor and is then honoured by the mayor for his heroism. With its emphasis on humanism and interpersonal reconciliation, *Tête de turc* aims to heal social divisions.[24] Still, the images inadvertently echo a host of clichés drawn from headlines and formulaic fiction: the gang of boys constantly enforcing loyalty and a code of silence, the beleaguered cop (sympathetically played by Zem, a popular Maghrebi-French actor), the liberal doctor, trying to understand why he has been targeted.

The fund's goal of promoting 'an understanding of the realities of the "priority neighbourhoods" of France' seems oddly served by a number of genre films meant for television, especially those depicting schools in urban areas (CNC(b)). These films constitute a veritable subgenre of this contemporary *banlieue* film, yet they vary widely in their sensitivity to the 'reality' of the *banlieue*.[25] Treating the embattled suburban (*banlieue*) school as a multicultural allegory for contemporary French society, the classrooms depicted stand in for the Republic in jeopardy. The worst of the genre aided by the fund, *La Journée de la jupe/Skirt Day* (Jean-Paul Lilienfeld, 2008) relies on a hysterical fear of the other.[26] Isabelle Adjani plays a teacher who holds her students hostage after being attacked by one student and becoming fed up with her students' resistance to their own education. *Les Héritiers/The Heirs* (Marie-Castille Mention-Schaar, 2014) attempts to show what an impassioned teacher can do to turn the lives of alienated students around. Based on the true story of teacher who motivates a failing class to work together to learn about the Holocaust and to go on to win the national contest for the representation of Resistance and Deportation. Despite its sentimentalism, students and audiences are moved by the testimony at the centre of the film, Holocaust survivor Léon Zyguel's description of his own deportation with his family to Auschwitz. The film also delicately, though briefly, has the Jewish teacher engage her Muslim students on the difference between the German genocide of the Jews and the Israeli occupation of Palestine. *Fracture* (Alain Tasma, 2010) depicts the school as a microcosm of both the social division haunting the Republic and the geopolitical conflicts in which these struggles are

Figure 13.2 Diversity in the Republican classroom; still from *Fracture*.

situated (see Figure 13.2). Also set in a multicultural classroom in a 'priority education zone', the film tackles racism and anti-Semitism. All express to differing degrees a felt social exclusion. Yet the multiethnic school film seems less likely to promote a rethinking of the Republican model of secularism than certitude that integration has failed and that Islam in France can only be conceived as a social problem.[27]

Mainstreaming French Muslims: The Family Comedy and Hip Hop Cinema to here

Against these potentially divisive images are films that assert the experience of being Muslim in France. In terms of impact, both the middlebrow television-series *Aïcha* by Yamina Benguigui and the rap autobiography of Abd al Malik, *Qu'Allah bénisse la France* merit closer analysis.[28]

The made for television series, *Aïcha* (2008–11) by veteran director Yamina Benguigui offers a poignant view of life in the suburbs. Without being socially or artistically daring, Benguigui tackles the glass ceiling, discrimination against Maghrebi-French and Muslims, the appeal of radical Islam, as well as the social mores specific to Maghrebi-French families. Part of youngest generation depicted in the series, Aïcha and her cousins are French Muslims: culturally Maghrebi, culturally and or religiously Muslim and still culturally French.

Figure 13.3 Still from *Aïcha*, featuring sympathetic and strong female and Muslim characters. Pictured from right to left; Aïcha (Sofia Essaïdi), Madame Maillard (Bunny Godillot), her Aunt (Biyouna), and her mother (Rabia Mokkadem).

The first episode of *Aïcha*, 'Un Job à tout prix' ('A Job at All Costs') opens with a French-Algerian wedding, with men and women dancing in opposing groups, a choreography of a gender division still oppressing the youngest generation. Aïcha's voice-over introduces us to each family member. She loves them all, but wants to be like none of them. In other words, the culture animating this traditional wedding ceremony belongs to Aïcha, but does not have to determine her, and yet, Aïcha's postal address just might. She jokes about dreaming to make the longest voyage of her life, to the other side of the *périphérique*, the motorway that separates inner-Paris from the northern suburb, where Aïcha has grown up.

By foregrounding the geographic and cultural divide that restricts the employment opportunities of Maghrebi-French youth so early in the film, Benguigui's comedy situates itself in the sociological realities, now well publicised, that frustrate the dreams of French Muslims from the *banlieues*. Yet in a style appropriate for a television audience, Benguigui's *Aïcha* seeks multicultural consensus. At the same time, it aspires to sensitise its audiences to the diversity within France, as well as within ethnic communities. The strength of Benguigui's body of work is its humanism and its focus on women of immigrant origins. *Aïcha* continues this focus, giving more airtime to the aspirations and tribulations of Aïcha, her cousins, her mother and her aunt (see Figure 13.3). As in many of the contemporary dramas discussed above, the French we hear is heavily accented or demographically specific, revealing the linguistic creativity of the slang of the suburbs, the accents of France's regions and cities, or French learned abroad as a second language. When Aïcha's mother (Madame Bouamazza, played to great comic effect by Rabia Mokkedem) complains in Arabic-inflected French about finding a Chinese businessman incomprehensible, Aïcha retorts, 'And your French is perfect?' Her mother protests, 'I come from Marseille!' 'Aha', says Aïcha, 'that's different'.[29]

The contrast of beliefs between the generations occupies a central place in the television series, with the myths and traditions of the parents shadowing their children, a generation decidedly French, though struggling to make their own way into adulthood. The superstitions, prejudices and pettiness of the older women are affectionately lampooned by Benguigui, and quite effectively through the casting of Biyouna, the Algerian singer and comic actor. In the women-only spaces of the spa and Biyouna's hair salon, the ladies play out their jealousies and moral policing via their children: Farida (Linda Bouhenni), Aïcha's cousin, is pregnant out of wedlock, the busybody neighbour's son is caught bellydancing in women's clothing, Aïcha is spotted smoking with a French boy, her childhood friend, Patrick (Axel Kiener). While the women trade herbs and try to ward off the evil eye, the older men jockey for their family's honour and survey marriage propositions for their daughters. As for the younger men in the suburbs, well, they mostly seem to harass Aïcha and her cousin, Nedjma (Shemss Audat). The girls constantly resist their advances. Though we suspect it is the young women's better prospects and dreams of leaving the *cité* that nettles, the boys taunt Nedjma and Aïcha for the excesses of Nedjma's sister (the pregnant Farida).

Some of these preoccupations reflect Benguigui's generation more than that of Aïcha. Though circling familiar topical ground with tales of taboo inter-racial love and restrictive parents, Benguigui does well to highlight obstacles facing later generations of French Algerian families in the suburbs. For Nedjma, it is the fact that she cannot get an internship even though she finished top in her class. When her work counsellor asks Nedjma if she has considered changing her family name, humiliated and fuming, Nedjma turns to a Muslim support society. There other young Muslim women share her frustrations and say that Islam gave them stability and identity. Aïcha attends the meeting with Nedjma, but finds the context and the leader of the group to be extremely manipulative. Nedjma defends the group, but it is Aïcha who turns out to be right. The leader of the group, having heard of Farida's pregnancy, seduces Nedjma into a 'temporary' marriage, sleeps with her and then denounces her. And yet, Nedjma doesn't abandon Islam and later takes up wearing a veil. While the weight of the drama supports secularism, Benguigui's portrayal deftly resists a media-ready instrumentalisation of Nedjma's choice.

Aïcha, for her part, must trick her family in order to win her independence. She agrees to marry her horrible, macho boss in order to escape the oppressive home atmosphere, where her father has imposed patriarchal rule following Farida's unexpected pregnancy (and failed efforts at suicide to conceal the fact). Ultimately, Aïcha's photography wins the attention of a Parisian businessman. When Aïcha makes it to the interview, her rendez-vous is with a white French woman who is disappointed to learn that Aïcha doesn't speak Arabic, 'Quel dommage'. Benguigui lampoons this exemplar of a politically correct bohemian-bourgeoise, as she explains to Aïcha that the idea was to hire 'the next girl from Tehran with that "street feeling"'. Aïcha gets the job, but, tragicomically, discovers that she will be working at the firm's Bobigny offices. Her dream of crossing the périphérique into Paris is thwarted by the firm's hope that Aïcha will help them understand and draw in the urban market as their new director of 'ethnic trends'. The irony is not lost on Aïcha, as she smiles and the camera follows her gaze to Bobigny's towers, the horizon that limits Aïcha's world as a French Muslim born on the wrong side of the freeway.

Aïcha, for all its middlebrow, mainstream trappings and emotional catharses, does not present a simple, redemptive or integrative narrative. The limit point of the *périphérique* remains intact. Social mobility and freedom depend on generation, gender and class. While, visually and narratively, we are encouraged to identify with the strong cast of Arab women, Benguigui portrays the diversity of their motivations and fortunes. Success is inextricably tied to indices of integration: mastery of French, French social conventions, and mobility beyond the domestic spaces of the *banlieue*.

Qu'Allah bénisse la France (Abd al Malik, 2014) brought rapper Abd al Malik's autobiography of the same title to the screen. While the film reached fewer viewers than Benguigui's telefilm, it is notable for its hard-hitting portrayal of the options available to young men of the *cités* and for its defence of French Islam.

Abd al Malik shot the film in the projects where he grew up, the Neuhof suburb of Strasburg.[30] As in *Aïcha*, the opening scene establishes the distance between suburb and town centre, as signs pointing to Neuhof bring us into a troubled zone where, over a soundtrack of rap, shots of police in riot gear raiding homes or picking up suspects are intercut with the faces of watching locals. Many of the reaction shots are those of adolescent boys of various ethnic backgrounds. These are not subtle oppositions: visually and dramatically, the lines are drawn. Al Malik (called by his birth name Régis, prior to his conversion) is hauled off with his brother, Oscar.

Figure 13.4 Still from *Qu'Allah bénisse la France* echoing the multi-racial composition of Mathieu Kassovitz's *La Haine* (1995).

Oscar screams at a female cop in dense urban slang, calling her a bitch in colourful terms (*connasse*). She teases him, 'oh this is France's beautiful, new generation. Long live France.' 'Fuck France,' he responds. To the query 'Why don't you go elsewhere?', he retorts 'Because I'm squatting here now. Do you think that uniform gives you the right to break my balls?' Al Malik interrupts his brother, 'Aren't you ashamed?' When the father picks up the boys from the station, he reminds them that they need to understand that while no one suffers in France, that does not mean they are entirely welcome: 'While we love France, France doesn't love us. Be careful. You are not at home here.'

While social oppositions remain as acid as they are black and white throughout the film, al Malik's depiction of the affective draw of popular culture (especially American), of music, poetry and rap, insists on the creativity of urban youth culture. As the camera pans the posters on the brothers' bedroom, these influences are the ones al Malik keeps in view: Raekwon (an American rap artist), boxing, the Koran and Jesus (an immigrant from the Congo, al Malik's mother raised them as Catholics).

Yet the draw of easy money, drugs, and crime is also great. The film oscillates between al Malik's passion for poetry, slam, and rap, his spiritual awakening, and his dalliances with petty crime. Filmed in black and white as a homage to Mathieu Kassovitz's *La Haine/Hate* (1995), al Malik's film also represents the multiethnic solidarity of Neuhof: his friends are Maghrebi and white (see Figure 13.4). Yet al Malik also confronts Arab racism against black Muslims. Al Malik's friend Mikey says 'the problem isn't religion, Muslim, Jewish, or Christian. The problem is people. Some people are just assholes.' Malik clearly supports the potential of Republican ideals, but sees them as having failed to live up to their promise in posing obstacles to freedom of expression and in the high rates of unemployment and hopelessness plaguing the ghettos. All the same, the boys reject this highly mediated interpretation of their lot. After being interviewed by a journalist, the boys are disgusted to hear themselves described as a 'social bomb' waiting to be radicalised given the misery and social inequality of the suburbs.

Though a first-time director, al Malik infuses the film with style, highlighting the limited options for urban youth with a triply split screen juxtaposing Islam, drugs, and rap. Alternating between split-screens and wipes, we come to understand that, as was the case for al Malik, young men are often seduced by some combination of these. The film, however, does not echo the diagnosis of the journalist. For al Malik, Islam is a source of peace and identity, but the social problems remain. The scenes depicting Islam as a community of brotherhood are rather heavy-handed (slow motion, Islamic prayer, shots of men praying, laughing and chatting together in a mosque). Yet the point is a salutary one – there is a social fracture in France, but Islam need not be villainised as menace. The urban peripheries are sites of misery, where al Malik lost friend after friend to overdoses, suicide, violence, or AIDS. Al Malik dramatises this in the scene depicting the funeral of a close friend killed by a rival gang. As the group of friends is pictured gathered around the casket, the ones who fall are 'disappeared' from the screen, with the cause of their early death and their names written over the space they had occupied seconds before. Islam, however, in al Malik's view, should not be dismissed in one stroke as predatory and radical. Social and ethnic discrimination betray the values that secularism – *laïcité* – is meant to protect. The answer for al Malik is peace and respect. By limiting freedom of religious expression in the Republic, France continues to fuel this social divide. Al Malik closes the film with this sentiment, in a devastatingly powerful and slow rap, '*Soldat de plomb*' ('Lead Soldier'). The first stanza of the rap recounts his youth, playing it tough, selling drugs, seeing too much blood too early:

> Tout maigre dans ma grosse veste qui me servait d'armure,
> J'avais du shit dans mes chaussettes et j'fesais dans mon . . . pantalon,
> Soldat de plomb, soldat de plomb.

> All skinny in my big jacket that served as my armour,
> I had hash (*shit*) in my socks, and I shit my pants
> Lead soldier, lead soldier.

And the last stanza outlines his vision of real equality and fraternity: 'For a better world, long live rainbow France, united, and unburdened of her fears.'[31]

Abd al Malik's film and music militate against effacement of identity and difference from the Republic. They draw on and play with the symbols and language of French youth culture, already in dialogue with global popular culture, with the audible sounds of American hip hop, Algerian Raï, and other African popular music. They, along with many of the other *Images de la diversité* films, refashion and re-envision a multicultural image of the French citizen. At the heart of the notion of cinéma-monde is such a rejection of the homogenous, tourist-ready Frenchness that sells as national culture. 'For "Francophone cinema" is everything that "French" culture purports not to be' (Marshall 2012: 41).

Conclusion

The geographic and linguistic breadth of themes, directors, and actors featured in *Images de la diversité* films extends the notion of *la Francophonie*, emphasising France's strong cultural connections with former colonies and overseas territories, as well as the flourishing of that diversity in the heart of the *métropole*.[32] Broadcast both in France and in its overseas territories and departments, these productions contribute not only to familiarity with the cultural heritage of these territories, but also to the internationalisation of French language content via digital and satellite channels, with diverse audiences listening to a proliferation of accents, creoles, and dialects. Within the Hexagon, the fund directly aided the creation of French films by women and underrepresented minorities. The groups represented are decidedly hyphenated: French-Cambodian, French-Roma, French-Polish, French-African, French-Jewish, French-Maghrebi and French-Arab.[33] In these ways, the films feature various inflections of French. Furthermore, Arabic is frequently present as a language of the French metropole – a language peppering French phrases or used exclusively in certain domestic contexts.

Indeed, in theme, reach and language, *Images de la diversité* has helped to erect a notion of cinéma-monde, a kind of cinema militating against the false homogeneity of the concept of national cinema. As Marshall outlines the potential of cinéma-monde:

> Instead of national integration, there is uncertainty of definition, lack of unity (as well as lack of clear-cut silos or hermetically sealed divisions), no claim to universalism, porosity with regard to what is outside, and no centripetally marked cultural capital. Indeed, there is a constantly visible and lived tension between centripetal and centrifugal forces, with the balance of power reversed in favour of the latter. (2012: 41)

Taking stock of the impact of the *Images de la diversité* fund, the films flesh out the kind of casual recognition of difference that Michelin championed as an 'official state struggle'. Perhaps, then, the programme constitutes a salient counterweight to banal nationalism in promoting an image culture built on the casual recognition of irreducible difference – colour and cultural – at the heart of the Republic. The films participate in the mainstreaming of diversity, inserting a new image culture of French everyday life that counteracts the stereotypes that frame urban youth, ethnic minorities, and French Muslims for the majority. The *Images de la diversité* fund, then presents a model for how audiovisual policies – if diverse in their approach (from art film to lowbrow comedies) – might contribute to the creation of a casual multiculturalism as a corrective to a banally homogenous version of the nation.

Notes

1. Unless otherwise noted, films appearing in this chapter were produced in France.
2. The fund was established on 8 November 2007 by the Minister for Culture and Communication and the Minister responsible for the promotion of equal opportunities (Blocman 2007).
3. 'Beur' is a term for 'Arab' that hails from the French urban slang *verlan,* a creative slang based on syllabic reversals and phonetic play. The term was initially an 'in' joke that eventually came to be seen as offensive, though still embraced by some. '*Beur* cinema' denotes films of second generation Maghrebi-French directors of the 1980s and into the early 1990s. Shortly thereafter, one notes a shift to the more geographic term, *cinéma de banlieue.* A *banlieue* is a working class enclave of France's urban peripheries. *Banlieue* used to be analogous in social and economic terms to the American term, the 'inner city'.
4. Riots that began in October 2005, following the accidental deaths of two youths fleeing police in the ethnic suburb of Paris, Clichy-Sous-Bois.
5. At the end of 2014, ACSÉ was folded into the *Commissariat général à l'égalité des territoires* (General Commission for Territorial Equality, CGET), with the aim of consolidating urban policy under the *Ministère de la ville* (Ministry of Urban Affairs).
6. See note 2.
7. France's *politique de la ville*, an urban development plan for the 'urban priority zones.'
8. One commission makes the decision regarding how to disburse the funds from both agencies. ACSÉ funds tend to support production promoting diversity in the audiovisual sector, including television programmes, magazines, televised documentaries, as well as a few interactive and web

documentaries. The CNC emphasises fiction features, documentary, animation, and shorts intended for projection in cinemas (CNC [a]).
9. Films can receive up to two kinds of support from the Images of Diversity fund, e.g. a development grant and/or a production grant. Producers can also seek other forms of aid from the CNC and the Ministry of Culture in the form of selective aid (such as the advance on revenues) or automatic aid (a loan based on previous box office success, a type of funding less available to young and new directors of less mainstream films). Selective aid often goes to smaller projects (Davies and Wistrich 2007: 331; Buchsbaum 2015: 49).
10. The grant marks one of the first times the government has openly supported a form of 'discrimination positive', and particularly, in terms of the CNC's standard criteria for funding, for films that do not always fit the familiar profile of auteurist art cinema. Thus, the fund opens up a new channel of support for first-time directors and for minority or socially-engaged artists who do not already have the reputation that would entitle them to automatic aid.
11. The mandate of the fund addresses diversity in the full sense of the term, including films about ethnic difference, gender equality, sexual orientation, and disabilities. Yet the great majority of the films selected focus on ethnic difference, with few films treating questions of gender and sexual orientation. Moreover, while ethnic difference remains the principal focus of diversity funding, supporting films about the Roma, other significant communities of immigration (French West Africans, Caribbeans, Vietnamese), and the cultures of France's overseas departments and territories, the most frequently funded films address Maghrebi-French communities.
12. It is interesting to note that the language of 'exception' was ultimately changed to one of 'cultural diversity'. Presumably, the diversity of world cultures could be ensured by protecting *national cultures*, though the image of 'Frenchness' and French cinema for these debates tended to reify tourist-friendly pictures of national identity (see Hayward 1993; Buchsbaum 2006).
13. Michelin refers here to Huntington's 'clash of civilizations' concept. Held on 29 October, 2009, the participants were Pierre Murat, Nabil Ayouch, Michel Miaille, Alexandre Michelin, and Marie Vanaret.
14. A weekly review of French television, radio, and cinema, somewhat akin to the American *TV Guide*.
15. Murat's comments at the 2009 roundtable (cf. fn. 11). The film was popular at the box office, with nearly 2.5 million entries, <http://www.allocine.fr/film/fichefilm-143035/box-office/> (last accessed 14 July 2017).
16. A producers' cinema, as opposed to a *cinéma d'auteur* (or author's cinema/art cinema). See Will Higbee (2013) for an exhaustive discussion of the ways in which producers have been drawn to (and helped to mainstream) Maghrebi-French cinema.

17. Higbee's data on the subject are compelling: 'In virtually every year of the 2000s a film directed by or starring Maghrebi-French or North African émigré filmmakers is placed in the top 10 most popular French films of the year, with more films arriving in the top 20. This consistent presence at the top of the box-office is even more impressive when it is understood that, since 1999, no more than eight features produced or co-produced in France by directors of Maghrebi origin have been released in any given year' (32).
18. Higbee classes Kechiche's work among this *cinéma du milieu* (middle cinema). Middle cinema, in this usage, refers only to the moderate nature of the production costs and should not be confused with middle-brow fare.
19. Author's translation of Michelin's comments at the 2009 roundtable on diversity (cf. fn. 11).
20. Yet, it should be noted that Cantet has just the kind of reputation in art cinema that the CNC has tended to favour.
21. The intense controversy surrounding the film demonstrates the necessity for such alternative histories. Indeed, critics of the film attacked what they saw as distortions of history, some suggesting that film fiction, in fact, requires abbreviation and dramatisation, both inimical to truth, according to the film's detractors. The fund also supported Bouchareb's *Frères d'armes/Brothers in Arms* (2013).
22. cf. fn. 3
23. These documentaries depict the *banlieues* and outer neighbourhoods of Paris proper as communities, e.g. *Des Hommes debout* (Maya Abdul-Malak, 2015) which centres on users of a taxiphone in Belleville and *L'Ame du Panier: le plus vieux village de France* (Olivier Poli and Sofiane Mammeri, 2014) about Le Panier neighbourhood in Marseille. There are also several documentaries that address subsidised housing projects in France, notably, *Cité Balzac: L'autre regard* (Daniel Kupferstein, 2009), *Le village vertical* (Laure Pradal, 2009) about the Assas tower in Montpellier, and *Sarcellopolis* (Bertrand Deve and Sébastien Daycard, 2015), a documentary film and interactive website about the multicultural Paris suburb Sarcelles, as well as several that approach the *banlieues* through the lens of local arts intitiatives in 'urban priority zones' or via the *banlieue* school, with *Nous, princesses de Clèves* (Régis Sauder, 2011) and *La Cour de Babel/School of Babel* (Julie Bertuccelli, 2013) being two excellent examples of the latter.
24. In this regard, it is significant that the film depicts events that erupted on the anniversary of the October 2005 riots mentioned at the beginning of this chapter.
25. The documentaries mentioned in fn. 23 counterbalance the ways in which fictional melodramas about the *banlieue* school teeter either towards feelgood narratives of liberal redemption or, to the other extreme, multicultural crisis.
26. In a measured analysis of this and other films centring on the Republican school, Geneviève Sellier suggests that *La Journée de la jupe* 'stigmatize[s]

Muslim communities as the primary element responsible for the discrimination against women' (2011: 155).
27. One should perhaps include Philippe Faucon's *Désintegration / The Disintegration* (2011, France/Belgium) here.
28. The first instalment of *Aïcha*, a four-part mini-series that aired on French 2 in May 2009 garnered over five million viewers.
29. Here, Benguigui recognises with humour both the Algerian origins (and lingering accent) of Aïcha's mother and the fact that Marseille, a port city on the Mediterranean with a large population of French Algerians, connects France historically and socially to Algeria and the Maghreb.
30. Al Malik proudly identifies his ties to Neuhof and Strasburg in these opening shots. Urban identification has been one way that minority youth have negotiated if not refused forms of racism tied to national belonging. In terms of *Images de diversité*, the strong regional identity of denizens of Strasburg puts into relief an interesting absence in the fund's construction of internal diversity: regional identity and languages are not targeted. This could be a structural echo of the complex relationship between centralised national government (of which the CNC is an agency) and the decentralised power bases of France's regions and departments, which each have their own funding mechanisms and even cinema funds that promote regional dialects and accents, as well as local tourism.
31. 'Pour un monde meilleur, vive la France arc-en-ciel, unie et débarrassé de toutes ses peurs.'
32. To emphasise the strength of the fund in fulfilling the second objective listed above, ACSE publicised the success of *Toussaint Louverture* (Philippe Niang, 2012), a historical telefilm celebrating the life of the legendary leader of Haiti's revolution. According to the Commission of Images of Diversity's summary report from 2010 to 2012, the film garnered over 3.7 million spectators when it aired on France 2, approximately 12.7% of the audience for France 2, an above-average viewership. The film aired on 14 February 2012 (*Commission*). The fund also supported a number of smaller films reflecting the geographic breadth of francophony, with many featuring artists, singers, actors, and directors from Martinique, Guadeloupe, Guyana, and Ile de Réunion.
33. The notion of hyphenated identity has not yet gained the ground in France that it has in the US, Canada, and perhaps the UK. In France, one's identity still seems to rest on one's 'origins', the immigration history of one's parents, grandparents, or even great grandparents, should one be a visible minority (see Alec Hargreaves 2007; Durmelat and Swamy 2011).

Works Cited

Barlet, O. (2014), '*Les Héritiers* de Marie-Castille Mention-Schaar: Mirage Sentimental', *Africultures*, 12 December, <http://www.africultures.com/php/index.php?nav=article&no=12652> (last accessed 17 July 2017).

Billig, Michael (1995), *Banal Nationalism*. London: Sage.
Blocman, A. (2007), 'France: Establishment of an "Images of Diversity" Fund', *IRIS Observations juridiques de l'Observatoire européen de l'audiovisuel*, 3.14/21, <http://merlin.obs.coe.int/iris/2007/3/article21.fr.html> (last accessed 17 July 2017).
Buchsbaum, J. (2006), 'The Exception Culturelle Is Dead', *Framework: The Journal of Cinema & Media*, 47:1, p. 13.
Buchsbaum, J. (2015), '"Do We Have the Right to Exist?" French Cinema, Culture, and World Trade', in A. Fox and M. Marie et al. (eds), *A Companion to Contemporary French Cinema*, New York: Wiley-Blackwell, pp. 45–73.
CNC (a), *CNC Images de la diversité – Commission images de la diversité. Bilan 2010–2012*, <http://www.cnc.fr/web/fr/images-de-la-diversite> (last accessed 17 July 2017).
CNC (b), *CNC Images de la diversité–Dossier appel à projets*, <http://www.cnc.fr/web/fr/images-de-la-diversite-descriptif-complet> (last accessed 17 July 2017).
Davies, A. P. and N. Wistreich (2007), *The Film Finance Handbook: How to Fund Your Film*, Glasgow: Netribution Ltd.
Durmelat, Sylvie and Vinay Swamy (2011), *Screening Integration: Recasting Maghrebi Immigration in Contemporary France*, Lincoln: University of Nebraska Press.
Hargreaves, Alec (2007), *Multi-ethnic France: Immigration, Politics, Culture and Society*, New York: Routledge.
Hayward, Susan (1993), *French National Cinema*, London: Routledge.
Higbee, Will (2013), *Post-Beur Cinema: North African Émigré and Maghrebi-French Filmmaking in France since 2000*, Edinburgh: Edinburgh University Press.
Kiwan, N. (2007), 'Equal opportunities and republican revival: post-migrant politics in contemporary France (2002–2005)', *International Journal of Francophone Studies*, 10:1–2, pp. 157–72.
Marshall, B. (2012), 'Cinéma-monde? Towards a concept of Francophone cinema', *Francosphères*, 1:1, pp. 35–51.
Rothberg, Michael (2009), *Multidirectional Memory: Remembering the Holocaust in the Age of Decolonization*, Palo Alto, CA: Stanford University Press.
Sellier, G. (2011), 'Don't Touch the White Woman: *La Journée de la jupe* or Feminism at the Service of Islamophobia', in Durmelat, Sylvie, Swamy and Vinay (eds), *Screening Integration: Recasting Maghrebi Immigration in Contemporary France*, Lincoln: University of Nebraska Press, pp. 144–60.

CHAPTER 14

Youth and *Média-engagé*: Is This West Africa's Heterolinguistic Cinéma-monde?

Carina Yervasi

'*La parole, c'est quelque chose. Quand tu l'as sur le coeur, ça te saisit. Si tu ne la sors pas, ça ne va pas . . . Ma parole ne restera pas en moi'.*
['Speech is something powerful. When it's in your heart, it grabs you . . . My voice will not stay inside me.'] An elderly witness (played by Zégué Bamba) spoken in Bambara to the court in *Bamako*. (Abderrahmane Sissako, 2006, Mali/USA/France)

'J'ai toujours essayé de me servir de ma voix, que ce soit en chantant ou en parlant, pour combattre l'injustice et les inégalités.'
[I have always tried to use my voice – singing and spoken – to fight injustice and inequality.]
Angélique Kidjo[1]

On 17 March 2014, #TweetUp226, Sawat Production and Adiska Entertainment published the lively music video entitled 'We Are Happy From Ouaga' on YouTube. Using Pharrell Williams's 'Happy' as a soundtrack, the filmmakers beautifully shot and edited a video of citizens from the capital city of Burkina Faso, Ouagadougou, lip-synching and dancing to Williams's words of joy and insouciance. While there are many 'Happy: We Are From . . .' videos on YouTube that use this same conceit of lip-synching Williams's song, this one had particular poignancy in Burkina Faso. A mere seven months later, these images of citizens offering a soundless lip-synched 'Happy' became the active voice of a nation during the October 2014 insurrection against president Blaise Compaore as he tried to change the nation's constitution in order to run for office yet again. Something had to give and it would not be the Constitution. People took to the streets in a popular grassroots movement called Le Balai Citoyen (The Citizen's Broom), initially waving push brooms and then small hand-held brooms, familiar to many in West Africa for sweeping away, both literally and figuratively, unwanted pests and debris. Images of this popular uprising and of a government overturned were captured on cell phones and amateur and professional cameras throughout the crisis. Droit Libre TV,[2] a Burkina Faso-based web television production company, for example, reported on the 27 October women's March of the Spatulas in a short documentary entitled *Ouaga: Les spatules battent le macadam* (2014), in which women speak out against the government and demonstrate in the city streets brandishing the ubiquitous large wooden cooking utensil. Many videos throughout October 2014 including *Modification de l'article 37: La révolte s'intensifie* (*Change to Article 37: The Rebellion Intensifies*) and *Avec le Balai Citoyen, au coeur de la lutte* (*At the Heart of the Fight with the Citizen's Broom*), were made by Droit Libre TV to depict the citizen-led anti-government demonstrations, which culminated on 30 October. After this violent day of discontent in the capital, which included the burning of the national assembly building, the president dissolved parliament, called for a state of emergency and resigned. Blaise Compaore fled the country on 31 October to neighbouring Ivory Coast.

Now, the people of Burkina Faso had something to celebrate. Their voice did not stay inside them; the voice of the citizens had been heard. Theirs was a citizens' movement that changed their country's political fate. It unfolded in sound and image on the world stage of the Internet.[3] And like its counterpart in Senegal, Y en a Marre (Fed Up), youth and music were front and centre, starring in videos of their own political triumph. The use of youth and music in these videos is not by chance. Rather it is a deliberate strategy used by the organisers of both movements. Y en a Marre, Senegal's largest youth-led hip hop-centred civic organisation (Appert 2011, Bryson 2014, Gueye 2013), was founded in January 2011 by musicians FouMalade (Malal Talla), Thiat (Cheikh Omar Cyrille Tour) and Kilifeu (Mbessane Seck) and journalists Fadel Barro, Alioune Sané, and Denise Sow. Le Balai Citoyen was founded in the summer of 2013 by reggae musician Sams'K Le Jah (Karim Sama), hip hop/rap artist Smockey (Serge Bambara) and lawyer Me Guy Hervé Kam. In order to maintain their grassroots character, neither group is affiliated with any official political party. In francophone West Africa[4] these two groups are at the forefront of civic engagement (see Figure 14.1), having won the 2016 Amnesty International Ambassador of Conscience Award for their work with youth activism. For Le Balai Citoyen the vehicular language is French, whereas Y en a Marre almost exclusively uses the urban Wolof of Dakar, which mixes Wolof, French, Arabic, and some English (McLaughlin 2001; Versluys 2006). Yet despite their linguistic differences both movements are witness to the ways that digital media can share political engagement and energy (Bryson 2014; Enz and Bryson 2014; Appert 2011).

Figure 14.1 Young activists with homemade signs attend a rally organised by Y en a Marre co-founders and musicians Matador and Thiat in early 2011, *Y en a marre / Fed-Up* (Adams Sie, 2013, Senegal).

At the heart of these documentaries and reportages that depict engaged activism is civic voice. Civic voice attends not only to language and discourse, but also to the role of speaking out in a democratic process, making speech 'something powerful' indeed. It is a voice that engenders the potential of the political towards organised politics (Dahlgren 2009: 101) and participation in the democratic processes of each country, whether it is youth voter registration, governmental oversight, or public action. This engagement is similar to the concept of 'democratic-participatory culture' theorised by Nico Carpentier in conversation with Henry Jenkins. (Jenkins and Carpentier 2013: 272). The films and videos produced as a result of and for the voice of engaged citizenship can best be described as *média-engagé*, due to their emphasis on political engagement. By analysing language, voice – a democratic civic voice – and worldwide collective access through the Internet, it seems evident that locally produced documentaries by and about Le Balai Citoyen and Y en a Marre are part of a growing trend of transnational francophone media using new technologies of image-making and distribution. They have much to offer recent scholarly debates about world cinema and media, particularly francophone cinéma-monde.

How do these videos use the combination of sound and voice to cooperate as key connectors to the francophone world in cases where French is not always used? How does the authority to speak, either literally or figuratively, develop as a long-term social and political goal in these documentaries? How might youth-centred media across West Africa redefine political media in terms of 'civic voice' to engage local viewers as well as the world audience looking in at that nation? And, finally, how can these civically engaged West African documentaries as *média-engagé* support the larger claims of a 'francophone' media enterprise and complement or expand the concept of cinéma-monde?

To answer these questions, this chapter is concerned with the audible – the play and interplay of speakers, listeners and participants; of voice, music and sounds on the soundtracks of politically engaged francophone media – and its relation to francophone documentaries about citizen- and youth-led movements in Senegal and Burkina Faso. The voice of young people in Burkina Faso's Le Balai Citoyen and Senegal's Y en a Marre democracy movements becomes a unified 'civic voice' and captures the energy of a local movement for a global audience. Theirs is a media distinctly motivated for political change in their countries, lending credibility to the idea that this documentary work is not only media entertainment, but is also *média-engagé*. Through discussions of four documentaries, I focus on the development of civic voice in young citizens in these two countries: *Avec le Balai Citoyen, au coeur de la lutte* (Droit Libre TV, 2014,) and *'Le Balai Citoyen': Smockey et Sams'K le Jah veulent assainir le Burkina!* (*The Citizen's Broom': Smockey and Sams 'K want to sanitise Burkina Faso!*) (Droit Libre TV, 2013) from Burkina Faso and *Y en a marre/Fed-Up* (Adams Sie, 2013) and *Yoole (Le sacrifice)/ Yoole: The Sacrifice* (Moussa Sene Absa, 2010) from Senegal. These documentaries have an objective: communicate to and with their citizens and be understood by the world.

Expanding the Concept of Cinéma-monde

While neither documentary nor civic voice are explicitly discussed in Bill Marshall's 2012 article, 'Cinéma-monde? Towards a concept of Francophone cinema', his articulation of cinéma-monde as a potentially 'francophonising,' (44) and therefore 'minorising' (47) process of world cinema in French can be broadened to embrace documentaries. Even as Marshall pays primary attention to fictional films, language and finances, his reading of a 'documentary mode' (47), developed in an analysis of *Loin* (André Téchiné, 2001, France), highlights 'borders, movement, language, and lateral connections' (Marshall 2012: 47) and a sense of realism or constructed reality that documentaries share with narrative film. Both the digitally shot documentary films of Adams Sie and Moussa Sene Absa in Senegal and the dynamic videos made by and of youth voices found, for example, in Droit Libre TV's Burkinabè documentaries on the Internet fit within the larger frame of Marshall's 'world cinema' and attend to those four key themes. Additionally, by referencing Deleuze and Guattari's *Kafka: pour une littérature mineure* (Marshall 2012: 44), Marshall invites a closer examination of any media, including documentaries, considering the characteristics that these two philosophers use to define 'des littératures mineures' (Deleuze and Guattari 1975: 29). Minor works in Deleuze and Guattari's taxonomy feature deterritorialised language and are 'attuned to politics' ['immédiatement branché sur la politique'] (30) and forge new alliances (32). These three traits of minor literature seem particularly significant for the media projects of these two activist groups.

As Marshall proposes, 'put[ting] the accent back' (2013: 45) in cinéma-monde theoretically echoes Hamid Naficy's work in *An Accented Cinema* and practically probes the complicated relationship that the French language has to francophone film. Marshall is inarguably right to reveal the 'guilty secret' of francophone cinema: 'that these films are not always in French, or rather, that the term "Francophone" forces a problematisation of what "French" is and what its relationship is with other languages' (43). What Marshall calls the 'Francophone cultural and linguistic world' (45) of films, he claims 'is interesting only when all its accents, contexts, and mixings are *made audible*' (45; emphasis in the original). That Marshall brings the 'audible' and linguistic relationships between French and its 'accents' into his definition of francophone cinéma-monde is the clearest example of the importance of language for his argument. Marshall's 'accents, contexts, and mixings' support my attention to voice, engaged politics and language of contemporary transnational francophone documentaries. Film critic Olivier Barlet offers in his article 'Enjeux documentaires' (2012) an insightful definition of documentary to better understand these videos and the ways in which the public's interaction with the language and voices of the social actors are fundamental to getting political messages to cross borders:

> Making a documentary means establishing a listening relationship with the filmed subjects ... In fiction, the actor is supposed to ignore the camera, but in documentary being conscious of the camera allows the spectators to be interlocutors of the filmed subject, who addresses not only the other people being filmed around them and/or the filmmaker (who may choose to appear on screen), but all who will see the film.[5] (291)

The videos for and by these groups must 'establish a listening relationship' with all constituents of the film. This includes addressing cross-border communities for international audiences, making use of this movement to convey their voice, and developing lateral connections with other such nascent youth and civic groups as LUCHA or Filimbi (Democratic Republic of Congo) or Sassoufit (Congo-Brazzaville). Put together, these features represent a new kind of media, touching on Marshall's 'francophonising' and 'minorising' processes, as they harness political engagement when the voice of the documentaries becomes 'civic voice'. In what follows, I will show how 'civic voice' can be used in place of Marshall's concept of making 'audible' accents, contexts and mixings (2012: 45), especially in relationship to the current popular movements of Le Balai Citoyen and Y en a Marre, whose documentaries critically engage image and sound.

From Voice to 'Civic Voice' to Political Engagement in the Era of Digital Media-making

The energised voice that Smockey uses in '*Le Balai Citoyen': Smockey et Sams'K le Jah veulent assainir le Burkina!* when talking about 'democratic rule' (1:30) or the quietly emphatic way that Thierno, a young citizen, communicates 'mal gouvernance, quoi' [badly run government] in Moussa Sene Absa's *Yoole: The Sacrifice* (4:25–4:30) are both evidence of 'civic voice.' The popular music of reggae and rap/hip hop artists featured at many of the recorded public rallies and on soundtracks are key elements that promote civic voice in these documentaries as a form of 'social collective' (Chanan 2007: 16). But the combination of youth, voice, language, and music to create civic voice is not new. In writing about earlier Ghanaian hiplife music, Jesse Shipley defines this youth-centred music form as a 'polylinguistic lyricism' (2013: 13), or a voice that must transcend one national language. For sociolinguist and film scholar John Kristian Sanaker, voice is a part of 'language behavior as cultural expression' (2010: 106). For film scholar Boulou Ebanda B'béri voice is 'the specificity of the practices of expression themselves' (2009: 812), and for Shipley, voice is the possibility of 'socially authoritative and free-thinking public speakers' (2013 4). But whereas B'béri lays claim to the need for an authoritative voice –using, for example, the leitmotiv of 'Ma mère raconte . . . ' in Haitian film director Raoul Peck's film, *Lumumba: la mort du prophète/Lumumba: The Death of A Prophet* (Peck, 1992, France/Germany/Switzerland) – Shipley asserts that hiplife 'provides the youth with transformative possibilities' (6), that they need no other authority than themselves. For Shipley, the youth in that movement 'are their own authority' (24). The voice and music of youth, as Shipley defines them, are all the authority that the movements of Le Balai Citoyen and Y en a Marre need to develop civic voice in their media.

While youthful music is crucial to these movements (and I analyse examples of this later), I would argue that more than holding the authority to speak and be heard, this media and its music must attend to publics and the networks they participate in. Defining these networked publics, which need a sense of agency and an openness to participate in social and political change, can be linked to the idea of 'democratic-participatory rhizome' advocated in the work of Nico Carpentier (Jenkins and Carpentier 2013: 272). In other words, for any public to succeed as a participatory culture it needs to be attached to civic engagement and the promise of change. This is how an ordinary citizen like Sabarane Lam in Adams Sie's *Fed-Up* can voice his concerns (5:30–6:24) and become invested in the social movement implicitly promised in Y en a Marre's 'democratic-participatory' civic voice. Being able to analyse this essential move from individual voice to civic voice in documentary is indebted to the work of media scholars Kate Nash (2014) and Trish FitzSimons (2009). Before the publication of their recent work, many theories around 'voice' in documentaries relied on Bill Nichols's concept of voice as a quality of the filmmaker's presence or self-reflexivity in film. Nichols's metaphor of voice as filmic texture or what he describes as the 'moiré-like' quality of a film's fabric (Nichols 1983: 18) functions more generally like the 'modes' of documentary film (Nichols 2010), rather than a clearly defined way to discuss the complexity of voices and sound in documentary.

The voice as 'civic voice' that I am postulating is more closely related to the features of voice and its place in creating a democratic 'discursive community' (Nash 2014: 384) that Nash and FitzSimons theorise. FitzSimons in particular is the first to question the role of voice both as a metaphor of authorship and its privileging over other voices that had become prominent in documentary studies (2014: 133). In critiquing the way 'voice' is unproblematised by Nichols, she examines the multiplicity of voices 'braided' throughout the documentary that share 'the authority . . . with subjects and broadcasters. . . film-makers and audiences' (FitzSimons 2009: 139). Nash picks up this thread of multiple voices in her 2014 article, 'What is interactivity for? The social dimension of web-documentary participation' by focusing on how interaction online is a form of democratic participation and investigates how 'documentary's social functions' (Renov 2004: 12) can create a 'documentary community' (389) around such voices. Along with Nash, media culture theorists

Jenkins and Carpentier (2013), Peter Dahlgren (2009) and Chelsey Hauge (2014) examine and explain how youth activists, who are invited to share 'equal power relations' (Jenkins and Carpentier 2013: 271), can become vocal participants through and in the new technologies of both traditional and web-based documentaries. While Nash warns against the easy slippage of 'voice-as-authorship with those of social voice' (2014: 393), this 'community' has the political potential to make the documentary address 'the viewer as a citizen, as a member of a social collective, as a putative participant in the social sphere' (Chanan 2007: 16). Droit Libre TV, for example, posts its videos both on its own website and in social media. With nearly 11,000 YouTube subscribers, Droit Libre TV creates and simultaneously relies on this 'documentary community' to promote its democratic programmes. Their six-minute short *Avec le Balai Citoyen, au coeur de la lutte* has over 19,000 views and multiple comments. After viewing this video and reading the comments – not all of which are positive or in French – one is left with the impression that through this media posted online, anyone with access to the Internet (and not only those who want to demonstrate in the streets) is given an opportunity to participate in a democratic 'social collective' like Le Balai Citoyen.

Voice, music and political engagement work simultaneously for Y en a marre and Le Balai Citoyen to create their participative civic voice of internationally engaged citizens. In short, these documentaries focus on documenting democratising voices for the nation and transnationally across borders. But both voice and crossing borders bring back the troubled question of language.

French Language in 'Francophone' World Media

No one can deny that the francophone world exists because of France and this nation's wide arm of geopolitical interventions over the past several centuries, including colonialism, (so-called) civilising missions, economic aid, neo-colonialism and finally, more recently, ongoing diplomacy. West African francophone cinema, a recent mid-twentieth century art form and commercial venture, survives in part as a consequence of this past as well as from ongoing funding from such organisations as Fonds Images de la Francophonie, Organisation internationale de la Francophonie, CIRTEF (Conseil international des radios et televisions d'expressions françaises), and Ministère des Affaires étrangères et européennes, all of which are linked in one way or another to the French government (Hoefort de Turégano 2005). France's interest in having a media presence in West Africa could be considered benevolent when it comes to maintaining the

French language[6] and funding media projects, but it has also created a handicap that, in the past, pressured filmmakers to rely on this funding because their home nations were often too poor or had difficulty justifying funding for the arts. At the same time, while French is present in West African francophone nations either as an official language of government or the language of education, it is not necessarily the predominant language of films and locally produced media.

Most films and videos across West Africa have been redefining the visual and linguistic medium for decades. Francophone cinema, from its very early years, was created in a paradoxical space, where international economic and artistic co-productions, not to mention transnational projects, were (and are) the rule rather than the exception. Francophone cinema creates a heterolinguistic space where French and local languages comingle or where no French is spoken at all (Bourget 2015). Francophone media share this same multinational and polylinguistic quality of earlier francophone cinema. One trait of heterolinguistic spaces is that they reflect language usage in unpredictable ways such as 'denaturalis[ing] the monolingual concept of language' or rendering the construction of all languages in a linguistic landscape visible or audible (Simard 2015). Here, I am referring to all sorts of linguistic and multivalent intermingling such as in Ousmane Sembène's cinema, in which the interplay of French, Wolof and occasionally Arabic is used to political effect. For example, in *Xala* (1975, Senegal) the main character's daughter advocates speaking Wolof as a political act, refusing to speak French with her father, while in *Guelwaar* (1992, Senegal) the son of the dead activist refuses to speak or understand Wolof in favour of a French that matches his French passport. This heterolinguistic space is taken to the extreme in Abderrahmane Sissako's most recent film *Timbuktu* (2014, France/Mauritania), where the role of linguistic miscommunication is deeply developed through the interplay of speech with no less than six languages spoken and translated (Arabic, Bambara, English, French, Songhay and Tamashek) throughout the film by occupying Jihadists, mercenaries, courts, and local and immigrant populations. Media works featuring Y en a Marre communicate in both French and Wolof and both are used to question power and invite critical reflection. Rap musicians Xuman (Makhtar Fall) and Keyti (Cheikh Sène) offer weekly Internet news bulletins, *Journal Rappé*, in French and Wolof respectively, which present ready examples of this linguistic co-habitation and give rise to a participatory 'civic voice' in a multivalent space. John Kristian Sanaker (2010) suggests that films and videos made in such 'incompletely Francophone countries' as those in francophone Africa as well as Algeria, Canada, Morocco and Tunisia, for example (105) – where 'francophone' is defined as much by a sociocultural phenomenon as ideological structure (105) – use local languages to paint a clearer picture of the plurilingual societies in which the films and videos are made. In addition to the use of multiple languages in these films, space is the single most important signifying feature of African film, claims film scholar Justin Ouoro in 'Enjeux esthétiques du cinéma d'Afrique noire francophone':

> Reminiscent of the manner in which new sovereignties permitted Africans to reappropriate their territory after independence, African cinema yolked itself to the return of African space for Africans with its goal of reterritorialising African values.
>
> The realistic reproduction of material space, whether the space of the bush, the concession, the village or the city, appears as a distinctive mark of cinematographic expression in sub-Saharan Africa. (2011: 58)

The 'audible' of Sanaker's heterolinguistic space of francophone West African media is comparable to Ouoro's 'reterritorialized space' in film and video of 'Africa for Africans.' Together, the combination of language and space, which are the material and 'distinctive marks' of media expression in sub-Saharan African, defines, along with civic voice and music, the *média-engagé* by and about Le Balai Citoyen and Y en a Marre. National, transnational, and Pan-African by nature, using local terrain, and French and local languages in sub-Saharan Africa, *média-engagé* cuts across and connects countries where French and other languages are still audible in daily life and where representation of the local landscape itself is a reterritorialisation of the nation through the visual medium.

Grassroots Message and Participatory Democracy

Droit Libre TV's *média-engagé* offers Le Balai Citoyen both local participation and a global presence by way of its Internet short entitled *Avec le Balai Citoyen, au coeur de la lutte*. In one of the many short featured interviews, Rasmane Zinaba, member of Le Balai Citoyen, remarks on the strength of young people to create local change: 'C'est un jour historique (4:10–4:20) . . . la jeunesse de Burkina est en train de créer l'histoire, une histoire positive de son pays . . .' (4:50–4:59) [This is a historic day . . . The youth of Burkina Faso are making history, a positive history for their country . . .]. That Zinaba's emotional and politicised address to an Internet audience is in French whereas Y en a Marre's is predominantly in Wolof, should not be lost on us, but it is not something to become obsessed by within a heterolinguistic landscape. The vehicular language of Burkina Faso is French and Le Balai Citoyen uses it almost exclusively, whether representing Le Balai Citoyen in Bobo-Dioulasso or in Ouagadougou. What is important in Zinaba's testimony is that the youth are speaking out and making changes at that historic moment in October 2014. Furthermore, the exclusive use of French by Droit Libre TV should not be seen as a 'betrayal' of local languages (Adejunmobi 2004: 53). Rather, according to linguist Moradewun Adejunmobi, using French even where local languages are available may 'signify a redrawing of the borders of belonging in order to reflect the acquisition of new affiliations spread over a wider territory than previous affiliations' (2004: 54). With about 70 living languages in Burkina Faso, French allows for such 'lateral connections' and affiliations across other Burkinabè ethnic and linguistic groups as well as other francophone nations in Droit Libre TV's sphere of communication. This is why privileging local voice turned civic voice, as opposed to national origin, is a crucial element to be analysed in any consideration of cinéma-monde's 'audible' and heterolinguistic space of francophone media.

As I pointed out earlier, music, another element of the 'audible,' has a long-standing relationship to these organisations and creates a dynamic intersection between voice and nation and political engagement. To raise consciousness about the immigration crisis in coastal sub-Saharan West Africa, Senegalese filmmaker Moussa Sene Absa, for example, highlights the role of local music in his film *Yoole: The Sacrifice* (hereafter *Yoole*). Moving between Barbados with its English- and Arabic-speaking Muslim community and Dakar's French narration and youth-centred interviews and hip hop songs in Wolof, this digitally shot documentary focuses on sound as the expression of youthful disillusionment in Dakar. Sene Absa's use of heterolinguistic audible elements, places emphasis on local voices using French, English, Arabic and Wolof to do so. Through short and often disjointed vignettes, punctuated by music and poetry, the documentary aims to trace the desire to leave, but also wishes to reveal the causes of this national sacrifice.

In *Yoole*, which uses the true story of the tragic discovery of the corpses of eleven young Senegalese men in a boat drifting in the Caribbean to talk about challenges facing young people in Dakar, Sene Absa pieces together an imaginary and unavoidably fragmented narrative of agency, frustration, disappointment and resignation. Sene Absa places black and white images of former Senegalese President Abdoulaye Wade's early campaign speeches of 'Sopi' ('change' in Wolof) alongside extreme close-up, colour images of young men (0:08–1:15). After telling the story of Barbados, Sene Absa sets up the comparison between the ghost ship and youth in Dakar by returning to the extreme close-ups of young men who are sometimes silent, sometimes speaking in both French and Wolof about governmental disarray and economic hardship (4:20–5:42). For Sene Absa the ghost ship was tantamount to a sacrificial offering. In an online interview at the Tarifa African film festival published on YouTube in 2012, he laments that

> These young men were sacrificed ... When an African offers up a sacrifice, he chooses the most beautiful animal. We are sacrificing our most beautiful youth, which is the beauty of our world. That is the thing that most moved me ... These young men are so disappointed. That is the truth that this reality revealed to me.[7] (2:15–2:55)

This collective sacrifice is echoed in *Yoole*'s sound track featuring Daara-J's 'Exodus,' which begins with a lyrical French voice singing 'au revoir famille et terre ...' ['good-bye family and homeland'] and continues by rapping in Wolof about young men being forced to leave their country for 'Barsah ou Barsakh' (7:07–7:37). This Wolof expression meaning 'Barcelona or death,' a play on words of Barsah as Barcelona and Barsakh as paradise, is explained in the documentary by psychologist Serigne Mor Mbaye speaking French. Towards the end of the documentary Ousseynou, a Senegalese immigrant in Portugal, is interviewed (1:01:11–1:01:45) and reveals the temptation of leaving by sea and arriving in Europe for the reality it is: a false hope for change: 'Europe is only a lure' (1:01:30). Where the young voices of the ship remain forever silent, the young men interviewed by Sene Absa, who directly witness the problems of a collapsing economy and rising unemployment, begin to use a rhetoric of accusation and protest, that Y en a Marre would further develop in January 2011 as civic voice in its platform for democratic participation, contributing to the collapse of Abdoulaye Wade's government in 2012.

The interplay of languages as civic voice in Sene Absa's documentary marks the rise of politically engaged music and of Wolof in Dakar as the use of French declines. This is evident with Y en a Marre's 2013 hit single 'Dox ak sa Gox' [literally 'marcher avec sa collectivité'/ 'walking with your community'] – the lyrics of which can be found on Y en a Marre's Facebook page in Wolof. Sponsored by Oxfam, the United States Agency for International Development (USAID), and OSIWA (Bryson 50), *Dox ak sa Gox* is also the title of Y en a Marre's own web-series and Internet platform created as Observatoire Citoyen de la démocratie et bonne gouvernance [Citizen's Observatory of Democracy and Good Governance], which alternates between French and Wolof.

Further evidence of this civic voice made of languages, youth and music is in Adams Sie's short film *Fed-Up*, when young rappers Matador

Figure 14.2 Young participants cheer and hold up their brooms at the end of a rally in Ouagadougou with Le Balai Citoyen co-founders and musicians Smockey and Sams'K le Jah in *'Le Balai Citoyen': Smockey et Sams'K le Jah veulent assainir le Burkina!* (Droit Libre TV, 2013, Burkina Faso).

(Mohamed Bendjabar) and Thiat address huge crowds at a demonstration in 2011 demanding that the government listen to the people and stop cutting the electrical current in Dakar. Speaking in Wolof, Thiat tells the crowd that the government is wrong about young people being 'unhealthy', because 'the world today will say that we're . . .' and without a pause adds in French 'une jeunesse consciente et éveillée' [conscious and awakened youth] (4:59–5:01). The message in *Fed-Up* of youth culture's fully awakened consciousness, civic voice, and political participation is also present in the 2013 documentary *'Le Balai Citoyen': Smockey et Sams'K le Jah veulent assainir le Burkina!*, in which the narrating voice says over an image of young people demonstrating in the street that the government would have to start listening to the 'opposition and the youth' (00:15–00:17) in the 'popular movement' to which Smockey et Sams'K le Jah lend their voice. They appear on the platform with brooms and incite the demonstrators to get out their brooms to 'clean up' their country. They repeat more than once 'on est là pour faire le balai' [we're here to get our brooms out, to clean up] (00:30). The two musicians understand that the voice of the country's youth should not be discounted in an election. Through the metaphor of cleaning house, they want to activate youth participation to change their government via the democratic process of elections. Sams'K le Jah declares very explicitly that they are there to respond to the interests of youth, who want real results and real change ('une jeunesse qui veut d'un movement des choses concrètes') (5:14–5:22), where each person has a voice and each person has a force to offer to the movement ('Chacun compte une voix. Chacun compte une force') (6:55–7:06) (see Figure 14.2). In other words, with civic voice comes the possibility to share power in a democracy.

Conclusion

Francophone media representations of such recent youth-led popular movements as Senegal's Y en a Marre and Burkina Faso's Le Balai Citoyen engage local political and democratic renewal in their respective nations by sparking a participatory civic voice that acquires transcultural and transnational viewership. These documentaries symbolise new technological trends in media-making worldwide, especially as democratising tools for youth and *média-engagé*. This is done in true minorising fashion that francophone cinéma-monde advocates by deterritorialising language in favour of civic voice, by attending to local democracy, and by forging alliances internationally across a heterolinguistic landscape. While these documentaries problematise the privileging of 'cinema' in cinéma-monde, they can also be included in an expanded understanding of cinéma-monde; one that would recognise multiple platforms for producing, viewing, and participating in the visual culture of the twenty-first century; would engage multiple publics in multiple languages; would critique assumptions about authority; would not easily untangle the complexities of belonging. These documentaries ought to be a part of the revolutionising of cinéma-monde so that it embraces its most minorising and democratising forms.

Notes

1. Angélique Kidjo, in a press release from Amnesty International, is quoted as saying 'I have always tried to use my voice – singing and spoken – to fight injustice and inequality' when she won, along with Le Balai Citoyen, Y en a Marre and LUCHA (Lutte pour le changement, Democratic Republic of Congo), Amnesty International's prestigious Ambassador of Conscience Award 2016. Available at <http:/www.amnesty.org/en/press-releases/2016/05/musician-angelique-kidjo-and-african-youth-activists-honoured-with-amnesty-international-award> (last accessed 1 August 2016).

2. Droit Libre TV is an Internet television station that broadcasts in French. Its programming can be found at <http://www.droitlibre.net> and, according to their website, the station covers human rights issues across Francophone West Africa in Benin, Burkina Faso, Guinea, Ivory Coast, Mali, Niger, Senegal, and Togo.
3. During and after the period of the Arab Spring, covering late December 2010 through to mid-2012, it is important to acknowledge the ways that the Internet and social media contributed to other social movements including Y en a Marre (January 2011) and part of Le Balai Citoyen (summer 2013). See Elisa Adami (2016) and Maximillian Hänska-Ahy (2016).
4. The nations most commonly grouped together as Francophone West Africa are Benin, Burkina Faso, Guinea, Ivory Coast, Mali, Mauritania, Niger, Senegal and Togo.
5. All translations from French are my own, unless otherwise noted.
6. According to the *Organisation internationale de la Francophonie* (hereafter OIF), which publishes statistical analysis every four years on the usage of French in the world, there were 274 million French speakers in the world in 2014. Use of French in Europe is down 8% from statistics of 2010, but has grown substantially in sub-Saharan Africa. Sub-Saharan Africa represents 54.7% of all speakers of French worldwide (OIF 2014: 20–22). One of the more interesting findings in Senegal (some 29% of the population speaks French) is that in Dakar French usage is declining with the rise of Wolof and English (45–51). With French as the language of instruction in some thirty-two countries in the world, including both Burkina Faso and Senegal, one could argue that maintaining the French language in sub-Saharan Africa is about developing a linguistic as well as a cultural sphere of influence.
7. (2:15–2:55) Available at <https://www.youtube.com/watch?v=FehKoqNG-zg> (last accessed 6 January 2016).

Works Cited

Adami, E. (2016), 'How Do You Watch a Revolution? Notes From the 21st century', *Journal of Visual Culture*, 15:1, April, pp. 69–84.

Adejunmobi, Moradewun (2004), *Vernacular palaver: imaginations of the local and non-native languages in West Africa*, Clevedon: Multilingual Matters.

Appert, C. (2011), 'Rappin' Griots: Producing the Local in Senegalese Hip Hop,' in Paul Khalil Saucier (ed.), *Native Tongues: An African Hip Hop Reader*, Trenton: Africa World Press, pp. 3–22.

Avec le Balai Citoyen, au coeur de la lutte (2014), Droit Libre TV, <https://www.youtube.com/watch?v=c-fTakOhmpM> (last accessed 4 January 2016).

Barlet, Olivier (2012), 'Enjeux documentaires' *Les cinémas d'Afrique des années 2000: Perspectives critiques*, Paris: L'Harmattan, pp. 291–306.

B'béri, B. E. (2009), 'Transgeographical Practices Of Marronage In Some African Films', *Cultural Studies*, 23:5–6, pp. 810–30.

Bourget, C. (2015), 'Francophone Films to the Rescue: Indigenous Languages and Francophone Studies', *The French Review*, 88:4, May, pp. 117–26.
Bryson, D. (2014), 'The Rise of a New Senegalese Cultural Philosophy', *African Studies Quarterly*, 14:3, March, pp. 33–56.
Chanan, Michael (2007), *The Politics of Documentary*, London: British Film Institute.
Dahlgren, Peter (2009), *Media and Political Engagement: Citizens, communication, and Democracy*, Cambridge: Cambridge University Press.
Deleuze, Gilles and Félix Guattari (1975), *Kafka: pour une littérature mineure*, Paris: Les Éditions de Minuit.
Enz, M. K. and D. Bryson (2014), 'Fed-Up: Creating a New Type of Senegal through the Arts', *African Studies Quarterly*, 14:3, March, pp. 1–12.
FitzSimons, T. (2009), 'Braided Channels: A Genealogy of the Voice of Documentary', *Studies in Documentary Film*, 3:2, pp. 131–46.
Gueye, M. (2013), 'Urban Guerilla Poetry: The Movement *Y'en a Marre* and the Socio-Political Influences of Hip Hop in Senegal', *The Journal of Pan African Studies*, 6:3, pp. 22–42.
Hänska-Ahy, M. (2016), 'Networked communication and Arab Spring: Linking broadcast and social media', *New Media & Society*, 18:1, January, pp. 99–116.
Hauge, C. (2014), 'Youth media and agency', *Discourse: Studies in the Cultural*, 35:4, pp. 471–84.
Hoefort de Turégano, T. (2005), 'Sub-Saharn African Cinemas: The French Connection', *Modern & Contemporary France*, 13:1, February, pp. 71–83.
Jenkins, H. and N. Carpentier (2013), 'Theorising Participatory Intensities: A Conversation About Participation and Politics', *Convergence: The International Journal of Research into New Media Technologies*, 19:3, pp. 265–86, doi: 10.1177/1354856513482090.
'Le Balai Citoyen': Smockey et Sams'k le Jah veulent assainir le Burkina! (2013), Droit Libre TV, Burkina Faso, <https://www.youtube.com/watch?v=tLY4CLu_vVw> (last accessed 4 January 2016).
Marche de la Spatule (2014), Droit Libre TV, Burkina Faso, <https://www.youtube.com/user/droitlibre> (last accessed 14 January 2016).
Marshall, B. (2012), 'Cinéma-monde? Towards a concept of Francophone cinema', *Francosphères*, 1:1, pp. 35–51.
McLaughlin, F. (2001), 'Dakar Wolof and the Configuration of an Urban Identity', *Journal of African Cultural Studies*, 14:2, December, pp. 153–72.
Naficy, Hamid (2001), *An Accented Cinema: Exilic and Diasporic Filmmaking*, Princeton: Princeton University Press.
Nash, K. (2014), 'What is interactivity for? The social dimension of web-documentary participation', *Continuum: Journal of Media & Cultural Studies*, 28:3, pp. 383–95.
Nichols, B. (1983), 'The Voice of Documentary', *Film Quarterly*, 36:3, pp. 17–30.
Nichols, Bill (2010), *Introduction to Documentary*, 2nd ed., Bloomington: Indiana University Press.

Organisation internationale de la francophonie (2014), *La langue française dans le monde*, Paris: Nathan.

Ouoro, J. (2011), 'Enjeux esthétiques du cinéma d'Afrique noire francophone', *Poétique des cinémas d'Afrique noire francophone*, Ouagadougou: Presses universitaires de Ouagadougou, pp. 51–73.

Renov, Michael (2004), *The Subject of Documentary*, Minneapolis: University of Minnesota Press.

Sanaker, John Kristian (2010), *La rencontre des langues dans le cinéma francophone*, Paris: L'Harmattan and Quebec: Presses de l'Université Laval.

Sene Absa, M. (2010), Interview, Festival Cine Africano Tarifa, <https://www.youtube.com/watch?v=FehKoqNG-zg> (last accessed 6 January 2016).

Shipley, Jesse (2013), *Living the Hiplife: Celebrity and Entrepreneurship in Ghanaian Popular Music*, Durham, NC and London: Duke University Press.

Simard, M. (2015), 'Une critique radicale de "la langue",' *Acta fabula* 16. 1, January, <http://www.fabula.org/acta/document9123.php> (last accessed 18 May 2016).

Versluys, E. (2006), 'Multilingualism and the City: The Construction of Urban Identities in Dakar', *Conferencias ISCTE* (International Conference of Young Urban Researchers), <http://conferencias.iscte.pt/viewpaper.php?id=141&cf=3> (last accessed 15 December 2015).

We Are Happy from Ouaga (2014), #TweetUp226, Sawat Production and Adiska Entertainment, Burkina Faso, <https://www.youtube.com/watch?v=rhsmmKYMvi4> (last accessed 14 January 2016).

Y en a Marre. 'Dox ak sa Gox', <https://www.facebook.com/permalink.php?id=218479604856155&story_fbid=571767706194008> (last accessed 2 January 2016).

Epilogues

Worlds Within; In the World
Bill Marshall

Cinéma-monde always came with a question mark: it was a hypothesis, a heuristic device, conjuring up a 'what would happen if' we looked at francophone film production through a slightly different lens. Simultaneously, it diverted us from, or even re-energised and re-focused, that 'F' word which so bedevils work in the discipline due to its baggage of implied binaries and hierarchies. The centrality of language invoked by 'francophone' might be re-harnessed not according to official unifications and diversities, and not just to 'francophonise' the non-decolonised metropole, but to make audible that 'Frenchness' in a special way, as Edouard Glissant says he writes, 'en présence de toutes les langues du monde' [in presence of all of the world's languages] (1996: 40). And to paraphrase and adapt Michel de Certeau, there was an opportunity to surpass the official *carte de la francophonie* and even the industrial-strategic hubs of new production formations in favour of the *parcours* of non-hierarchical connections and wanderings of creative personnel and ideas.

As the editors in their introduction, and other contributors, point out, cinéma-monde thus contains an ethical dimension, linked to 'gestures of solidarity' and 'interest in others' (page 10). Certainly, for example, contemporary refugee crises have led themselves to new patterns of transnational filmmaking, and, indeed, to a corpus of films within cinéma-monde that have profound ethical implications (e.g. *Le Havre* [Aki Kaurismäki, 2011, Finland/France/Germany]; *Dheepan*, [Jacques Audiard, 2015, France]). However, I wish to develop this further by emphasising the *monde*/world element in all its force. For, as Glissant continues :

> ma langue, je la déporte et la bouscule non pas dans des synthèses, mais dans des ouvertures linguistiques qui me permettent de concevoir les rapports des langues entre elles aujourd'hui sur la surface de la terre – rapports de domination, de connivence, d'absorption, d'oppression, d'érosion, de tangence, etc. – comme le fait d'un immense drame, d'une immense tragédie dont ma propre langue ne peut être exempte et sauve. (1996: 40)

[I deport my language and jostle it not with syntheses, but with linguistic openings that allow me to consider the relationships between languages today on earth – relationships of domination, connivance, absorption, oppression, erosion, tangent, etc. – as one of immense drama, of immense tragedy from which my own language can be neither exempt nor safe.[1] (1996: 40)]

The logic here is not simply of an ethical interest in the plight of other humans, but of an erasure of the self/other binary in favour of a recognition of mutual entanglements, of an unstable and changing continuum of universal culture and living-in-the-world marked by profound inequalities of power. The ethical always implies the political, even if it may be the first stage in a journey that comes to recognise the pervasiveness of politics. The implications for cinema are many, ranging from thematic choices (e.g. migration, refugees) made by filmmakers, through ways of looking and viewing, to the potentially creative role of film academics, teachers and critics – in their role as curators rather than gatekeepers – in enabling insightful juxtapositions of heterogeneous texts.

However, these possibilities raise further questions, firstly about audiences. I am reminded here of Joseph Mai's intervention in Chapter 1 of this volume about Rithy Panh, and the difficulties in speaking about intended (Khmer) and subtitled (French and English) audiences, about the way in which the film thus crosses 'many different global and linguistic worlds', and the need to construct, for the purposes of film analysis, 'a particular idealised viewer' (page 28). Clearly, an interesting but challenging project here would be some empirical audience research linked to reception study, for the perpetual risk of transnational research is precisely of losing a 'situatedness' that, paradoxically, is universal. This brings to mind discussions I have had about Xavier Dolan's latest feature film, *Juste la fin du monde/It's Only the End of the World* (Canada/France), released in 2016. The dazzling camerawork and use of close-up, and the inspired acting performances, cannot completely erase the fact of a non-place: actors with French accents filmed in an unnamed Quebec are not vehicles for 'universality', on the contrary, the absence of spatial particularism – where are these people? – takes away one element of living which is universally shared, that is a 'place'. Much further work needs to be done on the reception of French/francophone cinema that travels: what meanings can the latter term have in the identity and marketing of 'French' film festivals? What meanings do practices of translation – dubbing and subtitling – impelled by the presence of other languages in francophone film, or by the need to translate in non-francophone contexts, have in relation to audiences differently situated in terms of nation or class?[2]

To the instabilities associated with audience and reception can be added those of text. Audiard's *Dheepan* is a French film the majority of whose dialogue is in Tamil, and which includes key translation sequences that: foreground the language issue and language's capacity both to block and protect; contribute to the film's examination of lies, performance and the creation of new 'truths/identities' (the scene where the Tamil translator encourages a different refugee tale in the presence of the uncomprehending French bureaucrat); speak to questions of integration; and potentially defamiliarise or 'make strange' French itself via an 'alien's' view of France. On the other hand, usually contradictory modes of cinema are forced to coexist: the well-established social realism of French *banlieue* cinema, the auteurist stylistic and thematic tics of Audiard himself (marginalised men, 'the presence of unexplained lights' [Dobson 2016: 266]), and especially the irruption of genre – gangster, western, revenge – in the final shootout (an ending panned by many critics, although fully explicable in terms of the narrative's central post-traumatic scenario; see for example Tessé 2015). Whatever the complexity or the shortcomings, according to viewpoint, of *Dheepan*'s text, what is clear is that an ethics cannot automatically be 'read off' from this or other films, but that it requires quite complex textual work on film's ambiguity to do so, or, to put it another way, the work of recognising ambiguity of text, position and identity is itself a labour of ethics.

Moreover, the mention of genre impels an examination of the ways in which the transnational emphases of cinéma-monde are affected by established binaries of auteur and popular cinema. How and where is the latter constituted, and how does it circulate, if at all? Famously, massively successful metropolitan French comedies such as *Les Visiteurs* (Jean-Marie Poiré, 1993, France) and *Bienvenue chez les Ch'tis/Welcome to The Sticks* (Dany Boon, 2008, France) failed to gain the same traction in the Quebec film market; the period melodrama *Séraphin, un homme et son péché* (Charles Binamé, 2002, Canada) and the bilingual police buddy movie *Bon Cop Bad Cop* (Érik Canuel, 2006, Canada) are the two most successful Quebec films at the domestic box office, but inexportable – because incomprehensible – to audiences overseas, even and especially francophone audiences. (Here I broaden Jean-Pierre Jeancolas's definition of the 'inexportable' out from the original discrete corpus of films he examines: 'films as inexportable, because they were too insignificant and/or unintelligible to be appreciated by spectators outside a given popular cultural area, which was at once uncouth, coded, and based on recognition', and therefore 'based on a form of complicity that is limited both spatially and temporally' [1992: 141]).

Thus, the 'popular' is by and large constructed in the space of the 'national', and scholars of transnational film neglect these two terms at their peril. The nation is not going away, as the national-populisms of 2016 and after tell us. At the moment, the nation is still the main site of political mobilisation, for good or for ill, and here shifting arguments and paradigms concerning Quebec cinema are relevant. In previous work, I argued that Quebec films, and indeed those of any 'national cinema', were to be understood not as national allegories but as 'national-allegorical tensions' between forces of assertion and dispersal, homogeneity and heterogeneity: '"National" film texts are thus always inevitably pluralized and even destabilised by the competing discourses of and on the nation that exist in the culture and polity, the work of aesthetic form on non-aesthetic (ideological) discourses, and the contradictions and paradoxes inherent in the idea of the nation itself' (Marshall 2001: 3). Bakhtin ('centripetal/centrifugal') and Deleuze-Guattari ('territorialisation/ deterritorialisation') were deployed to help navigate this idea. The book ended on a discussion of modernity and postmodernity, and the ways in which globalisation was affecting the national-allegorical tension in contemporary film texts. Robert Lepage's *Le Confessionnal/The Confessional* (1995, Canada/UK/France) in the end summarised this tension in its staging of extreme contraction (the – incestuous – family kitchen in the home in the walled city of Quebec's national origin) with dilation (the opening out to modernity associated with Hollywood and television, the bridge to the suburbs, the outside, a world of difference exemplified by the references to Asian cultures).

This paradigm needs to be qualified by, but also in turn qualifies, the frequent discussion of a 'global' or 'transnational' turn in Quebec cinema since 2000, fuelled by Oscar and other international successes, the Hollywood careers of Jean-Marc Vallée and Denis Villeneuve, the Xavier Dolan phenomenon (Kotte 2015).[3] Rather than the 'national' being replaced, we might refer to an intensification of the processes and tensions previously outlined: not only is the nation not going away, it is to misrecognise 'the national' to see it as not already implicated in a relation to plurality and the world. This can be seen when centripetal national shared recognitions of popular comedy coexist with transnational agendas.

In Quebec popular cinema, one (partial) exception to inexportability has been *La Grande Séduction/Seducing Doctor Lewis* (Jean-François Pouliot, 2003, Canada; 1,197,843 entries at the domestic box office), which spins the tale of a remote and dispossessed fishing village on the north shore of the St Lawrence River 'seducing' a doctor from the city to settle there so that they meet the requirements of a potential employer who will install a factory. Thus binary oppositions are established, between rural/ urban, past/present, tradition/modern, community/individualism, face-to-face relations/anonymity, walking/motor car, truth and authenticity/ falsehood and corruption. Here the terms are very differently valorised but also become blurred. 'Truth' is already compromised by the social security fraud perpetrated by the leader of the section who becomes mayor (Raymond Bouchard), and the lies told to Dr Lewis (David Boutin) before the final reveal. Gossip, usually associated with communities having face-to-face relations, has its source here in technological surveillance as the women of the village are assigned to listening in and reporting on Dr Lewis' phone conversations. As befits popular culture, an imaginary solution to the real contradictions around Quebec national identity and the relation of present to past (the church is now completely secularised) is offered, with a new 'truth' upheld in the mayor's confession and in Lewis' acceptance; the rural community is 'urbanised' and even 'globalised', but remains intact. Things return to their rightful place (jobs, male sexual potency rediscovered, gender roles) while 'newness' is contained.

The film's destiny extended beyond its initial success in Quebec. Not only did the original film find overseas markets (including South Korea), achieving the fourth best ever box office success in France for a Quebec film, it spawned three remakes: *The Grand Seduction* (Don McKellar, 2013, Canada); *Un Village presque parfait* (Stéphane Meunier, 2015, France); *Un Paese quasi perfetto* (Massimo Gaudioso, 2015, Italy). These must be understood as requiring 'a description of exchange and difference; the unbroken vertical axis which leads from the "original" text to the remake as "copy" is replaced by the circles of intertextuality and hybridity' (Mazdon 2000: 27). While the English-Canadian remake shared the same production company (Max Films) and screenwriter (Ken Scott), and located its village in Newfoundland in a very analogous setting, even then, telling differences remain: the homology between male heterosexual potency and communal identity plenitude has a history in Quebec that goes back to 1960s nationalism; the original also continues an older Quebec tradition of associating modernity with the Anglo, here dealt with very ambivalently through the francophone doctor with an anglophone name whose sporting obsession is with cricket. In contrast, *Un Village presque parfait* is set in the Pyrenees, with the money solicited coming from Brussels to enable the installation of a 'bio-plastic' factory (which conveniently squares the circle of modernity and ecology). The doctor, unlike in the Canadian versions, is played by Loràant Deutsch for comedy more than sex appeal, and the final celebration is a communal affair in the French populist tradition rather than being consummated in bed. The cricket reference remains. The setting is remote but also at a frontier that is crossed, hence the mayor's Spanish wife (Carmen Maura).

The film's exportability and its remakes point to shared real contradictions around issues of the local and the global, economic change and belonging, that are visible and genuinely felt by participants in the world economy, including cinema audiences. It is these lateral connections that a 'francophonising' view of Quebec cinema can begin to explore, I argue, as a starting-point for other links. For the examples of the Pyrenees setting, as well as of that of one of the adapters of the screenplay for the French version, the *beur* director Djamel Bensalah, indicate what connections can be formed in terms of parts of wholes, in other words of the *worlds within* Quebec or French national cinema which can form productive and challenging, and even subterranean or rhizomatic, links outside the general official picture. However, it is essential to recall that the 'national' is not erased by this process, but actively participates in it.

At the dawn of Quebec cinema during the Quiet Revolution, these productive links out to the world were being forged even as Quebec nationalism was on the rise. Claude Jutra's key feature film *À tout prendre/Take it All* (1963, Canada/France),[4] the first fictional feature to be made in the private sector in Quebec, is an outstanding exemplum of this. A quasi-autobiographical piece, it portrays the affair between filmmaker Claude (Jutra) and a black model (Johanne Harelle). The vicissitudes of the relationship are here less important than the way the film combines formal experimentation with a sustained problematisation of identity itself. A dazzling array of rapid camera movements, rapid montage, extensive use of zoom, freeze frame and slow motion, discontinuous interruptions from Claude's fantasy life, a soundtrack that veers from synchronous dialogue to music to Claude's stream of consciousness and his ironic voice-over commentary, track the apprenticeship of difference that Johanne forces Claude to experience, in terms of race (her refusal of exoticisation), her own masquerade (she fabulates for herself a Haitian identity), and in the knowledge of his own homosexual inclinations that she in fact provokes. She renders visible Claude's 'identity' or rather plurality of identities, which is thus predicated on a dialogue with otherness, a becoming-other.

This becoming-other can lead Jutra, and the film, to embrace the process of decolonisation, as in his documentary *Le Niger jeune république* (1961, Canada), which reminds us of the homologies some versions of Quebec nationalism in the 1960s set up between the conquered French-Canadian people, other colonised peoples, and the anti-colonialist rhetoric which heavily shaped discourses at the time. At the end of *À tout prendre*, Claude walks past graffiti for 'Québec libre', with the preceding voice-over, at the end of the affair with Johanne, suggesting 'Il faut penser à autre chose' ('It is necessary to think differently'). The implication is that such a project is worth pursuing, but is qualified and tempered by what occurs in the film, namely with full knowledge of the contradictions of identity and its assertions, of their performativity and provisionality: a cinematic playing-out of the national-allegorical tension between an aspiration to identity and wholeness and a falling away or line of flight from it.

As this volume attests, cinéma-monde is about convergences of production as well as culture and politics. Film historiographies of the years 1957–1964, for example, tend to neglect the 'French Atlantic' dimension of the French *nouvelle vague* and Canadian *cinéma direct*, via collaborations among, for example, Jean Rouch, Michel Brault, Claude Jutra, and François Truffaut (who makes a cameo appearance in *À tout prendre*). Jutra had met Truffaut at a film festival in Tours in 1957 at which their respective productions of that year – the collaboration with animator Norman McLaren (*A Chairy Tale*, 1957, Canada) and *Les Mistons* (1957, France) were screened. They also made a short film together, *Anna la bonne* (1958, France), based on a theatrical poem by Jean Cocteau. As a major – and early – example of a 'coming out' film, *À tout prendre* also of course deserves its place in the 'Hypervisibilities' project of conferences and publications on queer francophone cinemas (Grandena and Johnston 2011). The film is also an interesting example of a Montreal text, that is of a city in translation (Simon 2013), both in the hierarchical way English is used (the bank manager's speech), and the way in which the English version is the fruit of a collaboration with Leonard Cohen, Claude's now English-language voice-over combining with an extremely ludic use of subtitles for dialogue which joins the formal experimentation of the rest of the film.

So far, my remarks have dwelt on the imbrication of ethics and politics, and on the persistence of place and the national: their compatibility with plurality, with Glissant's 'presence of other languages', and even with nomadic connection, even if lived as a tension always-already there. If the anti-colonial activism of 1960s Quebec and the lateral connections it provoked now seem remote, it is important nonetheless to historicise it, and even from a *longue durée* perspective. For the rest of this essay, I wish, via two more films, to push further the implications of thinking cinema and *cinéma* in terms of world and *monde*. Questions of language remain central, but will be understood by fully emphasising the implications of the 'world' in 'world cinema' and world history, the better potentially to articulate new radical politics of humanity and the planet that befits the ethical and therefore political urgencies of this volume, and the activism they might generate.

The first film may seem an outlandish choice: Jean-Jacques Annaud's *La Guerre du feu/Quest for Fire* (1981, Canada/France). Based on the 1911 French source novel – a *roman de la préhistoire* by J.-H. Rosny aîné – it is basically a journey narrative whose goal is to restore a lost source of fire to a prehistoric tribe that does not have the secret of making it. The film telescopes millions of years of human evolution into its short time frame, with a spectrum of types ranging from proto-humans to sophisticated *homo sapiens* who hold the secret of fire, as well as pottery and other indicators of 'the modern'. Predictably, this modern human – complete with the discovery of moonlit romance and the missionary position in sex – marks the teleological outcome of the whole affair. However, the film is important to our analysis for three reasons. Firstly, it is by far the most successful of a – technically – Canada/Quebec film in France, drawing five million spectators, far beyond the million-plus enjoyed by *Les Invasions barbares/The Barbarian Invasions* (Denys Arcand, 2003, Canada/France) and *Mommy* (Xavier Dolan, 2014, Canada). When Fox withdrew its support for the project, Annaud and his producer Michael Gruskoff went to Canada, where favourable tax shelter laws brought in by the federal government had kickstarted what was to become the 'branch-plant' of films made there with little or no reference to Canadian content. The main production company is therefore International Cinema Corporation, founded in 1979 by Denys Héroux and John Kemeny, veterans of the emerging Quebec commercial (and even soft-porn) film industry of the 1960s. The reason the film could so easily span the francophone North Atlantic was that its language was not French but a concoction of grunts and Indo-European roots invented by Anthony Burgess, and a repertoire of gestures and mime proposed by the anthropologist Desmond Morris. Secondly, the film launched Jean-Jacques Annaud's subsequent career as director of transnational middlebrow (or, here, protruding brow) co-productions, usually in English (*The Name of the Rose/Der Name der Rose* [1986, Italy/West Germany/France]; *L'Amant/The Lover*, [1992, France/UK/Vietnam]; *Stalingrad/Enemy at the Gates* [2001, USA/France/Germany/UK/Ireland]), or in no language at all (*L'Ours/The Bear*, 1988, France/USA). It seems equally important for cinéma-monde to be deployed to analyse this field of production and its audiences, in addition to the auteur/activist films in this volume, or the ambiguities and wanderings of the 'national-popular' outlined earlier.

However, the most important reason for invoking this film at this point is to force attention to, and consideration of, world history when considering world cinema and world cinema in French. For how to conceive Glissant's 'relationships between languages today on earth', the divisions, dominations, community-making, story-telling, image-creation activities of a common humanity in relation to the *longue durée* of human history? How can cinema offer a window on to that duration, in terms of filmmaking itself and the way it is viewed?

'World history', as far as modernity is concerned at least, has been most commonly associated with Immanuel Wallerstein and world-systems theory, with categorisations such as core (north-west Europe and its offshoots), semi-periphery, and periphery situated in relation to the emergence of capitalism and surplus value exported to that core (e.g. Wallerstein 1992). Here, however, I draw on the work of the Argentinian philosopher Enrique Dussel, who argues that such accounts fail to break free of Eurocentrism: 'Europe has only been "central" in the last two centuries, so what has not been subsumed by Modernity may emerge, thrive and be rediscovered not as an anti-historical miracle, but as the resurgence of many political traditions concealed by the dazzling "shine" of Western politics, of the Modernity whose technical and economic globality is not a *cultural globalization of the valued daily life* of the majority of humanity' (Dussel 2011: 129). Instead, Dussel proposes the idea of 'trans-modernity', the ripostes and resources emanating beyond that Eurocentric category: 'To speak of "trans"-Modernity will demand a new interpretation of the whole phenomenon of Modernity, to count on moments which *were never incorporated into European Modernity*, and which subsuming the better of European and north American Modernity, will affirm "from *outside*" itself *essential components of the excluded cultures*' (131). Importantly for our purposes, he pinpoints 'the two historical modes of Exteriority: the Alterity of the original American inhabitant [. . .] and the African slave' (182), 'an unheard-of inhuman bloody violence, origin of the process of Modernity, as the hidden face of the Exteriority of the system' (183). In addition, as David Martin-Jones has argued, if we reflect upon Dussel via the concept of the Anthropocene, vast ecological agendas open when we consider the Earth itself as exterior and excluded: 'The transmodern encounter between humanity and its "nonhuman" other provides one way of considering together films that, when viewed across borders, can be seen to place ecological concerns in relation to the global imbalances created by coloniality/modernity' (2016: 76).

What are cinéma-monde, or the francophone world, or the French Atlantic, but spatio-temporal contexts for processes of modernity that carry along with them industrial capitalist development and organisation, slave and wage labour, city life, individualism, migrations, dispossession, domination and exclusion of, but also composition and compromise with, pre-existing human, social and natural environments which 'reply' (Dussel 2002: 221)? As far as cinéma-monde is concerned, this is partly about ways of looking – the ethics of 'watching without borders', as Dina Iordanova calls it (Slapšak, n.d.) – partly about film production and its mappings, including critiquing the nexus of coloniality and modernity, and making lateral links between the excluded.

One obvious place to go here is that of the presence of indigenous communities and cultures in Quebec cinema. The three best known directors relevant here are: the Canadian National Film Board documentary filmmaker Alanis Obomsawin, who made *Kanehsatake: 270 Years of Resistance* (1993, Canada), from the Abenaki community; the playwright Yves Sioui Durand, of Huron origin, whose *Mesnak* (2011, Canada) was the first fictional feature film by an indigenous director in Quebec; and the French-born/Gascon Arthur Lamothe, whose prolific, mostly documentary, output (e.g. *Mémoire battante*, 1983, Canada) posits a universalism of the exploited and economically marginalised, be they workers, peasants or hunter-gatherers, and sees that native peoples' disruption of the master Quiet Revolution narrative of technical progress is a disruption of all narratives of modernity.

I shall focus briefly here, however, on the award-winning 2016 feature film by Chloé Leriche, *Avant les rues / Before the Streets* (Canada). Working with the Atikamekw community at Manawan 250 kilometres north of Montreal, following her experience with the Wapikoni project that travels to indigenous communities with fully equipped mobile filmmaking studios, Leriche weaves a narrative that takes place almost entirely in the Atikamekw language. The film was released at a time when the brutal historical experience of indigenous peoples in Canada – under a colonialism that is ongoing – was occupying a fuller space in the public sphere, and perceptible shifts were taking place, first in some academic discourse, to the role of the French-Canadians as settler colonialists rather – or as well as – a colonised people (e.g. Cornellier 2013; Simpson 2014). A lost, unemployed young man, Shawnouk (Rykko Bellamare) living on the reservation with his policeman stepfather, mother, teenage sister and her baby is drawn by a white Québécois from the city, Thomas (Martin Dubreuil) into burgling nearby second homes. In a confrontation, Shawnouk saves the returning chalet owner by shooting Thomas dead. The journey that follows, including an attempted suicide, sees him reconnecting with his community's traditions by joining a group of other troubled men and following rituals that end in the sweat lodge.

Leriche draws on approaches associated with neo-realism and direct cinema: use of non-professional actors, shooting entirely on location, extensive use of hand-held camera, and, skirting any possibility of exoticism, enabling performances and story to emerge from within the community. Parallel with this quasi-documentary approach, an aesthetic strategy emphasises the natural scene and its components: sun, stars, moon, forest. The success of these twin strategies lies not only in their mapping of contemporary native alienation and traditional native relations to nature, but the way in which camera and soundtrack eloquently speak of uneven development and differently embedded temporalities. The spaces of the film – domestic, village street, desolate waste ground, even at times the forest – render visible objects of consumerism (e.g. the ubiquitous mobile phone) and the detritus of industrial civilisation (e.g. car tyres and other parts). The film is both very situated in time and space, *and* possesses a *longue durée* that not only offers a 'reply' to modernity, a non-incorporation (Dussel's 'technical and economic globality [as] not a *cultural globalization of the valued daily life*') but is even cosmic in scope. The hand-held point-of-view shots of Shawnouk glimpsing the sun through the trees (and the moon when he emerges from the sweat lodge), often circular in nature to contrast with the shots of the ceiling before his suicide attempt, echo the astronomy and cosmology essays by the Quebec scientist Hubert Reeves recorded on his portable tape machine: the sun is a star, one of billions, light and time are intrinsically linked. The film makes visible – and audible – the history and reality of colonial modernity in a 'francophone' space.

Since *Avant les rues* lent an insight into Native Canadian spirituality, I shall end these remarks with a Deleuzian proposition. Drawing on Bergson, Deleuze famously suggests that 'le temps n'est pas l'intérieur en nous [the misunderstanding of the idea of durée/duration as 'our' inner life], c'est juste le contraire, l'intériorité dans laquelle nous sommes, nous nous mouvons, vivons et changeons'/'Time is not the interior in us, but just the opposite, the interiority in which we are, in which we move, live and change' (Deleuze 1985: 110; Deleuze 1989: 82). These formulations emphasise the interconnectedness of memories, of all memories, within a world memory (*mémoire-monde*) as distinct from world history. A Deleuzian approach to the cinema of Alain Resnais, for example, emphasises the way in which memory is a membrane separating the present from the vast non-chronological archive of the past, whose sheets are raided to create circuits of meaning. Might not we as scholars, for as long as it is useful, see cinéma-monde as more than simply a space of language(s), ethics, industry, audiences, and texts? Because of its relevance to durations and temporalities of world history, cinéma-monde might also be approached as an archive of cinematic memory and practice, which we, as curators, may raid to create new circuits and juxtapositions that, like this volume, carry forward debates in teaching and research.

Notes

1. Translation is ours (the editors).
2. For example, see the discussions of dubbing and subtitling in Britain in Mazdon and Wheatley 2013.
3. This is also the topic of a panel at the 2016 Society for Cinema and Media Studies conference and of my forthcoming contribution to the *Oxford Handbook of Canadian Cinema*.
4. The film is available via the Cinémathèque québécoise at <http://collections.cinematheque.qc.ca/dossiers/a-tout-prendre/2-le-film> (last accessed 14 July 2017).

Works Cited

Cornellier, B. (2013), 'The "Indian thing": on representation and reality in the liberal settler colony', *Settler Colonial Studies*, 3:1, pp. 49–64.
Deleuze, Gilles (1985), *Cinéma 2: L'Image-Temps*, Paris: Minuit.
Deleuze, Gilles (1989), *Cinema 2: The Time-Image*, translated by Hugh Tomlinson and Robert Galeta, London: Athlone Press.
Dobson, J. (2016), Special issue of *Studies in French Cinema*, 16:3, September.
Dussel, E. (2002), 'World-System and "Trans"-Modernity', *Nepantla: Views from South*, 3:2, pp. 221–44.
Dussel, Enrique (2011), *Politics of Liberation: A Critical World History*, translated by Thia Cooper, London: SCM Press.
Glissant, Édouard (1996), *Introduction à une poétique du divers*, Paris: Gallimard.
Grandena, Florent, and Cristina Johnston (eds) (2011), *Cinematic Queerness: Gay and Lesbian Hypervisibility in Contemporary Francophone Feature Films*, Bern: Peter Lang.
Jeancolas, J.-P. (1992), 'The Inexportable: the case of French Cinema and Radio in the 1950s', in *Popular European Cinema*, Richard Dyer and Ginette Vincendeau (eds), London: Routledge, pp. 141–8.
Kotte, C. (2015), 'Zero Degrees of Separation: Post-Exilic Return in Denis Villeneuve's *Incendies*', in *Cinematic Homecomings: Exile and Return in Transnational Cinema*, Rebecca Prime (ed.), London: Bloomsbury, pp. 287–302.
Marshall, Bill (2001), *Quebec National Cinema*, Montreal: McGill-Queen's University Press.
Martin-Jones, D. (2016), 'Trolls, Tigers and Transmodern Ecological Encounters: Enrique Dussel and a Cine-ethics for the Anthropocene', *Film-Philosophy* 20, pp. 63–103.
Mazdon, Lucy (2000), *Encore Hollywood: Remaking French Cinema*, London: British Film Institute.

Mazdon, Lucy, and Catherine Wheatley (2013), *French Film in Britain: Sex, Art and Cinephilia*, Oxford: Berghahn Books.

Simon, Sherry (2013), *Cities in Translation: Intersections of Language and Memory*, London: Routledge.

Simpson, Audra (2014), *Mohawk Interruptus: Political Life Across the Borders of Settler States*, Durham, NC: Duke University Press.

Slapšak, S. (n.d.), 'One must watch across borders Interview with film specialist Dina Iordanova', <http://www.versopolis.com/interview/150/one-must-watch-across-borders> (last accessed September 2016).

Tessé, J.-P. (2015), 'Audiard, la palme c'est son genre', *Cahiers du cinéma*, 712, June, 9.

Wallerstein, Immanuel (1992), *Le Système du monde, du XVe siècle à nos jours: 1, Capitalisme et Économie-Monde 1450–1640*, Paris: Flammarion.

Cinéma-monde as a Call to Arms
Lucy Mazdon

The 2017 Academy Awards' ceremony will indubitably be best remembered for the confusion over the Oscar for best film. As the team behind Damian Chazelle's *La La Land* (2016, USA/Hong Kong) began their acceptance speeches for the award, they were interrupted to be told that the Oscar should in fact have gone to Barry Jenkins' *Moonlight* (2016, USA). The first Oscars' ceremony of the Trump presidency was always going to be a turbulent occasion as Hollywood's stars used their moment on the global stage to air their opposition to the new administration. However, the embarrassment caused by Faye Dunaway's reading out of the wrong envelope caused quite unexpected levels of consternation, not least as some commentators felt that *Moonlight*, a film about African-American life with an African-American director, had been robbed of its chance to fully celebrate its success. After 2016's 'Oscars so white' protests the award to *Moonlight* was of particular significance so it was not surprising that some saw the mix up over the prize as yet another curtailment of diversity and difference.

Rather less high profile, but extremely significant nevertheless, was another Oscar acceptance speech that similarly played into questions of diversity and difference. The Oscar for best foreign language film went to Asghar Farhadi's Franco-Iranian co-production *Forushande/The Salesman* (2016). Farhadi had initially intended to travel to Los Angeles for the ceremony in order to highlight 'the unjust circumstances that have arisen for the immigrants and travellers of several countries to the United States' (Shoard 2017). However, he ultimately decided against attending the ceremony saying that, following Trump's recent attempts to block entry to the US for the citizens of Iran, Iraq, Syria, Sudan, Somalia, Libya and Yemen, the conditions that would be attached to a potential entry visa were unacceptable. The award was collected instead by Iranian-American engineer Anousheh Ansari who read out a statement on Farhadi's behalf:

> I'm sorry I'm not with you tonight, my absence is out of respect for the people of my country and those of the other six nations who have been disrespected by the inhumane law that bans entry of immigrants to the US. Dividing the world into the 'us' and 'our enemies' categories creates fear. A deceitful justification for aggression and war, these wars prevent democracy and human rights in countries which have themselves been victims of aggression. Filmmakers can turn their cameras to capture shared human qualities and break stereotypes of various nationalities and religions. They create empathy between us and others, an empathy that we need today more than ever.

Farhadi's words are worth quoting as they underline the extent to which his film and its receipt of the best foreign language Oscar were bound up with broader discourses of nationalism, race and prejudice. Indeed, the last minute surge in votes for Farhadi's film was believed by some commentators to be an explicit protest at Trump's travel ban. In London on the night of the Awards' ceremony, a free public screening of the film was introduced by mayor Sadiq Khan, again in an explicit protest at the visa restrictions.

Why begin this epilogue with reference to the Oscars and Farhadi's film? First and foremost, it seems to me that both the anxieties over *Moonlight*'s brief usurpation and, more significantly, Farhadi's non-attendance at the ceremony, underline the extreme timeliness of this collection of essays. As the volume goes to press a growing rejection of otherness and difference can be witnessed in the US through the Trump administration, in the UK through Brexit, and in France as Marine le Pen's extreme right *Front National* makes great strides in the build up to the presidential elections. As Farhadi's acceptance speech declared, the role of film, and culture more widely, in the deconstruction of nationalism and other forms of oppression and exclusion becomes ever more vital. As producer Christine Vachon wrote in *The Guardian* on the eve of the Oscar ceremony:

> At times like these it can seem hard to care about the Oscars. But recognition for films such as *Moonlight*, *Fences*, and *Hidden Figures* is something we should care about. Celebrating other people's stories is, in a small way, a protest against the current political agenda to oppress and silence the narratives and stories of the perceived other. (Vachon 2017: 33)

In particular, an engagement with an understanding of cinema that rejects the national in favour of various forms of decentring or othering, precisely the engagement which underpins this volume, feels ever more pressing.

In their introduction Gott and Schilt argue persuasively for cinéma-monde 'as an optic or framework through which to approach a flexible corpus' (page 8), a corpus which expands a francophone discursive category 'emphasising the linguistic and cultural diversity that might be hidden behind that term if it is understood in binary terms or as derivative from French colonialism' (page 8). According to this definition, *The Salesman* can precisely be seen as part of a cinéma-monde, of a cinema which resists plenitude in favour of porosity and difference. In this sense then cinéma-monde takes on a vital political urgency. It becomes, as did Farhadi's film, a tool in the resistance to cultural nationalisms of all kinds.

The need to resist homogenising definitions of French cinema underpins much of my own research. Indeed, both my work on the Hollywood remake of French film (2000) and on the distribution, exhibition and reception of French film in Britain (2013) reveal the instability of definitions of 'French' cinema and the limitations and reduction provoked by such definitions. Any notion of a 'national' cinema is always already unstable. That which may be constructed and marketed as 'French' for a domestic audience is not identical to that which will be sold as 'French' elsewhere. The specificities of region and class, readily available to audiences in Lyon or Paris, will be either lost to or subsumed within a general 'Frenchness' by audiences in London or New York (Mazdon and Wheatley 2013: 9). As the essays in this volume demonstrate so persuasively, there is no single French cinema or indeed francophone cinema. Rather there is a diverse and porous body of work which engages in varying ways with different aspects of 'France' or 'Frenchness' and which once viewed through the prism of cinéma-monde reveals itself in all its flexibility and diversity. Gott and Schilt stress the diversity of cinéma-monde:

> We will focus in particular on exploring the porosity of various kinds of borders in and around francophone spaces and the ways in which languages and identities 'travel' in contemporary cinema. Cinéma-monde, as we understand it, is not simply cinema in French from outside of France. Nor does it exclude France. (page 3)

It seems to me that this is a crucial gesture, not least because the market imperatives of distribution and exhibition work so hard to limit or obscure that diversity. If we return once more to the Academy Awards we can see precisely that process of curtailment at work. A prize is awarded to the best 'foreign language film' and the shortlisted films are described and defined by their national identity. Thus *The Salesman* becomes an Iranian film. Yet, as we have noted, it is a Franco-Iranian co-production. Its dialogue is in Persian which, although the official language of Iran, is not of course the only language spoken, reminding us of the fluidity of any concept of Iranian nationhood. The plot is inspired by that classic of American twentieth-century theatre, Arthur Miller's *Death of a Salesman*

(1949) and the film premiered in competition at the Cannes festival in 2016 where it won two awards. Clearly, to describe this film as an Iranian film is to impose a plenitude which neither its plot nor production permit. And yet it is safe to assume that, following the precedent set by the Oscar, it will be marketed and distributed as an Iranian film, thus precisely curtailing that potential for empathy building and boundary destabilising which its cinéma-monde status is able to offer.

A conception of cinema resistant to homogenising forces and attuned to accommodation or at least acknowledgement of differences is then more than a scholarly exercise. It is rather a call to arms, a demand for the importance of culture in resistance to the ideological forces which are currently proscribing and threatening freedoms, exchanges and movements of all kinds. One of the great strengths of this volume is its mapping of a new geography of French and francophone cinema. It proposes a 'decentring', a rejection of the binaries and limitations of hyphenated identities in favour of a complex, protean and interchangeable understanding of francophone cinematic geography. Again this seems to me to be a crucial gesture. As borders are increasingly threatened with closure and dividing walls are planned, so the remapping undertaken here plays a vital role in resisting this reassertion of nationalism (cultural and other). Just as we must question and problematise our understanding of what constitutes 'French' or 'francophone' cinema so we should ensure an open and always mutable understanding of what constitutes francophone space. Where is '*la France*' which underpins the ideological discourse of Marine le Pen's *Front national* when London is France's fifth or sixth largest city in terms of population? Where or what is francophone space when parts of the Hexagon are rendered transnational through border fluidity, immigration and other forms of exchange? The mappings and journeys of this volume – from London to Senegal to Quebec and so on – provide answers to these questions, revealing the spaces and places of francophone cinema. Yet in the sheer diversity of their focus they reveal the porosity, the always unfinished, always changing nature of what we can understand to constitute the francophone world.

The essays in this collection are organised via three main categories: auteurs and actors; representations; production and industry. One could add a fourth category; that of reception. As I have explored in my own work, to a great extent a film's national identity (and indeed other identities) is a product of specific modes of reception. A film only becomes straightforwardly 'French' outside France. In similar fashion the status of the films discussed here as part of a francophone cinema will also depend on modes of reception. In other words, the porosity or shifting nature of identity which lies at the heart of the notion of cinéma-monde as outlined in this volume will be extended further by the different conditions and methods of reception accorded to the films. As I have already noted, in the Anglophone market the imperatives of distribution and exhibition typically work towards curtailing this plurality in favour of a more easily marketable 'national' identity. This both limits the films made available to audiences (those 'French' films selected for distribution in the US/UK will tend to match with certain dominant conceptions of what constitutes 'French' cinema) and serves to manage and contain audience selection and response; the films will play to certain types of audience who are likely to come armed with particular expectations of the film defined by its national identity. So it seems to me that a thorough exploration of these modes of reception could extend even further this volume's wonderfully rich and politically timely engagement with the plurality of cinéma-monde. But that is perhaps subject matter for a second volume.

Works Cited

Mazdon, Lucy (2000), *Encore Hollywood: Remaking French Cinema*, London: British Film Institute.

Mazdon, Lucy and Catherine Wheatley (2013), *French Film in Britain: Sex, Art and Cinephilia*, Oxford: Berghahn Books.

Shoard, Catherine (2017), 'The Salesman Wins Best Foreign Language Oscar', *The Guardian*, <http://www.theguardian.com/film/2017/feb/27/the-salesman-wins-best-foreign-language-oscar-asghar-farhadi> (last accessed 27 February 2017).

Vachon, Catherine (2017), 'At Times Like This, Hollywood Can Offer Hope', *The Guardian*, 25 February, p. 33.

Cinéma-monde and the Transnational
Will Higbee

From the documentaries of Cambodian director Rithy Panh, and an analysis of the road movie in Quebec, to the transnational roles played by the Maghrebi-French actress Hafsia Herzi, the chapters within this collection explore the notion of exactly what cinéma-monde might be from a multiplicity of (appropriately diverse) perspectives. Although, as Florence Martin has explained, the term itself first appeared in a quite different context as a means of 'decrying Hollywood's hegemony in global cinema' (Martin 2016: 462), the starting point for the discussion of cinéma-monde in these pages comes from Bill Marshall's call to engage with a critical framework that could offer a 'de-centred' view of francophone cinema (Marshall 2012). It is to this challenge, in their analysis of a range of films and filmmakers linked to the Francosphere, via a combination of cultural and linguistic connections, production contexts, funding structures, geographical locations and reception networks, that the authors and editors of this collection respond. Viewed in the broader academic context of French and francophone studies, this collection also contributes to the ongoing challenge towards the existing hierarchy of French or francophone culture within the discipline, moving away from a centre/periphery binary and towards a perception and practice of 'French Studies' that is both transcultural and intercultural (Forsdick 2015).

Despite the range of cultural perspectives and geographical territories covered in the individual chapters of this book, a number of common themes nonetheless emerge. Firstly, the notion of cinéma-monde as a form of encounter and transcultural exchange that takes place within multiple contact zones or interstitial spaces, referred to by the editors of this collection as 'franco-zones'. Whilst not necessarily free from the imbalances of power inherent in the established binaries of French/francophone, such encounters nonetheless challenge the debilitating notion of francophone as exclusively and immutably 'other' to 'French'. As a number of contributors to this volume make clear, these cinematic contact zones are often constructed in and around border spaces, in narratives that are frequently concerned with movement or the act of migration (legal and illegal) and the consequences of such displacement. A second common concern is the means by which cinéma-monde can transcend the problematic and contested label of 'francophone', through rendering multiplicity and difference visible. As Gott and Schilt state in the Introduction to this collection:

> A cinéma-monde approach, then, would simultaneously be concerned with expanding a francophone discursive category and emphasising the linguistic and cultural diversity that might be hidden behind that term if it is understood in binary terms or as derivative from French colonialism. (page 8)

Through the mapping (rendering visible) of such multiplicities in these films, cinéma-monde thus 'makes us conscious of our own "global situation" and our own "geopolitical orientation"' (page 27), as Joseph Mai suggests in his chapter for this book.

Moreover, by foregrounding these cultural, linguistic and cinematic differences on screen, such mapping also reveals how, even though they may well be profound sites of transcultural exchange, these spaces (as well as the contact zones that produce them) can be fragmented or partial in the way that they relate to the broader experiences of those who inhabit the socio-cultural settings or nation-space in which they are located. In other words, as Mireille Rosello (cited by Gott in this collection) explains it: 'Rather than homogeneous and circumscribed territories symbolized by blocks of solid colours, global and local francophone practices form a multitude of dots with various levels of concentration in several continents and cities' (Rosello 2009: 54). We need to recognise, then, that in the context of cinéma-monde such flows and encounters are multidirectional, and not solely determined by the postcolonial axis between the (former) metropole and (former) colonial territory. Nor are they limited by movement from 'centre' to 'periphery'. Rosello's description of the uneven, scattered and yet concentrated nature of such transcultural encounters in the Francosphere brings to mind the patterns created by dispersal and settlement of diasporas. In this context, Laura Reeck's chapter for this collection highlights a potential blind-spot in Marshall's initial discussion of cinéma-monde: whilst evoking the notion of accented cinema, virtually no attention is paid to the wealth of minority or accented filmmakers working *in* France, whose work performs precisely the function of francophonising the (former) *métropole* and who are bringing a different aesthetic and vision to French cinema.

In her chapter, Reeck elects to focus on the guerrilla filmmaking practices of Franco-Algerian director Rachid Djaïdani, a diasporic/

postcolonial filmmaker whose films challenge preconceived notions of insider and outsider that are central to a 'national' construction of French identity and French cinema. Reeck's analysis thus suggests a potential link between Djaïdani (and by extension this concept of cinéma-monde) to both Lionnet and Shih's notion of minor transnationalism (2005) but also to the kind of 'critical transnationalism' evoked by Higbee and Lim (2010). In the former, the transnational is conceived as 'a space of exchange and participation wherever processes of hybridization occur and where it is still possible for cultures to be produced and performed without necessary mediation by the center' (Lionnet and Shih 2005: 5). In the latter, scrutinising the tensions and dialogic relationship between the national and the transnational allows for a consideration of how local, regional and diasporic film cultures can connect globally at the same time as they affect, subvert and transform (politically speaking) national cinemas. If there is an area in which this collection's formulation of cinéma-monde could extend its engagement with contemporary debates within film studies, it is arguably in relation to the concept of the transnational. My aim in the remainder of this essay is therefore to argue for cinéma-monde as a subset of transnational cinema and, by using the example of contemporary Moroccan cinema, to suggest that, by thinking-through the 'transnationality' of cinéma-monde, we can further appreciate the potential of this critical approach, its search for cross-lingual and cross-cultural cinematic connections within *and* beyond the Francosphere, not to mention the value in bringing such relationships (cultural, linguistic, political, economic) into some form of critical focus.

Cinéma-monde and the Transnational: Whose Cinema and Which World?[1]

Writing in 2000, Andrew Higson defined the transnational as a subtler method of understanding cinema's relationship to the cultural and economic formations 'that are rarely contained within national boundaries' (Higson 2000: 64). Seven years earlier, Marsha Kinder, in her analysis of Spanish 'national' cinema presciently identified the need to 'read national cinema against the local/global interface' (Kinder 1993: 7). Following on from these early attempts to theorise cinema in a context that moves beyond the boundaries of the nation, the past decade has seen transnational cinema established as a key area of enquiry in film studies within the Anglo-American academy. Higson's initial focus on the triad of production circulation and reception of transnational cinema has been extended by other scholars across the 2000s to consider the transnational as a regional phenomenon, often in relation to issues of funding, co-production and distribution (Nestingen and Elkington 2005; Steele 2015), and, in ways that are directly political, through an analysis of diasporic, exilic and the postcolonial cinema (Higbee 2007; Naficy 2001; Marks 2000; and Enwezor 2007), or a consideration of cinema's response and resistance to the consequences of neo-liberal globalisation and cultural homogenisation more generally, which demands an examination of 'the relationships of cinema and geopolitics through, between, and beyond the state' (Galt 2016).

What, then, are the specific benefits of thinking 'transnationally'? Why not speak in terms of cinema and globalisation, World Cinema or, indeed, cinéma-monde? As Tim Bergfelder (2005) suggests, one advantage of the term 'transnational' is that it offers an alternative to the generalised and imprecise application of the term 'globalisation', a term that is frequently applied to any and every process or relationship (political, social, cultural or economic) that crosses a national boundary. In contrast, the transnational (following Hannerz's definition) is more attuned to the scale, distribution and diversity of such exchanges and their impact at a local level as well as an understanding that they may have effects within and beyond the nation-state. In certain cases, the transnational may even bypass the mechanisms of the nation-state altogether (Hannerz, cited in Bergfelder 2005: 321). As Ďurovičová and Newman note (2009: x), 'relationships of unevenness and mobility' are implicit in the prefix 'trans-' and it is the relative openness of the transnational to 'modalities of geopolitical forms' that permits the concept a dynamic force and greater degree of flexibility than the notion of 'World Cinema'. This ability for a transnational approach to accommodate and reflect the complex and shifting dynamic both within, across and beyond the national is undoubtedly one of its strengths.

The reality is, then, that, with the exception of films that are specifically produced for an ethnic or regional audience, cinema has been, almost from its very inception, a transnational medium. The Lumière brothers sent camera operators out across the French empire to bring back short travelogues and exotic views of the colonies as early as 1897, while the movement of filmmakers, actors and technicians between countries and continents throughout cinema's long century, the global reach of Hollywood or Bollywood's popularity in the diaspora and beyond, the necessity of international co-productions for many national cinemas and the international circulation of film through film festivals and distribution networks (both legal and illegal) whose reach has only expanded in the digital age, make it virtually impossible to think or theorise cinema solely within the framework of the nation-state. And yet, the concept of national cinema remains heavily embedded in our understanding and organisation of funding and regulating cinema within territories, as well as a means of historicising film cultures through a series of key films, directors, stars as well as movements and moments that are, more often than not, organised through the national: French New Wave, German Expressionism, New Taiwanese cinema (the list goes on). Consequently, there is a critical need to understand the shifting dynamic between the national and the transnational within a given film culture, as well as the lateral connections made between the participants in individual national cinemas on a regional and supranational level.

From the above summary, the common ground between transnational cinema and cinéma-monde should be obvious: both try to understand the production, circulation and reception of films beyond the nation state; both celebrate a diversity of representations that are simultaneously local (culturally specific) and global (with the potential to connect with audiences and other film cultures beyond the country of origin); both display a strong preoccupation with borders, border crossing and intercultural 'contact zones'; both engage with a range of films that could be described as postcolonial, accented or diasporic; both are also concerned with the politics of production and circulation of film, recognising the imbalances of power and the possibilities for multiple sites of production and reception that challenge the primacy of the nation-state and the doxa of centre/periphery relations.

Where the two terms diverge is in relation to their cultural, linguistic and geographical reach. The concept of cinéma-monde as presented in this collection is, necessarily 'limited by design' to what the editors describe as 'franco-zones', the constellation of sites of intercultural exchange across the Francosphere that are not solely linguistic and might be predominantly narrative, cultural, symbolic, practical, or financial. Nevertheless, the anchorage in the French language, writ large in the very nomenclature cinéma-monde, imposes a restriction from which it is hard for the term to escape.

The predicament is acutely summarised by Charles Forsdick (2010: 127) in his analysis of the related concept of *Littérature-Monde* as 'a phenomenon that claims a global reach but persists with a monolingual definition'. The problem for employing cinéma-monde as an approach for analysing these films and, as importantly, the politics and aesthetics of the transcultural connections they articulate, therefore lies less in what Marshall (2012: 43) describes as francophone cinema's 'guilty secret' (that many of the films are not in French) as it does in the fact that it can too readily be misinterpreted (and not, I hasten to add, by the contributors to this collection) as a cinema that is defined by its inescapable relationship to a reductive French/francophone binary, a partial map, whose view of the world is determined by Franco-centric norms that elide an engagement with 'social, cultural, religious and political formations that are themselves increasingly both transnational and cross-lingual' (Forsdick 2015: 2).

According to Marshall (2012: 37–8), such a problematic entanglement with the ideology of *francophonie* and the political and economic imbalance that it generates, leads cinéma-monde to a critical impasse. The problem can be summarised thus: how can we speak of a cinematic community of production and transcultural exchange across the Francosphere in a system where the means of production and, just as importantly, access to distribution networks, are so comprehensively stacked in favour of French cinema? Marshall concludes by offering 'post-francophone' and 'cinemas of the Francosphere' as alternative conceptual neologisms that might succeed where cinéma-monde cannot (Marshall 2012: 51). In her recent article 'Cinéma-monde: De-orbiting Maghrebi Cinema' (2016), Florence Martin offers a potential solution to Marshall's perceived impasse; namely, to liberate cinéma-monde (in its Maghrebi context at least) from the hegemonic pull of French cinema's orbit, though an approach that

> allows one to still identify points of convergence and divergence between a local production in the South and the cinema production in the North or West, but without subsuming these various criss-crossings into a 'francophone; or even a 'post-francophone' reality and order [. . .] What now best explains on-screen creation that emanates from North or West Africa for instance is the age of globalism, the diversity of cinematic relationships that are woven transnationally away from France. (2016: 473)

The model proposed by Martin is one that 'would force critics and academics to anchor their arguments differently in the evolving field of transnational French studies', ultimately helping to 'steer scholars away from *francophonie* altogether' (474). What interests me most in Martin's approach is how the transnational[2] arguably becomes the key to realising the potential of cinéma-monde and thus articulating the dynamic and complex socio-political reality of transcultural exchange within, across and (crucially) *beyond* the cinemas of the Francosphere. It furthermore supports the conviction that cinéma-monde is best conceptualised as a subset of transnational cinema, due to its concerns with border crossing, 'contact zones', cross-national, regional and diasporic narratives and the desire to make lateral or 'minor-to-minor' connections. By engaging with a more overtly political critical transnationalism, liberated from the ideological and historical legacy of *francophonie*, cinéma-monde can identify its place as simultaneously within and beyond the Francosphere – forging connections based on a shared political and ethical commitment to resist Eurocentric practices and representation of domination and subordination that inform both postcolonialism and, in an earlier period, Third Cinema (which, in its politics of anti-imperialism and desire to make lateral connections between formerly colonised nations acts as something of a precursor to cinéma-monde).

Cinéma-monde and the Transnational Reach of Moroccan Cinema

In the final section of this epilogue, I want to use the context of contemporary Moroccan cinema, as a specific example of how to view the concept of cinéma-monde through a transnational optic in three specific areas: the impact of diasporic filmmakers, the role of festivals, and finally the (politics) of international co-production. As the veteran Moroccan director M. A. Tazi proclaimed in an interview with Kevin Dwyer (drawing a memorable parallel with the way a bumblebee seems to defy the laws of aeronautics but is still able to fly) the paradox of Moroccan cinema is that films have been made despite not because of the conditions of development, production, distribution and exhibition and by overcoming obstacles put in place by the political climate in the Kingdom (Tazi in Dwyer 2004: 103). And yet, even in the face of such challenging conditions for filmmakers at all stages of the value chain, a growing range of Moroccan films aimed at local, national and international audiences have been produced since the late-1990s. As a result of targeted institutional support from the Centre Cinématographique Marocain (CCM) under the leadership of Noureddine Saïl between 2003 and 2014, Moroccan cinema has come to be seen as a model of production for other African and Arab nations (Awad 2017), even if the autonomy of the CCM has been complicated somewhat in recent years by increased interference from the ruling conservative Islamist Justice and Development Party (PJD).[3] Today, Moroccan cinema, so long the poor relation of Algerian and Tunisian cinema in terms of prestige, levels of production and international reach, has emerged as arguably the Maghreb's most important national cinema. From a position where only a handful of features were being produced in the country each year in the 1960s, 1970s and 1980s, Morocco has now established itself as the third largest national cinema in Africa behind Egypt and South Africa, producing an average of 20–25 features and 50–80 short films annually.[4]

As Moroccan cinema has grown in stature and influence since the mid-1990s, so multiple nodes with either a global or local reach have enhanced or established their presence within the network of Moroccan 'national' cinema: Amazigh cinema, popular genre films produced for a domestic or pan-Arab audience, urban neo-noir films popular with Moroccan youth, auteur-led productions that rely on a relationship with European producers and festivals for a portion of their funding and international circulation, co-productions with the Global North but also with partners in the Global South, even studios in southern Morocco that specialise in location services for foreign productions. One further 'node' within (trans-)national Moroccan cinema that is also relevant to the concept of cinéma-monde, concerns filmmakers of the Moroccan diaspora. Such films and filmmakers are inherently transnational in the sense that their work frequently questions how fixed ideas of a national film culture are transformed by the protagonists (and indeed filmmakers) who have a presence within the nation, even if they exist on its margins, but find their origins quite clearly beyond it.

The success of Moroccan cinema since the late 1990s has also come about because of a reengagement on the part of the CCM and audiences with filmmakers from the Moroccan diaspora. Through a targeted funding initiative, the CCM has actively encouraged non-resident Moroccan filmmakers to 'return' to the Maghreb and make films (undoubtedly the most stunning example of the success of this policy being Nabil Ayouch). These filmmakers, working for the most part between Europe and the Maghreb (not only in France but also Belgium and Spain) are at once inside and outside of the configuration of 'national' cinema as it is traditionally understood – forcing us to re-think what constitutes Moroccan 'national' cinema, where it is located, created and disseminated. Moreover, these diasporic filmmakers may well be concerned with the consequences of return to the homeland for the diasporic subject (see, for example, *Tenja* [Hassan Legzouli, 2004, France/Morocco]) or may immerse their narratives directly within the socio-political realities of contemporary Morocco (offering a perspective as both insider and outsider), most evident in the work of Nabil Ayouch. However, they may also choose to depict the experiences of Moroccan migrants outside of the Kingdom within the broader geopolitical system of neo-liberalism – such as Belgian-Moroccan director Jawad Rhalib, whose documentary *El Ejido, la loi du profit* (2006, Morocco/Belgium/France) explores the exploitation of illegal African migrants (including Moroccans) within the intensive agricultural systems of southern Spain.

A transnational approach to analysing the contribution of diasporic filmmakers to both Moroccan 'national' cinema and, by association, the relationship of filmmakers of the Moroccan diaspora to cinéma-monde is beneficial in that it allows us to consider the ongoing, postcolonial legacies of French (and to a lesser degree Spanish) colonial rule in Morocco on Moroccan cinema. For example the use of French language in Moroccan films, the long and sometimes fraught history of co-production between France and Morocco, as well as the impact of filmmakers from the Moroccan diaspora working in France – without viewing more recent developments exclusively through a postcolonial lens. The problem of applying the terms postcolonial to contemporary Moroccan cinema is one of the socio-political and cultural blind spots that it creates. Whilst the spectre of French colonial rule is still experienced strongly in contemporary Moroccan society, its culture, politics and indeed cinema are not shaped solely by the colonial legacy or a postcolonial dynamic between the former colonised and coloniser. For Moroccan filmmakers dealing with socio-political realities in the Kingdom today (especially the vast majority of filmmakers from a post-independence generation who did not live through the struggle for independence and who, in historical terms, have been more profoundly marked by the transition from the repressive rule of Hassan II to the relatively more moderate political climate of Mohammed VI) the concerns of inequality and injustice articulated in their films are directed as much towards the ruling Moroccan elite (the *Makhzen*) and the impact of neo-liberal globalisation, as they are to the former (French) coloniser.[5]

The pivotal function of film festivals in Morocco (and abroad) as a means of promoting international investment as well as creative and institutional collaboration in the Moroccan film industry is a second area in which viewing Moroccan cinema as cinéma-monde may benefit from a transnational perspective. International film festivals are now central to the construction of cinema knowledge as well as the behind-the-scenes mechanics of finance, distribution, and exhibition. The importance of such festivals to Moroccan cinema can be seen in the way that the CCM supports the activities of its filmmakers, while increasingly promoting Morocco as a service location for foreign productions (especially those from Hollywood) at key international festivals and film markets. The CCM thus maintains a regular presence at the two largest international festivals and film markets, the Berlinale and European Film Market in February, and Cannes and the Marché International du Film in May, as well as activity at key Arab film festivals such as the Arab Film Festival in Malmö (Sweden) and the Dubai International Film Festival. In 2016, alongside selection and exposure at domestic festivals, twenty-nine Moroccan films circulated in official competition at forty-five international festivals, garnering a total of twenty-one awards (CCM 2016: 72–80). The importance of this transnational film circuit to Moroccan filmmakers can be seen in the way that since 2015

Hicham Lasri has established his international reputation through successive appearances in the official selection at the Berlinale, rather than at French-language festivals. Indeed, I would argue that the importance of Cannes and the Marché for Moroccan filmmakers has little to do with a link to a French-speaking country (and the former metropole) and more to do with Cannes' status as the *world's* leading international film festival and market.

The increasing maturity, sophistication and internationalisation of Moroccan cinema can also, in part, be explained by the role of its own film festivals as a hub for film production and distribution as well as a point of contact and exchange for Moroccan filmmakers and industry figures with filmmakers from other nations. In 2016 the CCM recognised and provided financial aid for 16 festivals in Morocco (categories A – C) and a further twenty-two smaller festivals and film 'events' (*manifestations cinématographiques*) (CCM: 2016: 65–8). Many of these, such as the Festival International du Cinéma Marocain et Ibéro-Américain (Martil), Festival du Cinéma Africain de Khouribga, and the Festival International du Cinéma Méditerranéen (Tétouan) are decidedly transnational in their programming and ethos, with the festivals seeking to establish connections with filmmaking communities and audiences that are not limited to the Francosphere. The Marrakech International Film Festival (FIFM), held annually since 1999, has grown in stature and significance as one of the most important international film festivals – its success and status directly reflecting the global ascendency of Moroccan cinema over the past two decades. In its programming and outlook, the festival is decidedly international, arguably doing more to promote filmmakers from outside of the Francosphere than within it, as reflected by the composition of festival juries, retrospectives, lifetime achievement awards and the inclusion each year of a selection of films from a specific national cinema that is, more often than not, from a non-French speaking nation. However, the success of the FIFM has not been without its problems, which have often been linked to the perceived French influence on the festival. Before the CCM took joint stewardship of the festival in the mid-2000s, it was conceived and programmed exclusively by festival directors based in Paris, with all of the potential problems and baggage that this entails in terms of the paternalistic influence of the former coloniser on Moroccan cultural events. More recently, at the 2016 edition of the FIFM there was outrage from many Moroccan filmmakers at the fact that Public System, the festival's Paris-based directors, had decided not to include any Moroccan films in the official selection for the first time in the FIFM's sixteen-year history. Whether as a result of this decision or not, the FIFM foundation, which is under direct patronage of Prince Moulay Rachid, has since broken ties with Public System, with the festival in abeyance for 2018. The politics surrounding the FIFM thus raises the question as to what happens when a national cinema from a former French colony (in this case Morocco) asserts its own identity – can it ever entirely disentangle itself from this colonial past when analysed within the context of the Francosphere? We might well interpret the actions of the FIFM as a 'de-centring' move from *francophonie* along the lines proposed (albeit in different ways) by both Marshall and Martin. However, the very act of de-centring suggests that the spectre of Franco-centrism still exerts an influence in one form or another. Does Moroccan cinema really become a hub or one of many centres for francophone culture? Or does it, more productively, exist in its own right as part of a broader transnational system of production, distribution and exhibition? Here, again, we return to this notion of 'which cinema?' and 'whose world?' we are referring to in cinéma-monde, a question of perspective that brings to mind the quote by the giant of Arab cinema, Youssef Chahine when interviewed in Férid Boughedir's documentary *Caméra arabe* (1987, Tunisia): 'The Third World is England, the US and France. I'm from the First World, I've been there for seven thousand years!'

The role of the CCM during the late 1990s and 2000s in providing funding and institutional support for Moroccan filmmakers has obviously been key in promoting the development of Moroccan cinema both at home and abroad. Facilitating international co-productions with Morocco has been part of this ongoing strategy. According to CCM data, during the period 2009–16, Moroccan producers participated in thirty-two international co-productions – an average of four a year, just under a fifth of annual production – with production companies from eight nations: Argentina, Belgium, Canada, France, Holland, Italy, Spain and the UK.[6] Of course, when identifying the shared 'nationality' of a given co-production, we need to proceed with caution, mindful of what Hjort refers to as the 'scalar' characteristics of 'marked' and 'unmarked' transnationalism (Hjort 2010). For example, despite the Algerian origins of the film's director and its narrative focus on the story of the French son of an Algerian immigrant who returns to the *bled* (family village) in order to protect their home from land developers and corrupt local politicians, the comedy-drama *Né quelque part/Homeland* (Mohamed Hamidi, 2013, France/Morocco) is in fact a Franco-Moroccan, not Franco-Algerian, co-production. The Moroccan co-producers, Agora films, became involved when, for logistical reasons, the film's French producers decided on rural Morocco rather than in Algeria as the stand-in location for the *bled*, making it necessary to bring on board a trusted team of Moroccan producers.[7] The production history of the film thus contains elements of 'unmarked' (Moroccan) transnationalism that complicate any reading of the film's representational politics in relation to a Franco-Algerian return narrative or indeed, collaboration between France and Algeria as francophone nations, illustrating how reading cinéma-monde 'transnationally' can provide us with a more nuanced view of the politics and practicalities of co-production.

As a Franco-Moroccan co-production, *Né quelque part* forms part of the majority of the international co-productions with Morocco between 2009–16. The fact that eighteen out of a total of thirty-two co-productions during this period involve French production companies seems to support Marshall's claim about the economic and political imbalance between France and the rest of the Francosphere rendering the notion of cinéma-monde 'counter intuitive' (Marshall 2012: 37). Nevertheless, if we delve deeper, we can see that of those eighteen films, the lead producer (with a majority stake in the production) was French on eight (less than half) of the productions, with five of the Moroccan-French co-productions involving one or more companies from other countries – nearly all from the Global North, but not all of them francophone nations. Moreover, the CCM data also reveals that Moroccan producers acted as lead producer on four of these eighteen French co-productions, with a further three of them functioning as an equal (50/50) partnership (in terms of financing and thus producer control) between France and Morocco.

Marshall is therefore correct when he suggests that there is a considerable imbalance between France and the rest of the Francosphere in terms of cinema production. However, this does not mean that Moroccan producers were secondary or marginal players in every co-production with France. Nor does it mean that every Moroccan film looks to the former metropole as its central or sole source of funding: based on the CCM data, French co-productions represent just under 10% of annual production in Morocco. This sense of filmmakers from the Francosphere seeking alternative sources of funding away from France is also emphasised by the growing importance to filmmakers in Morocco and across the Arab world of the post-production bursaries offered by the Doha Film Institute, which in recent years has offered support to Moroccan filmmakers such as Hicham Lasri and also to Oliver Laxe, a Galician director who has lived in Morocco for more than a decade and was the first foreign director to receive selective aid for production from the *avance sur recettes*, for the Spanish/Moroccan/French co-production *Mimosas* (2016). Further investigation of the CCM's co-production data[8] reveals that, between

2009–16, the CCM has co-produced additional films (a range of documentary, narrative features and short films) with producers in Iran, Nigeria, Portugal and Spain, and across the Francosphere in Algeria, Angola, Benin, Burkina Faso, Cameroun, Cape Verde, Guinea, Ivory Coast, Mali, Senegal and Tunisia. The majority of this co-production activity from the CCM thus focuses on 'lateral' collaborations with other francophone nations in the Maghreb and sub-Saharan Africa in an attempt to develop alternative production hubs away from the former metropole. Indeed, such initiatives should also be seen as part of what Van de Peer (2016: 5–6) identifies as a more recent trend visible in both African festivals and production practices for greater pan-African (rather than francophone) collaboration, particularly between the Maghreb and sub-Saharan Africa.

Of course, the choice of co-production partner based on nationality alone offers no automatic guarantee of their politics. Similarly, the fact that a film is co-produced equitably between France and Morocco does not mean that the resulting work will be free from Eurocentric, Franco-centric or, indeed, 'Morocco-centric' bias. To fully comprehend the nature of collaboration and intercultural exchange at play in these international co-productions demands a detailed analysis of the individual conditions of each production history, as well as the politics of funding and co-production agreements between the respective national film agencies. It would also require a critical reading of the resulting film itself in order to unpick its ideological positioning and cultural politics. Nevertheless, approaching these Moroccan international co-productions from a transnational perspective – one that is conscious of the geopolitics of the Francosphere but which analyses the financing and politics of co-production between individual nations or regional blocks, rather than through a distorted France/francophone lens – allows us to better comprehend how these Moroccan films function within the multi-directional context of cinéma-monde at the same time as they may operate within and beyond the 'franco-zones' of the French-speaking world.

Notes

1. I have reformulated this question from the title of a review article of three books exploring the topic of 'World Literature' by Charles Forsdick (2010).
2. In her original article, Martin actually evokes the transnational/translocal/transvergent.
3. The PJD came to power in 2011 following the first national elections in the Kingdom as a result of major constitutional reform in Morocco, instituted in response to the popular protests in the country and across the region that formed part of the so-called Arab Spring. The PJD is predominantly

conservative and, significantly for Moroccan cinema, oversees the CCM via the ministry of Communication (not culture). It has attempted, through the Ministry of Communication, to promote and impose its idea of *art propre* (clean art) in film and TV through both censorship and in attempting to influence public funding of film and TV. This threatens Moroccan cinema's ability to explore social taboos (notably around sex, sexuality and prostitution) and came to a head in 2015 when Nabil Ayouch's feature on illegal heterosexual prostitution in Marrakech, *Much Loved* (Ayouch, 2015, France/Morocco) was banned from Moroccan cinemas by the government, despite having appeared to critical acclaim in the *Quinzaine des réalisateurs* at Cannes only a week before.

4. In 2016 a slight reduction in the number of feature films produced, combined with a sharp drop at the Moroccan box-office for indigenous films and the fact that, for the first time in the festival's history, a Moroccan film was not selected for the Marrakech International Film Festival, led to outcry from many Moroccan filmmakers and a concern that Moroccan cinema was in crisis. Other commentators saw this simply as a blip: pointing to the success of Moroccan films on the international festival circuit, the CCM's plans to expand the number of multiplexes in major urban centres of the Kingdom and the fact that many of Morocco's most prominent contemporary directors (Bensaïdi, Lakhmari, Kilani, and Nejjar) were due to release films in 2017.

5. See, for example, the film by Moroccan activist filmmaker, Nadir Bouhmouch, *My Makhzen and Me* (2012, Morocco), available at <https://vimeo.com/36997532> (last accessed 14 July 2017).

6. Figures provided by the CCM to the Transnational Moroccan Cinema research team, January 2017.

7. Any clean lines surrounding the national identity of this co-production are further disrupted by the fact that the Moroccan production company Agora films is run by an all-female French and Moroccan producer team, while one of the French producers of *Né quelque part* was Maghrebi-French star Jamel Debbouze (the son of Moroccan immigrants) who also appears in the film.

8. <http://www.ccm.ma/docs/liste-cooperations-internationales> (last accessed 27 March 2017).

Works Cited

Awad, David (2017), 'Could foreign partners help to revive an ailing Arab Film industry?', *Almonitor*, 29 March, <http://www.al-monitor.com/pulse/originals/2017/03/egypt-film-festival-europe-joint-production-movies.html> (last accessed 14 July 2017).

Bergfelder, Tim (2005), 'National, transnational or supranational cinema? Rethinking European film studies', *Media, Culture & Society*, 27:3, pp. 315–31.

Centre Cinématographique Marocain (CCM), *Bilan Cinématographique 2016*, <http://www.ccm.ma/bilan-cinematographique.php> (last accessed 14 July 2017).

Ďurovičová, N. and K. Newman (eds) (2010), *World Cinemas, Transnational Perspectives*, New York: Routledge.

Dwyer, Kevin (2004), *Beyond Casablanca: M. A. Tazi and the Adventure of Moroccan Cinema*, Bloomington and Indianapolis: Indiana University Press.

Enwezor, Okwui (2007), 'Coalition Building: Black Audio Film Collective and Transnational Post-colonialism', in Kodwo Eshun and Anjalika Sagar (eds), *The Ghosts of Songs: the film art of the Black Audio Film Collective*, Liverpool: Liverpool University Press, pp. 106–29.

Ezra, Elizabeth and Terry Rowden (eds) (2006b), 'General Introduction: What is Transnational Cinema?', in Elizabeth Ezra and Terry Rowden (eds), *Transnational Cinema: The Film Reader*, London: Routledge, pp. 1–12.

Forsdick, Charles (2010), 'World Literature, *Littérature-Monde*: Which Literature? Whose World?', *Paragraph*, 33:1, pp. 125–43

Forsdick, Charles (2015), 'Beyond Francophone postcolonial studies: exploring the ends of comparison', *Modern Languages Open*, pp.1–24.

Galt, Rosalind (2016), 'Choosing the Transnational', *Frames Cinema Journal*, <http://framescinemajournal.com/article/choosing-the-transnational> (last accessed 14 July 2017).

Higbee, Will (2007), 'Locating the Postcolonial in transnational cinema: the place of Algerian émigré directors in contemporary French film', *Modern and Contemporary France*, 15:1, pp. 51–64.

Higbee, W. and S. H. Lim (2010), 'Concepts of transnational cinema: towards a critical transnationalism in film studies', *Transnational Cinemas* 1:1, pp. 7–21.

Higson, Andrew (2000), 'The limiting imagination of national cinema', in Mette Hjort and Scott MacKenzie (eds), *Cinema and Nation*, London: Routledge, pp. 63–74.

Hjort, Mette (2010), 'On the Plurality of Cinematic Transnationalism', in N. Ďurovičová and K. E. Newman (eds), *World Cinemas, Transnational Perspectives*, New York: Routledge.

Kinder, Marsha (1993), *Blood Cinema: The Reconstruction of National Identity in Spain*, Berkeley, California: University of California Press.

Lionnet, Françoise and Shih, Shu-mei (2005), *Minor Transnationalism*, Durham, NC: Duke University Press.

Marks, Laura (2000), *The Skin of the Film: Intercultural Cinema, Embodiment, and the Senses*, Durham, NC and London: Duke University Press.

Marshall, Bill (2012), 'Cinéma-monde? Towards a Concept of Francophone Cinema', *Francosphères* 1:1, pp. 35–51.

Martin, Florence (2016), 'Cinéma-monde: de-orbiting Maghrebi cinema', *Contemporary French Civilisation*, 41:3–4, pp. 461–75.

Naficy, Hamid (2001), *An Accented Cinema: Exilic and Diasporic Filmmaking*, Princeton and Oxford: Princeton University Press.

Nestingen, Andrew and Trevor G. Elkington (eds) (2005), *Transnational Cinema in a Global North: Nordic Cinema in Transition*, Detroit: Wayne State University Press.

Newman, Kathleen (2010), 'Notes on Transnational Film Theory', in Ďurovičová, N. and K. Newman (eds) (2010), *World Cinemas, Transnational Perspectives*, New York: Routledge.

Rosello, Mireille (2009), 'We, the Virtual Francophone Multitudes? Neo-Barbarisms and Micro-Encounters', in *Empire Lost: France & its Other Worlds*, Elizabeth Mudimbe-Boyi (ed.) Lanham: Lexington Books, pp. 47–67.

Steele, Jamie (2015), 'Towards a "transnational regional" cinema: the francophone Belgian case study', *Transnational Cinemas*.

Van de Peer, Stefanie (2016), 'Introduction to the Special Issue: The North in African Cinemas', *Journal of African Cinemas*, 8:1, pp. 3–9.

Index

Note: n indicates endnote; *italic* indicates illustration

32 août sur terre, Un/August 32nd on Earth (Villeneuve), 212n5
400 coups, Les/The 400 Blows (Truffaut), 169
5150 rue des Ormes (Tessier), 193

À tout prendre/Take it All (Jutra), 328
Abbass, Hiam, 13, 124, 204, 213n17
   Héritage/Inheritance, 112, 122, 123, 124
Abd al Malik: *Qu'Allah bénisse la France!/May Allah Bless France!* 290, 295–8, *296*
Abderrezak, Hakim, 137, 147
Abdul-Malak, Maya: *Des Hommes debout*, 301n23
Abeid, Maata Mohamed Ould, 95
Abel, Dominique and Gordon, Fiona: *La Fée/The Fairy*, 143
Abel, Dominique, Gordon, Fiona and Romy, Bruno: *L'iceberg*, 142
Abiabdillah, Kenza, 203
Abouna/Our Father (Haroun), 158
accented cinema, 7–8, 70–1, 72, 217–18
   Aïcha, 293–4
   and bilingualism, 209
   Bouchareb, Rachid, 49
   Djaïdani, Rachid, 76, 78
   and *Francophonie*, 308
   and Frenchness, 66
   Herzi, Hafsia, 111, 118
   Juste la fin du monde, 324
   Le Havre, 222–3
   Provençal, 19n3
   Samba, 220
'activist' films, 10, 245, 255
actors
   archetypes, 52
   choice of, 51–2
   polyglot, 13
   see also Herzi, Hafsia
Adamu, Semira, 207
Adejunmobi, Moradewun, 314

Adesokan, Akin, 93
Adjani, Isabelle, 291
affaire Farewell, L'/Farewell (Carion), 11, 177
Africa
   cinema: fantasy, 171; first generation films, 90; funding, 88; historical highlights, 162–4; production, 87–8, 104; road movies, 214n26
   colonialism, 169
   economic development, 90
   and globalisation, 90
   incomes, 90
   magic, 162
   migration from, 146
   stereotypes of, 85, 87
   see also Burkina Faso; Chad; Côte d'Ivoire; Ghana; Maghreb; Mali; Senegal; West Africa
Afrique-sur-Seine (Vieyra and Sarr), 163
Afropolitanism, 85–6
Aftab, Kaleem, 46–7
Aguid, Hamza Moctar, 169
Ahmarani, Paul, 207
Ahmed, Ibrahim, 99
Aïcha (Benguigui), 290, 292–5, *293*
Akerman, Chantal, 13
Akika, Ali, 67
Alegi, Peter, 160, 162, 166
Alexakis, Vassilis, 248–9
Algeria, 147, 149, 177, 203
Alice et moi (Wald), 273, 274
All Quiet on the Western Front (Milestone), 177
Allen, Woody: *Match Point*, 207–8
Allman, Jean, 163
Allouache, Merzak, 13
   Harragas, 146–8, 149, 151, 214n26
   Salut cousin, 147, 148
   Terrasses, Les, 120
Alsace-Lorraine, 182, 231
Amant, L'/The Lover (Annaud), 330

Amar, Armand, 206
Amari, Raja: *Les Secrets/Secrets*, 112, 122, 123, 124
Ame du Panier, L': le plus vieux village de France (Poli and Mammeri), 301n23
âmes grises, Les/Grey Souls (Angelo), 177
Ameur-Zaïmech, Rabah
 Dernier maquis, 60n7
 Histoire de Judas/Story of Judas, 82n6
 Wesh Wesh, qu'est-ce qui se passe? 60n7
Amores perros (Iñarritu), 207
Amouache, Nassim: *Des Apaches/The Apaches*, 290
Andrew, Dudley, 25–7, 234
Andrien, Jean-Jacques, 264, 265, 266
ange de goudron, L' (Chouinard), 202–7, 210
 Arabic language, 213n22
 autobiographical dimension, 213n17
 bridge metaphor, 204, 213n19
 homages, 205–7
 Québécité, 211
 as a road movie, 205
 soundtrack, 206
Angel's Share, The (Loach), 268
Angelo, Yves: *Les âmes grises/Grey Souls*, 177
Anna la bonne (Jutra), 329
Annaud, Jean-Jacques
 Amant, L'/The Lover, 330
 Guerre du feu, La/Quest for Fire, 330–1
 Name of the Rose, The/Der Name der Rose, 330
 Ours, L'/The Bear, 330
 Stalingrad/Enemy at the Gates, 330
anti-Semitism, 292
anticoste, L' (Gosselin), 212n9
Apollonide, L': souvenirs de la maison close/ House of Pleasures (Bonello), 112, 120–1, 124
apprenticeships, 97
Arab Spring, 318n3
Aractingi, Philippe
 Mirath/Heritages, 14
 Sous les bombes/Under the Bombs, 13–14
Arcand, Denys, 192
 Les Invasions barbares/The Barbarian Invasions, 330
Archambault, Louise, 192
Ardant, Fanny
 Cadences obstinées/Obsessive Rhythms, 14
 Cendres et sang/Ashes and Blood, 14
Arestrup, Niels, 176
Arletty, 79, 222–3, 228
Armée du crime, L'/Army of Crime (Guédiguian), 289
Armenia, 4
Arrivée d'un train en gare de La Ciotat/Arrival of a Train at La Ciotat (Lumière), 104
Artist, The (Hazanavicius), 66

Asli, Nabil, 148
Association du cinéma indépendant de sa diffusion (ACID), 67
Atalante, L' (Vigo), 228
Atlantic Ocean, 137–8, 141, 145–6
Attia, Kader, 73
Au delà des collines/Beyond the Hills (Mungiu), 268
Aube du monde, L'/Dawn of the World (Fahdel), 112, 115, 122–3, 124
Audat, Shemss, 294
Audiard, Jacques
 De rouille et d'os/Rust and Bone, 271
 Dheepan, 14, 183, 323, 325
 Un prophète/A Prophet, 183, 221
audiences, 49, 58, 89, 338, 340
Augé, Marc, 175–6
Autre émoi, L' (Catteau), 118
avant-garde, 81, 258
Avant les rues/Before the Streets (Leriche), 14, 332–3
awards
 Academy Awards (Oscars), 177, 336, 337, 338
 Ambassador of Conscience Award (Amnesty International), 317n1
 Association Trophées Francophones du Cinéma (ATF ciné) (Canada), 1, 4
 Césars, 68, 110, 177
 d'Orano prize, 68
 Genie, 192
 International Critics Prize (FIPRESCI), 68
 'Leopards of Tomorrow' competition, 273–4
 Marcello Mastroianni Prize for Most Promising Actress, 110
 Petit Rail d'or, 274
 Prix Jutra (later Gala Québec Cinema/*Prix Iris*), 4, 192
Ayouch, Nabil, 13, 300n13, 348
 Much Loved, 354n3
Ayverdi, Firat, 217
Azabal, Lubna, 13

Baier, Lionel, 13
Bakhtin, Mikhail, 326
Balibar, Étienne, 133
Baltic Sea, 137, 150
Bamako (Sissako), 85, 158, 166–7
Bamba, Zégué, 304
banlieue cinema, 55, 290–2, 299n3, 325
 Aïcha, 293–5
 see also beur films
banlieues, 49, 50, 51, 188
Barbé-Petit, Françoise, 41
Barbery, Muriel et al: 'For a *littérature-monde* in French' manifesto, 1–2, 65
Barlet, Olivier: 'Enjeux documentaires', 308–9
Barnes, Leslie, 41–2

barrage contre le pacifique, Un/The Sea Wall (Panh), 41
Barro, Fadel, 305
Bartas, Sarunas: *Indigène d'Eurasie/Eastern Drift*, 11, 14
bataille d'Alger, La/The Battle of Algiers (Pontecorvo), 61n13
bataille dans le ciel, La/Battle in Heaven (Reygadas), 268
Baton Rouge (Bouchareb), 49–50
Bausch, Andy: *Three shake-a-leg-steps to Heaven*, 267
B'béri, Boulou Ebanda, 309
Bekhti, Leïla, 114, 119
Bélanger, Louis: *Route 132*, 197
Belgium
    Antwerp, 258
    ateliers (workshops), 262, 263
    audiovisual clusters/hubs, 259–60, 265–6, 268
    bilingualism, 209
    Brussels, 11, 273; World Fair 'Expo 58', 208; Bruxellimage, 260, 266; Centre de l'Audiovisuel à Bruxelles (C.B.A), 262; 'Cinema made in Brussels', 260
    Centre du Cinéma et de l'Audiovisuel (CCA), 266, 269, 272, 273, 274–5
    Charleroi, 258
    Ciné-regio, 257
    Cinéfinance, 267–8
    Cinéma Belge (journal), 273
    Cinémathèque Royale, 268
    CLAP bureau, 269, 272, 274
    Dérives Collective asbl, 263, 267, 273
    Digital Graphics, 270–1
    documentaries, 267–8
    film schools, 274
    Films de la Drève, Les, 265
    Films de la Passerelle, Les, 264
    Films du Fleuve, Les, 264, 267, 268, 271, 276n9
    Fleur Maigre co-operative, 264
    Francophonie, 2, 4, 268, 271, 272–5
    HoverLord, 270–1
    IMG (Invest Minguet Gestion SA), 270
    international co-productions, 269, 271–2, 274
    Latitudes Productions, 272, 273
    Liège, 11–12, 257–75; funding, 267; as a hub, 269–72; Pôle Image de Liège (PIL), 257, 261, 263, 265, 267, 268–9, 270, *270*, 271, 272
    Médiaform Production, 264
    Meusinvest, 261, 270
    Mons, 258
    Namur, 258; Festival international du film francophone de Namur, 12
    Need Productions, 272
    postcolonialism, 208
    Versus Productions, 267, 272, 273–4, 277n12
    refugees, 207
    regional filmmaking, 265
    Saga Films, 277n10
    Screen Flanders, 257
    short filmmaking, 272–5
    SofiPôle, 266
    subsidies, 273
    Tarantula (production company), 268
    Tax Shelter, 257, 267, 270, 272
    television, 266, 270; Canal Emploi, 276n3; RTBF (Radio Télévision Belge Francophone), 261–2; *Vidéographie*, 261, 262, 263
    TSF (equipment provider), 271
    videomaking, 261, 262, 263, 264
    Wallonia: 'Cinema Made in Wallonia' DVD series, 274; Cinéma Wallonie, 265; Fédération Wallonie-Bruxelles (CFWB), 262, 272; Inwa (later Wallimage Entreprises), 266; Sowalim (later Wallimage Coproductions), 266; T.W.I.S.T scheme (Technologies Wallonnes de l'Image, du Son et du Texte), 260; Wallimage, 257, 266, 267, 268, 271, 273, 274; 'Walliwood', 268–72; Wallonie Effets Visuels (FX), 271; Wallonie Image Production (W.I.P.), 262–3
Bellamare, Rykko, 332
Belmondo, Jean-Paul, 233
Beloko, Jean-Pierre: *Le Président/The President*, 171n5
ben Mahmoud, Mahmoud
    Fatwa, 276n9
    Les siestes grenadine/Grenadine siestas, 267
Ben Yadir, Nabil: *La Marche/The Marchers*, 112, 121
Bendjabar, Mohamed, 316
Benguigui, Yamina
    Aïcha, 290, 292–5
    Inch'Allah dimanche, 213n18
Bensalah, Djamel, 287, 328
    Beur sur la ville, 282, *282*, 287
    Neuilly sa mère, 286
Bergfelder, Tim, 131, 187, 344
Bergson, Henri, 333
Berri, Claude
    Jean de Florette, 19n3
    Manon des sources/Manon of the Spring, 19n3
Bertuccelli, Julie: *La Cour de Babel/School of Babel*, 301n23
Besson, Eric, 67
Bessora, 240
bête humaine, La (Renoir), 228

beur films, 49, 50, 55, 299n3
Beur sur la ville (Bensalah), 282, *282*, 287
Bienvenue chez les Ch'tis/Welcome to the Sticks (Boon), 7, 66, 325
Billig, Michael, 287–8
Binamé, Charles: *Séraphin, un homme et son péché*, 193, 325
Bingo (Lord), 204
Binoche, Juliette, 4, 125, 241
Biyouna, 286, *293*, 294
Blethyn, Brenda, 46, *53*
Blondeel, Michèle *see* Lehman, Boris and Blondeel, Michèle
Boer, Inge, 133
Bohas, Alexandre, 19n2
Bollywood, 344
Bon Cop Bad Cop (Canuel), 192, 193
Bonello, Bertrand: *L'Apollonide: souvenirs de la maison close/House of Pleasures*, 112, 120–1, 124
Bonmariage, Manu, 262
  Malaises, 276n2
Bonsanti, Maria, 72
Booder, 286
Boon, Dany, 7, 12, 181
  Bienvenue chez les Ch'tis/Welcome to the Sticks, 7, 66, 325
borders, 132–3, 149, 157, 345
  border-crossing films, 131, 180–1
  and boundaries, 187
  Europe, 135, 175, 178
Borleteau, Lucie: *Fidelio, l'odyssée d'Alice*, 140–3, 149, 150, 151
Bornaz, Kalthoum, 13
Borom Sarret (Sembène), 163
Bosch, Rose: *La Rafle/The Round Up*, 176
Bouchard, Raymond, 327
Bouchareb, Rachid
  Baton Rouge, 49–50
  choice of actors, 51–2
  diversity, 289
  Frères d'armes/Brothers in Arms, 301n21
  Hors-la-loi/Outside the Law, 177, 183, 289
  Indigènes/Days of Glory, 176, 289
  Little Senegal, 50–1
  London River, 45, 46–8, 51, 52–8, 183
  and the national, 49
  Poussières de vie, 50
  route d'Istanbul, La/The Road to Istanbul, 60n10
  and space, 51
Boufares, Habib, *111*
Boughedir, Férid: *Caméra arabe*, 351
El Bouhati, Souad: *Française/French Girl*, 112, 114–15, 118, 119, 122
Bouhenni, Linda, 294
Boukhrief, Nicolas: *Made in France*, 59n1
Bourgeois, Chloé, 139, 140

Bourouissa, Mohamed, 73
Boutin, David, 327
Bouzid, Leyla, 13
Bozon, Serge: *La France*, 177
Braeckman, Colette *see* Michel, Thierry and Braeckman, Colette
Brahimi, Salem, 204, 213n16
Brakni, Rachida, 114, 246
Brault, Michel, 196, 329
  Entre la mer et l'eau douce/Between Sweet and Salt Water, 205–6, 212n9
  see also Perrault, Pierre and Brault, Michel
Brazil, 146
Bresson, Robert: *Pickpocket*, 231
Briand, Manon, 192
Brocard, Isabelle: *Ma compagne de nuit/My Night Companion*, 112, 117, 120, 123
Bronckart, Jean-Henri, 274
Bronckart, Olivier, 274
Brühl, Daniel, 180, 181
Bûcherons de la Manouane (Lamothe), 196
Buren, Daniel, 73
Burgess, Anthony, 330
Burkina Faso
  Balai Citoyen, Le (The Citizen's Broom) movement, 304–5, 306, 307, 310, 311, 313, 314, 316–17, *316*
  Droit Libre TV, 304, 305, 308, 311, 313
  Festival panafricain du cinéma et de la télévision de Ouagadougou (FESPACO), 12
Butler, Judith: *Frames of War*, 47–8
Bye Bye Africa (Haroun), 168

Cadé, Michael, 55
Cadences obstinées/Obsessive Rhythms (Ardant), 14
Cages (Masset-Depasse), 274
Cahiers du cinema (journal) 110, 263
Calais, 135, 230
Cambodia, 4, 12, 28–9
  Khmer Rouge, 29, 30, 31, 32, 33–4, 39
  language, 27
  music, 33
  refugee camps, 30–40, 42
  United Nations Border Relief Operation (UNBRO), 30, 31, 34, 38–9
camera
  Chaos, 246
  hand-held, 333
  Heremakono/Waiting for Happiness, 98
  power of, 47
  and understanding, 61n13
  video, 262
  Vie sur terre, La/Life on Earth, 92
Caméra arabe (Boughedir), 351
Cameron, James: *Titanic*, 141
Camion (Ouellet), 197

Canada
    Association Trophées Francophones du
        Cinéma (ATF ciné), 4–5
    cinéma direct, 329
    co-productions with Belgium, 272, 274
    colonialism, 332
    female directors, 192
    Festival international du cinéma
        francophone en Acadie (FICFA), 12
    International Cinema Corporation, 330
    Lévis, 139–40
    Montreal *see under* Quebec
    National Film Board, 332
    *Organisation internationale de la
        francophonie* membership, 4
    Ski-Doos, 194–5, 198, 199, 205, *206*, 210
    see also Quebec
Canary Islands *see Farbe des Ozeans, Die*;
    Pirogue, La
Canet, Guillaume, 180
Cantet, Laurent: *Entre les murs / The Class*, 288
Canuel, Eric: *Bon Cop Bad Cop*, 192, 193
capitalism, 227–8
Carion, Christian
    affaire Farewell, L' / Farewell, 11
    Joyeux Noël / Merry Christmas, 9, 11,
        176–86, 188, 189–90
Carle, Gilles: *La vie heureuse de Léopold Z*, 198
Carné, Marcel
    Hôtel du Nord, 79
    Le Quai des brumes, 228
Carpentier, Nico, 306, 310, 311
Carpignano, Jonas: *Mediterranea*, 152n1
Carrenard, Djinn: *Donoma*, 69
Carrier, Mélanie and Higgins, Olivier
    Québékoisie, 197
    Rencontre, 197
Cartier, Jacques, 195
Cartouches gauloises / Summer of '62 (Charef),
    289
Cassel, Jean-Pierre, 207
Castiel, Elie, 208
Cathars, 56
Catteau, Raphaëlle: *L'Autre émoi*, 118
Celik, Ipek A., 230
Cendres et sang / Ashes and Blood (Ardant), 14
censorship, 41, 354n3
Certifiée Halal / Certified Halal (Zemmouri),
    112, 117–18, 120
Césaire, Aimé, 170–1
    Cahier d'un retour au pays natal, 93
Chad, 12, 168
Chahine, Youssef, 351
Chairy Tale, A (Jutra), 329
chambre des officiers, La / The Officers' Ward
    (Dupeyron), 177
Champlain, Samuel de, 195
Chaos (Serreau), 239, 246–9

Chaplin, Charlie: *The Kid*, 170
Charef, Mehdi
    Cartouches gauloises / Summer of '62, 289
    fille de Keltoum, La / Daughter of Keltoum,
        214n24
    Graziella, 82n6
Charlebois, Lyne, 192
La chasse au Godard d'Abbittibbi (Morin), 197
Le chat dans le sac / Cat in the Sack (Groulx),
    195–7
Le château de ma mère / My Mother's Castle
    (Robert), 19n3
Chazelle, Damien: *La La Land*, 336
Chikly, Chemam: *La Fille de Carthage / The
    Girl from Carthage*, 163
children
    Heremakono, 97
    Poussières de vie, 50
    Site 2 (Panh), 35, 36–7, 38, 40, *40*
Choudens, Denis and Wadimoff, Nicolas:
    Clandestins, 152n1
Choudens, Xavier de: *Joseph et la fille / Joseph
    and the Girl*, 112, 120, 125
Chouf (Dridi), 6–7
Chouik, Néma Mint, 97
Chouinard, Denis, 5
    L'ange de goudron, 202–7, 210, 211,
        213nn17, 19, 22
Chouinard, Denis and Wadimoff, Nicolas:
    Clandestins, 197
Christianity: *London River*, 55–7
*Chronique d'une cour de récré / Chronicle of a
    Playground* (Fritah), 290
Chronique des indiens du nord-est du Québec
    (Lamothe), 197
cinéma de banlieue see banlieue cinema
cinéma des producteurs, 287
cinéma direct, 196–7, 201, 205, 211, 213nn17,
    21, 329
cinéma du milieu (middle cinema), 301n18
Cité Balzac: L'autre regard (Kupferstein),
    301n23
civic voice, 306, 307–8, 309
    West Africa, 310, 312, 314, 315–16, 317
Cixous, Hélène, 240
Clandestins (Chouinard and Wadimoff), 5,
    152n1, 197
Closets, François de, 72
clothing, 163
clusters: audio-visual, 259–60, 265–6, 268
Cocteau, Jean, 329
*Code inconnu: Récit incomplet de divers voyages /
    Code Unknown: Incomplete Tales of
    Several Journeys* (Haneke), 239, 241–5,
    244, 251
Cohen, Leonard, 329
Cold War, 177
Collard, Marie-France, 262, 265

Collinson, G., 60n8
colonialism, 51, 87, 332; *see also* decolonisation; empire; postcolonialism
comedic films, 286
  Aïcha, 292–5
  Beur sur la ville, 282
  Quebec, 325
'coming out' films, 329
communications
  inequalities in, 102–3, 104, 105
  and modernity, 89, 90–1, 93–4, 96
  multicultural, 176
  see also language; media
Compaore, Blaise, 304, 305
Confessional, Le / The Confessional (Lepage), 326
Congo, Republic of, 192, 208, 309
Congorama (Falardeau), 6, 194
  cultural symbols, 210
  homages, 207–8, 209
  identity, 208
  metaphor, 209
  as a road movie, 207, 209–10
  soundtrack, 209, 211
Conley, Tom, 169
Consortium audiovisuel international, 88
Continental, un film sans fusil / Continental, a Film Without Guns (Lafleur), 198
Corsini, Catherine: *Trois mondes / Three Worlds*, 239, 252–5
Costa-Gavras, 204
  Eden à l'ouest / Eden is West, 136, 152n1
Côté, Denis, 193
  Les états nordiques / Drifting States, 196
Côte d'Ivoire *see* Ivory Coast
Cotillard, Marion, 125
Cour de Babel, La / School of Babel (Bertuccelli), 301n23
C.R.A.Z.Y. (Vallée), 193
Crialese, Emanuele: *Terraferma*, 136

Daara-J: 'Exodus', 315
Dahlgren, Peter, 311
Daigle, Michel, 199
Damas, Léon-Gontran, 170–1
Damia, 232
Damrosch, David: 'World Literature', 10, 25, 26
Dans l'ombre / In the Dark (Masset-Depasse), 273–4
Dans la vie (Faucon), 60n7
Daratt / Dry Season (Haroun), 172n115
D'arbres et de charbon / About Trees and Coal (Lienard), 263
Darby, Paul, 160, 161, 164
Dardenne, Jean-Pierre, 266, 267
Dardenne, Luc, 42, 262

Darroussin, Jean-Pierre, 228
Dardenne Brothers, 265
  cooperation with Mungiu, 268
  Dérives Collective asbl (association sans but lucratif), 263
  Deux jours, Une nuit / Two Days, One Night, 257
  and Liège, 262, 263, 271
  Lorsque le bateau de Léon M. descendit la Meuse pour la première fois / When Léon M's boat went down the Meuse for the first time, 263
  promesse, La / The Promise, 267
  R … ne répond plus / R … No longer responds, 264
  Regarde Jonathan, Jean Louvet, son oeuvre / Look at Jonathan, Jean Louvet, his work, 263
  Rosetta, 267
Daycard, Sébastien *see* Deve, Bertrand and Daycard, Sébastien
De rouille et d'os / Rust and Bone (Audiard), 271
Debbouze, Jamel, 354n7
decentring process, 1, 3, 11
decolonisation, 328
Deleuze, Gilles, 2, 91, 308, 326, 333
Denmark: World War I, 184
Depardieu, Gérard, 80
Dernier maquis (Ameur-Zaïmech), 60n7
Des Apaches / The Apaches (Amouache), 290
Des étoiles / Under the Starry Sky (Gaye), 5, 11
Des Hommes debout (Abdul-Malak), 301n23
Deshaies, Raymond, 209
désintégration, La / The Disintegration (Faucon), 61n13, 302n27
Dessay, Natalie, 184
Détour (Guy), 193
Deux jours, Une nuit / Two Days, One Night (Dardenne), 257
Deutsch, Loránt, 327
Deve, Bertrand and Daycard, Sébastien: *Sarcellopolis*, 301n23
Dheepan (Audiard), 14, 183, 323, 325
Diakité, Nana, 95
dialects
  and accent, 66
  Arabic, 123, 124
  French, 7, 288, 298
  Herzi, Hafsia and, 111
  Picard, 7
  see also accented cinema; language
Diawara, Manthia, 172n7
Diego Star (Pelletier), 139–40, 141, 146, 149, 151, 197–8
Diop, Mbissine Thérèse, 163
Diot, Pascale, 269, 271
Diplomatie / Diplomacy (Schlöndorff), 176

directors
  actors: choice of, 51–2
  French, 175–7; *see also* Carion, Christian; Gatlif, Tony; Lojkine, Boris; Nakache, Olivier; Tati, Jacques; Toledano, Eric
  and French language, 4, 6–7, 13
  and Frenchness, 49
  and identity, 6, 50
  Maghrebi-French, 282, 285, 287, 288, 289, 290–8
  minority, 298
  Québécois, 192–211, 332–3; *see also* Chouinard, Denis; Falardeau, Pierre; Pelletier, Frédérick; Poulin, Julien
  and race, 240
  sub-Saharan *see* Saleh, Haroun; Sissako, Abderrahmane; Touré, Moussa
  'regional', 12
dissidence, 49, 104
diversity, 240, 336, 338, 339; *see also* under France
Dixon, Wheeler Winston, 45
Djadjam, Mostefa: *Frontières/Borders*, 214n26
Djaïdani, Rachid, 66–9, 342–3
  and the avant-garde, 82n4
  and Dogme95 manifesto, 81n3
  films
    Encré, 68, 72–5; *La Ligne brune*, 67, 68; *Quinquennats*, 67–8; *Rengaine*, 68, 75, 76–80; *Sur ma ligne*, 67, 71–2, 75; *Tour de France*, 80
  and Kassovitz's *La Haine*, 81n2
  micropractices, 81
  novels: *Boumkoeur*, 67, 72; *Mon nerf*, 71, 72
documentaries
  Barlet on, 308–9
  Belgium, 267–8
  Canada, 332–3
  French housing projects, 301n23
  Morocco, 348
  music in, 309, 315–16
  Naficy on, 71
  performative, 82n9
  Quebec, 332
  Senegal, 307–9
  Tunisia, 351
  voices in, 310–11
  Wadimoff, Nicolas, 5
  youth and, 311, 313–14, 316–17
  see also Djaïdani, Rachid; Panh, Rithy
Dolan, Xavier, 193, 326
  Juste la fin du monde/Only the End of the World, 324
  Mommy, 330
Donoma (Carrenard), 69
Dozo, Marie-Hélène, 149
Dramé, Malaminé, 165

Dridi, Karim, 12, 13
  Chouf, 6–7
dubbing, 147, 324
Dubois, Laurent, 160, 161
Dubreuil, Martin, 332
Dudrah, Rajinder *see* Nagib, Lucia, Perriam, Chris and Dudrah, Rajinder
Dufaux, Guy, 205–6
Dumont, Bruno, 12
Dunaway, Faye, 336
Dupeyron, François: *La chambre des officiers/The Officers' Ward*, 177
Durand, Yves Sioui: *Mesnak*, 332
Duras, Marguerite: *Un barrage contre le pacifique/The Sea Wall*, 41
Durmelat, Sylvie, 241
Ďurovičová, Nataša, 344
  World Cinemas, Transnational Perspectives, 9
Dussel, Enrique, 331–2
Dussollier, André, 176
DVDs, 274, 284; *see also* videomaking
Dwyer, Kevin, 347

Écran Total (journal), 269
Eden à l'ouest/Eden is West (Costa-Gavras), 136, 152n1
Eder, Klaus, 135
Egypt, 4, 122
El Ejido, la loi du profit (Rhalib), 348
Elbé, Pascal: *Tête de turc/Scapegoat*, 290–1
Eldorado (Lanners), 274
elites, 104, 349
Elkabetz, Ronit, 13
Elle s'appelait Sarah/Sarah's Key (Paquet-Brenner), 176
Elmaleh, Gad, 148
Elvis Gratton: le King des Kings (Falardeau and Poulin), 5–6, 8, 10
émigré filmmakers, 287
empire, 41, 112, 289, 344; *see also* colonialism; imperialism
En terrains connus (Lafleur), 198–203, *202*, 210, 211
Encré (Djaïdani), 68, 71, 72–5, *74*
England *see* London
Entre la mer et l'eau douce/Between Sweet and Salt Water (Brault), 205–6, 212n9
Entre les murs/The Class (Cantet), 288
Envahisseur, L'/The Invader (Provost), 149, 152n5
Ergüven, Deniz Gamze: *Mustang*, 14
Ervine, Jonathan, 245
Esquive, L'/Games of Love and Chance (Kechiche), 60n5
Essaïdi, Sofia, *293*
états nordiques, Les/Drifting States (Côté), 196
ethics, 10, 33, 143, 147, 245, 246, 323–4

Europe
  boundaries, 151, 175, 176
  conceptions, 148
  cultural zone, 134–5
  Europeanness, 133, 151, 187, 235
  Fortress Europe, 132, 133, 135, 147, 188
  globalisation, 234
  immigration to, 315
  'mosaic Europe', 187–8
  and world history, 331
European Commission, 272–3
European Union
  borders, 135, 178, 188
  European Cinema Communication, 271
  European Structural Funds, 260–1
  Eurotransmedia project, 276n1
  ideal, 178, 186
  role, 188
Eurovillage (Pirot), 263
Exit Marrakech (Link), 113, 122, 124
Express, L', 111
Expressionism, 345
Ezra, Elizabeth and Rowden, Terry: *Transnational Cinema: The Film Reader*, 82n5

Fadel, Yassine, 140
Fahdel, Abbas, 124
  L'Aube du monde / Dawn of the World, 112, 115, 122–3, 124
Falardeau, Philippe, 192
  Congorama, 6, 194, 207–10
Falardeau, Pierre and Poulin, Julien: *Elvis Gratton: le King des Kings*, 5–6, 8, 10
Fall, Laïty, 165
Fall, Makhtar, 312
El Fani, Nadia, 13
Fanon, Frantz, 158, 159
fantasy, 156
  African cinema, 168–70, 171
  football, 160, 161, 168
  Freud on, 158–9
  neocolonial, 159, 166
  objet petit a, 159, 160, 170
  and posters, 170
  West as, 165
Farbe des Ozeans, Die / The Color of the Ocean (Peren), 136–7
Farhadi, Asghar
  Academy Awards acceptance speech, 338
  Farushande / The Salesman, 336, 338–9
fashion *see* clothing
Fatwa (ben Mahmoud), 276n9
Faucon, Philippe, 288
  Dans la vie, 60n7
  La désintégration / The Disintegration, 61n13, 302n27

faute à Voltaire, La / Poetical Refugee (Kechiche), 183
Fed-Up (Sie), 310, 315–16
Fée, La / The Fairy (Abel and Gordon), 143
Ferns, Alex, 180
Ferroukhi, Ismaël, 13
  Le Grand Voyage / The Great Journey, 11
  Les Hommes libres / Free Men, 289
festivals, 12–13
  Arab Film Festival, 349
  Bucharest International Film Festival (BIFF), 13
  Cannes Film Festival, 3, 67, 68, 80, 177, 274, 339, 349, 350, 354n3
  Cinéma du Réel, 68
  COLCOA French Film Festival (Hollywood), 12
  Deauville Film Festival, 68
  Dubai International Film Festival, 349
  Festival de Montbéliard, 263
  Festival du film francophone d'Angoulême, 13
  Festival du film francophone de Vienne, 12
  Festival international de cinéma méditerranéen de Montpellier (Cinémed), 12, 137, 285–6
  Festival international du cinéma francophone en Acadie (FICFA), 12
  Festival international du film francophone de Namur, 12, 265
  Festival international du film policier de Liège, 267
  Festival panafricain du cinéma et de la télévision de Ouagadougou (FESPACO), 12
  identity and marketing, 324
  Institut du Monde Arabe (Paris): Biennale des cinemas arabes, 67
  Journées Cinématographiques de Carthage, 12–13
  Journées internationales du film sur l'art (Louvre, Paris), 68
  Locarno Film Festival, 273
  MoMA New Directors/New Films (New York), 68
  Morocco, 349, 350; Marrakech International Film Festival (FIFM), 12, 350–1
  Rencontres internationales des cinémas arabes, 12
  San Sebstian Film Festival, 263
  Tarifa Film Festival, 315
  Venice Film Festival, 110
fetishism, 157–8
Fidelio, l'odyssée d'Alice (Borleteau), 140–3, 149, 150, 151
Fille de Carthage, La / The Girl from Carthage (Chikly), 163

Fille de Keltoum, La / Daughter of Keltoum (Charef), 214n24
Film Socialisme (Godard), 152n1
Filme Falado, Um / A Talking Picture (Oliveira), 152n1
Fils de Jean, Le (Lioret), 213n23
Fin de carrière (Widart), 263
Finland, 234
Flaherty, Robert, 196
  Nanook of the North, 212n8
'floating films', 11, 131–51
  connections, 149–51
  European boundaries, 151
  as metaphor, 150
  ports, 138
  settings, 133, 134
  water, 135–8
Foer, Franklin, 157
Fontaine, Camille: *Par Accident / By Accident*, 112
football
  Africa, 160–2
  Barcelona Football Club, 165, 167–8
  and extremism, 167
  France, 167
  Internazionale Milano, 169
  in *Joyeux Noël / Merry Christmas*, 188
  and Negritude movement, 170–1
  phantasmagorical quality of, 171
  and politics, 161–2
  and racism, 171
  Real Madrid, 167
  as slavery, 164
  and violence, 171
  West African cinema, 155–71
Forestier, Sara, 250
Forsdick, Charles, 345–6
FouMalade (Malal Talla), 305
Fracture (Tasma), 290, 291–2, 292
fragments d'Antonin, Les / Fragments of Antonin (Le Bomin), 177
Française / French Girl (El Bouhati), 112, 114–15, 118, 119, 122
France
  and African film, 88
  co-productions with Morocco, 348, 351–2, 354n3
  colonialism, 169
  diversity, 283–99; *Images de la diversité* Commission, 282, 283, 284, 287, 288, 289–90, 291, 298–9, 301n30; National Agency for Social Cohesion (ACSÉ, *L'Agence nationale pour la cohésion social*), 283, 299n8; National Film and Moving Image Centre (CNC, *Centre national de la cinématographie et l'image animée*), 283, 288, 300n8, 302n30
  ethnic minorities, 284–5

Fonds sud, 88
football, 167
Front National party, 68, 337, 339
globalisation, 227
incomes, 90
Institut des hautes études cinématographiques (IDHEC, now La Fémis), 30
Islam, 290
Mikros Images, 271
multiculturalism, 283–4, 298
Muslims, 292–8
national identity, 67, 286
television, 292–5, 302n32; *Bouillon de culture* talk show, 67, 72; Canal +, 3, 19n2, 67–8, 118; *Telerama*, 286TV5, 4
see also Alsace-Lorraine; Calais; Frenchness; La Rochelle; Le Havre; Lyons; Marseille; Mont Saint-Michel; Montpellier; Nantes; Paris; Provence; Sète; Strasbourg
France, La (Bozon), 177
France est notre patrie, La / France is Our Homeland (Panh), 41
Francophonie, 2, 9, 342
  and accented cinema, 308
  Belgium, 2, 266, 267, 268, 272–5
  and cinematic geography, 339
  in co-productions, 272
  and cultural diversity, 134
  Francophone cinema, 1, 65–6, 157, 219, 298; West African, 311–13
  and heterolingualism, 142
  in *Images de la diversité* films, 298–9
  limits of, 132, 133, 134
  in *London River*, 58
  Organisation internationale de la francophonie, 4
  and 'post-francophone', 346
  and 'Pour une " littérature-monde" en français' manifesto, 65
  Quebec, 328
  and space, 333
  and world media, 311–13
Francosphères (journal), 65
Frankel, Jeffrey, 87
French, Lindsay, 30–1, 35, 40, 43n5
French cinema: definitions, 338
French language
  Algerians, 147–8
  Burkina Faso, 305, 314, 315
  and cinéma-monde, 219
  as a common language, 145
  dialects, 7, 288, 298
  and francophone film, 308
  in *Joyeux Noël / Merry Christmas*, 181
  in *London River*, 58
  in Moroccan films, 349

French language (*cont.*)
  and 'plateaus', 260
  as a subaltern tongue, 142
  and transnationalism, 150
  see also accented cinema; dialects: French; Francophonie
Frenchness, 49, 125, 323
  and accented cinema, 66, 288, 294
  Atlantic Ocean and, 137
  Bouchareb and, 50
  Images de la diversité Commission and, 285
  in *Samba*, 227
Frères d'armes / Brothers in Arms (Bouchareb), 301n21
Freud, Sigmund, 158–9
Fritah, Brahim: *Chronique d'une cour de récré / Chronicle of a Playground*, 290
Frontières / Borders (Djadjam), 214n26
Frot, Catherine, 246
funding, 3, 4, 41, 88, 267
Fürmann, Benno, 180
fusillés, Les (Triboit), 177

Gabriel, Teshome, 172n7
Gainsbourg, Charlotte, 216
Galeano, Eduardo, 165
Galt, Rosalind, 133
Galt, Rosalind and Schoonover, Karl: *Global Art Cinema*, 10
Gamblin, Jacques, 250
Gatlif, Tony, 13
  Geronimo, 290
  Korkoro / Freedom, 289
  Transylvania, 4, 153n8
Gaudioso, Massimo: *Un Paese quasi perfetto*, 327
Gaudreault, Emile: *Mambo Italiano*, 193
Gaye, Dyana: *Des étoiles / Under the Starry Sky*, 5, 11
Gens d'Abitibi (Perrault), 212n9
Gens de la rizière / Rice People (Panh), 41
Geronimo (Gatlif), 290
Getino, Fernando, 161
Ghana, 309
Gheorghiu, Luminita, 241
Gilroy, Paul: *The Black Atlantic: Modernity and Double Consciousness*, 51, 137–8
Giroux, Maxime, 193
Gitai, Amos, 13
Gleeson, Erin, 28
Glissant, Édouard, 26, 323–4
globaletics, 90
globalisation, 87, 89, 167, 216
  Africa, 90–1, 102, 103, 163
  alter-globalist movement, 213n16
  and cinema, 104, 105, 344
  Europe, 234
  France, 227
  legitimisation of, 89–90
  Morocco, 349
  Sissako and, 91–4, 95, 98
  and terrorism, 45, 46, 47, 48, 49
  and violence, 54
  see also transnationalism
gloire de mon père, La / My Father's Glory (Robert), 19n3
Godard, Jean-Luc: *Film Socialisme*, 152n1
Godbout, Jacques, 195, 196
Godillot, Bunny, 293
Godin, Gérald, 207
Goldblatt, David, 162
Gomis, Alain, 13
Gordon, Fiona *see* Abel, Dominique and Gordon, Fiona
Gosselin, Bernard: *L'anticoste*, 212n9
Gourmet, Olivier, 207
Graine et le mulet, La / The Secret of the Grain (Kechiche), 110, 112, 116, 121, 183
Grand Seduction, The (McKellar), 327
Grand Voyage, Le / The Great Journey (Ferroukhi), 11
Grande Illusion, La / Grand Illusion (Renoir), 177
Grande Séduction, La / Seducing Doctor Lewis (Pouliot), 192, 326–7
Graziella (Charef), 82n6
Great War *see* World War I
Greece, 4
  Lesbos, 136
Grigris (Haroun), 172n15
Groulx, Gilles, 196
  Le chat dans le sac / Cat in the Sack, 195–7
Gruskoff, Michael, 330
Guardian, The (newspaper), 46, 337
Guattari, Félix, 326
Guédiguian, Robert, 12
  L'Armée du crime / Army of Crime, 289
  Les Neiges du Kilamandjaro, 152n6
Guelwaar (Sembène), 312
Guernsey, 52, 53, 54, 56
Guerre du feu, La / Quest for Fire (Annaud), 330–1
guerrilla filmmaking, 69, 342–3; *see also* Djaïdani, Rachid
Guiraudie, Alain: *Le Roi de l'évasion / The King of Escape*, 112, 115–16, 120
Guy, Sylvain: *Détour*, 193

Hada, Moussa: *Harraga Blues*, 152n1
Haidara, Omar, 99
Haine, La / Hate, (Kassovitz), 59n3, 81n2, 296
Haïti, la terre / Haiti (Riga), 263
Halle, Randall, 2–3, 134, 150, 151
Hamidi, Alexandre, 241
Hamidi, Mohamed: *Né quelque part / Homeland*, 351–2

Haneke, Michael: *Code inconnu: Récit incomplet de divers voyages/Code Unknown: Incomplete Tales of Several Journeys*, 239, 241–5, *244*, 251, 255
Hansen, Miriam Bratu, 89
Harelle, Johanne, 328
Hargreaves, Alec G., 2, 283
Haroun, Mahamat-Saleh, 13, 168–70
  Abouna/Our Father, 158, 168–9
  Bye Bye Africa, 168
  Daratt/Dry Season, 172n15
  Grigris, 172n15
  Un homme qui crie/A Screaming Man, 172n115
Harraga Blues (Hada), 152n1
Harragas (Allouache), 146–8, 149, 151, 214n26
Harrow, Kenneth, 96, 156, 163
  Postcolonial African Cinema: From Political Engagement to Postmodernism, 157
Hattau, Messaoud, 148
Hauge, Chelsey, 311
Havre Libre (newspaper), 230, *230*
Hayward, Susan, 88, 219
Hazanavicius, Michel: *The Artist*, 66
Heremakono/Waiting for Happiness (Sissako), 85, 95–8, 166
Héritage/Inheritance (Abbass), 112, 122, 123, 124
Héritiers, Les/The Heirs (Mention-Schaar), 291
Héroux, Denys, 330
Herzi, Hafsia, 110–25, *111*, *120*
  accent, 118
  awards, 110
  biography, 113–14
  ethnic identity, 119–20, 121
  films, 110–11; *Apollonide, L'*, 120–1; *Aube du monde, L'*, 115, 122–3, 124; *Certifiée Halal*, 117–18, 120; *Exit Marrakech*, 122, 124; *Française*, 114–15, 118, 119, 122; *Graine et le mulet, La*, 110, 114, 116, 121; *Héritage*, 122, 123, 124; *Homme et son chien, Un*, 120; *Joseph et la fille*, 120, 125; *Ma compagne de nuit*, 112, 117, 120, 123; *Marche, La*, 121; *Roi de l'évasion, Le*, 115–16, 120; *Sac de farine, Le*, 118; *Secrets, Les*, 122, 123, 124; *Source des femmes, La*, 118, 119, 122, 124; *War Story*, 122, 124
  global roles, 122–5
  linguistic ability, 13, 111, 114, 121, 122–4
  Marseillaise identity, 113–14, 116–17, 118 and Paris, 117
  and stereotyping, 115, 116, 121
Hesme, Clotilde, 252
Higbee, Will, 58, 82n7, 88, 188, 189, 219, 287, 290, 343
  Post-Beur Cinema, 69

Higelin, Izïa, 221
Higgins, Olivier *see* Carrier, Mélanie and Higgins, Olivier
Higson, Andrew, 343
hip hop cinema *see Qu'Allah bénisse la France!*
Histoire de Judas/Story of Judas (Ameur-Zaïmeche), 82n6
historical films, 289; *see also Guerre du feu, La*
history: world, 329, 330–1, 333
Hjort, Mette, 10, 268, 351
Holden, Stephen, 46
Hollywood
  COLCOA French Film Festival, 12
  distribution networks, 87
  French film remakes, 338
  and globalisation, 45, 334
  and neo-liberalism, 89
Homme et son chien, Un/A Man and His Dog (Huster), 112, 115, 120
homme qui crie, Un/A Screaming Man (Haroun), 172n115
homme qui répare les femmes, L': La colère d'Hippocrate/The man who mends women: The wrath of Hippocrates (Michel and Braeckman), 263
Hommes libres, Les/Free Men (Ferroukhi), 289
Hong Kong, 260
Hop (Standaert), 208, 214n26
Hope (Lokjine), 152n3
Hors-la-loi/Outside the Law (Bouchareb), 177, 183, 289
Hors les murs/Beyond the Walls (Lambert), 272
Hôtel du Nord (Carné), 79
Hou Hsiao-Hsien: *Le voyage du ballon rouge/Flight of the Red Balloon*, 4
Houle, Denis, 199
hubs: audiovisual, 12, 259–60, 265–6, 268, 269–72
human rights, 338
  in *Site 2*, 38–9, 40
  Universal Declaration of Human Rights, 31
Human Zoo (Rasmussen), 186–7
Huntington, Samuel, 285
Huster, Francis: *Un Homme et son chien/A Man and His Dog*, 112, 115, 120

I Hired a Contract Killer (Kaurismäki), 231
iceberg, L' (Abel, Gordon and Romy), 142–4
identity
  in *À tout prendre*, 328–9
  and belonging, 133
  in *Congorama*, 208
  and difference, 297
  in *En terrains connus*, 201
  historical, 231
  hyphenated, 298
  images of, 284
  in *Joyeux Noël*, 183–4

identity (*cont.*)
   and language, 220, 221–2, 224
   local, 229
   and names, 250
   national, 187, 227, 286, 287–8, 339–40
   neocolonial, 162
   Québécois, 192, 196, 197
   women and, 119
Iland, Cédric, 270
Illégal / Illegal (Masset-Depasse), 214n26, 274
immigrants, 314–15, 338; see also migrants; refugees
immigration cinema, 148, 216–17; see also *Le Havre*; *Samba*
imperialism, 164; see also colonialism; empire
Iñarritu, Alejandro: *Amores perros*, 207
Inch'Allah dimanche (Benguigui), 213n18
India see Bollywood
Indigène d'Eurasie / Eastern Drift (Bartas), 11, 14
Indigènes / Days of Glory (Bouchareb), 176, 289
inexportable films, 325, 326–7
Inrockuptibles, Les, 110
Internet: West Africa, 305, 306, 308, 311, 312, 313, 315, 318n3; see also Skype; YouTube
Intouchables / The Untouchables (Nakache and Toledano), 218, 221
Inuit cinema, 197
Invasions barbares, Les / The Barbarian Invasions (Arcand), 330
Iordanova, Dina, 332
Iosseliani, Otar, 13
Iran, 338
Isaac, Elisapie: *Si le temps le permet / If the Weather Permits*, 197
Islam
   France see *Qu'Allah bénisse la France!*
   Morocco, 347
   representations of, 48, 54, 55, 98, 290
   see also Muslims
Italy see Sicily
Ivory Coast, 4, 50–1

Jackson, Mark: *War Story*, 112–13, 122, 124
Jaoui, Agnès, 67
Jarmusch, Jim: *Stranger Than Paradise*, 170
Je suis à toi / All yours (Lambert), 272
Je suis mort mais j'ai des amis / I'm Dead but I Have Friends (Malandrin), 212n7
Jean, Rodrigue
   Panique, 204
   Yellowknife, 197
Jean de Florette (Berri), 19n3
Jeancolas, Jean-Pierre, 325
Jeffries, Stuart, 46
Jenkins, Barry: *Moonlight*, 336, 337
Jenkins, Henry, 306, 311

Jeunet, Jean-Pierre: *Un long dimanche de fiançailles / A Very Long Engagement*, 175
Jimmy Rivière (Lussi-Modeste), 112, 124
Jonas, John, 262
Joseph et la fille / Joseph and the Girl (Choudens), 112, 120, 125
Journée de la jupe, La / Skirt Day (Lilienfeld), 291
Jouvet, Louis, 79
Joyeux Noël / Merry Christmas (Carion), 9, 11, 176–86
   awards, 177
   barriers, 178, 179
   boundaries / borders, 181–2, 186
   European mission, 189
   identity, 183–4
   language, 181, 182–3, 184, 185, 186
   multiculturalism, 189
   music, 180, 184
   no-man's land, 179, 180, 188
   production, 185
   religion, 183–4
   symbolism, 183
   themes, 177–8
Julien-Laferrière, Gabriel: *Neuilly sa mère / Neuilly Yo Mama*, 286–7
Juste la fin du monde / Only the End of the World (Dolan), 324
Jutra, Claude
   À tout prendre / Take it All, 328–9
   Anna la bonne, 329
   Chairy Tale, A, 329
   Mon oncle Antoine, 198
   Niger jeune république, Le, 328

Kaci, Nadia, 13
Kader, Khatra Ould Abder, 95
kaleidoscopes: as metaphor, 98
Kam, Me Guy Hervé, 305
Kampuchea see Cambodia
Kanehsatake: 270 Years of Resistance (Obomsawin), 197, 332
Kapoor, Anish, 73
Karabache, Christophe, 13
Karaman, Onur, 13
Kasmi, Baya, 251; see also Leclerc, Michel and Kasmi, Baya
Kassari, Yasmine, 265
Kassovitz, Mathieu: *La Haine / Hate*, 59, 81n2, 296
Kaurismäki, Aki
   I Hired a Contract Killer, 231
   Le Havre, 152n6, 216, 217, 218, 220, 222, 224, 225, 227–33, 323
   Leningrad Cowboys Go America, 213n14
Kechiche, Abdellatif, 13
   Esquive, L' / Games of Love and Chance 60n5

INDEX

faute à Voltaire, La / Poetical Refugee, 183
Graine et le mulet, La / The Secret of the Grain, 110, 116, 121, 183
Keita, Salif, 165–6
Kemeny, John, 330
Kennedy, John F., 209
Khan, Siddiq (Mayor of London), 337
Kid, The (Chaplin), 170
Kidjo, Angélique, 304
Kiener, Patrick, 294
Kiernan, Ben, 28
Kiki, Toulou, 99
Kilifeu (Mbessane Seck), 305
Kinder, Marsha, 343
Kiwan, Nadia, 284–5
Klapisch, Cédric: *Ma part du gâteau*, 152n6
Korkoro / Freedom (Gatlif), 289
Koutras, Panos: *Xenia*, 14
Kouyaté, Sotigui, 51, *53*, *56*
Kramsch, Claire, 179
Kruger, Diane, 184
Kuper, Simon, 162, 172n12
Kupferstein, Daniel: *Cité Balzac: L'autre regard*, 301n23
Kurys, Diane, 12
Kusturica, Emir, 13

La Haye, Francis, 198, *202*
La La Land (Chazelle), 336
La Rochelle, 137
Labed, Ariane, 140–1, *141*, 149
Lacan, Jacques, 157, 159
Laderman, David, 152n7
Lafleur, Stéphane, 193
 Continental, un film sans fusil / Continental, a Film Without Guns, 198
 En terrains connus, 198–203, 210, 211
Lafosse, Joachim, 274
Lambert, David
 Hors les murs / Beyond the Walls, 272
 Je suis à toi / All yours, 272
Lamothe, Arthur, 196, 332
 Bûcherons de la Manouane, 196
Lamothe, Willie, 211
language
 adolescents, 60n5
 Arabic, 5, 7, 54, 55, 97, 111, 122–3, 147, 213n22, 221, 243, 244, 298, 305, 312, 314
 barriers to, 179
 bilingualism, 209
 boundaries of, 138
 Cambodia, 27, 29
 Canada, 139–40; Atikamekw, 332
 as cultural expression, 309
 and democracy, 306
 English, 124, 153n8, 181, 185, 187, 305, 314, 329

 German, 181
 heterolinguistic spaces, 312, 313–14
 and identity, 220, 221–2, 224
 Inuktitut, 132, 144
 Khmer, 33
 Latin, 180, 182–3, 184
 linguae francae, 11, 181
 Mauritania, 97, 98
 metaphors of, 8–9
 monolingualism, 179
 multilingualism, 9, 177, 178, 179, 184, 185
 Palestinian, 123
 '*parole filmée*', 32
 Persian, 338
 Polish, 151
 and solidarity, 133, 134
 Spanish, 145, 148
 Tamil, 325
 translation, 324
 and *Trophées francophones*, 4, 5
 Wolof, 305, 312, 314, 315, 316
 see also accented cinema; dialects; *Francophonie*; French language
Lanners, Bouli, 274
 Eldorado, 274
 Travellinckx, 273
 Ultranova, 274
Laroche, Josepha, 19n2
Lasri, Hicham, 350, 352
Latin America: and Third Cinema, 161; *see also* Brazil
Latour, Bruno: *We Have Never been Modern*, 59n2
Laxe, Olivier, 13
 Mimosas, 352
Le Bomin, Gabriel: *Les fragments d'Antonin / Fragments of Antonin*, 177
Le Havre, 228, 234; *see also Fée, La*
Le Havre (Kaurismäki), 138, 216–33, 323
 filmic language, 233
 newspapers, 229–30
 police, 231, 232, 233
 port, 152n6
 soundtrack, 232
 transnationalism, 232
Le Pen, Marine, 337, 339
Léaud, Jean-Pierre, 228
Lebanon, 4
Leclerc, Kadija: *Le Sac de farine / The Bag of Flour*, 112, 118
Leclerc, Michel and Kasmi, Baya: *Le Nom des gens / The Names of Love*, 239, 250–2, 251
Legzouli, Hassan: *Tenja*, 348
Lehman, Boris and Blondeel, Michèle, 259
 Marcher, ou la fin des temps modernes, 262
Lekbeid, Mamma Mint, 97
Lemoine, Nathalie, 199

Leningrad Cowboys Go America (Kaurismäki), 213n14
Lepage, Robert: *Le Confessional / The Confessional*, 326
Leriche, Chloé: *Avant les rues / Before the Streets*, 14, 332–3
Letort, Delphine, 51
Lewis, Gary, 182
Liberski, Stéphane: *Tokyo Fiancé*, 272
Lie, Anders Danielsen, 150
Liénard, Bénédicte
  D'arbres et de charbon / About Trees and Coal, 263
  Une part du ciel / A Piece of Sky, 257
Ligne brune, La (Djaïdani), 67, 68
Lilienfeld, Jean-Paul: *Journée de la jupe, La / Skirt Day*, 291
Lindon, Vincent, 217, 246
Linh Dan Pham, 13
Link, Caroline: *Exit Marrakech*, 113, 122, 124
Lionnet, Françoise, 248, 343
Lionnet, Françoise and Shi, Shu-mei, 3, 69–70, 134
Lioret, Philippe
  Le Fils de Jean, 213n23
  Welcome, 135, 153n8, 214n26, 217
literature: minor, 308
littérature-monde, 10, 25, 219, 345
  and Afropolitanism, 85–6
  mapping of, 32
  'Pour une "littérature-monde" en français' manifesto, 1–2, 25, 65, 219
Little Bob, 231, 232
Little Senegal (Bouchareb), 50–1
Loach, Ken: *The Angel's Share*, 268
Loin (Téchiné), 307–8
Lojkine, Boris, 136
  Hope, 152n3
Lon Nol, 29, 32
London
  bombings, 7th July, 2005, 46
  as a 'franco-zone', 12
  French population, 339
  screening of *Farushande / The Salesman*, 337
London River (Bouchareb), 51, 52–8, 183
  criticisms of, 46–7
  as a Francophone film, 58
  as a global story, 52
  Islamophobia in, 47, 54–5
  as a political film, 47, 48
  religion, 54, 55–7
  soundtrack, 52
  stereotypes, 58
  terrorism, 53, 57–8
  theme, 46, 47, 52
long dimanche de fiançailles, Un / A Very Long Engagement (Jeunet), 175
Lord, Jean-Claude: *Bingo*, 204

Lorenzi, Jean-Louis: *La tranchée des espoirs / Trench of Hope*, 177
Lorsque le bateau de Léon M. descendit la Meuse pour la première fois / When Léon M's boat went down the Meuse for the first time (Dardenne), 263
Louvet, Jean
  Conversations en Wallonie, 263
  L'homme qui avait le soleil dans sa poche, 263
  Le train du bon Dieu, 263
Lumière, Auguste and Louis, 104, 194, 344
  Arrivée d'un train en gare de La Ciotat / Arrival of a Train at La Ciotat, 104
  La sortie des usines Lumière / Workers Leaving the Lumière Factory, 104
Lumumba: la mort du prophète / Lumumba: The Death of A Prophet (Peck), 309–10
Lussi-Modeste, Teddy: *Jimmy Rivière*, 112, 124
Luxembourg, 12
Luyckx, Eddy, 262
Lyons, 73

Ma compagne de nuit / My Night Companion (Brocard), 112, 117, 120, 123
Ma part du gâteau (Klapisch), 152n6
McKay, Claude: *Banjo*, 138
McKellar, Don: *The Grand Seduction*, 327
McLaren, Norman, 329
Made in France (Boukhrief), 59n1
Maghreb
  Al Qaeda, 98
  co-operation, 353
  films, 2, 18, 69, 82n7, 112
  relationship with France, 147
  see also Algeria; Morocco; Tunisia
Maghrebi-French directors, 282, 285, 287, 288, 289, 290
Magrini, T., 150
Mai, Joseph, 276n
mainstream filmmaking, 69
Makhlouf, Samir, 291
Malaises (Bonmariage), 276n2
Malandrin, Guillaume and Stéphane: *Je suis mort mais j'ai des amis / I'm Dead but I Have Friends*, 212n7
Mali
  Ansar Dine jihadist group, 98, 99
  communications, 102–3
  Dogon, 102
  football, 166
  globalisation, 102, 103
  incomes, 90
  National Movement for the Liberation of Azawad (MNLA), 99, 102
  portrayal of, 91, 93, 94; see also Timbuktu
  transnationalism, 103–4
  Tuareg, 98, 99, 102
  water, 99–100, 101

Mallette, Fanny, 198–9
Mambety, Djibril Diop: *Touki Bouki*, 90
Mambo Italiano (Gaudreault), 193
Mammeri, Sofiane *see* Poli, Olivier and Mammeri, Sofiane
Mankiewcz, Francis: *Le temps d'une chasse*, 205
Manon des sources / Manon of the Spring (Berri), 19n3
maps, 26–7
   Atlantic Ocean, 146
   and borders, 187
   Cambodia, 29–30
   cognitive, 234, 235
   and disorientation, 147
   of European novels, 32
   European Union, 189
   in *iceberg, L'*, 145
   in *Joyeux Noël / Merry Christmas*, 182
   Quebec, 195
   in *Site 2*, 34, 38, 42
   travel films, 144
   World War I trenches, 178–9
Marcel, Sylvain, 199
Marche, La / The Marchers (Ben Yadir), 112, 121
Marcher, ou la fin des temps modernes (Lehman and Blondeel), 262
Marder, Marc, 33, 40
Mariage, Benoît, 266
   Les Rayures du zèbre / Scouting for Zebras, 172nn8, 10, 16
marketing, 88
markets, 349, 350
Marseille
   films set in, 111, 116–17, 140–1, 301n23
   French language in, 7
   Herzi, Hafsia and, 113–14
   and identity, 138
   Rencontres internationales des cinémas arabes, 12
'Marseille Trilogy' (Pagnol), 19n3
Marshall, Bill, 5, 7, 26, 135, 137, 157, 176, 187, 193, 218, 260, 265, 285, 288, 298, 341, 345, 346, 352
   'Cinéma-monde? Towards a Concept of Francophone Cinema', 1–2, 65–6, 307–8
Marsolais, Gilles, 196
Martin, Catherine, 192
Martin, Elaine, 61n12
Martin, Florence, 3, 19n2, 341
   'Cinéma-monde: de-orbiting Maghrebi cinema', 2, 346
Martin, M. Phyllis, 163–4
Martin-Jones, David, 331
Martz, Philippe, 144
Masset-Depasse, Olivier, 274
   Cages, 274

Dans l'ombre / In the Dark, 273–4
Illégal / Illegal, 214n26, 274
Massey, Doreen, 141–2
Mastroianni, Marcello, Prize for Most Promising Actress, 110
Match Point (Allen), 207–8
Maura, Carmen, 328
Mauritania
   language, 97, 98
   television, 96
   see also Heremakono
May, Carine and Zouhani, Hakim: *Rue des cités*, 69
Mbaye, Serigne Mor, 315
Mbembe, Achille, 86, 241, 246, 248, 249, 252
media, 13
   média-engagé, 306, 307, 313
   see also Internet; newspapers; radio; Skype; television; YouTube
Mediterranea (Carpignano), 152n1
Mediterreanean Sea, 136, 137, 147, 148–9
Meier, Ursula, 13
Mekhnache, Yassine (Yaze), 68, 72–5
Melgar, Fernand, 13
melodramas *see banlieue* cinema
memories, 289, 333–4
Mennour, Kamel, 73
Mention-Schaar, Marie-Castille: *Les Héritiers / The Heirs*, 291
Mesnak (Durand), 332
Messi, Lionel, 167, 168
metaphors
   archipelagos, 26
   fathers, 169
   kaleidoscopes, 9
   mosaics, 8–9
   mothers, 168
   oceans, 170
Meunier, Stéphane: *Un Village presque parfait*, 327–8
Meyer, Paul, 265
Miaille, Michel, 300n13
Michel, Thierry, 257, 262, 264
Michel, Thierry and Braeckman, Colette: *L'homme qui répare les femme: La colère d'Hippocrate / The man who mends women: The wrath of Hippocrates*, 263
Michelin, Alexandre, 284, 285–6, 287, 289, 299, 300n13
middle cinema *see cinéma du milieu*
Migraine-George, Thérèse, 10
migrants, 342
   crisis of, 132, 135–6, 348
   and French culture by, 150
   hostility towards, 188
   interzones, 151
   invisibility of, 246, 249

migrants (cont.)
  otherness of, 148, 245, 246, 247, 249, 252, 253, 254
  representations of, 143, 144
  shared spaces of, 241
  and solidarity, 151
  'touring', 136
  see also immigrants
Miguel, Blondin, 216
Mihaileanu, Radu, 13
  La Source des femmes / The Source, 112, 118, 119, 122, 124
Milestone, Lewis: All Quiet on the Western Front, 177
millennium, 91–3
Miller, Arthur: Death of a Salesman, 338–9
Miller, Christopher: The French Atlantic Triangle, 51
Mimosas (Laxe), 352
Minassian, Lévon, 206
Mirath / Heritages (Aractingi), 14
Mistons, Les (Truffaut), 329
mobility
  and borders, 175, 188–9
  and cities, 260
  and globalisation, 210, 216
  and immobility, 194, 198, 200
  and space, 189
modernism, 41
modernity, 331–2
Mohamed, Layla Walet, 99
Mohamed, Mahmoud Ould, 95
Mokkadem, Rabia, *293*, 294
Moknèche, Nadir, 13
Mommy (Dolan), 330
Mon oncle Antoine (Jutra), 198
Mont Saint-Michel, 231
Montpellier, 12, 137, 301n23
Moonlight (Jenkins), 336, 337
Morel, Gaël, 12
Moretti, Franco, 26, 27, 32, 234
Morin, Éric: La chasse au Godard d'Abbittibbi, 197
Moroccan Gigolos (Saidi), 272
Morocco
  Agora Films, 351
  censorship, 354n3
  Centre Cinématographique Marocain (CCM), 347, 348, 349, 350, 351, 352–3
  co-productions, 347, 348, 349, 351–3
  Doha Film Institute and, 352
  as a film location see Française; Source des femmes, La
  Islamist Justice and Development Party (PJD), 347
  Marrakech, 74, 75
  Marrakech International Film Festival, 12
  national cinema, 347, 348

television, 354n3
transnationalism, 347–53
Morris, Desmond, 330
Mort à Vignole (Smolders), 273
Mosley, Philip, 276n
Mouithys, Arnaud, 207
Moussa, Ahidjo Mahamat, 169
Much Loved (Ayouch), 354n3
multiculturalism, 283–4, 288, 293, 298
Mulvey, Laura, 156, 157–8
Mungiu, Cristian: Au delà des collines / Beyond the Hills, 268
Murat, Pierre, 286, 287, 300n13
Murphy, David, 85, 156, 157–8
music
  ange de goudron, L', 206
  Congorama, 209
  documentaries, 309, 315–16
  hip hop, 296, 297
  Joyeux Noël / Merry Christmas, 180, 184
  Mediterreanean, 150
  Samba, 224
  Site 2, 33, 38, 39, 40
  Timbuktu, 168
  'We Are Happy From Ouaga' (YouTube video), 304
  and youth, 305, 309–10
Muslims, 292–8; see also Islam
Mustang (Ergüven), 14

Naficy, Hamid, 7, 70–1
  An Accented Cinema, 66, 71, 72, 76–7, 78, 217–18, 308
Nagib, Lucia, Perriam, Chris and Dudrah, Rajinder: Theorizing World Cinema, 10
Nakache, Olivier and Toledano, Éric, 216
  Intouchables / The Untouchables, 218, 221
  Samba, 216–17, 218, 220–2, 223–4, *226*, 228, 232, 233–4
Name of the Rose, The / Der Name der Rose (Annaud), 330
Nanook of the North (Flaherty), 212n8
Nantes, 137
narrative films, 89–90
Nash, Kate, 310, 311
Nasr, Siamak, 206
national cinema, 104–5, 326, 338, 343, 347, 348
nationalism, 105
  'banal', 287–8
  deconstruction of, 337
  Quebec, 328–9
  see also transnationalism
Ndiaye, Soulaymane, 156
Né quelque part / Homeland (Hamidi), 351–2
Nebbou, Mehdi, 13
Negritude movement, 170–1

Neiges du Kilamandjaro, Les (Guédiguian), 152n6
Nejjar, Narjiss, 13
neocolonialism, 158, 159, 162–3, 164, 165, 169
neo-liberalism, 89
Nestingen, Andrew, 231
Neuilly sa mère / Neuilly Yo Mama (Julien-Laferrière), 286–7
Neuvic, Thierry, 245
Névé, Éric, 149
new wave cinema, 193, 329, 345
New York
  in *Encré*, 75
  MoMA New Directors/New Films 2013, 68
  terrorist attacks on (11 September 2001), 45
New York Times, 46
Newman, Kathleen, 3, 344
newspapers, 229, 230
Ngũgĩ wa Thiongo, 90
Nguyen, Kim: *Rebelle / War Witch*, 192
Nguyen, Quoc Dung, 223
Niang, Philippe: *Toussaint Louverture*, 302n32
Nichols, Bill, 82n9, 310
Niemandsland / Hell on Earth (Trivas), 177
Niger, Paul: 'Petit oiseau', 98
Niger jeune république, Le (Jutra), 328
Noire de …, La / Black Girl (Sembène), 90, 163
Nom des gens, Le / The Names of Love (Leclerc and Kasmi), 239, 250–2, 251
non-lieu (non-place), 175–6
Norindr, Panivong, 34
Nous, princesses de Clèves (Sauder), 301n23
nouvelle vague cinema see new wave cinema
nuit tous les chats sont gris, La (Wald), 273

Obomsawin, Alanis: *Kanehsatake: 270 Years of Resistance*, 197, 332
O'Healy, Aine, 137
Oliveira, Manoel de: *Filme Falado, Um / A Talking Picture*, 152n1
O'Shaughnessy, Martin, 240, 245
otherness, 148, 245, 246, 247, 249, 252, 291
Ouazani, Sabrina, 13, 119
Ouedraogo, Idrissa: *Yaaba / Grandmother*, 169–70
Ouellet, Raphaël, 193
  Camion, 197
Ouoro, Justin, 313
Ours, L' / The Bear (Annaud), 330
Outinen, Kati, 222–3
outsiders: artist-, 71–5
Ouyahhia, Raba Aït, 203

Pabst, Georg Wilhelm: *La tragédie de la mine / Comradeship*, 177
Paese quasi perfette, Un (Gaudioso), 327

Pagnol, Marcel: 'Marseille Trilogy', 19n3
Paik, Nam Jun, 262
Panh, Rithy, 27, 30, 324
  barrage contre le pacifique, Un / The Sea Wall, 41
  élimination, L' / The Elimination, 29
  France est notre patrie, La / France is Our Homeland, 41
  Gens de la rizière / Rice People, 41
  papier ne peut pas envelopper la braise, Le / Paper Cannot Wrap Ember, 41–2
  Site 2, 27–8, 30–40, 42
  terre des âmes errantes, La / The Land of Wandering Souls, 34, 41
Panique (Jean), 204
papier ne peut pas envelopper la braise, Le / Paper Cannot Wrap Ember (Panh), 41–2
Paquet-Brenner, Gilles: *Elle s'appelait Sarah / Sarah's Key*, 176
Par accident / By Accident (Fontaine), 112
Paris
  accented cinema see Djaïdani, Rachid: *Rengaine*
  'activist' films, 10, 255
  ATF ciné award ceremonies, 4
  Bir Hakeim bridge, 78–9
  Centre national du cinéma et de l'image animée (CNC), 7, 68, 147
  Défense, La, 225, 233
  Eiffel Tower, 234
  filming foreigners in, 239–55
  Foire Internationale d'Art Contemporain (FIAC), 73
  Forum des Images: Festival Pocket Films, 67
  globalisation, 220
  Institut du Monde Arabe: Biennale des cinemas arabes, 67
  silent films, 106
  urban space, 228, 234, 290
  Vie sur terre, La / Life on Earth, 91–3
  World War II films, 176
part du ciel, Une / A Piece of Sky (Liénard), 257
pays sans bon sens!, Un (Perrault), 212n9
Paysage imaginaire (Widart), 263
Peck, Raoul, 13
  Lumumba: la mort du prophète / Lumumba: The Death of A Prophet, 309–10
Pelletier, Frédérick: *Diego Star*, 139–40, 141, 146, 149, 151, 197–8
Penley, Constance, 159
Peren, Maggie: *Die Farbe des Ozeans / The Color of the Ocean*, 136–7
Perin, Anne-François, 262
Perrault, Pierre, 196
  Gens d'Abitibi, 212n9
  Un pays sans bon sens! 212n9
  Un royaume vous attend, 212n9

Perrault, Pierre and Brault, Michel: *Pour la suite du monde/Of Whales and Men*, 196
Perriam, Chris *see* Nagib, Lucia, Perriam, Chris and Dudrah, Rajinder
Peur sur la ville/Fear over the City (Verneuil), 233
Pickpocket (Bresson), 231
Pilote, Sébastien, 193
Pireaux, Christine, 264
Pirogue, La (Touré), 145–6, 148, 149, 156, 158, 164–6, 214n26
Pirot, François: *Eurovillage*, 263
Pitiot, Pierre, 137
Pitts, Rafi, 13
Pivot, Bernard, 67, 72
Playtime (Tati), 200
Poelvoorde, Benoît, 172n8
Poiré, Jean-Marie: *Les Visiteurs*, 325
Poirier, Anne Claire, 192
Pol Pot, 29, 30, 32; *see also* Cambodia
Poland
  Gdańsk, 151
  migrants from, 150
Poldalydès, Denis, 68
Poli, Olivier and Mammeri, Sofiane: *L'Ame du Panier: le plus vieux village de France*, 301n23
Polytechnique (Villeneuve), 193
Pontecorvo, Gillo: *La bataille d'Alger/The Battle of Algiers*, 61n13
Pool, Léa, 192
'popular' film, 325–7
postcolonialism, 5, 208, 221, 222, 349; *see also* colonialism
Poulin, Jacques: *Volswagen Blues*, 194
Poulin, Julien *see* Falardeau, Pierre and Poulin, Julien
Pouliot, Jean-François: *La Grande Séduction/Seducing Doctor Lewis*, 7, 192, 326–7
Pour la suite du monde/Of Whales and Men (Perrault and Brault), 196
Poussières de vie (Bouchareb), 50
Pradal, Laure: *Le village vertical*, 301n23
Pratt, Mary Louise, 2, 3, 178
Président, Le/The President (Beloko), 171n5
promesse, La/The Promise (Dardenne), 267
Promio, Alexandre, 104
prophète, Un/A Prophet (Audiard), 183, 221
Provost, Nicolas: *L'Envahisseur/The Invader*, 149, 152n5

Qatar: Doha Film Institute, 352
Qu'Allah bénisse la France!/May Allah Bless France! (Abd al Malik), 290, 295–8, 296

Quai des brumes, Le (Carné), 228
Quebec
  cinéma direct, 196
  Crisco (les compagnons de la crise), 203, 204, 205, 206
  films made in, 192–211, 330, 332; *see also* Montreal
  films set in, 192, 325, 326–9; road movies, 193–5, 196, 197–201, 203–11
  First Nations, 197
  globalisation, 207–10
  identity, 5–6, 8, 196, 197, 211
  independence referenda, 197
  map of, 195–6
  Montreal: film production, 3–4, 12, 193, 260, 329; National Film Board of Canada, 3; nationalism, 328–9
  new wave cinema, 193, 329
  Prix Jutra (later Gala Québec Cinema/*Prix Iris*), 4, 192
  Quiet Revolution, 192, 328, 332
  refugees, 203, 206, 207
Québec-Montréal (Trogi), 197
Québékoisie (Carrier and Higgins), 197
queer cinema, 193, 329
Quinet, Patrick, 266
Quinquennats (Djaïdani), 67–8

Raag, Ilmaar, 13
Rabbath, François and Sylvain, 73
racism, 241–2, 249
  football, 171
  Fracture, 292
  'Marche pour l'égalité et contre le racisme' ('March for Equality and Against Racism') (1983), 121
  in *Qu'Allah bénisse la France!* 296
radicalisation, 60n10
radio, 94
Rafle, La/The Round Up (Bosch), 176
Rahim, Tahar, 220
Rancière, Jacques, 47
Rascaroli, Laura, 10, 135, 138, 228–9, 233
Rasmussen, Rie: *Human Zoo*, 186–7
Rayures du zèbre, Les/Scouting for Zebras (Mariage), 172nn8, 10, 16
Real: and Reality, 156–7
Rebelle/War Witch (Nguyen), 192
Reeves, Hubert, 333
refugees
  camps: Cambodia, 30–40, 42
  crisis, 132, 136, 175–88, 203, 206–7, 222, 223–4, 229–30, 233–4, 325
  see also immigrants
regionalism, 85
religion
  in *Joyeux Noël/Merry Christmas*, 183–4
  in *London River*, 54, 55–7

in *Rengaine*, 79
see also Christianity; Islam
Rencontre (Carrier and Higgins), 197
Rengaine (Djaïdani), 68, 75, 76–80, *77*
Renoir, Jean
   La bête humaine, 228
   La Grande Illusion/Grand Illusion, 177
Resnais, Alain, 36, 333
Reuchamps, Robert, 266
Reygadas, Carlo: *La bataille dans le ciel/Battle in Heaven*, 268
Reynaert, Philippe, 257, 266, 268, 270, 272
Rhalib, Jawad: *El Ejido, la loi du profit*, 348
Riga, Jean-Claude, 262, 264, 265, 273, 276n3
   Haïti, la terre/Haiti, 263
road movies, 11, 152n7, 210
   African, 214n26
   Congorama, 207, 209–10
   En terrains connus, 199–200, 201
   getting lost, 147
   Quebec, 193–5, 196, 197–201, 203–11
   Tour de France, 80
   urban, 205
   see also 'stopover film'; travel cinema
Robert, Yves
   château de ma mère, Le/My Mother's Castle, 19n3
   gloire de mon père, La/My Father's Glory, 19n3
Roi de l'évasion, Le/The King of Escape (Guiraudie), 112, 115, 120
Roma communities, 188
Romania, 4, 13
Rombout, Bob, 262, 276n3
Romy, Bruno *see* Abel, Dominique, Gordon, Fiona and Romy, Bruno
Rosello, Mireille, 8, 11, 134, 138, 175, 187, 232, 342
Rosetta (Dardenne), 267
Rothberg, Michael, 289
Rouch, Jean, 234, 329
Roumas, André, 262
Route 132 (Bélanger), 197
route d'Istanbul, La/The Road to Istanbul (Bouchareb), 60n10
Rowden, Terry *see* Ezra, Elizabeth and Rowden, Terry
royaume vous attend, Un (Perrault), 212n9
Rue des cités (May and Zouhani), 69

Sac de farine, Le/The Bag of Flour (Leclerc), 112, 118
Sadek (rapper), 80
Said, Edward: *The Essential Terrorist*, 61n12
Saidi, Ismaël: *Moroccan Gigolos*, 272
Saïl, Noureddine, 347
Salo, Elina, 222
Salut cousin (Allouache), 147, 148

Samba (Nakache and Toledano), 216–17, 218, 220–2, 223–4, 225–7, *226*, 228, 232, 233–4
Sams'K Le Jah (Karim Sama), 305, 316, 317
Sanaker, John Kristian, 309, 312–13
Sané, Alioune, 305
Sarcellopolis (Deve and Daycard), 301n23
Sarr, Mamadou *see* Vieyra, Paul and Sarr, Mamadou
Sauder, Régis: *Nous, princesses de Clèves*, 301n23
Sawadogo, Isaka, 13, 139–40, 152n5, 221
Sayad, Abdelmalek, 225
Schlöndorff, Volker: *Diplomatie/Diplomacy*, 176
Schoonover, Karl *see* Galt, Rosalind and Schoonover, Karl
Scorcese, Martin: *Taxi Driver*, 213n20
Secrets, Les/Secrets (Amari), 112, 122, 124
Selasi, Taiye, 85, 86
Sellier, Geneviève, 301n26
Sembène, Ousmane, 163
   Borom Sarrett, 163
   Guelwaar, 312
   Noire de..., La/Black Girl, 90, 163
   Xala/The Curse, 158, 312
Sène, Cheikh, 312
Sene Absa, Moussa, 308
   Yoole: Le sacrifice, 153n9, 309, 314–15
Senegal, 12
   documentaries, 307–9
   films set in, 50–1
   football, 161
   languages, 318n6
   Y en a Marre (Fed Up) movement, 305, 306, *306*, 307, 310, 311, 312, 313–14, 315, 317
Senghor, Léopold Sedar, 170–1
Séraphin: Un homme et son péché (Binamé), 193, 325
Serreau, Coline: *Chaos*, 239, 246–9
Sète, 110, 116, 148
Seuil (publisher), 72
sexism, 249
Shih, Shu-mei, 343; *see also* Lionnet, Françoise and Shi, Shu-mei
Shipley, Jesse, 309–10
Shohat, Ella, 9, 171n2
short filmmaking, 272–5
Si le temps le permet/If the Weather Permits (Isaac), 197
Sicily, 124, 136
Sie, Adams, 308
   Fed-Up, 310, 315–16
Siege, The (Wright), 45
siestes grenadine, Les/Grenadine siestas (Mahmoud), 267
Sight and Sound (magazine), 257

Sihanouk, Norodom, 28–9
silent films, 105, 106
Silverman, Kaja, 159
Sissako, Abderrahmane, 85–6
   aesthetics of, 91
   and ATF, 4
   Bamako, 85, 158, 166–7
   and football, 166–8
   and globalisation, 91–4
   Heremakono / Waiting for Happiness, 85, 95–8, 166
   and montage, 87, 106
   on speech, 304
   Timbuktu, 85, 98–104, *103*, 158, 167, 312
   and transnationalism, 87, 89, 91, 95–6, 105–6
   Vie sur terre, La / Life on Earth, 85, 91–4, 166
Site 2 (Panh), 27–8, 30–40, *40*
   allegory, 39
   children, 35, 36–7, 38, 40
   encounters, 42
   human rights, 38–9
   humanising effect of, 33
   language, 32
   maps, 34, 38, 42
   mise en scène, 32, 37
   music, 33, 38, 39, 40
   self-awareness, 36
   soundtrack, 34
   spaces, 35
Skype, 142
slavery, 51, 164, 165, 172n8, 227
Smith, Alison, 183, 185
Smockey (Serge Bambara), 305, 309, 316
Smolders, Olivier: *Mort à Vignole*, 273
Smrt u Sarajevu / Death in Sarajevo (Tanovic), 14
Sneid, Hervé, 83n13
Solanas, Octavio, 161
solidarity
   in *iceberg, L'*, 143
   and language, 133, 134
   migrants, 151
   pan-European, 178
   in *Pirogue, La*, 146
Sorfa, David, 255
Soualem, Zinedine, 13, 203–4, 213nn17, 18
Source des femmes, La / The Source (Mihaileanu), 112, 118, 119, 122, 124
Sous les bombes / Under the Bombs (Aractingi), 13–14
Sow, Denise, 305
Spain, 145, 147, 165, 343
Spartiates (Wadimoff), 5
Spivak, Gayatri, 94
Stalingrad / Enemy at the Gates (Annaud), 330
Standaert, Dominique: *Hop*, 208, 214n26
Stéphane, Robert, 261–2

stereotypes
   Africa, 85
   in *Esquive, L'*, 60n5
   ethnic minorities, 282, 287
   Herzi, Hafsia and, 115, 116, 121
   in *London River*, 58, 60n5
   in *Nom des gens, Le*, 250
   racial, 251
   in romantic comedy, 83n12
   'stopover film' see Diego Star
Stranger Than Paradise (Jarmusch), 170
Strasbourg, 182
subalterns, 94
subjectivity, 89, 92, 93, 158
subtitles, 324, 329
Sur ma ligne (Djaïdani), 67, 71–2, 75
Swamy, Vinay, 241
Switzerland, 2, 4, 12
Sy, Omar, 216, 220

taboos, 59n1, 76, 79, 80
Tagbo, Claudia, 207
Taghmaoui, Saïd, 13
Tanovic, Danis, 13
   Smrt u Sarajevu / Death in Sarajevo, 14
tape machines, 333
Tarr, Carrie, 41, 131, 188–9, 225
Tasma, Alain: *Fracture*, 290, 291–2
Tati, Jacques: *Playtime*, 200
Taxi Driver (Scorcese), 213n20
Téchiné, André: *Loin*, 307–8
television
   Belgium, 261–2, 266, 270, 276n3
   Burkina Faso, 305, 308, 311, 313, 314
   CNN, 45
   France, 4, 19n2, 67–8, 72, 98, 286
   Maghrebi-French, 300n16
   Mauritania, 96
   Morocco, 354n3
   newscasts, 230
television films, 177, 302n32
temps d'une chasse, Le (Mankiewcz), 205
Tenja (Legzouli), 348
Terraferma (Crialese), 136
Terrasses, Les (Allouache), 120
terre des âmes errantes, La / The Land of Wandering Souls (Panh), 34, 41
terrorism
   in *bataille d'Alger, La / The Battle of Algiers*, 61n13
   and globalisation, 46, 47, 48, 49
   in *London River*, 53, 57–8
   Mali, 99
   representation of, 45–6
   see also Al Qaeda; radicalisation
Tessier, Eric: *5150 rue des Ormes*, 193
Tête de turc / Scapegoat (Elbé), 290–1
TGV (Touré), 145, 164

Thiat (Cheikh Omar Cyrille Tour), 305
Third Cinema, 61n12, 161, 347
Thomas, Dominic, 12, 188
Thompson, David, 45
Three shake-a-leg-steps to Heaven (Bausch), 267
Timbuktu (Sissako), 4, 85, 98–104, *103*, 158, 167–8, 312
Tissières, Hélène, 98
Titanic (Cameron), 141
Toint, Hubert, 266
Tokyo Fiancé (Liberski), 272
Toledano, Éric *see* Nakache, Olivier and Toledano, Éric
Toubab Bi (Touré), 164
Touita, Okacha, 147
Touki Bouki (Mambety), 90
Tour de France (Djaïdani), 80
Touré, Moussa
    La Pirogue, 145–6, 148, 149, 156, 158, 164–6, 214n26
    TGV, 145, 164
    Toubab Bi, 164
Touré, Yaya, 161–2
Toussaint Louverture (Niang), 302n32
tragédie de la mine, La / Comradeship (Pabst), 177
tranchée des espoirs, La / Trench of Hope (Lorenzi), 177
transculturalism, 341
transnational: definitions, 343, 344
transnational cinema, 3, 9–10, 219
transnationalism, 87, 88–9, 105–6, 312, 341–53
    aesthetics of, 89–91
    and civic voice, 317
    French language, 150
    French population, 339
    and genre, 325
    in *Joyeux Noël / Merry Christmas*, 180
    Mali, 103–4
    and *média-engagé*, 313
    minor, 69–70, 134
    Moroccan cinema, 347–53
    in *Pickpocket*, 232
    and the 'popular', 325–6
    Sissako and, 91, 95–6
    typologies of, 268
    see also Afropolitanism
Transylvania (Gatlif), 4, 153n8
travel cinema, 144, 193–4
    Quebec, 194, 195–6, 197–8, 211
    see also road movies
Travellinckx (Lanners), 273
Tréfois, Jean-Paul, 262
Tribiot, Philippe: *Les fusillés*, 177
Trivas, Victor: *Niemandsland / Hell on Earth*, 177
Trogi, Ricardo: *Québec-Montréal*, 197

Trois mondes / Three Worlds (Corsini), 239, 252–5
Trudeau, Catherine, 203
Truffaut, François
    Les 400 coups / The 400 Blows, 169
    Les Mistons, 329
Trump, Donald, 336, 337
Tsai, Ming-liang
    Visage / Face, 268
    Voyage en occident, Le / Journey to the West, 14
Tunisia, 4, 123, 351
    Journées Cinématographiques de Carthage, 12–13
Turkey, 188
Tyner, James A., 29–30, 34

Ulrich, Barbara, 195
Ultranova (Lanners), 274
United Kingdom
    Brexit, 188, 337
    French film in, 338, 340
    see also Guernsey; London
United States
    and Cambodia, 29, 32
    Chicago, 260
    CNN, 45
    COLCOA French Film Festival, 12
    entry into, 336
    films set in, 49–50, 51
    French film in, 340
    immigrants, 338
    marketing, 88
    see also Hollywood; New York
United States Agency for International Development (USAID), 315
Urry, John, 133

Vachon, Christine, 337
Vallée, Jean-Marc, 192, 326
    C.R.A.Z.Y., 193
Van de Peer, Stefanie, 353
Vanaret, Marie, 300n13
Vernet, Joseph, 80
Verneuil, Henri: *Peur sur la ville / Fear over the City*, 233
Vertov, Dziga, 196
videomaking
    Belgium, 261, 262, 263, 264
    West Africa, 304–5, 306–7
    see also DVDs; YouTube
vie heureuse de Léopold Z, La (Carle), 198
Vie sur terre, La / Life on Earth (Sissako), 85, 91–4, *92*, 166
Vietnam, 4, 50
Vieyra, Paul and Sarr, Mamadou: *Afrique-sur-Seine*, 163
Vigneault, Gilles, 209, 211

Vigo, Jean: *L'Atalante*, 228
Village presque parfait, Un (Meunier), 327–8
village vertical, Le (Pradal), 301n23
Villeneuve, Denis, 192, 326
   32 août sur terre, Un / August 32nd on Earth, 212n5
   Polytechnique, 193
Virgil, 25
Visage / Face (Tsai), 268
Visiteurs, Les (Poiré,), 325
Voleurs de chevaux / In the arms of the enemy (Wald), 274
voyage du ballon rouge, Le / Flight of the Red Balloon (Hou), 4
Voyage en occident, Le / Journey to the West (Tsai), 14

Wade, Abdoulaye, 314, 315
Wadimoff, Nicolas, 13
   Clandestins, 5, 152n1
   Spartiates, 5
   see also Chouinard, Denis and Wadimoff, Nicolas
Wahl, Chris, 176, 183
Wald, Micha
   Alice et moi, 273, 274
   La nuit tous les chats sont gris, 273
   Voleurs de chevaux / In the arms of the enemy, 274
Wallerstein, Immanuel, 331
Walli, Hasse, 232
war films *see* Cold War; World War I; World War II
War Story (Jackson), 112–13, 122, 124
Welcome (Lioret), 132, 153n8, 214n26, 217
Welsh, Henry, 4
Wendrick, Willeke, 97
Wesh Wesh, qu'est-ce qui se passe? (Ameur-Zaïmech), 60n7
West Africa
   civic voice, 310, 312, 314, 315–16, 317
   football cinema, 155–71
   francophone cinema, 311–13
   immigration crisis, 314–15
   Internet, 305, 306, 308, 311, 312, 313, 315, 318n3
   média-engagé, 306, 307, 313
   videomaking, 304–5, 306–7
   see also Burkina Faso; Ghana; Senegal
Wheatley, Catherine, 245
Widart, Nicole, 262, 276n3
   Fin de carrière, 263
   Paysage imaginaire, 263
Williams, Pharrell, 304

Wilms, André, 216, 228
Witter, Frank, 181
Wolton, Dominique, 2, 133, 134, 241
women
   Agora Films (Morocco), 354n7
   Burkina Faso, 305
   as filmmakers, 82n6, 192, 262
   and identity, 119
   immigrant *see* Aïcha
   Maghrebi, 112, 114
   in male settings *see* Fidelio, *l'odyssée d'Alice*; *Pirogue, La*
   as protagonists, 46, 52–4, 55, 57, 58, 60n3, 140–1, 247–8, 251–2
   and sexism, 249
   in *Timbuktu*, 104
world cinema, 9–10, 135, 219, 234
world literature *see littérature-monde*
World War I, 176–90
World War II, 176, 289
   Holocaust, 291
Wright, Lawrence: *The Siege*, 45

Xala / The Curse (Sembène), 158, 312
Xenia (Panos), 14

Yaaba / Grandmother (Ouedraogo), 169–70
Yellowknife (Jean), 197
Yenke, Ona Lu, 241
Yoole: Le sacrifice (Sene Absa), 153n9, 309, 314–15
youth
   documentary making, 311, 313–14, 316–17
   in *L'Esquive*, 60n5
   and music, 305, 309–10
   see also banlieue cinema
YouTube, 304, 311

Zem, Roschdy, 290, 291
Zemmouri, Mahmoud: *Certifiée Halal / Certified Halal*, 112, 117–18, 120
Zglinski, Greg, 13
Zidane, Zinedine, 162, 167
Zinaba, Rasmane, 313
Zinga, Marc, 172n8
Zizek, Slavoj, 156, 158, 160
zones
   contact, 2, 9, 178, 341–2, 345
   franco-, 9, 11–12, 341, 345
   inter-, 2, 150, 151
Zouhani, Hakim *see* May, Carine and Zouhani, Hakim
Zyguel, Léon, 291

EU representative:
Easy Access System Europe
Mustamäe tee 50, 10621 Tallinn, Estonia
Gpsr.requests@easproject.com

www.ingramcontent.com/pod-product-compliance
Lightning Source LLC
Chambersburg PA
CBHW052139300426
44115CB00011B/1446